THATCHER'S SECRET WAR

THATCHER'S SECRET WAR

SUBVERSION, COERCION, SECRECY AND GOVERNMENT, 1974-90

CLIVE BLOOM

Prospero: You do yet taste
Some subtleties o' th' isle, that will not let you
Believe things certain.

William Shakespeare, The Tempest V.I

Next to these public things were the dreams of old
women, or, I should say, the interpretation of old
women upon other people's dreams; and these put
abundance of people even out of their wits.

Daniel Defoe, A Journal of the Plague Year, 1722

The truth is an acquired taste.

Gordon Thomas and Martin Dillon, The Assassination of Robert Maxwell

Government is not about truth.

Clive Ponting, Whitehall: Tragedy & Farce

In a democracy, government claims that only the
guilty have anything to fear are as insidious as they
are specious.

Andrew Neather, Evening Standard, 15 May 2014

For our three little musketeers,
who will sort this mess out when we're gone.

Cover illustration: *Her First Year.* (Courtesy of Michael Leonard)

First published 2015

The History Press
The Mill, Brimscombe Port
Stroud, Gloucestershire, GL5 2QG
www.thehistorypress.co.uk

British Library Cataloguing in Publication Data.
A catalogue record for this book is available from the British Library.

ISBN 978 0 7524 9974 1

Typesetting and origination by The History Press
Printed in Great Britain by TJ International Ltd. Padstow

CONTENTS

ACKNOWLEDGEMENTS AND PERMISSIONS

The author would like to thank the History Press for permission to reprint an extract from his book *Restless Revolutionaries: A History of Britain's Fight for a Republic* (Stroud, 2010)

The author would like to thank Gerry Gable; James Goddard of the TUC Library at the London Metropolitan University Archives; the Margaret Thatcher Archives; the archivists of the Scottish National Party and those of the National Archives of Scotland; Maria Castrillo, curator of Political Collections at the National Library of Scotland; the librarian, the Library and Museum of Freemasonry; John McGill, founder of Scotland-UN; David Powell, archive manager at D.C. Thomson for the *Sunday Post*; Professor Warren von Eschenbach of the University of Notre Dame; Lesley Kacher; and Mark Beynon and Lauren Newby at The History Press

1

MONSTER TIME

What machinations brought Thatcher to power and what secrets helped sustain the Thatcherite revolution? This is the story of the state-within-the-state which warped Thatcher's premiership from its inception. How was the population convinced to support an ideology designed to defeat those whom Thatcher defined as the 'enemies within': everyone she could not see eye to eye with? It is also about how her supporters recognised whether a civil servant, journalist, union leader or simple member of the public was 'one of us' rather than one of 'them': the subversive and unwashed socialists of whom her government was so wary. It led to a world of dirty tricks and murder.

The central argument of this book is that there was an undeclared and internal 'cold war' fought throughout the 1980s in which rogue elements in the government, military and secret services seemed to have free rein to distort facts and even kill opposition voices under the camouflage of black propaganda.

Everything in this book is true; everything is false. It all depends on which side of the looking glass one is standing. There will be those who might be sceptical that the evidence represented here is only a multiplicity of coincidences, nevertheless, the coincidences do start to make patterns – a matter of point of view, perhaps.

This is not another book on the story of Thatcher or a history of her premiership; nor is it a retelling of the long (and often secret) war with the Irish Republican Army. However, it is about aggression and the world that partially grew from the Irish Troubles, much of which was exported to mainland Britain and much of which was kept secret.

My central argument is that there was not only a secret and undeclared *internal* 'cold war' fought throughout the 1980s (a war that had started in the 1970s), but that the consequences of the decisions and events that occurred in those years have huge implications for the importance and role of the state as it has evolved into the twenty-first century. It is in the years between the mid 1970s and the early 1990s that the state became a direct arm of government policy; one which pursued an undeclared agenda unexamined by parliament or voters. This led, by degrees, to the secret bureaucracy of the state metamorphosing into the real and uncontrolled hidden political power in Britain today – a power no longer decided or directed by parliamentary process.

This was a particularly contradictory situation, as Thatcher always seemed opposed to the 'wets' of the old-boy networks who made up the servants of the state. Indeed, after the final exposure of Sir Anthony Blunt's role as a double agent in 1979, Thatcher was apparently prepared to expose the system and destroy it. Sir Bernard Ingham, Thatcher's press secretary, recalled her attacking the duplicity of those controlling MI5: 'I believe she did it because she didn't see why the system should cover things up. This was early in her Prime Ministership. I think she wanted to tell the Civil Service that the politicians decide policy, not the system. She wanted them to know who was boss.'[1]

It was not, however, without irony that Thatcher came to rely more and more on the secretive and American-inspired free-market experiments of economists such as Milton Friedman. Free markets (about which Thatcher insisted, 'There [was] no alternative') were needed if individual enterprise was to be revived in Britain. Yet the free-market system would have to be created against fierce, entrenched, organised and mainly socialist (and liberal) opposition. To achieve the changes required for the correct social engineering (although 'There [was] no such thing as society'), Thatcher needed conservative-orientated state organisations and government policies to face down the perceived 'enemy' (the unions, militant activists, the anti-nuclear lobby, anti-Cruise-missile feminists, New Agers, homosexuals) and destroy them in the name of freedom of choice. This would be achieved through the narrowing of the political framework and the growing authoritarianism of state decisions.

Thatcher's years saw the growth and frequent deployment of the Special Air Service (SAS), the Security Service (MI5), the Secret Intelligence Service (MI6), Special Branch, GCHQ surveillance and police powers. All were increased to deal with internal threats to perceived security. The 'enemy within' was to be interpreted far beyond the miners to include the real fear of the break-up of the United Kingdom through the defeat of British forces in Ireland and the potential victories of secret 'Trotskyist' cells planted inside unions, GCHQ and the Labour Party. Enemies grew to include Greater London councillors, Scottish nationalists, ecological protesters, poll-tax activists, inner-city youths and, it seemed, most of the population of Liverpool.

My story follows the many accusations of conspiratorial politics in the late 1970s until the early 1990s, from those of the paranoid right to those of an equally paranoid left. Because the right ultimately won the political battle, this story is framed in terms of those who were cast into the wilderness for over ten years and whose tales were dismissed as the ravings of lunatics and renegades. For the most part, the stories of murder, cover-ups, lying and institutional corruption that emerged at the time have never been proven. Nevertheless, taken together, they provide a hidden story of an era; one that, because there was prosperity and economic well-being, could be dismissed as a fantasy as long as the cash flowed. By the time the cash ran out, the stories had gone cold, or, like the miners' strike, had become the stuff of legend, or even, like the Irish troubles, fallen on deaf ears because things needed to be forgotten if peace was to be achieved.

The period that stretches from Harold Wilson's last term to Margaret Thatcher's three terms in office was perhaps the most authoritarian since the first two decades of the nineteenth century and the most secret in modern history. In effect, this is the story of the emergence in Britain of two forces: that of economic regeneration and that of Britain as a nuclear (-energy) state entangled with the United States and paranoid about communist subversion. These two propositions have immensely important significance if taken together. To achieve one of these aims required the other coming into play. Economic regeneration was intimately tied to the international arms trade which, in turn, was tied to the centrality of nuclear fuel for a modern, regenerated and internationally significant United Kingdom.

The 1980s were not just a story of yuppie success, defeated northern workers and the rise of Estuary English; they were also a tale of secret machinations, top-secret civil defence bunkers, the ever-present fear of nuclear annihilation and the overwhelming belief that Britain had been penetrated by dark forces bent on the destruction of the British way of life.

The United Kingdom is rapidly changing, and Thatcher's ideals seem to have vanished – all except one: the power and importance of the extra-parliamentary state and its surveillance methods and hidden powers in a new age of terrorism. This narrative is, therefore, an exploration not only of the myth of Thatcher, but also a reminder of the real and perceived threats in a period which has been remembered in recent histories as a story entirely to do with surface matters, and sanitised and mythologised in films such as *The Iron Lady*.

In her beginnings were her ends. In 1971 Margaret Thatcher was voted 'the most unpopular woman in Britain' by readers of the *Sun* which even asked, 'Is Mrs Thatcher Human?'[2] On 29 October 1986, Tam Dalyell broke parliamentary rules and accused Thatcher, when she was Prime Minister, of being a 'bounder, a liar, a deceiver, a cheat and a crook'.[3] A reckoning of sorts occurred at the Ritz on 8 April 2013 when the Iron Lady passed away, aged 87. By the time of her death, Margaret Thatcher had already reached a type of international sainthood, especially with the release of numerous films and documentaries. Her funeral on 17 April 2013 was called 'ceremonial', but was a state affair by another name. It had been planned before her death and was sufficiently grand to give the British people pause for thought. No commoner had had this type of funeral since Winston Churchill. The crowds watching the military procession began arriving the night before, the occasion was packed with dignitaries and there was full television coverage.

On the whole, the day was dignified. Yet, all was not well. The wounds of thirty years ago were opened and examined again; Thatcher's divisive nature was revisited. In northern towns, people built bonfires in celebration of her demise as they had done hundreds of years ago for other folk demons. There was a small but vocal demonstration at the funeral; someone threw something from the crowd as the bier passed and the song 'Ding Dong! The Witch is Dead' almost reached number one in the music charts.

All the evidence presented here is verifiable from sources elsewhere. The facts, such are they are, have accumulated in books, articles, newspapers, television programmes, government reports, parliamentary debates, individual letters, memoirs, and on the Internet. This is the first time it has all been brought together in one volume, and various patterns have emerged. The evidence paints a picture of an almost lost world. Most of the books I have used for research are out of print and many hard to find; the documentary programmes are now forgotten or half-remembered; the news just yesterday's tittle-tattle. Nevertheless, these tales paint a certain picture of Britain, which appears, in hindsight, both more violent and certainly more authoritarian than is usually remembered, something recognised by those in the headlights of the authorities at the time. The history that emerges is of a country not just in deep crisis before Thatcher came to power, but in a crisis that lasted throughout her three terms and continued into those of John Major – a crisis managed by unseen and dangerous people, wholly unelected and nameless.

Many of the relevant books from the 1970s and 1980s have long been out of print, and each was directed at only a single injustice. I have endeavoured to gather the numerous arguments and put them back into public view to be read alongside long-forgotten reports and pamphlets mouldering in archives and the new proliferation of Internet material. The book is a compendium, of sorts, of wrongdoing, bad management and lies. It is not a particular attempt merely to put new evidence on the table, but to act as a synthesis for the great babble of competing voices which urgently need to be heard in a format easily available and in one place, where all the evidence may be impartially judged.

As such, what is recorded here is the disparate investigations of different people often working in isolation and never quite sure of what was true or false. In a sense, these pages represent speculation of a rather particular research type, half history and half the innuendo that history is made from. I am only too aware that different registers of significance will be attached to the various pieces of the jigsaw which I offer. I am also aware that conjecture does not make for facts, but my point is that in the scenarios described in this book there are few facts, if any, and the investigator is forced to make a pattern out of fragments and hearsay.

The stories are sometimes garnered from testimonial evidence, which occasionally lacks forensic corroboration. Yet testimony can be powerful, and testimony joined by logic and the overwhelming coincidence of events becomes evidence, especially when squared with the documents available and the conjectures made by political historians, investigators and journalists

This was a world where records regularly went missing and documents were too often shredded and the media were fed misinformation and reproduced it as fact. When 'details dovetail neatly with those of others' (to borrow a phrase from a notorious series of articles in the *Independent* in 1987, which were fed to journalist David McKittrick by British intelligence sources to blacken the name of whistle-blower Colin Wallace),[4] we might be rationally inclined to agree that the pattern in the wallpaper is wholly produced from a willingness on the part of readers to fill in the blank spaces with shapes that don't exist.

This refusal to accept that there is no pattern except in the reader's head is what David Aaronovitch of the *Times* calls 'voodoo' history.[5] Yet the intelligence services will regularly feed stories to a newspaper in order to defuse accusations that the pattern does exist and that the dots could and should be joined; evidence dovetails because it has the traction of not being coordinated. It is the rational denial printed in the quality media or reproduced on the news which proves to be the false decoy by embarrassing readers and viewers into believing that they have been duped by their own credulity.

On the whole, I have used investigations into particular events and works interpreting those events to provide a micro-history which concentrates on the unfortunate men and women, some half remembered, some almost forgotten, who formed what came to be known as the 'enemy within', people who wittingly or unwittingly found themselves bunched together as unacknowledged conspirators in a war of ideologies, which they lost. Their defeat was the triumph of the state machine. These oppositional voices have never been fully vindicated and they probably never will. The villains of the piece were universally crowned with laurels, their crimes securely hidden and guarded, their motivations largely unknown. Officially sanctioned villainy is at the heart of this book, whether it be policy towards parliamentary procedure, the safety of British citizens or the protection of state 'secrets'.

I have also looked at the many half-remembered actors who formed a Thatcherite right even before Thatcher knew she stood for an ideology: ideologues on both sides determine this debate. Those right-wing thinkers are not, however, characters from the fringe, but figures from the centre who, for one reason or another, have been expunged from the record or have faded into the background. By revisiting the documents relating to their activities, the reader can check every fact as well as every 'fact' and make their own mind up about those years leading to the end of the Cold War and just beyond.

I have tried to use only information in the public domain, being increasingly distrustful of memoirs, Thatcherite hagiographies and reminiscences that seem to skirt vital connections, or books on espionage that clearly only tell the particular 'truth' of those who are granted access to the information in the first place. I have also avoided those synoptic histories of the period which pour everything into a mix which includes high politics and pop music, excellent though they are.

The book is not just about Thatcher, and to blame her premiership for all that is said in the following pages would be absurd. As always, this is a story of accumulation and adaption. Nevertheless, the book does concentrate on Thatcher's time in office, as well as concentrating on her time as Leader of the Opposition. To complete the story,

I have strayed beyond either end of her premiership. To me it seems clear that, despite the numerous books written on her and on the different aspects of the Conservative government's decisions in office, much of the sense of the period still needs to be joined up. Unfortunately, the right's flattery and the left's opprobrium have left much of the field still to be explored. Indeed, the paranoia felt by the left was matched by paranoia on the right, and the usual suspects in socialist opposition may be matched by a host of figures on the Conservative and traditionalist right who felt embattled and almost defeated during the run-up to Thatcher's first premiership.

What interests me is the activity that seems to have fallen through the net or been sidelined or ignored as if it was all merely a matter of conspiracy theory and pseudo-history. Even the nature of paranoia in the period is worth its own special study, and much of that paranoia is itself based on the deliberately disseminated half-truths and distortions put out by the Home Office, police, intelligence services, Ministry of Defence, Atomic Energy Agency, Royal Ulster Constabulary and army. It is hardly surprising that official versions of events, many of which appeared to the public ephemeral at the time, are distinctly more interesting when put into a pattern. It is for the reader to decide if the patterns I have made are mere fantasy or not. They can check the records. I have tried to apply a certain logic which I hope is not false, but may seem exaggerated to some.

The debate over the role of Thatcherism's influence on the state and the state's influence on Thatcher has, for the most part, been ignored in the histories, but, for me, these things are central to the period and make us think again about the truth of the world around us. Thatcher's years in office were determined by three areas of principle: the need to curb union power (and its apparently communistic corporatism); the need to create wider liberty (through authoritarian means); and the need to keep Britain central to Cold War diplomacy (by the maintenance of nuclear weapons, civil nuclear technology and military exports). The government and its servants were not always as particular as they might have been over the means to achieve these principles.

In this respect, the issue of ownership of the Falkland Islands which had festered for a long time before Thatcher came to power and caught her government by surprise is central to the distortion of ideas relating to the period. Because the resultant war was successfully concluded, it not only skewed the overall aims that Thatcher professed, but also seemed to confirm them to voters. It was a most fortuitous accidental symptom of her politics, but not fundamental to them. In this respect, investigative journalists and nosy politicians at the time have proved more powerful voices than recent historians in uncovering state abuses and systematic obfuscation.

Many of the situations described in this book were originally there to deceive and, in order to cover them up, more lies had to follow. Many of the circumstances occurred before Thatcher came to power, but she was not merely the guardian of those who lied; she also had to lie in turn to protect herself. Thatcher was aware of deceits which made the difficulties over the sinking of the *General Belgrano* or the Westland affair seem trivial. This other register of deception went to the heart of modern Conservatism and later fatally infected New Labour. It concerned activities during a time when those who wanted an authoritarian and strictly conservative (and Conservative) government were devising 'Thatcherism' and were still looking for the person who would bear the name of the ideology they had created. Indeed, Alan Sherman, one of her closest advisors, believed that, 'Mrs Thatcher never "thunk" any thoughts,' rather her instinct was 'to do', that is, put into effect the various ideas that were coalescing around her.[6]

This book charts the significance of government policy and state action across four Prime Ministers: Ted Heath and Harold Wilson, who feared those who ran the secret state; Jim Callaghan, whose government unwittingly ushered in the rule of the new politics; and Margaret Thatcher, who was the protector of the secret state and its greatest beneficiary. This was politics by other means, which journalists Stephen Dorril and Robin Ramsey named 'para-politics' in 1983. It was militaristic and aggressive from the start, an assault on legitimate political parties and political figureheads as well as union leaders. It was, in effect, a crusade against unionisation, liberals and the welfare state carried out on both an economic and a military front. The result was pure conspiracy come true, a coincidence of intention by person or persons unknown and social and economic circumstances:

> Brutally summarised … Mrs Thatcher and Thatcherism grew out of a right-wing network in this country with extensive links to the military-intelligence establishment. Her rise to power was the climax of a long campaign by this network which included a protracted destabilisation campaign against the Labour and Liberal Parties – chiefly the Labour Party – during 1974–1976.[7]

Is such a thesis to be believed and is it credible? Was there one plot, or many that seemed to overlap and intertwine? In the late 1980s, there seemed a case for thinking so. The scenario seemed, at face value, to be improbable, but everything about what was revealed by whistle-blowers such as Colin Wallace, Cathy Massiter, Fred Holroyd, Gary Murray, Clive Ponting and Peter Wright seemed bizarre and it was only the similarities and coincidences of their stories that gave credence to their arguments. Investigative journalists such as Martin Dillon, Paul Foot, Duncan Campbell, Gerry Gable and Judith Cook pursued stories which corroborated evidence. Amateurs such as Peter Green would not let explanations lie, however plausible, and continue even now to search for the flaws. Members of Parliament such as Tam Dalyell were tenacious. Against these voices must be taken the millions of voters who did not know, did not understand, did not concern themselves or did not care. In one or two instances things are now clearer.

These tangled stories are linked by reoccurring patterns or reoccurring names while some only appear to be tangential. Political machinations are often hard to follow, and information is complex and contradictory. Simply stated, this history offers a view of much of what had been already been investigated in the late 1980s regarding the secret state as revealed by whistle-blowers, former army information officers, the nuclear authorities, rogue intelligence officers and journalistic and private investigators. These stories are linked to the central thesis that Thatcher was privy to secrets and circumstances that it was convenient to ignore in the name of the ideology that satisfied and reassured so many and allowed the Conservatives to hold onto power for over a decade.

Only in the twenty-first century are some of the secrets kept by the security forces at the time coming to light. Only in the last few years, for instance, has the full extent of paedophilic activity been revealed, although MI5 certainly seemed to know that certain MPs, such as Cyril Smith, were paedophiles as early as 1974. This was also the year when the mysterious file relating to the Wilson 'plot' known as 'Clockwork Orange' (perhaps named as such by a wag who knew it was about aversion therapy) appeared for the first time and which would have so much impact on later revelations.[8]

Yet did the corruption and machinations of politicians, secret service personnel and police carry on much later into the 1980s and beyond? Did the forces of subversion and deception unleashed in the 1970s sink into the very fabric of the Thatcherite state to a point where corruption and deceit could not be recognised as corrupt because they served the ends of power and the interests of a certain party line? At the end of his 1989 book, *Who Framed Colin Wallace*, on the man whose revelations predate all the rest regarding contemporary state corruption, Paul Foot concluded:

> from the early 1970s onwards, and particularly in Ireland, the British secret state stepped far beyond any line which should be tolerated by a democratic and civilised society; and that if such things, once exposed, are ignored or covered up by the authorities, the one certainty is that they will continue, to excesses even more horrific.[9]

By 1985, it had become quite clear to many that the cover-ups and the deceits of the 1970s, especially those in Northern Ireland, were now embedded in numerous cancerous ways in such diverse fields as mainland policing, Scottish independence, the Falklands War, the economic fight with the miners and, above all, the centrality of secrecy concerning both the civil and military nuclear industries.

Although I have known at least three of the participants in this book for many years, I have never knowingly met a member of the Secret Intelligence Service (MI6), Security Service (MI5), Special Branch, the Royal Ulster Constabulary, the SAS, the Fourteenth Intelligence Company, 'E Squadron', Group 13 or the secretive – and possibly fictitious – 'Increment'. Nor have I met the numerous bankers or security and arms consultants who started life as intelligence agents before receiving knighthoods and moving into the private sector. (The Increment appeared to be a group of serving SAS soldiers employed in black ops abroad. It was reborn as E squadron in 2007 and noted by the BBC as operating during 2012.)

In the 1970s and 1980s, the men (and occasionally women) who formed the intelligence network were a cadre and followed a profession which was, in their eyes at least, an honourable one. For the most part, their peccadilloes and eccentricities were their own: they were all (whatever their private tastes) socially conservative and traditional, and their allegiance was primarily to the Crown (unless they had switched to the Soviets). A government dedicated to fighting leftism could count on their necessary support so long as that support was unaccountable and certainly unattributable.

Generally, such mandarins were beyond criticism, leaving lesser men to take the blame. To question such people and expect an indiscreet answer is relatively pointless and so I have confined my research to written or recorded comments. Nevertheless, much of the tangible evidence has vanished, sometimes in mysterious circumstances, and some has occasionally miraculously reappeared. The written evidence has, at one time or other, been challenged or discredited. The physical evidence has been literally reduced to rubble or left as mouldering files in archives. Most of the men and women recorded in these pages have died and so are beyond questioning anyway, and those who haven't are unlikely to face justice so many years later. Few records may be trusted at face value as to their intentions or origins.

Intelligence work is meant to be dull and unglamorous, but the very nature of unthinking routine may breed indifference to active abuse and encourage those who have the energy for plots to work unheeded by the multitude of their pen-pushing colleagues. The worst abuses may be those committed by overzealous persons working in an indifferent atmosphere where their activities may be carried out in full sight but remain invisible.

The murky world of secrecy and conspiracy that these worlds represent during the period is of sufficient interest, however, to allow an inquirer to question the fashionably bland histories and biographies of the period that litter the bookshelves, and dig up those accounts of forgotten intrigues and scandals that surfaced briefly, but seemed to evaporate with the passing of time. There is at least prima facie evidence of all sorts of black propaganda and smoke and mirrors to suggest that Parliament and voters were deliberately deceived for long periods and that there certainly seemed to lurk deep in the darkest unrecorded bowels of the state certain organisations that did the intelligence service's dirty work, which, on occasion, would entail burglary and intimidation and might even have come to murder.

Too much thinking like this (one hears the reader say) leads straight down the Pont d'Alma road tunnel with Princess Diana and the 'confessions' of soldier N, but thinking like this may also lead to the Straits of Gibraltar, which provided the scene for the most controversial of all the army's actions in the period, and to possible clandestine operations designed to destabilise government, re-engineer the social fabric and remove anyone who got in the way.

2

THE FAT SPIDER

In retrospect, it is difficult to remember just how shadowy some elements of the state and secret intelligence were in the 1970s and 1980s. The SAS first made their spectacular public appearance on television dressed in black ninja costumes when they stormed the Iranian Embassy; the secret services were only covered by new regulations in 1989; the world of underground bunkers and nuclear war preparations, although known about in the 1980s, really only became publicly known when it was sold off as surplus; army dirty tricks and collaborations in connection with assassinations in Northern Ireland and elsewhere, which seem to have begun in the 1970s, only became public knowledge after three IRA members were killed on Gibraltar. The public order role of the police throughout the 1980s was questionable and occasionally illegal; the actions and cover-ups of senior politicians and civil servants galling; a large number of murders linked to the security services left unsolved; even local councils were steeped in a network of deceit. Government Communications Headquarters (GCHQ), although it employed hundreds of staff, was itself a well-kept secret until Thatcher decided to make an issue of union membership.

GCHQ had started life as the cover name for Bletchley Park in 1939, but the name was retained for a network of intelligence and listening posts reporting back to the central hub at Cheltenham. Here, signals from around the world were deciphered and interpreted. Indeed, when Tam Dalyell asked a written parliamentary question on 19 December 1983 on the subject of the sinking of the *Belgrano*, he recalled that he:

> had the haziest notion only that there was a major communications centre in the Cheltenham area. Even for Defence-oriented MPs, GCHQ was an elusive subject of which we knew little ... Remember – these questions appeared at a time when 600 Members of the House of Commons would have been quite blank, if asked what or where GCHQ was.[1]

Dalyell was right. As late as the mid-1980s, almost nothing was known regarding the set-up and organisation of the British intelligence network. When journalists went looking for clues regarding the suspicious death of nuclear protester Hilda Murrell in the spring of 1984, almost everything they discovered came as a revelation even to the point of needing explanations regarding exactly what the difference was between branches of the secret services. It would come as a bigger revelation that GCHQ, rather than functioning independently, seemed to be merely an outpost of the equally secret National Security Agency (NSA) based in the United States, which was itself hidden within the labyrinthine CIA.

Thus parliamentarians knew that MI5 reported nominally to the Home Office and MI6 to the Foreign Office, but they might not have known, which very few voters would have imagined possible, that both services were not bound to anybody and acted, to all intents and purposes, as independent wings of the permanent state outside any real government control and answerable to a nebulous entity called 'the Crown'. The services were supported in their enterprise by 'entrepreneurial' and unlicensed and unregulated private agencies hired to do 'dirty jobs', trained by army or intelligence specialists and let loose with equipment often bought freely on the high street.

Hinting at where the services were based was likely to have those nosing around placed under surveillance. Nevertheless, in the 1980s, MI6 was at Century House at 100 Westminster Bridge Road SE1, and MI5 at Curzon House, Curzon Street W1, while Special Branch, the political police, was based at Scotland Yard. If you wanted to inform on your neighbour there was also an address: Box 500, 14–17 Great Marlborough Street W1. These were all (even the last address) officially secret locations in 1985. MI5 was also colloquially known as Box 500.

There were no official records of the cost of any of these organisations, which ran at around £1 billion a year by the mid to late 1980s. The money was part of the annual intelligence budget known as the Single Intelligence Vote. This was meant to run at around £800 million, but records of payments from the Exchequer remain secret even to this day and seem to have exceeded the billion threshold. As for GCHQ, Sir John Adye told a news conference in 1993 that it employed at least 3,000 members of the armed forces. The specific job of all the intelligence branches was the 'defence of the realm'. Not until 1994, when the Intelligence Services Act was passed, was there any real mention of what the services should *not* do, and even this had an opt-out clause:

> Britain's 1994 Intelligence Services Act prohibits MI6 agents, or anyone else who might act on behalf of MI6 … from taking part in any criminal activity for which they would normally still be liable in the United Kingdom even if it occurs abroad. They are thereby prevented from committing genocide, murder, kidnapping or indeed bigamy – unless the Foreign Secretary deems it necessary

for the proper discharge of one of the service's statutory functions, in which case the agents will be absolved of all liability under British criminal law.[2]

Moreover, Sir Gerry Warner, who was intelligence coordinator in the 1990s, considered it would be 'unthinkable' for MI6 officers to be armed. Yet:

> Given the nature of their work, which now includes not just espionage operations abroad but also 'the prevention or detection of serious crime', it is simply not credible that MI6 agents involved in that type of operation could be left unarmed in the face of what would inevitably be a serious risk of violence.[3]

Maximum secrecy remained in place until Thatcher left office, and then it was only partially lifted. This led to the ludicrous situation that Sir Robert Armstrong found himself in during the government's civil action in the New South Wales Supreme Court when the British Government tried to suppress the publication of Peter Wright's *Spycatcher*. When cross-examined, Armstrong refused to say whether MI6 existed or not. Yet he was confronted with his own admission that Sir Dick White had been head of MI6 between 1956 and 1968. Armstrong remained insouciant, however, only admitting that the organisation had existed between those dates and that he could not confirm whether it existed before or after the period in question.[4]

What rules or laws were enacted to control the secret forces of the state? The answer was none. This continued right up until 1989. Instead, there was only one directive, produced on 25 September 1952, by the Conservative Home Secretary David Maxwell-Fyfe and it laid out the accountability of the head of MI5 to Parliament:

1. In your appointment as Director General of the security services you will be responsible to the Home Secretary personally. The security service is not, however, a part of the Home Office. On appropriate occasions you will have right of direct access to the Prime Minister.
2. The security service is part of the defence forces of the country. Its task is the Defence of the Realm as a whole, from external and internal dangers arising from attempts at espionage and sabotage, or from actions of persons and organisations whether directed from within or without the country, which may be judged to be subversive of the State.
3. You will take special care to see that the work of the security services is strictly limited to what is necessary for the purposes of their task.
4. It is essential that the security services should be kept absolutely free from any political bias or influence and nothing should be done that might lend colour to any suggestion that it is concerned with the interests of any particular section of the community, or with any other matter than the Defence of the Realm as a whole.

5. No inquiry is to be carried out on behalf of any Government Department unless you are satisfied that an important public interest bearing on the Defence of the Realm , as defined in para. 2, is at stake.

6. You and your staff will maintain the well-established convention whereby Ministers do not concern themselves with the detailed information which may be obtained by the security service in particular cases, but are furnished with such information only as may be necessary for the determination of any issue on which guidance is sought.[5]

These guidelines (with no legal status) were still the only method by which the intelligence community might be called to account throughout the 1980s. On 1 March 1985, Margaret Thatcher wrote to Neil Kinnock expressing confidence in the secret services, 'It is for the Home Secretary and me to satisfy ourselves that the security services operate entirely within the letter and spirit of its directive ... I do not believe there are any grounds for changing the present system of accountability to ministers which has stood through successive governments.'[6]

It was a bland and derisory assurance lacking all substance, and, eventually and reluctantly, would have to be changed into formal law. The statement reassured no one. Indeed, given Thatcher's conviction of the trustworthiness of the security services, the statement was guaranteed to produce more concern in people opposed to her policies.

That was the amount of control that Parliament or the government could hope to apply. It gave carte blanche to any operation designed to defend the status quo. Yet this also allowed the defence of the status quo as it was *fantasised* by any element of the secret services. This required finding constant 'threats' that had to be dealt with. One investigative journalist at the time concluded that, 'It is now abundantly clear that the security services are not absolutely free from any political bias. The label "enemy within", which Prime Minister Margaret Thatcher applied to the 180,000 miners who went on strike in 1984, now applies to most of us.'[7]

Thatcher's continued assurances effectively gave the security services, especially MI5 in conjunction with Special Branch, the appropriate leeway to spy on anyone deemed 'subversive', including union leaders, journalists, political activists and 'suspicious' ordinary people. MI5 was an organisation that veered increasingly towards over-complexity and non-accountable control systems, all out of the purview of parliamentary procedure: a state-within-the-state where telephone bugging by unit A4 and professional burglary carried out by sections of MI5 known as A1(D) and A1A seemed routine. In the late 1970s, private detectives working for the security services were regularly trained by the SAS and at the Army Special Branch training school in interrogation and surveillance. It was true that the SAS itself kept out of mainland affairs except in exceptional circumstances – the Iranian Embassy siege and intervening in the Peterhead Prison riot in 1987 being two occasions.

Such sweeping powers meant that the very act of communication was suspect. Phone tapping became de rigueur in these years in an alarming way and was run by a unit called the Tinkerbell Squad. Junior ministers and MPs had their phones regularly tapped. On 3 February 1980, the *Observer* exposed the tapping of the phones of three Labour MPs: Neil Kinnock, Bob Cryer and Michael Meacher. In July 1980, the Post Office Engineering Union was concerned enough about this clandestine attack on civil liberties to publish information on the subject:

Most members of the public would be amazed and concerned by the range and sophistication of surveillance technology which now exists. Most official tapping – whether authorised by warrant or not – is carried out on behalf of the relevant agency by specially selected Post Office personnel. These personnel volunteer for the task and are drawn from grades represented by a number of trade unions (including, of course, the POEU). During their time on tapping duties, they are under the operational control of the Home Office.[8]

Such operations were directed from a headquarters at 113 Grove Park, Camberwell SE5 which was guarded by steel doors and, although nominally part of C Division of the Metropolitan Police, was certainly a 'wireless receiving centre' which passed on information to R12 Division of British Telecom (created 1980) at Martlesham Heath near Ipswich, which in turn was linked to GCHQ and from there to NSA in the United States which effectively had overall 'control' of British operations. The men and women who undertook telephone tapping were part of a secret British Telecom or police unit who were 'unknown to their Post Office colleagues and operated out of sight and in most cases without their support'. The union's comments ended, 'The ordinary Post Office engineer has nothing whatsoever to do with telephone tapping and has the same mixed feelings about this practice as most members of the community.'[9]

The problem was twofold. Special operational groups seemed to exist, yet didn't ever seem to have substance. On the one hand, it would appear that those who might have reason to know about such shadowy organisations from their own experiences within the intelligence services or the SAS tantalised those interested with enough hints and allegations in their 'memoirs' to make things seem plausible, while, on the other, they used these hints for their own commercial purposes which re-fictional-ised the issues and obscured the truth.

Typical of this teasing method is the former SAS soldier-turned-author Chris Ryan who on his blog writes:

I've been asked if the Increment [a black ops/murder gang consisting of former SAS members] is real, and if the kind of deniable 'black' ops I depict … really happen. The Increment most definitely exists. It's a small group of badged guys who are part of E Squadron. They are specially selected for their skill, which is amazing even by SAS standards. They have to undergo incredibly stringent background security checks because they are entrusted with the most sensitive operations within the entire military. To be a member of the Increment is to be the best of the best.

As for whether these kind of deniable 'black' ops really exist ... well, that would be telling, wouldn't it?! [10]

Yet the very success of this derring-do, James Bond lifestyle was only to produce more obscurity and more 'faction', especially during the early 1990s when SAS histories, memoirs and survival manuals were big business. The very protection that Thatcher had lavished on the regiment was stripped away as soon as she left office. By 1998 there was a flood of books and 'memoirs' from disaffected soldiers. This outpouring of material was ironically due to the intransigent attitude of the commander of 22 SAS who demanded complete silence from his former soldiers who, having left the service, hoped to cash in on the public's interest in 'special ops'. Indeed, even General Peter de la Billiere, who had commanded A Squadron in Aden, was banned from publishing his own memoirs because of the potential leak of sensitive material. As a result of the ban on publications, the public was even more intrigued, a situation that led to an equal flood of dubious reminiscences.

Such was the case with Paul Bruce, whose book *The Nemesis File* supposedly recorded his enlistment into the SAS and then his involvement with SAS murder squads in Northern Ireland during the 1970s. [11] Although his book is accompanied by photographs, Bruce was allegedly exposed as a fraud when he was questioned over the allegations by the Royal Ulster Constabulary (RUC). Just as with another bestselling SAS 'fraud' called Tom Carew (actually Philip Sessarego), who committed suicide in 2014, Bruce seems never to have been in any covert operations or possibly not even in the regiment. The waters are further clouded by the fact that Bruce's *The Nemesis File* was reprinted in 2010 with the subtitle *The true story of an SAS execution squad*. The original book was, however, endorsed by Captain Fred Holroyd, someone who knew first-hand what really went on in Ireland; fiction by such an endorsement turns into 'faction'.

Captain Holroyd was stationed in Portadown, where he ran intelligence operations for the army and MI6. He resigned his commission in 1976, thereafter accusing the British army and the RUC of collusion in dirty ops and assassination. Holroyd claimed that the SAS operated under cover of the '4 Field Survey Troop, Royal Engineers' also known as the 14 Intelligence Company. The soldiers in this unit were part of something called the Northern Ireland Training and Tactics Team and appeared to be active members or former members of the SAS.

Holroyd was apparently confined to a mental hospital after he made public the turf war which raged between MI5 and MI6 over who ran operations in Northern

Ireland. He met Ken Livingstone when Livingstone was on the election trail in Brent and told Livingstone his story. Concerns that Holroyd was framed by intelligence or the army for his revelations led Livingstone to name Holroyd in his maiden speech to Parliament on 7 July 1987, a speech which also alluded to the undisclosed battle between MI5 and MI6 and the operations of a number of classified units so secret as to have no official military position. When asked to give evidence at the inquiry into the Dublin and Monaghan bombings, in front of Justice Henry Barron, Holroyd was considered a Walter Mitty character who, nevertheless, told enough of the truth to be believed in his accusations.[12]

Holroyd's accusation that Edmund Garvey, assistant commissioner of the Garda, was on the British 'side', led, in part, to Garvey being sacked.[13] So, why did Holroyd endorse a book he knew might be fiction when he knew more of the facts? When I contacted Blake Publishing, the publisher of *The Nemesis File*, it prevaricated. So, no further light has been thrown onto whether the book is fact or merely fantasy based on overheard facts, and the reason for the endorsement remains obscure.

Then there is the 'deception' of a more serious kind, committed by someone well known and taken seriously. Ranulph Fiennes' 'biography' of a group of killers called the Clinic, which he published as *The Feather Men*, was exposed as 'faction' at a Cheltenham Literature Festival publicity appearance.[14] The book, Fiennes admitted later, was 'all fiction', but used the names of real people. Each of these apparent hoax fictions contain enough 'fact' to seem plausible and, more importantly, for the reading public to want them to be plausible.

Were any security services engaged in outright murder or planned assassination during the 1970s and 1980s? Even in 2014 there was no definitive evidence to suggest MI5 or MI6 were engaged in planned assassinations. In his book *Enemies of the State* Gary Murray says: 'Despite the tremendous amount of circumstantial evidence that exists to support these allegations, there is no first-hand evidence to bring a prima facie case against MI5 for any illegal act, especially not for murder.'[15] Nevertheless, there also seemed to be an inner cadre of MI5 known as IP (the Inner Policy Club) which may or may not have had the direction of such practices through their employment of private agencies whose relationship can always be denied. 'This so-called IP Club is alleged to consist of a group of staunch traditionalists who believe that it is their God-given right to use MI5 facilities to advance their own political aims. In the armed forces, such conduct would more than likely be classified as "mutiny".'[16]

The 1980s almost made conspiracy theory a legitimate mode of history. The most problematic exposé of all was that of Peter Wright, whose uncorroborated allegations in his book *Spycatcher* were enough to put real fright into the government. It has subsequently become abundantly clear that 'illegal' methods were employed during the period, including, perhaps, SAS-style assassinations by methods which seemed to have been learned in Northern Ireland.

Were certain 'rogue' elements in all levels of the security services out of control after all, or was some of this apparent illegal activity authorised at the highest level? The fact that there were shadowy assassination groups did not fully emerge until 1989, when an ultra-Protestant group consisting of politicians, businessmen, police officers, ex-SAS soldiers and paramilitaries calling itself the Committee began a murderous campaign across Ireland. Were such groups, or those with similar purposes, active on the British mainland during the 1980s? Did such groups even exist?

No one really knew (or knows) if all these rogue elements were a strange fantasy or a reality. Serious corruption, manipulation and political interference just became another weary joke exemplified by writers such as Willie Rushton of *Private Eye* (a publication with otherwise exemplary credentials during the period) whose satirical book *Spy Thatcher: The Collected Ravings of a Senior MI5 Officer – an Insult to British Intelligence* reduced the whole thing to an Edwardian pantomime:

> He had the basis of a plan to get a listening device into the Russian Embassy. I became more and more excited as he outlined it to me. What he asked of me fell well without my bailiwick as it simply involved hovering a kite or balloon over the Embassy itself … We must experiment at once … I have applied for a fortnight's use of an old Artillery Range on the Gower Peninsular. I had never been to Wales. My word, these were exciting times … We were to meet at Paddington Station next morning. Dress garishly. We are Variety Artistes on our way to an engagement at the Old Alhambra, Tenby. A trunk will be delivered to you shortly with the name of our Act stencilled upon it. Cloak and Dagger. Rather good I thought.[17]

It seems clear, nevertheless, that successive Thatcher governments accepted the dubious secret roles of intelligence and 'other' services. On the whole, the government stuck to the line formulated by Austen Chamberlain in 1924, and reiterated by every government up to the late 1980s: 'It is of the essence of a Secret Service that it must be secret, and if you once begin disclosure it is perfectly obvious to me … that there is no longer any Secret Service and that you must do without it.'[18]

This continuing attitude led the secret services into areas of 'neglect' and 'maladministration', but it also led to abuse and non-accountability too. In 1985, the historian Sir Michael Howard suggested the ridiculousness of too much secrecy: 'So far as official government policy is concerned, the British security and intelligence services do not exist. Enemy agents are found under gooseberry bushes and intelligence is brought by the storks.'[19] Indeed, Nigel Lawson noted in his memoirs how Thatcher confused fiction for fact when it came to intelligence:

> In general, however, the security services, their establishments and their hardware, were one of the very few areas of public life virtually untouched by the rigours of

the Thatcher era. Most Prime Ministers have a soft spot for the security services, for which they have a special responsibility. But Margaret, an avid reader of the works of Frederick Forsyth, was positively besotted by them.[20]

This was certainly in marked contrast to Harold Wilson, who entertained a morbid fear of the security forces. Indeed, as soon as he had handed over to Jim Callaghan after resigning on the morning of 16 March 1976, he felt the need to unburden himself to journalists freelancing for the BBC over his fears. Barrie Penrose and Roger Courtiour were summoned to 5 Lord North Street for an extraordinary interview. Wilson had already spoken on record as to his belief 'that democracy … [was] in grave danger' from 'anti-democratic agencies' in South Africa and 'else-where'.[21] The South African connection was supposedly through the infiltration of British institutions by BOSS (Bureau of State Security, the South African intelligence service), then seen as the most ruthless of western intelligence agencies and one determined to discredit the Labour Party over its opposition to apartheid. The 'else-where' referred to was Britain's own security services, who Wilson thought had a vendetta against him and the Labour Party:

> I am not certain that for the last eight months when I was Prime Minister I knew what was happening, fully, in Security … They would naturally be brought up to believe … that Socialist leaders were another form of Communist. They are blinkered; the sort of people who would have spread the stories of Number 10 and the Communist cell … They were saying I was tied up with the Communists … The arch link was my Political Secretary Marcia [Lady Falkender]. She was sup- posed to be a dedicated Communist.[22]

So worried had Wilson become that he had hauled in Sir Maurice Oldfield, the head of MI6, and Sir Michael Hanley, head of MI5, to answer the charges that rogue elements were acting on their own agenda within the services. Wilson had also contacted George Bush, then head of the CIA, to see if there was an American connection, and written privately to Senator Hubert Humphrey for further reassur- ances. The reassurances duly came, but to Wilson it all smacked of another Watergate. He bought a huge safe to protect his papers and looked under every stone for con- spiracy. He became obsessed by a mysterious 'doctor' who had apparently worked for the Israelis, and started to talk to journalists in a sort of peculiar gobbledegook code that suggested he might be losing his senses:

> I see myself as the big fat spider in the corner of the room. Sometimes I speak when I'm asleep. You should both listen. Occasionally when we meet I might tell you to go to the Charing Cross Road and kick a blind man standing on the corner. That blind man may tell you something, lead you somewhere.[23]

It all seemed very mysterious, and, as with all paranoia, everything was connected. Thus it was that the peculiar machinations of one Norman Scott – who had been peddling since the 1960s a story that he had had a torrid affair with the leader of the Liberal Party, Jeremy Thorpe – were also woven into the fabric of Wilson's concerns. Wilson believed that Scott was a spy for BOSS working to discredit the Liberals for their anti-apartheid stand, which in due course would smear the Labour Party (Thorpe and Wilson were good friends) and thereby let the Conservatives win power.

No one wanted to believe Scott, who openly accused Thorpe, at every opportunity of turning him 'homosexual'. Scott was seen as a dangerous neurotic and a notorious blackmailer. On 24 October 1975, he went for a drive with a new friend called Andrew Newton, who had been hired (on Thorpe's behalf) to kill him. In the car was Scott's large dog Rinka which bounded at Newton, who was terrified of dogs. Newton panicked and shot Rinka and then went up to Scott to kill him, but thought better of it and left. The bizarre story made a small splash in the newspapers and was quickly forgotten. On 18 November, Newton was arrested, but the whole affair was seen as a huge joke. Even when Newton was sentenced to two years in prison for illegal possession of a firearm and intent to endanger life, the case was still seen as a minor bit of peculiarity. The judge summed up: 'As a matter of law … You are not allowed to shoot blackmailers. If people were allowed to take the law into their own hands you see what the result could be: chaos.'[24] Newton later changed his name to Hann Redwin and died in 2004.

The full story took many more years to emerge, but by then it seemed certain that Scott was the victim of a long-running personal conspiracy which had ended when Thorpe had decided on a 'final solution' to his problems in 1974.[25] Indeed, he had decided to embezzle Liberal funds to have Scott bought off:

> Then Thorpe had a brainwave: he said that [his colleague] Peter Bessell should lure Scott to the States with the promise of a job, where Holmes would kill him. Bessell said that this had potential … such as burying Scott's body in Florida … having killed him … Bessell would dispose of the body in the swamps, where alligators would consume it.[26]

Thorpe was quite capable of framing his friends and lying to colleagues to gain his own ends, as he did continuously to both Wilson and his party whip, Cyril Smith (a man hiding his own secrets). Thorpe was a man hiding in plain sight. When journalists Penrose and Courtiour approached the BBC with their story, they were met by the stonewall of the old-boy network. They were made to understand that, 'even if our information all turned out to be true, it set an organisation like the BBC so many problems. The overwhelming reaction was one of intense worry, either way. It involved too many difficult factors. The truth wasn't necessarily the overwhelming consideration.'[27]

Wilson was paranoid, but not without cause. He was wrong about trusting Thorpe, who later had his own day in court (even though he was acquitted in one of the most biased trials in British history). Scott did not work for BOSS, but neither was he a liar or blackmailer, and Peter Wright later confirmed many of Wilson's fears in his memoirs.

MI5 and Special Branch had kept files on Jeremy Thorpe for years. Indeed, Reginald Maudling, Conservative Home Secretary, and Sir John Waldron, Metropolitan Police Commissioner, both knew in 1971 that Thorpe was a homosexual with a taste for 'cruising' because Special Branch and MI5 had taken a watching brief as part of their quite unofficial and illegal surveillance of political figures.[28] The files were probably begun during the early 1960s when Alex Keller was head of F Branch at MI5, the unit set up to monitor political parties. Keller was a dapper and rather camp homosexual himself, nicknamed Liberace by colleagues. It was Keller who had compiled a vast list of Communist Party sympathisers at Oxford and Cambridge in order to identify possible Soviet moles, especially among the secretive homosexual community. He therefore must have been aware early on of Thorpe's proclivities. Keller retired in 1965 when the file would have been quietly passed on.[29] Marcia Williams recalled later, 'MI5 knew about Thorpe but did not tell Harold [Wilson] because they wanted to destabilise us [the Labour government].'[30]

Wilson was actually interviewed by Special Branch detectives about Thorpe's prevarications, but the meeting went entirely unremarked by the national press even though he was the first Prime Minister in British history to be questioned by police. Marcia Williams refused to meet the detectives, fearing another plot to entrap Wilson.

Thorpe's lies landed him in the dock of the Old Bailey, but his fellow conspirators made themselves scarce as Thorpe continued to con his way out of prison. He didn't have to try too hard because the trial judge, Justice Joseph Cantley, was sufficiently enamoured of the defendant and his 'class' of person that he allowed himself to be blinded to the obvious – that Thorpe was guilty and a habitual liar. Cantley delivered a summing up both ridiculously biased and inadvertently comic. Of Scott he opined: 'He is a crook. He is a fraud, a sponger … He is a whiner. He is a parasite. But of course he could still be telling the truth … I am not expressing any opinion.'[31] Of Andrew Newton, the judge suggested that 'He is a chump, a conceited bungler. I doubt whether he has paid any income tax. One has to look at his evidence with great care.'[32] The trial's atmosphere had been captured well before the event by an article in the *Sunday Times* which summed up (in earnest) the deadly mixture of old-boy networking and plain secrecy and lying that marked the establishment's attitude to an attack on one of its own and the threat to their own supremacy:

> To ask a public man whether he has ever been a homosexual is as indefensible as
> to ask him if he has ever committed adultery. It scrapes the barrel of journalistic
> slime. Backwards and ever backwards the innuendoes go. That is the stuff of
> McCarthyism and its whispering agents deserve no honour.[33]

It was not because Thorpe was a closet homosexual (there were many of them) or a liar or a conspirator to murder that meant he was protected for so long, but because he appeared the perfect gentleman, and, in attempting to ruin Thorpe, the vindictive, 'cowardly' and effeminate Scott wished somehow to damage England.[34]

In 1979, politicians in Britain were still intrinsically trusted (as were the police) and attacks upon them were malicious spite, class hatred or some personal vendetta represented as being pursued by a 'weirdo'. The *Sunday Times* and Mr Justice Cantley stood for the older subservient conservatism that upheld the 'unwritten rules' of social etiquette, rules that Margaret Thatcher always lived by. Inadvertently, these same rules were destroyed in her vision of a property-owning Britain, best summed up in her third term by the culture of red-braced greed in the City of London, the appearance of the yuppie and Harry Enfield's comic creation Loadsamoney, itself the triumph of Essex Man.

3

CLOCKWORK ORANGE

Harold Wilson had a right to be concerned. The Labour Party had much to fear in the 1970s, for its support of left-wing regimes in South America, its intimate links to the unions, and its opposition of apartheid, all of which fuelled right-wing paranoia. Socialists and liberals had even more to fear from opponents hidden in the state machinery.

This poisonous atmosphere was fuelled by what was going on in Northern Ireland. The increasingly desperate and violent measures of the Republicans were being met by increasing force and subterfuge from the forces sent against them. At the centre of much controversy was the figure of Colin Wallace. Wallace was born into a Scottish Presbyterian family in 1943 and lived in Randalstown in Unionist County Antrim. As a patriotic boy, Wallace had joined the Territorial Army and later the Ulster Special Constabulary or B Specials, who were hated by Catholics. In 1968, Wallace joined the regular army and quickly rose through the ranks, becoming assistant command public relations officer based at Lisburn, the army's headquarters.

The IRA was fizzling out until internment inadvertently resurrected it. Wallace was to be employed producing 'psyops' (psychological operations) or black propaganda in the emerging conflict. It was during 1974 that Wallace was approached by an intelligence agent called 'John Shaw' and asked to participate in Operation Clockwork Orange – an operation to destabilise the IRA through false media stories, but which soon spread to include problems that needed dealing with at 'home': alleged communist infiltration of the Labour Party.

The information which Wallace transcribed seemed not to have originated in Ireland. He kept notes of what appeared to be an attempt to undermine British sovereignty that led all the way from Ireland to the Prime Minister, Harold Wilson. It was all apparently part of a bigger conspiracy. Wallace's Clockwork Orange notes were being collated while he continued work in psyops. In this regard, he produced an influential paper called 'Ulster – A State of Subversion' which argued (alongside other black propaganda papers then held at Lisburn and available to Northern Irish journalists) that Irish terrorism had to be defeated rather than merely allowed to peter out. Defeating the Provisional IRA would effectively defeat *those in government* (the real terrorists and subversives) who tied the hands of the army because of secret leftist sympathies and Soviet connections.[1]

Things went badly for Wallace as he became more concerned about his 'role' and told his story to David McKittrick of the *Irish Times*. Employment prospects had already been soured, as Wallace had been dealing with a Protestant murder group and paedophile operation out of the Kincora Boys' Home, a situation that had to be kept under wraps. Wallace soon found himself out of a job and under investigation both for divulging secrets and for the murder of a friend, Jonathan Lewis, whom he was alleged to have killed in August 1980 because of an affair with Lewis's wife, Jane. Whether he killed his friend or his friend was killed to frame him, Wallace went to prison, his case a salutary lesson in keeping state secrets forever secret.

Harold Wilson was correct to be vigilant but wrong in his belief that the things he feared were directly connected to the people he liked and trusted. Paul Foot in his exposé of the workings of the secret state concluded his investigative book on Colin Wallace (published in 1989) with this damning indictment of the 'state within the state':

> By the middle of the 1970s sections of the security services were completely out of control. They were running their own operations without anyone with demo-cratic responsibility knowing about them, let alone controlling them. The chief victim of these campaigns was not 'the enemy' as it is widely known – foreign powers, perhaps, who threaten invasion – but 'the Left' in general and in this particular [case] the elected government of the country. So powerful was this secret state that it was … able and keen to operate against that part of the state for which elected people have to answer. In the hothouse atmosphere created by irresponsibility to the outside world, those sections of the Intelligence services tried to change the outside world to their best taste: a taste which by the very nature of the type of organisation, and the secrecy with which it worked, was inevitably of the most bizarre and terrifying variety.[2]

Only when John Major became Prime Minister and brought in a policy of parlia-mentary accountability did the government feel able to confirm the existence of the Secret Intelligence Service (MI6) at all and this almost 100 years after it came into existence.[3]

This veil that hid alleged conspiracy and innuendo was, however, finally pulled aside when Christopher Andrew produced his official history of MI5 in 2009, based on confidential material kept in the files at the Security Service's archives. Were all those involved in underhand army operations, such as Holroyd and Wallace, simply mistaken in their understanding of the situation, and the journalists and politicians they enlisted simply gullible? Wilson had certainly been misled by Jeremy Thorpe in believing that there was a South African connection, but that had already been corrected some time before the Wilson 'plot' was exposed.

According to Andrew, other accusations by Colin Wallace and Fred Holroyd were merely hot air. Andrew repeats the assertion by Sir Anthony Duff, then director general of the Security Service, that the allegations 'were baseless'.[4] To Andrew, the re-emergence of the allegations in Peter Wright's *Spycatcher* were the outpourings of a delusional and embittered man who first suggested that the Wilson plot was known to eight or nine conspirators, then changed his tune and suggested that only 'one' person was actively involved.[5]

When James Callaghan and Neil Kinnock met Sir Anthony Duff on 31 March 1987, Duff was soon put on the spot regarding the revelations in Wright's book:

> Callaghan fixed [Duff] with a fairly penetrating, not to say hostile, glance and said that even if only a tenth of what Wright had said about destabilising the Wilson government was true, it was still a 'bloody disgrace' that it had happened. [Duff] said that it was all in any case untrue.[6]

According to Andrew, Wilson was 'paranoid' (possibly leading up to his illness) and Marcia Williams had been 'responsible for a lot of it'.[7]

Were any of these tales true? Colin Wallace had, after all, released his story to Paul Foot ten years after the event and about the same time that Peter Wright released *Spycatcher*. Certainly, academics who write about intelligence matters are often more sceptical than investigative journalists in search of a scoop, and those on the right are more willing to argue that the whole thing was some put-up job by angry ex-soldiers or civil servants involved with dirty work trying to clear a tainted conscience. This is best captured by the comments of Bernard Porter, an academic writer on intelligence affairs who suggests that Wallace was a man with a 'grievance' whose 'horse's tale' was the result of embitterment and 'flakiness'.[8]

Yet this solves nothing. Both Porter and Andrew quote hearsay and counter-accusation, not hard facts, nor does either offer evidence that MI5 was not involved. Neither author offers evidence (for or against) to show what a number of unrelated journalists (such as Seumas Milne), writers and politicians came to think – that much of what was whispered might be supported by facts. Otherwise, why waste government time and money in the prosecution of non-existent plotters and bother with the expense of pointless prosecution of books that were allegedly pure fiction? Nor does such scepticism answer the question of the evidence provided or the veracity of witnesses. We know, for instance that later cover-ups (in regard to paedophile accusations or the tragedy of Hillsborough) have never been fully investigated until now and the whole truth is unlikely ever to be revealed. This does not make the allegations regarding the activities of rogue members of the state or even the activities of authorised members untrue, just unproven and, much more importantly, unprovable.

As we shall see, the importance of absolute proof is an especially important idea when applied to allegations regarding 'death squads' in Northern Ireland or politicians in paedophile rings, but absolute proof is what rarely comes to light unless the intelligence services will it to do so, in which case it will already be tainted! Take the official history of MI5, for instance. Christopher Andrew's ability to determine the truth is itself coloured by his reliance on his friend, Soviet defector Oleg Gordievsky, with whom he had written another book and whose evidence is used to accuse the union leader Jack Jones of being a Soviet mole (an accusation going back to the 1960s). More damningly, Andrew clearly approves of the illegal surveillance of left-wing groups, the Communist Party of Great Britain and the Revolutionary Socialist League or Militant and which was, according to Andrew, 'unquestionably subversive', an accusation that I explore later. Moreover, the number of internal subversives who might have lurked in these organisations was minuscule and the likelihood of their causing such a breakdown in civil life as to create a 'revolution', or even exploiting one, was laughable.

The threat from the extreme left may be gauged from their micro-internecine struggles. In April 1978, the Spartacists announced in their paper *Spartacist Britain* that they had split from the Workers' Socialist League, which in turn was a splinter group of the Socialist Labour League and Workers' Revolutionary Party. They spent more of their time on doctrinaire squabbles than on any real belief that a revolution or a socialist coup was on the cards.

In contradistinction to the thoughts of their opponents, these groups usually hated each other on a personal level and were incapable of uniting to take over the country even if they had had the means. There certainly was never an overall secret organisation that linked these warring factions (as there had been with the Bolsheviks before the 1917 revolution in Russia). More significantly, none of these organisations was proscribed and all were therefore legitimate. The practice of watching political subversives had grown out of Special Branch interest in foreign anarchists in the early twentieth century and turned into a practice wholly condoned, but on no legal footing, after the surveillance of 'reds' began in the 1920s.

Despite the great threat of subversion by communists and crypto-communists in the unions (the actual claim to 'subversion' was that the unions wanted 'unfettered wage bargaining', a standard union position), they appear to have been rendered impotent by the very strikes they had been secretly engineering. Indeed, even the Box 500 reports suggest no master plan for the Winter of Discontent in 1979 which brought Thatcher to power. MI5 reports state that:

Trotskyist groups are finding difficulty in keeping pace with events and in some places are being told by Party officials to concentrate their attention entirely on selling their newspapers … the industrial organiser of the Socialist Workers party (SWP), believes that many of their members are daunted by the scale of the action and are not clear how to take advantage of it.[9]

While Harold Wilson and James Callaghan were both happy to let the security services loose on the unions, Wilson became more paranoid about their activities in his second term and Callaghan became more dependent on them as industrial unrest seemed to go out of control.

On the other hand, Margaret Thatcher herself was fascinated by intelligence, and mesmerised by it too. On taking office, she actually thought she had carte blanche to oust the 'Trots' and 'wreckers' she thought had infiltrated every aspect of public life, including the unions, the broadcasting services, the Church, universities and the Civil Service. So she called an immediate meeting with the director general of MI5, Sir Howard Smith. Although the argument was forcefully put to her that her plan was against the spirit of the Maxwell-Fyfe Directive of 1952, she insisted that something be done.

This proved an impasse, so, at the next meeting to consider industrial subversion (a meeting so secret the security services were not informed), held in October 1979, the director general was simply not invited. This was the way that much of the business was handled. Thatcher 'Chair[ed] the Ministerial Steering Committee on Intelligence (MIS) which supervise[d] the community and fixe[d] its budget priorities. A permanent secretaries' steering group on intelligence (PSIS) chaired by the cabinet secretary prepare[d] briefs for the MIS [as it still does].'[10]

This led Thatcher to take a quite over-personal interest in the doings of GCHQ, to the point where her intransigence actually made the acronym and its activities widely known. Yet Thatcher and her associates may themselves have been subject to surveillance and destabilisation. If Thatcher was felt to be the creation of ultra-right-wing elements in MI5 still operating years after the Clockwork Orange dossier, it makes sense that they watched their investment carefully. This might explain a curious incident when she was in opposition in the run-up to the 1979 election.

Tim Bell was the main contact with Thatcher at Saatchi and Saatchi as she prepared for her attempt to oust Callaghan. It was Bell who had helped her change her appearance for television and who (with Gordon Reece) modified the tone of her voice. He also invented the famous 'Labour Isn't Working' slogan (itself a deception that used young Hendon Conservatives to 'play' at being unemployed). Thatcher and Bell recalled in their memoirs that she had telephoned him to discuss her disappointment that an election had not been announced by 7 September 1978. Suddenly Bell said, "'My God, I've been burgled ...'" He had managed to go to bed without noticing.'[11] It was a strange and unexplained incident, but it seemed evidence of intelligence burglary.

The security forces played dangerous games throughout Thatcher's time in office. These often related to the dispute between MI5 and MI6 over geographical jurisdiction, especially regarding Northern Ireland. Nevertheless, David Owen, the Labour Foreign Secretary between 1976 and 1979, said of Maurice Oldfield and his service (MI6) that:

They were scrupulous and that they had referred the right ones to me and they had been very good sorting out what was technical detail and what was something which involved political content and required the authorisation of the democratic political leadership ... I didn't get the feeling that I was dealing with a reactionary bunch of people at all. Dealing with things like South Africa and race, I found them very broad-minded and not by any means the sort of archetypal right-wing figure.[12]

So appreciated by the government was Oldfield that Thatcher approached him as security coordinator for Northern Ireland. He accepted, but he had a history. In April 1987, a story was leaked to the *Sunday Times* that suggested Oldfield had been a security risk when caught 'cottaging' in 1980. It was not exactly true, however, but plausible enough to cause damage. MI5 was at war with MI6 and wanted to create more power for itself by spreading a smear. During the 1970s, Oldfield had denounced the type of dirty tricksters that operated under Peter Wright.

Then, in 1979, Oldfield had actually been brought in to sort out the mess in Ireland and investigate MI5 in relation to the 'shoot to kill' policy which he tried to end. This intervention was probably Oldfield's downfall. Indeed, Oldfield had observed the CIA in action and deplored what he saw and did not want British intelligence to go down the same route. Specifically, he insisted that there should be no confusion between 'the collection of information' and 'sabotage and assassination'.[13] His carefully defined strictures embraced the two areas in which MI5 seemed to be mired. Oldfield had therefore, to be neutralised post hoc, a method that seems to have been used in the case of Wallace and numerous union leaders and left-leaning politicians.[14] Ironically, MI5 had been spying all along on the head of their rival service. Oldfield was finally forced out of office in June 1980 when his clearance was suddenly withdrawn after he admitted he was homosexual.

Oldfield had himself taken over from Sir John Rennie, who had resigned after both his son and daughter-in-law were jailed for drug offences. Oldfield died a year after his final retirement. Just before he died, he is alleged to have said to Sir Anthony Cavendish, 'I think they got me', by which he meant either an ironic black joke or that he had actually been poisoned by MI5 with chemicals stolen from Porton Down (where Peter Wright had contacts). Cavendish had noted how closely this fitted the same story told by Wallace, who had not met Oldfield, but who had repeated his narrative to Cavendish.[15] Oldfield's death was seen as part of the Wright 'plot' inside MI5 by investigators such as Gary Murray, whose work on the secret services and private investigations and their corrupt practices became a bible both for conspiracy theorists and those whose legitimate investigations suggested an actual series of conspiratorial situations.

Murray soon became disillusioned with his own dealings with MI5, which seemed to employ incompetent handlers and was tardy in its payments to those it ran on operations. Moreover, he also feared it was quite capable of some very dubious activities, including the infiltration of unions and the anti-nuclear lobby as well as regularly using burglary, phone tapping, bugging and intimidation for ends that were not always legitimate. This was the case throughout the 1970s and 1980s and certainly had its antecedents long before. Murray was also convinced that murder was not necessarily out of the equation as long as the intelligence service could employ a 'cut-out' system allowing it to deny all knowledge and discredit those it employed. Thus he recalled:

> Assassination is of special interest to me, for the simple reason that at one stage in my relationship with MI5 it was suggested that I take a subject of investigation, who was described as 'a menace', for a ride in my private aircraft and drop him out over the North Sea! I have no doubt in mind that this was an attempt to expand my function from spy to assassin. Sometime after this suggestion, the person referred to was involved in a mysterious road accident.[16]

Corruption was such that in 1971 Edward Heath, then Prime Minister, said of MI5's operatives that they were utterly untrustworthy to the point of suffering from professional paranoia, his assessment was quite at odds with that of David Owen, but in line with that of Gary Murray:

> I met people in the security services who talked the most ridiculous nonsense and whose whole philosophy was a ridiculous nonsense. If some of them were on an underground train and saw someone reading the *Daily Mirror*, they would say 'that is dangerous, get after him and find out where he bought it'.[17]

Murray also quotes an unnamed MI5 officer as suggesting that, 'Some officers live a very sheltered life and never work in the real world and the overall tone is right wing. Some of them thought people who wore jeans were potentially subversive.'[18]

Such dirty tactics were also attempted in the case of Margaret Thatcher's numerous links to Jewish politicians and businessmen, a number of whom were in her Cabinet. The inherent upper-class anti-Semitism of the intelligence services, which went back as far as the origins of the service itself when it was linked to fascism, never quite came to the surface. It is clear that the watching brief MI5 had on Wilson was attached to his fondness for Israel and to his friendship with the coat manufacturer Joseph Kagan, who in turn was in touch with a KGB agent called Dick Vaygauskas. This historical paranoia regarding the question of the patriotism of British Jewish citizens led to MI5 watching Leon Brittan and preparing a smear campaign and plotting against Robert Maxwell among others.

Wilson clearly had reason to be concerned, for the world of intelligence was entering a new and dangerous phase in which the rules were being bent with impunity.

It was hardly surprising that a left-wing Prime Minister, in this respect, came under suspicion too. Those whom the government designates as enemies become the enemy, but, far more powerful are those who designate the enemy on behalf of the Crown, those often unanswerable and ghostly figures who have been in the military and who are activated by equally distant figures in Whitehall. Paul Foot suggests that:

Peter Wright wrote that none of his colleagues in MI5 (by which he probably meant some of his own right-wing gang in MI5) felt themselves loyal to Parliament. They all, he said, felt loyal to the Queen. They never met the Queen, and were certainly never called to account by her. So the expression 'loyalty to the Queen' was a fiction; a mere excuse to be loyal to nothing except themselves.[19]

4

A COLDITZ WARRIOR
IN WHITEHALL

The spirit of the Thatcher years was one of messianism mixed with paranoia regarding communist infiltration. This paranoia was felt by a sufficient (if proportionally small) number of disenfranchised voters who brought her to power. In 1979, as she campaigned to be Prime Minister, Thatcher believed that the political and cultural breakdown of the 1970s, itself a consequence of the moral breakdown of the 1960s, had to be halted at any cost.

The National Association for Freedom (NAFF) was created precisely to stop the malaise. It was the vision of Ross and Norris McWhirter, best known for their involvement with the *Guinness Book of Records* (frequently appearing on television testing record-breaking claims). The two brothers were also involved in efforts to support several projects dedicated to beating the unions (at Grunwick and at Ford), halting comprehensive schools and stopping postal workers boycotting post for South Africa. In 1975, Ross McWhirter started publishing pamphlets on liberty, freedom and the dangers of union corporatism and state control under the imprimatur of the Current Affairs Press. He also produced a news-sheet called *Majority* which highlighted anti-union activists. Current Affairs Press, which was renamed Self Help (a favourite idea of Thatcher's), formed the core of NAFF. Self Help in its turn came under the direction of Jane Birdwood, a virulent anti-communist and anti-Semite. NAFF officially began in December 1975, just after Ross's assassination by the IRA in November. He had offered £50,000 to catch the perpetrators of numerous attacks, including two that targeted Edward Heath. Some time before, the brothers had had a chance meeting on a plane with Lord de L'Isle. Norris later recalled:

> [We] had a detailed discussion about the seriousness of Britain's decline since the death of Winston Churchill. Lord de L'Isle had just received a letter from Michael Ivens [the director of the anti-union pressure group Aims of Industry], asking him to consider leading a new association pledged to support individual freedom and to resist ever Bigger Government. As a result of the long flight, Ross

and Norris McWhirter were invited to Lord de L'Isle's home at Penshurst Place in Kent for a further discussion. It was on the hottest day of the year, Thursday 12 June 1975. At a light lunch on a small round table that Lord de L'Isle had acquired at an auction at Chartwell, home of Sir Winston Churchill, plans were hatched to convene a meeting of fifty prominent people from politics, business, the armed services, the church and the professions at the Grosvenor House Hotel in London on Thursday 31 July.

The day after Ross McWhirter was killed, Thatcher paid this tribute to him in the Commons:

We on this side of the House feel particularly deeply about this matter, because we knew Ross McWhirter well and admired him a great deal. He was one of the finest people of his generation. He was never timid or passive about his belief in liberty. He was active each and every day in protecting and preserving individual liberty. The terrorists may have killed him and others, but we are concerned that they must never conquer that indomitable spirit of unhesitating courage without which freedom would perish.[2]

Her admiration did not stop there, and she happily put her name to the letter appealing for donations for the Foundation that Norris McWhirter was setting up with journalist Brian Crozier, academic and journalist Robert Moss and John Gouriet. Of these, all were conspiratorial and suspicious of political leaders. The letter, which was published in the *Times* on 5 December 1975, stated that Ross McWhirter was 'a man of such fiercely held and uncompromising convictions [that he] was bound to provoke disagreement in some quarters as well as strong approval in others'. Thatcher also spoke at the inaugural meeting of NAFF protected by police who feared trouble. She had her soulmates in Ross McWhirter and Airey Neave and both were killed, almost as confirmation of the rightness of the 'cause' which could now not be abandoned. When Neave was killed by a bomb, Thatcher's eulogy was, in effect, the same as for McWhirter.

Airey Neave was perhaps the most influential but also one of the most shadowy of all the supporters of the liberal vision that emerged in the consensus of the right in the mid-1970s. Neave had been educated at Eton and Oxford and had served in the Royal Artillery until his imprisonment. He was the first Briton to escape from Colditz and was recruited to MI6 soon after. As MP for Abingdon, he proved an average parliamentarian rising to no great heights in the Conservative Party. Nevertheless, he kept strong contacts with the intelligence agencies and was deeply interested in problems relating to anti-subversive measures and keeping order in the slow retreat of the Empire from the colonies. A staunch traditionalist, Neave hated the swinging '60s, unions, lefties and the Soviets (in no particular order), and by the '70s he was

convinced that Britain was on the brink of a communist takeover in which Ted
Heath and Harold Wilson were equally culpable. To counter this threat, he had joined
Ross McWhirter and his brother Norris and was a founder member of NAFF when
it formed after Ross's death.

Neave's time came in 1974, when he was elected to the executive of the 1922
Committee of Conservative backbenchers, where he began to plot the return of his
form of 'patriotic' conservatism. In this respect, Heath was the enemy and had to be
eliminated. To this end, Neave had backed Keith Joseph as leader. Joseph had started
the Centre for Policy Studies and his arguments had inaugurated what became
known as Thatcherism, but he had also embarked on a crusade to restrict working-
class breeding which he had wheeled out on 19 October 1974, effectively ending the
possibility of his own leadership bid. Interestingly, Joseph was, in his own words, only
'converted' to real Conservatism (i.e. Thatcherism) in April 1974.[3] Joseph was too
loose a cannon. By a process of elimination, this only left Thatcher, to whom Neave
offered to become campaign manager. Heath, certain of treachery had exclaimed,
'He'll kill us! He'll kill us!'[4]

Patrick Cosgrove, a Conservative journalist and advisor to Thatcher, suggested
that Neave was 'cunning' and brilliantly manipulative of disillusion within the
Conservative Party when he backed Thatcher in the 1974-75 leadership election.
Nevertheless, his management was not so Machiavellian as to believe he could run
Keith Joseph as a stalking horse for his preferred candidate as many suggested at the
time. Thatcher, herself, represented everything contemptible to Heath who referred
to her (if ever he could bring himself to do so) as 'that woman'.[5]

Neave saw in Thatcher the hopes of NAFF and the less barmy ideas of Keith Joseph.
She could be moulded to fit the right-wing agenda of the 1970s. On 31 January 1974,
Thatcher had laid out her beliefs in a speech in her Finchley constituency.
These were:

> Concern for individual freedom; opposition to excessive state power; reward
> for the thrifty and hard-working, and the right to pass on those gains to their
> children; diversity of choice and defence of private property against the socialist
> state; and the right of a man to work without oppression by either employer or
> trade union boss.[6]

Neave applauded the sentiments and Thatcher's aggressive spirit, suggesting that:

> [He] would choose her great personal courage. It may be that she has many
> frightening experiences to come but the thing she will never lack is courage.
> That is her great quality. She is outspoken by nature and is essentially a fighter
> and nobody should be surprised if she tells the country a few home truths.[7]

Neave was now entering the world of intrigue that fascinated him. Things moved inexorably towards his own fate. On the day Thatcher declared against Heath – 21 November 1974 – a bomb went off in Birmingham killing nineteen and injuring 182. Six days later, Roy Jenkins rushed through the Prevention of Terrorism Bill.

For his help with the leadership manoeuvres, Neave had the pick of Cabinet posts. He chose Northern Ireland, a post then considered a political backwater. Thatcher had agreed because of Neave's 'intelligence contacts'. It appears then that Neave thought that he could resolve the problem of Northern Ireland by the use of greater force and greater use of intelligence. Yet such intelligence contacts were not exactly playing by the rules.

Neave enjoyed the power he had by the nature of the backstairs he inhabited. He had cultivated senior people in intelligence who, working together, had helped bring about a 'coup' in the Conservative Party of a type they would have deeply disapproved of if the same had occurred in Labour ranks. Neave was not only in contact with George Kennedy Young of MI6, but also Peter Wright, to whom Neave offered information as to 'traitors, or potential ones'.[8] Neave had strong connections with other far-right groups too, and with the 'stay behind' organisations of former intelligence agents who disliked the way the country was going.

Neave was also involved with those associated with Frank Kitson and those using 'colonial' tactics in Ireland. One of Neave's friends from the Second World War was David Stirling, the founder of the SAS, and Neave wanted to expand the role of the SAS should he take control in Ireland. For instance, the SAS squadron based in Birmingham was to be used to monitor social unrest and to be ready for the predicted 'communist takeover'. In July 1974, the Monday Club, with orchestration by Neave and help from Stirling, had begun to agree secret plans for the army to occupy government buildings in a civil 'emergency'.[9]

To see how this might be allowable, we have to turn to the Home Defence Planning Assumptions which were published as early as 1973 and look at what the government's priorities might be:

1. The security of the UK against *Internal* threat. [This against the background of labour militancy at a level unknown since 1926]
2. Measures to mitigate the effects of *External* attack.
3. The provision of an alternate machinery of government to increase the prospect of national survival.
4. Measures to enhance the prospect of national recovery after attack.[10]

This feeling of embattlement on both sides of the political spectrum fuelled the general unease over every move by the police, secret services, Special Patrol Group (SPG), SAS, GCHQ and army and the growth of privately funded private-security agencies such as GB75 set up by David Stirling.

It was a world of mavericks. Field Marshall Montgomery described the young Stirling as 'quite mad, quite, quite mad', but he also recognised the need for eccentrics in extreme situations. 'In war there is often a place for mad people.'[11] The war in Northern Ireland was a perfect training ground and test laboratory for mad people (who could be trusted) and for dangerously mad people, some of whom had lost their moral compass as well as their sanity. It gave hints of what might arrive on the British mainland, especially as those in charge of developments concerning urban warfare were now in positions of great authority.

Those in the position of forming policies were often themselves prone to the sort of paranoid thinking that might create attitudes and practical solutions either hidden from those in government or such as might need approval after the event. This was the situation with actions in Northern Ireland.

Covert actions occasionally became overt (if supposedly benevolent) social coercion. Such was the case with various 'war games' around Heathrow in 1974, the crucial year for those plotting the various options for a right-wing coup. The *Evening Standard* reported on 8 January 1974 that:

> There is now some belief that, to an extent, the weekend's surprise developments at Heathrow, were a public relations manoeuvre aimed at accustoming the public to the sight of troops on the streets. It is known that the Ministry of Defence has contingency plans, often under review, for moving in servicemen to take over areas of industry vital to the running of the country. Obviously, first priorities would be the moving of coal and other essential supplies. The Arab missile threat [or the IRA getting hold of a SAM missile] presented the authorities with a good opportunity to do this, and the approach helps to explain why Scorpion light tanks were moved in.

The atmosphere was becoming poisonous. The National Council for Civil Liberties (NCCL) expressed concern in its annual report for 1973, which was released in March 1974:

> 1973 was a year which civil libertarians would have been better off without. Parliament was dissolved in the midst of a red scare unparalleled in 30 years, with the declaration of a sixth State of Emergency, the continuation of a joint police-military operation at Heathrow – despite its doubtful validity – and the admission by the Home Secretary, Robert Carr, that troops might be used in industrial disputes.[12]

In February 1976, the *Sunday Times* exposed plans by the government to use the already existing scheme for 'a minor nuclear attack' as a basis for the recovery of civil order in the light of a violent trade union industrial dispute, rioting and apparent societal breakdown.

Of everyone who might have been concerned about lost freedom and parliamentary overview it was the Trotskyist Workers' Party which rang one of the first alarm bells. Its election manifesto published on 12 February 1974 claimed that a then-unknown brigadier was working in Ireland on long-term plans to make Britain an authoritarian dictatorship:

> The plans … are far more advanced than many people realise. A clique of militarists around Brigadier Frank Kitson are constantly developing plans for a civil war attack on the working class. These military conspiracies are being advanced in the closest consultation with extreme right-wing Tories, British intelligence and the most reactionary sections of the ruling class. Ulster was the training ground for the type of operations they want to launch here.[13]

Frank Kitson was a strange type of soldier who had been given leave to take time out of the army to write a seminal book on urban warfare. *Low Intensity Operations: Subversion, Insurgency and Peacekeeping*, published in 1972, was an attempt to discuss warfare by terrorists or subversives which would be fought among the population in an urban environment. Kitson, who had won two Military Crosses, based his ideas on the low-intensity warfare from his colonial experiences in the Second World War and in Kenya and Cyprus. The book was intended as a manual for counter-insurgency and armed response on the streets of Britain using the lessons of the United States learned during the height of the student protests against the Vietnam War.

In the early 1970s, Kitson was advising the government on fighting 'extremists'. He was clear about the new warfare:

> Subversion, then, will be held to mean all measures short of the use of armed force taken by one section of the people of a country to overthrow those governing the country at the time or to force them to do things they do not want to do. It can involve the use of political and economic pressure, strikes, protest marches and propaganda …
>
> The second half of the 1970s is going to see a further swing towards the lower end of the operational spectrum with large-scale insurgency giving way to civil disorder accompanied by sabotage and terrorism, especially in urban areas.[14]

He was also quite clear about the need to 'bend' the law if necessary to protect the state. Here, Kitson was taking his cue from Robert Thompson, whose *Defeating Communist Insurgency* had been published in 1967. Kitson recognised from Thompson a basic contradiction in democratic society and indeed that there were two legal alternatives in fighting insurgents. The first was to treat both sides with impartiality, which would advantage the enemy; but the other, more effective means was for the judiciary to work quietly and in cahoots within a partial and patriotic legal system aligned to government needs, which might include the need for 'a propaganda cover for the disposal of unwanted members of the public'.[15] Moreover:

> It has to be recognised that methods of tying down large numbers of policemen and soldiers have been developed for use against governments which rely on popular support and which cannot therefore afford to use the sort of ruthless brutality which a dictatorship could use in order to control the situation in an economic way. If a genuine and serious grievance arose, such as might result from a significant fall in the standard of living, all those who now dissipate their protest over a wide variety of causes might concentrate their efforts and produce a situation which was beyond the power of the police to handle. Should this happen the army would be required to restore the position rapidly. Fumbling at this juncture might have grave consequences even to the extent of undermining confidence in the whole system of government.[16]

Kitson's recommendations were to impact on soldiering in Ireland, and his emphasis on 'psychological operations' was a reading of developments in similar tactics in American urban warfare at home and in Vietnam:

> Although the British seem to persist in thinking of Psychological Operations as being something from the realms of science fiction, it has for many years been regarded as a necessary and respectable form of war by most of our allies as well as virtually all of our potential enemies. The Americans maintain a Psychological Operations capability in all their joint commands overseas as well as Psychological Operations Battalions in the Continental United States, grouped with Special Force Units and held ready for immediate deployment as required. Undoubtedly the British are 'bringing up the rear' in this important aspect of contemporary war.[17]

These ideas would have major consequences for Ulster. They would also be used as evidence for successful psychological social engineering so that Thatcher could adopt the Chicago School's economic experiment in Chile to promote her version of the free market when she was elected. Kitson went on to become the first head of military intelligence in Ulster, and, in 1982, was promoted to Major General, Commander-in-Chief of United Kingdom Land Forces.

Nowhere was the contradiction of defending democracy by unauthorised, underhand and very dirty and ungentlemanly tactics better exemplified than in Kitson. His tactical interests in the 1970s were directly served by the loss of strategic control of Northern Ireland by the Heath government. The tactics he proposed for the streets of Northern Ireland as the decade wore on progressed to the carte blanche secretive and illegal activities that appear to have been the field of operations in the 1980s, which were his direct legacy.

Warfare outside the law and in civilian areas, however, justified by immediate circumstances in the field, and carried out defending democracy, sooner or later turns against the aims which it serves if it has no legal or regulated basis. Kitson and his ilk had bent the rules to the point where democracy was no longer relevant and civilian lives were daily put at risk. His legacy was to train dangerous men who sooner or later might be available for hire.

❧ ♋ ☙

One disciple of Kitson's form of intervention was Captain Laurence Nairac, who was abducted, tortured and murdered by the IRA in May 1977. He was killed on his fourth tour of duty as he worked under cover. Nairac began his involvement with Northern Ireland while serving in the Grenadier Guards, but, after the battalion's tour of duty, he stayed on as a liaison officer with the Argyll and Sutherland Highlanders. Unlike his first tour, which was relatively bloodless, the rest of Nairac's time in Ireland became increasingly violent. As the violence increased, it appears that he volunteered for military intelligence in the 4 Field Survey Troop, Royal Engineers, which itself was a sub-group of the 14 Intelligence Company. Nairac was not, apparently, a member of the SAS, despite his affiliation with this predominantly SAS unit. Nevertheless, he became a liaison officer between the army and the Royal Ulster Constabulary.

On his final return to Ireland, he was abducted and assassinated by the IRA, but, by this time, he might have been involved with espionage into suspected IRA members and liaising with secret loyalist paramilitaries. Indeed, it was claimed in a 1993 Yorkshire Television documentary about the Dublin and Monaghan bombings that:

> Evidence from police, military and loyalist sources … confirms the links between Nairac and the Portadown loyalist paramilitaries. And also that in May 1974, he was meeting with these paramilitaries, supplying them with arms and helping them plan acts of terrorism against republican targets. In particular, the three prime Dublin suspects, Robert McConnell, Harris Boyle and the man called 'The Jackal' (Robin Jackson, Ulster Volunteer Force member from Lurgan), were run before and after the Dublin bombings by Captain Nairac.[18]

Given freedom to operate independently (it seems never to have been established by whom), Nairac might have associated with known loyalist killers. It seems possible that Nairac was also at the centre of a murderous cabal of police officers, security personnel, soldiers and Ulster volunteers involved with targeting terrorists.

Nairac certainly appeared to have boasted to Fred Holroyd of his help in the murder of Provisional IRA member John 'Francie' Green in the Republic on 10 January 1975. Green had been on the run from Long Kesh (Maze Prison) for two years, but to pursue him over the border was irregular and highly illegal. Numerous sightings of a red Ford Escort associated with Nairac lent credence to Holroyd's tale. Assistant Garda commissioner J.P. McMahon suggested that beyond the loyalists involved there appeared to be collusion with the British army, to whom the Escort with its number plate was traced.

Nairac's boast was perhaps bravado intended to make more of his role as a vigilante, but there seems less doubt about his involvement with the attack on the Miami Showband. John Weir, who was an Ulster Volunteer Force (UVF) volunteer and a member of the RUC SPG claimed that:

> The men who did that shooting were Robert McConnell, Robin Jackson and, I would be almost certain, Harris Boyle, who was killed in the Miami attack. What I am absolutely certain of is that Robert McConnell knew that area really, really well. Robin Jackson was with him. I was later told that Nairac was with them. I was told by … a UVF man, he was very close to Jackson and operated with him. Jackson told [him] that Nairac was with them.[19]

If Nairac was with Jackson, then he mixed with very dangerous company. Robin (the Jackal) Jackson was a loyalist paramilitary assassin who worked in County Armagh and was in cahoots with the authorities. He was the most successful of the United Kingdom's growing number of Protestant killers. Having murdered at least fifty civilians, Jackson was finally killed while in prison. Colin Wallace described Jackson, whom he had known in the mid 1970s as, 'A hired gun. A professional assassin. He was responsible for more deaths in the North than any other person I knew.'[20]

John Weir also corroborated the story of the murder of 'Francie' Green in the cross-border raid, although the investigative journalist Martin Dillon says the charges are unproven and the Pat Finucane Centre suggested Nairac's formidable reputation puts him at the centre of things of which he might not even have been aware.[21] Apparently careless of his own welfare or believing his Republican alter ego protected him, Nairac left his barracks in civvies to sing Irish republican ditties under an assumed name in a pub in a staunchly republican area. An altercation led to his unmasking and abduction. His body was never found. He was posthumously awarded the George Cross in 1979.

There is no doubt that Nairac was a staunch patriot and a very brave, if foolhardy, soldier, but he might also have been a dangerous vigilante operating as a one-man independent unit acting outside army rules and regulations – with long hair, non-regulation uniform and carrying a shotgun (which aligned him with the SAS, although he was never a member as is sometimes suggested) – who seems to have taken Kitson's advice to heart. He was one of many mavericks created by the conflict. Oddly, he was also a staunch Catholic.

There were enormous implications both for the army and the intelligence services when Nairac's activities were exposed, especially when linked to the revelations of

Colin Wallace regarding Clockwork Orange. It was Wallace who pointed out, 'Nairac could not have carried out this open association without official approval, because otherwise he would have been transferred immediately.'

Major Clive Fairweather, Nairac's commanding officer, observed of the situation in Northern Ireland that:

> The point I'm making is that Northern Ireland wasn't just about the Troubles. This was a coming-together of military people whose alternatives were Germany or exotica like Hong Kong or Belize, short-term postings where there was not the slightest chance of winning a medal or showing themselves off for rapid promotion. There was nowhere left, and that wasn't just SAS – that's everybody. There was nothing for our vast army of impatient troops to do and, to a certain extent, Northern Ireland had become good value for the military. The Troubles began in 1969, right on cue.[22]

The men who apparently came through Kitson's unofficial school of resistance and counter-terrorism formed, if rumour is to be believed, a cadre of highly trained, but patriotic, hardmen who would allow themselves to act on behalf of those in power when called upon to do so. This was the direct legacy of Northern Ireland and the Kitson mentality which suggested that the ends always justified the means.

Yet Frank Kitson would hardly have got started without the impetus gained from David Stirling, the founder of the SAS, who during the 1970s had branched out into security work and television film-making. Stirling harnessed the anger on the right at the election of Harold Wilson in 1974 to launch Greater Britain 1975 (GB75), a strike-breaking force that included all sorts of disgruntled intelligence operatives, former soldiers and arms dealers who were preparing for a coup against what they considered a communist government led by a communist agent – the Prime Minister himself. The organisation had evolved out of military experience gained abroad in the 1960s.

During the 1960s, vigilantes mixed with mercenaries, and mercenaries with the intelligence services. Former SAS soldiers had had their most spectacular success in the fight against Nasser in the Yemen, where around forty mercenaries from Belgium, France and Britain (around twelve former SAS men) were recruited to train the royalist Yemeni forces fighting against the Soviet-backed and Egyptian-led coup by republicans who had seized power in 1962.

This miniature army was to be led by Lieutenant Colonel Jim Johnson, former commanding officer of 21 (Territorial) SAS and at that time an underwriter at Lloyd's, who kept an arsenal of machine guns in his basement in Sloane Street in Knightsbridge. The plan had been hatched by Lieutenant Colonel Neil Mclean, a Conservative MP, and Colonel John Woodhouse, the commander of 22 SAS, over a chat in their gentlemen's club. Johnson was given immediate leave of absence and was able to 'borrow' soldiers from 22 SAS when Woodhouse allowed them to be 'permitted to be absent without leave'.[23] No questions were asked. The team was unofficially backed by the British, Spanish and French governments and part paid for by Israel against a backdrop of growing Arabism and American jealousy of Britain's role east of Aden.

To further the ends of counter-subversion, this loose mercenary organisation had evolved into Watchguard International, which was formed in 1967 to do the jobs that the government needed to keep secret or disown. The company was intended to provide mercenaries to prop up right-wing or royalist regimes which were mostly in the Middle East and opposing 'Nasserism' and 'Sovietism'. The organisation was also intent on fighting General Gaddafi, but the plans, code-named the Hilton Assignment, were aborted when the Foreign Office objected.

All these rather secretive private armies were the creations of a small group of enthusiasts at London clubs such as White's. It was entirely the work of members of an old-boy army network who thought it their right to organise the world and whose fierce patriotism even contemplated the overthrow of legitimate British governments if they were of the wrong hue. The failure of Hilton gave Stirling pause and he left Watchguard and began mixing more fully in SAS matters.

So it was that that when Harold Wilson came into office, Stirling was prepared to create another organisation called the Greater British League to oppose the 'totalitarian' state of socialism. Stirling considered:

> This near takeover of the governing Labour party by its parliamentary left-wing activists in alliance with the trade union extremists ... poses the most menacing crisis our country has faced – more dangerous by far than the worst period of the last World War ... This crisis, which is both organic and of the spirit, cannot possibly be resolved within parliament alone. The sickness lies at the heart of the country itself and of its people, and that is where the cure will come from ... Those who have studied socialism critically (and no one has done a better job ... than Hayek in the *Road to Serfdom* and Solzhenitsyn in his recent writings) acknowledge the inevitability of the final slide to totalitarianism once central planning, and what the left-wing socialists like to call rationalisation have gone beyond a certain point; and, without doubt, we are now at that point.[24]

The League evolved into GB75, which maintained contacts with Walter Walker's Unison Committee for Action and an ex-MI6 officer called George Young. George Kennedy Young had retired as deputy director from MI6 in 1961 and had joined Kleinwort Benson. He was an old-school Calvinist moralist, who, like John Reith, believed in his own overriding sense of morality. Indeed, when he had been involved with MI6, then riddled with traitors and Soviet agents, he had announced, 'The spy finds himself the main guardian of intellectual integrity.'[25]

Shortly after joining Kleinwort Benson (which had had connections to the fascist Right Club during the Second World War), George Young had joined the Monday

Club at the invitation of John Biggs-Davison. Here, he retailed other members with stories of how he had undermined the Iranian state with help from the CIA and had restored the Shah to the throne. Young had also encouraged the proliferation of Monday Club groups, but had been disappointed when he had been beaten to the chair of the organisation by Jonathan Guinness in 1973.

At that point, Young joined the Selsdon Group, which had emerged after a policy meeting held by Edward Heath at the Selsdon Hotel. With this group and with his Monday Club connections, Young had proposed that Tony Benn (then Anthony Wedgewood-Benn) should be impeached for his part in suggesting the nationalisation of the air industry. Met with horror as well as derision, Young then joined Unison in 1974 as an 'anti-chaos organisation'.

Chapman Pincher described Unison in the *Daily Express* as 'a formidable vigilante group to help protect the nation against a Communist takeover ... organised by former Service chiefs, senior ex-members of the Secret Service and MI5'.[26] Part of Unison's preparations may have been the peculiar military events around Heathrow airport. Later, in 1975, Young organised Tory action alongside Airey Neave and can be seen in that respect to be one of the secret architects of Thatcher's rise to power.

Walker's Unison was too gung-ho for David Stirling, who then dissolved GB75 in favour of the Better Britain Society, which, among other things, advocated a 'nationally scaled one-year citizenship course with a broad curriculum for the 15- to 16-year-old age groups as an alternative to remaining at school. Those taking the course would be boarded away from their homes except for usual holidays to combat "left-wing cancer".'[27]

As early as 1973, there had been rumours of insurrections from the top down. This was radicalism designed to protect the government form communism. On 4 April 1973, John Biggs-Davison, MP for Chigwell, a Monday Club member and member of the Society for Individual Freedom, chaired a meeting at the Royal United Services Institute for Defence Studies. Four brigadiers shared the platform to debate whether a 'third' force which was neither the army nor police might make the role of the army as 'peacekeepers' more palatable. One of the speakers, Brigadier 'Mad Mike' Calvert pointed out that:

> We are discussing the role of peace-keeping by the armed forces: how far should this extend into foreign and commonwealth territory, and indeed, Home Office territory? Should we form counter-insurgent schools, or would such a service be counter-productive? ...
>
> The role of the armed forces ... should take much more interest and be trained for and be prepared to operate in the grey world between the armed

forces and the Home Office, and the armed forces and the Foreign and Commonwealth Office.[28]

It was a hint of the possible changing role of the SAS in the 'grey' area of assassination and the accelerating arming of the police and the role of the SPG. And there was a target that such tactics might be used for. In 1972, while addressing a meeting of Conservative women in Epping, Biggs-Davison contemplated the use of a 'third force' against the militant unions:

> Today a 'thin blue line' contains the enemies of society. In [1973] we must be prepared for new outbreaks of industrial intimidation, urban terrorism and political violence. I have called for a special anti-terrorist force and a mobile squad of motorised troops to counter the forces of red fascism which have turned picket lines into storm troops [sic] and terrorised our building sites.[29]

General Walter Walker, having lectured the Monday Club on 'The Red Menace, Within and Without', contemplating armageddon in the streets of Kensington argued in the pages of the *Daily Express*:

> Do you mean to say that if the situation spilled over into this country we would adopt the same weak-kneed, wet, velvet-gloved, low profile we do in Northern Ireland? Of course we would not. If we are going to prevent London becoming like Belfast, then we must pull our finger out.[30]

Perhaps the country might 'choose rule by the gun in preference to anarchy' he mused in the *Evening News*.[31] The article was noticed by David Petrie, a sports-shop owner from Sussex and leader of the National Association of Ratepayer's' Action Group, who offered his organisation for any action – his personal choice for Prime Minister being Enoch Powell.

Increasingly frustrated, Stirling now called for the introduction of TRUEMID or 'true industrial democracy'. It did not seem ironic to him that in calling for more democracy, he had actually begun using the same style of phraseology as Oswald Mosley in the 1930s. It was an irony lost on a man who saw 'red' and liberal subversion everywhere; the satirical magazine *Private Eye* was even, according to Stirling, a Socialist Workers' Party organ.

The hysteria of the 1970s remained a factor in the apocalyptic language of the mid 1980s. In 1985, at the height of the last phase of the Cold War, General Sir John Hackett had published his fantasy scenario *The Third World War* in which he predicted hostilities in August that year.

The military arguments put forward in the book read like the best Cold War thriller and the book was hugely successful among readers fearful of their last days on Earth. Nevertheless, hidden within the book was another agenda about civil order. Hackett (and the colleagues with whom he wrote the book) was an advocate of legislation to create an 'army reserve' and 'auxiliary volunteer reserve' to be used 'in the management of a national emergency'. Hackett's main concern was civil defence, which had become so weak (how would anyone have known?) that 'public' pressure had forced the government to react to the creation of amateur vigilante groups such as the National Emergency Volunteers.

Why was this a priority? Because Britain, according to Hackett's futurology, no longer had the Blitz spirit; rather, Britain was on the brink of civil anarchy exacerbated by the threat of war. 'Lawlessness was particularly in evidence in the towns. Houses left untenanted were an open invitation to burglary. Mugging in the streets, even in broad daylight, was common.'[32] The movement of refugees from the north and Midlands was especially worrying, northern people being prone to utter lawlessness:

> Evacuation of children, food and petrol rationing, the activation of emergency services, the decentralization of administration – all worked smoothly enough. It was the exodus from the towns, particularly from the Midlands and the north towards the west and south, that did most to tax the authorities, even with their new-found powers and resources. It was in movement, too, that there occurred the ugliest scenes of mob violence, rioting and looting.[33]

All this military manoeuvring was itself the legacy of another covert group called the Resistance and Psychological Operations Committee (RPOC) set up in 1970 as a response to the Cold War in order to defend the country against a communist invasion. Closely linked to the Conservative Party and the military, the RPOC was trained, so it went, to undertake urban warfare against a Soviet aggressor. It was paid for through the Reserve Forces Association, an organisation of former soldiers and reservists under leaders such as Sir Collin Gubbins, the creator of the Special Operations Executive.

This group was linked to Group 13, a force of patriots who had trained in Northern Ireland between 1969 and 1972 and who were thought to be retained by elements in MI6 and the Foreign Office to perform necessarily unsavoury but also untraceable work. Group 13 also drew on private security firms with links to the security services and was itself supposedly linked to the group around Peter Wright and his attempts to prove that Harold Wilson was a Russian agent.

The plots and counter-plots of right-wing philosophers and political agitators were almost as fictitious as in George Shipway's prescient novel *The Chilian Club*, produced in 1971, three years before things came to a head. Shipway was a popular novelist, born in 1908, who lived in India for the first eleven years of his life, before being educated at Clifton College and Sandhurst from whence he graduated and joined the Indian Army. On retirement from the army, he became a schoolteacher in Hampshire. After retiring from teaching, this modern-day Mr Chips fantasised about the state of Britain.

The Chilian Club, Shipway's third novel, took as its premise a group of highly decorated retired army officers who meet at the Chilianwala, a gentlemen's club, where they plan to rid Britain of what they believe is an all-pervasive communist plot.[34] This plot, called 'Moondawn', has been put in place by Russia in order to conquer Britain without a fight. By the time the novel begins, there is a general strike, directed and commanded by the Kremlin, and ethnic protest is being led by an extreme 'racialist' and 'Black Muslim Negro calling himself Abdul Sharif'.[35]

In order to succeed, the group makes contact with a secret agent who runs a strange department called Int/Co-ord, a halfway house between the old establishment and MI5. With information leaked from the department, the five intrepid vigilantes begin to eliminate communist infiltrators in the unions, the BBC, universities and big business and the leaders of the black community, their final victim being the traitorous and communist-directed Prime Minister who is clearly based on Harold Wilson and who is vaporised by a new secret weapon aimed at Stonehenge!

By the end of the book, this club of retired officers has 'restored' Britain to a highly successful, business-led 'fascist dictatorship' through its policy of 'selective murder'. Thus Shipway peculiarly predicts in fiction what some army officers and others in their clubs across London were thinking might be possible in fact. Interestingly, Shipway calls his book 'a diversion', suggesting an amusing Edwardian fantasy in the vein of Dornford Yates or Edgar Wallace rather than the repressed wishful thinking of many of those who, like Shipway's heroes the blimpish General Sir Henry Mornay, K.B.E., C.B., D.S.O., M.C.; Lieutenant-Colonel Hugo Mayne-Armaury, D.S.O.; Brigadier Charles Cotterell, C.B.E., M.C.; and Group Captain Geoffrey Emtage, C.B.E., D.S.O., D.F.C., by the mid 1970s felt themselves the victims of Marxist repression and left-wing liberal bias towards ethnic groups: 'England, in effect, [had] become a Russian satellite.'[36]

It was in this hothouse atmosphere that George Young, David Stirling, Walter Walker and Airey Neave began to have meetings. On 30 April 1975, Neave had invited Walker to a reception organised by Sir Frederic Bennett, Conservative MP for Torbay, after which a network called Tory Action began to assert itself in the constituencies. It was this association that created the mobilisation of Margaret Thatcher's supporters. No wonder the lady was eternally grateful. Tony Benn was even threatened, by Neave, that if he should become leader of the Labour Party he would be 'eliminated', a threat Benn took seriously.

The likelihood of Tony Benn ever leading the Labour Party was slim, and not just because of internal opposition. The security services also were watching in the wings. They had bugged and burgled the Labour Party before. Wilson's Principal Private Secretary, Michael Halls; the Prime Minister's solicitor, Arnold Goodman; his Press Officer, Jean Denham; and supporters such as Marcia Williams and Bernard

Donoughue were all burgled in mysterious circumstances. This was apparently
undertaken by an MI5 group tasked with the oversight of political parties, a department, if it actually existed, which had been part of Roger Hollis's remit and set up
some time between 1947 and 1948. Tam Dalyell found evidence that:

> Operations against the Labour party did not cease with the retirement of Harold
> Wilson. Far from it. In 1981 there was a prospect of Tony Benn becoming leader
> of the Labour party and putative Prime Minister. According to Lee Tracey, as MI6
> electronics expert of long experience, discussions took place in the security
> services and the consensus was to make sure Benn was stopped. Tracey was quite
> clear that violent means were a possibility when he was interviewed by the *New
> Statesman* on 20 February 1981. Since that time I have been assured of Tracey's
> seriousness and factual accuracy by a source in a position to know, retired from
> a senior position in MI6.[37]

As a matter of fact, the intelligence services had always kept an eye on Tony Benn,
the aristocrat turned man of the people. To the operatives of MI5 he was an obvious
subversive if ever there was one.

This form of subversion of British democracy 'from the top', as it were, continued
when the Conservatives travelled abroad. Neave accompanied Thatcher when she
went to the United States as Leader of the Opposition. Here he spread the story of
Harold Wilson as a KGB agent, something he had intended to do with Thatcher's
tacit agreement, but the information for which was later suppressed by Thatcher.[38]
On 6 January 1976, Thatcher and Neave went to see Wilson about the deteriora-
tion in Northern Ireland. Neave thought the IRA was finished, but, the next day,
ten Protestants were killed and Wilson ordered in 600 troops, 150 of whom were
members of the SAS. In 1976 Wilson, exhausted and ill, announced his resignation.

Wilson may have known of Neave's part in his downfall, because Neave certainly
knew a great deal about Operation Clockwork Orange. Here all the threads came
together: Irish Catholic gunmen supplied by the Soviet Union and the trade unions,
and the Labour Party infiltrated by 'reds'. It was scenario that convinced Neave of
his own righteousness.

In August 1976, Neave met Colin Wallace. Wallace stressed how the Provisional
IRA had links with the Russians, Palestinians and Libya. The two men met three
times during that August, and Wallace updated his earlier analysis on the intelligence
problems in Northern Ireland for Neave to repeat at a speaking engagement in
Seaton, Northumberland. As Neave saw it, both parts of the IRA were one 'Marxist'
organisation dedicated to turning the Province into 'Cuba'.[39] Meanwhile, Wallace
was dismissed with £70 for his information.

Neave's plans, like those of other right-wingers with whom he mixed, had the
dual purpose of destroying communist subversion in England and ending the

possibility of an Irish Marxist independent state. The backing of Thatcher to lead the Conservative Party was the result of these two prime considerations. Neave's appointment as Shadow Secretary for Northern Ireland, and his predicted appointment as Secretary, were both predicated on his network of contacts in Unionist circles and perhaps beyond into the twilight world of loyalist paramilitaries and army and RUC collaboration in Protestant violence. Neave was always a 'queen and country' patriot which, by inclination, seems to have taken him into the company of those who regularly broke the law to prove their patriotic credentials. On the surface he appeared more than even handed. He was determined to 'gain victory over the murder gangs of the IRA and the loyalist thugs at war with the state'.[40] And he would use any means to do so. In a more aggressive tone he suggested, 'There may be 100 or 200 really hard men, who are known to our intelligence services. It is these people whom we have to get, and only special service troops can do it.'[41] This appears to have been the first public advocacy of the policy that later became known as 'shoot to kill'.

Why was Airey Neave so interested in the Northern Ireland office given the fact that it appeared to be a self-defeating exercise? The answer might lie in the sinister turn that occurred in Northern Irish terrorist activity between 1975 and 1976. As soon as Margaret Thatcher had become Leader of the Opposition, she was invited by Harold Wilson and Merlyn Rees to regular meetings to discuss the situation. At their meeting on 10 September 1975, Rees told both leaders that the situation had got out of hand and that there was sufficient collusion between the RUC and the UVF to make non-partisan judgements in Ulster impossible.

Rees told Wilson and Thatcher, 'Unfortunately there were certain elements in the police who were very close to the Ulster Volunteer Force and who were prepared to hand over information, for example, to Mr [Ian] Paisley.'[42] Moreover, he told them, 'The Army's judgement [was that] the Ulster Defence Regiment (UDR) were heavily infiltrated by extremist Protestants and that in a crisis situation they could not be relied on be loyal.'[43]

On 11 September, the UVF was proscribed for the second time. This made no difference to the levels of violence and to the numbers of Catholics being murdered, which exceeded those killed by the IRA. On 10 January 1976, Wilson had decided that Ireland had become 'apocalyptic' and that the government had to prepare for full-scale civil war. The next day, Wilson met Rees and Roy Mason, the Secretary of State for Northern Ireland, as well as the army's general staff and top civil servants, to discuss the crisis. At this meeting it was decided that the enemy remained the IRA and that Protestant paramilitaries were not the main focus of the war. It was also at this meeting that it was decided that the SAS and the security forces (meaning the RUC) would be 'given a free reign to demolish the provisional IRA'.[44]

Through connections in MI5, MI6 and the army, as well as through closeness to Thatcher, Neave would have been well aware of what was going on. The situation turned towards civil war after a particularly violent attack by the IRA on the village of Kingsmill. To counter such IRA atrocities, loyalist paramilitaries concocted a plan to attack Belleeks Primary School. It was intended to kill the teachers and all the pupils and essentially tip the conflagration.

If the attack had gone ahead it would have appeared that the policies adopted by the Labour Government had *wilfully* created a situation favourable to a 'one Ireland' solution under a 'socialist' government. Peculiarly, this would have 'proved' that Wilson was a Soviet stooge. The drift into civil war would have allowed a gloves off policy, which was exactly the type of scenario that Neave and others were angling for, to allow them to destroy the Labour Party and create a hard-line authoritarian government in Britain. Indeed, Neave's meetings with Colin Wallace might have been part of his attempt to gain information in the area.

⸻⸘⸻

It was the deteriorating situation in Northern Ireland rather than the Winter of Discontent that finally brought down Jim Callaghan's government through a vote of no confidence, behind which lurked the machinations of Thatcher's closest ally. It was now that Neave began the peculiar intrigue that might have led to Tony Benn's assassination. In the last days of Callaghan's government, Neave did have a meeting at the Cumberland Hotel in the West End with former MI6 electronics expert Lee Tracey, just as Dalyell had suggested. Neave wanted Tracey to help form a team to destroy Benn, with 'violent means [a] possibility'.[45] Benn recorded in his diary for 17 February 1981 that the television journalist Duncan Campbell had phoned him to tell him that, 'Two years ago he had heard from an intelligence agent that Airey Neave planned to have me [Benn] assassinated if a Labour government was elected, Jim Callaghan resigned and there was any risk I [Benn] might become leader.'[46] Benn mused, 'It doesn't ring true in a way; it sounds like the dirty tricks department trying to frighten me by implying that a serious assassination attempt was being planned. No-one will believe for a moment that Airey Neave would have done such a thing.'[47]

Airey Neave was killed by a car bomb on 30 March 1979 as he left the House of Commons. A relatively new organisation called the Irish National Liberation Army (INLA) had assassinated him. This group had been set up by Seamus Costello, who had been expelled by the official IRA in 1974. This new force, although small in number, seemed to confirm Neave's nightmares. It was dedicated to nationalism and revolutionary socialism.

It is clear that the INLA felt that the escalation of violence in Northern Ireland was certainly a preconceived plan by Neave and his colleagues in the intelligence services. Neave had after all had his eyes on wider preoccupations than just Northern Ireland, setting himself up as potential controller of both MI5 and MI6. It is possible Neave was going to suggest to Margaret Thatcher the appointment of Christopher

Sykes as the new head of MI6 and Christopher Tugendhat as head of MI5. Both were the subject of machine-gun attacks, from which Sykes died. Conspiracy theorists such as Gerald James, who had worked with Neave in the days of Tory Action and the Monday Club, believed the bomb that killed Neave had been planted not by the INLA but by the CIA working for Irish Catholic interests.

Neave's death was, nevertheless, later explained by his killers as a military target:

> He was in fact Margaret Thatcher's principal adviser on security. He was an advocate of order and increased repression against a nationalist people in the six counties … Mr Neave was not a civilian, did not act, or never acted like a civilian in regard to the Irish people. Mr Neave was an advocate of torture in Ireland. Mr Neave was an advocate of capital punishment for Irish freedom fighters.[48]

Neave's murder was a sharp reminder of the values Margaret Thatcher intended to live by as a conviction politician:

> He was one of freedom's warriors. Courageous, staunch, true. He lived for his beliefs, and now he has died for them. A gentle, brave and unassuming man, he was a loyal and very dear friend. He had a wonderful family who supported him in everything he did. Now, there is a gap in our lives which cannot be filled.[49]

His absence also stood to remind Thatcher that her values, expressed as they were in uncompromising terms, were likely to attract enemies who would not stop at the ballot box or the political leak, but, like her, would be willing to see things to their conclusion; one sort of intransigence met another, each side obstinately paranoid in its distrust of the other.

Ironically, the eulogies Thatcher offered on the death of two of her intellectual mentors was effectively the eulogy recited at her own passing. Boris Johnson, Mayor of London, intoned, 'You either gave in to the [Irish] hunger strikers, or you showed a grim and ultimately brutal resolve … You either accepted an Argentine victory or else you defeated Galtieri. You either took on the miners or else you surrendered to Marxist agitators.'[50]

5

SHINING LIKE SPUN GOLD

The tenor of right-wing paranoia in the period leading to Margaret Thatcher becoming Leader of the Opposition might be gauged from the activities of its organisers. In 1975, just around the time that Airey Neave was forming his inner circle, Norris McWhirter set about looking for a suitable memorial for his brother. He found it in the Ross McWhirter Memorial Essay competition aimed at people under the age of 30. The competition was to be judged by the Bishop of London, dissident Vladimir Bukovsky, lyricist Tim Rice and a school-teacher from Lancashire among others. The subject of the essay was 'How can a democratic country protect its citizens against subversion without sacrificing individual freedom?' The competition closed in autumn 1977 with ten winners gaining cash prizes.

The essayists duly concerned themselves less with freedom of the individual than for vigilance against the 'subversion of the state', as the winning essay from Simon R. Emdin showed.[1] Emdin argued for a stronger Special Branch and SAS and the employment of infiltrators to combat 'left-wing agitators' and the National Front. The final showdown was approaching, because 'since 1975 the working class have been marking time'.[2] Quite what for was never explained, but certainly no good, 'against which the government has made no sustained effort to challenge the revo-lutionaries' assumptions'.[3] Other essays repeated the mantra.

Norris McWhirter (who thought that Tom Paine was a socialist and that the Labour Party had included 'subliminal' messages in its party political broadcasts[4]) was a keen advocate of freedom against all sorts of 'centralised authoritarianism', but his ire was reserved for 'far-left socialism' which he equated with 'far-right national socialism'.[5] What was needed was a return to traditional or 'market' values, which were a type of 'continuous referendum', and the use of 'social engineering'[6] to defeat:

The active enemies of freedom in this country today (apart from those paid to undermine it) … the corporatists, the collectivists who take salaries and pensions to centralise economic and political power, and also those who get themselves elected (usually by tiny minorities) to life offices as leaders of trade unions.[7]

Moreover, these villains were the creations of centralisation and weakness at the heart of the British political system:

It is at last dawning on the people of this country that the Government of the day is not the solution to any problem: Government is the problem … By nationalising our bank accounts and our pension funds, by municipalising private enterprise, by abolishing non-State education and medicine, by union-ising the police and the armed services, the 20th century aim appears to be first to make life worse and second to make it impossible.[8]

Who could be relied upon to reverse the situation? McWhirter had found a saviour in the 'golden-haired leader of Her Majesty's Opposition'. This love letter to Thatcher was repeated in his memoir of his brother. In describing the scene at the memorial service at St Paul's Cathedral on 16 December 1975, Norris cannot help but notice 'Margaret Thatcher, her hair shining like spun gold under the lofty lights'.[9] Such praise was tantamount to a type of erotic hagiography, the sort that would help to cement Thatcher's persona as the 'iron lady' ruling as Britannia and Joan of Arc.

Thatcher saw both the comic potential of such drooling sycophancy and also the political capital of fragility, femininity and strength. She knew the pastiche effec-tively placed her ideologically alongside Neave and Ross McWhirter, but sealed her implacability in the language of women's fashion. In a speech to her Finchley constituency in 1976, ostensibly about foreign policy, she began in humorous mood to rapturous applause:

I stand before you tonight in my Red Star chiffon evening gown. (Laughter, Applause), my face softly made up and my fair hair gently waved (Laughter), the Iron Lady of the Western world. A cold war warrior, an Amazon philis-tine, even a Peking plotter. Well, am I any of these things? (No!) Well, yes … (Laughter) … Yes, I am an iron lady. After all, it wasn't a bad thing to be an iron duke. Yes, if that's how they wish to interpret my defence of values and freedoms fundamental to our way of life.[10]

It was only half a joke, for Thatcher believed her own notices and knew others needed to be reassured that she was as she was expected to appear. It was a type of masquerade which actually protected her inner feelings, which often clashed with her Cabinet, and joined her in spirit to the campaigners of the 1970s whom she might no longer acknowledge if she came to power. Those who felt embattled and against the wall knew what she meant; the enemies of freedom were everywhere and the fight unending. Her comment that we were 'waging a battle on many fronts' was not, therefore, confined merely to the Soviet threat, but effectively put a future Conservative government on a permanent war footing which allowed for actions inexcusable in other circumstances – you were either one of 'us' or one of 'them'.

Such extremism was hardly unusual in the rarefied atmosphere of right-wing fanaticism and desperation during the 1970s. Everyone from the television presenter Hughie Green to the newspaper magnate Cecil King seemed to smell reds under the bed and wished for, or actually conspired to bring about, a right-wing coup to restore order.

Walter Walker was just one of many who looked to Thatcher as a bulwark against communist infiltration, just as she had her own martyrs in Neave and (Ross) McWhirter. Walker was no amateur conspiracy theorist. He had, after all, been Commander in Chief, Allied Forces, Northern Europe between 1968 and 1972 and was the recipient of the KCB, CBE and DSO. Nevertheless, by 1983, he was convinced that the apocalypse was about to be fulfilled. 'The period 1982–85', he predicted, 'may prove to be the most crucial phase of history yet experienced by the Western World … It is no exaggeration to say that what is at stake is not only the whole future of the West, but civilisation itself and the Christian West.'[11]

The threat was not merely from the Soviet Union (the evil empire to Ronald Reagan), but from infiltration by 'the Marxist private army' led by Arthur Scargill.[12] Scargill's power lay in the use of flying pickets in his closure of the Saltley coal depot during the miners' strike of 1972. It was a wound that would not heal. Walker blamed Scargill for his actions over Grunwick too, a cause close to the heart of the McWhirters, and it was Scargill who was seen as mainly to blame for the 'present state of anarchy and subversion in Britain'.[13] Mrs Thatcher and her government were fully aware of the dangers.

In 1976, a number of these freedom associations were considering amalgamation. In October, Walter Walker became leader of Civil Assistance (CA), a group with a strong private army and vigilante image, which was negotiating with NAFF to form a libertarian bloc aimed at being at the right hand of Thatcher in any showdown with unions or communists. In order to woo NAFF, Walker sent an open letter to its county and area co-ordinators in which he tried to distance himself from his 'gung-ho' image:

> I intend to confine my activities to supporting any properly organised and viable campaign whose aim would be firstly, to prevent a breakdown of law and order, and secondly, to restore the power of judges and magistrates, including corporal punishment as a deterrent. Indeed, ever since CA started more than two years ago I have been highlighting our slide towards a lawless society …

I have never ceased to warn of the imminent threat from the 'Enemy Within' as well as the 'Enemy Without' …

From her strong pronouncements, it is perfectly clear that Mrs Margaret Thatcher is fully alive to both these threats. It is now my firm belief that the salvation of this country, which has sunk to an all time low, lies in the early return of a Conservative Government to power.

Therefore, another of my activities will be to campaign vigorously for the return of Conservative Government, with such a strong working majority that the will of the people – and not that of a small but immensely powerful clique of extreme left-wingers-shall prevail.[14]

NAFF resented Walker's intrusiveness and broke off talks. In January 1979, it became the Freedom Association to avoid its initials being confused with the National Front.

In 2010, Norman Tebbit wrote an extraordinary foreword to a new book by John Gouriet, co-founder of NAFF. Tebbit had known Gouriet since 1976 and recalled that Gouriet had long fought the 'unbridled power' of the closed shop, the block vote and flying pickets. For Tebbit, as for Gouriet, NAFF was at the forefront of defeating the 'tide of socialist extremism' which was being used to 'destroy capitalism and British Freedom'. NAFF, was in fact, actually 'in the vanguard … of Thatcherism' and had been for 'eighteen years'. No wonder that, to Tebbit, 'NAFF made an invaluable contribution to Margaret Thatcher's first victory in 1979.'[15]

Others too were quite willing to set themselves up as vigilantes for the right and keen-eyed guardians against communist terrorist subversives. One very active enthusiast was Brian Crozier whom Barrie Penrose and Roger Courtier had chanced upon while investigating Harold Wilson's accusations against MI5. Crozier, it appeared, had a rather shady background. An Australian brought up in France, Crozier had drifted into journalism and into a position of vehement anti-communism having once been a sympathiser.

In 1975, Crozier became director of Forum World Features, a CIA front set up to coordinate anti-communist journalism and propaganda and launder money. Crozier insisted the organisation was clean, but he kept links with American and other intelligence agencies. Previously, in 1968, Crozier had co-founded the Institute for the Study of Conflict which had its headquarters in the London School of Economics, but, in 1979 he was removed after a coup which included apparent interventions by both the CIA and MI6. The Institute was dedicated to the study of terrorism and subversion and specialised in 'exposing' Soviet peace plans. Crozier continued to work with the CIA and MI6 throughout the 1970s when Wilson was in power, telling army officers at the staff college at Camberley and at a dinner in Harrogate (and elsewhere) that it was their duty to intervene if the [socialist] government went too far. He was – according to his autobiography – applauded to the rafters.[16] In these meetings, he was occasionally accompanied by John Gouriet, campaign director of the Freedom Association.

In order to be ready for 'the day', Crozier formed 'the 61' in 1977, a private-enter-prise operational intelligence agency, the numbers standing for the 'sixth International'. It was involved in work in both Iran and South America. In 1981, the importance of the organisation was proven when it might have prevented a Russian invasion of Poland. Crozier believed he was involved in a new secret war of intelligence against universal communist subversion and he was taken very seriously by those in power. Crozier was someone capable of convincing politicians and businessmen that he somehow held the reins of power and knew the secret history of events.

In 1982, still at the centre of conspiracy, Crozier was shown to be involved in an attempt to rig the West German federal elections of 1980 through bribery, slush funds and black propaganda – the aim to make the fiercely anti-communist Franz Joseph Strauss, Chancellor. Crozier died in 2012, lauded and distinguished. For Crozier, as for Walter Walker, the enemy was communism, or communism disguised as socialism, collectivism or trade unionism, British or otherwise. It was the political, military and intelligence half of the economic arguments that formed the basis of Thatcherite thinking.

Crozier was determined to create a private space for anti-communist, anti-trade-union and anti-Labour-Party discussion. He was also in touch with various world leaders (later he had a meeting with Ronald Reagan), but he remained an outsider running the think tank and lobby group, the Institute for the Study of Conflict (ISC), which was related to the Information Research Department of the Foreign Office. So worried were the groups he was in touch with that Michael Foot would become Prime Minister that they wrote an open letter to the Queen calling for her to 'act'. [17]

Crozier and his ilk were part of a rapidly growing world of private intelligence agencies and spying which might be hired out to the highest bidder and, more importantly, could act as an intermediary stage between the state's intelligence work and any dirty or 'wet' operations that might need denying. In this way, it has always been true to the letter of the law that MI5 and MI6 have never been directly involved in murder. Most such companies worked for the private sector especially in industrial espionage, either within the workforce or between companies. Thus, by 1979, such private organisations were purchasing the latest and most sophisticated hardware:

> At [an] International Security Conference sponsored by the industry's house organ, *Security World*, there were more than a hundred exhibitors representing manufacturers of surveillance and counter intrusion equipment, ranging from Psychological Stress Evaluators to ultrasonic, infrared, ionization, and motion detectors. Amid surveillance cameras, 'multiplex security polling systems', stress, alarms, automatic encoders, 'cloaks' and window shock alarms, thirty-six lecturers sang the praises of Tasers and 'company undercover men'. [18]

So sophisticated were their arsenals that Tasers were utterly unknown outside the business. Moreover, in the United States alone, 3,000 personnel made redundant at the beginning of the 1970s by the CIA were in the market, as were many former British intelligence agents and former Special Branch police officers.

Alongside these freelance and free-market entrepreneurial spies, who were putting Thatcherism into practice in the most unlikely circumstances, were those professional civil servants who embraced the ethos of the 'market'. These formed small cadres of self-help individuals or vigilantes in the 1970s determined to correct the faults of government or, in the 1980s, to follow the instructions of government in their own eccentric and unregulated way. Just as the markets were to be freed from regulation, so were those who had to answer to no one.

It was this self-determined freedom that got Peter Wright accused of being a 'rogue' element and allowed the (usually) right-wing papers to vilify others as Walter Mitty types when they had outlasted their usefulness to the intelligence agencies. Such individuals rarely proved to be Walter Mittys. Instead, they represented a small but dangerous group (and Colin Wallace was just as much a part of this nasty business) who either thought the 'rules' didn't apply to them or were encouraged by their political, military or intelligence masters with hints and inducements to break the law with impunity.

⁓ ⁓ ⁓

The 1970s were an age of voluntary organisations; bodies set up by libertarian and free-market enthusiasts to beat the threat of unionisation and collectivist corporatism. Everything was seen in military terms, and for those who subscribed to these 'clubs', the issues appeared as matters of economic and social life or death. For the most part, these associations were middle class. As early as 1906, there had been a Middle Classes Defence Organisation and, after the First World War, this had partly reformed as the Middle Class Union, the British branch of an organisation called Middle Class International, itself becoming the National Citizens' Union in 1942.

As vigilante groups began to flourish, so too did purely economic ones. By 1974, economic fears had reached crisis point and yet another organisation called the Middle Class Association had been formed, this time by John Gorst, a Conservative MP and someone who was part of the parliamentary team that promoted Thatcher when she challenged for the leadership. The Association was set up to represent the self-employed and those in management in order to remedy 'the basic malaise common to individuals who find themselves [victims] of the economic policies followed by successive Governments since the Second World War [that] have deprived them of a fair return for their industry, enterprise or thrift'.[19]

Nevertheless, Gorst was not able to control the organisation, some of whose members were put off by the 'socialist' word 'Class' in the title. So was born the Voice of the Independent Centre whose more active members began baying for blood. A palace coup left the association with a new general council and a new 'strong man' in the figure of Joey Martyn-Martin. It turned out, however, that Martyn-Martin wanted to reorganise the whole thing as an anti-communist lobby group. Indeed, he finally left in November 1975 to join 'hard-line anti-communists' in Brussels.[20]

In 1974, another group also sprang up. This was the National Federation of Self-Employed led by the suitably named Norman Small, a retired soldier living in Lytham St Anne's in Lancashire who had been a recruiter for small shopkeepers unions. The idea had come to him while playing golf. Alongside Gerry Parker-Brown, a grocer from Lytham, Small toured the country and set up a head office funded by generous subscriptions from 10,000 members. Yet the fight they put up was not convincing and a breakaway body called the Reform Group was set up, causing Small to suffer complete physical collapse.

The two groups were, however, active in getting attention. Margaret Thatcher actually addressed the Federation at the Conservative Party Conference, and both Cyril Smith and Jeremy Thorpe endorsed the Federation at the Liberal Party Assembly. At its highest point there were 50,000 members.

In 1976, Patrick Hutber, the City Editor of the *Sunday Telegraph* and a supporter of NAFF, wrote a book called *The Decline of the Middle Class;* it was subtitled *And how it can fight back.* The book began with the truism (by the middle 1970s a right-wing mantra) that 'this is a time of crisis'.[21] Feeling that crisis most were the squeezed and neglected middle classes; those who were thrifty and cautious and believed in education and advancement. It was those people, and those who aspired to be middle class, who most suffered, and the suffering had increased. Since 1974, the middle classes had become the target of a sustained campaign to destroy them, a campaign that had even included the infiltration of education where anarchist influence had been detected, such as in the William Tyndale School in Islington.[22] Patrick Hutber said, 'Let no one under-estimate the importance of even this slight shift. At the February 1974 election, for example, the Labour Party called in its manifesto for "a fundamental and irreversible shift of power and wealth in favour of working people and their families".'[23]

For Hutber, this was no less than the sort of approach that was taken in the Soviet Union. It sapped national morale, making Britain reliant on an all-powerful state: 'There is much less belief in self-reliance, much less desire for independence, or belief in its possibility and, as a consequence, a belief that it is natural and good for the state to care for an individual in retirement or at moments of crisis in life.'[24]

Something had to be done to restore faith in middle-class values, especially as, in Hutber's analysis 'somewhere in the region of half the population [was] middle class'.[25] Hutber's arguments, alongside those of Norman Small and his National Association of the Self-Employed, formed yet another plank of Thatcherite beliefs: now the 'small man' and ordinary individual who aspired to be middle class were to provide the backbone of the Tory vote.

The destruction of the middle class at the hands of left-wing social engineers who wanted to create a non-aspirational and compliant working-class Britain, was tantamount to the undermining of core British values; values that suggested permanence and aspiration rather than state reliance and immediate gratification. Hutber's middle-class moral landscape was shown in a letter he quoted which referred to the financial provisions of the correspondent's father, whose wartime savings had been eroded. The letter represents the definition of middle-class, as well as Thatcherite values. It might have been written from Thatcher's own personal memories of Grantham:

A sense of personal pride and a desire to be self-supporting.

An ability to exercise self-discipline.

A desire to improve one's position in the world and to provide a better education for the children.

The recognition that an increase in income would only come through hard work and enterprise.

A desire to own a house, to have one's own family doctor, to be able to afford private nursing facilities, to possess a motor cycle or a car.

To be able to provide the family with a holiday, be it only a week at a local coastal resort and to ease the burden of household chores through domestic help.

A clear concept as to what constituted the necessities and what constituted the luxuries of life.

A respect for property and other persons.

An aspiration towards culture.

The ability to distinguish between material and spiritual.

A code of personal conduct and personal judgement as to what is right and what is wrong – a judgement which was derived from religious faith.

A respect for law and order.

A pride in being British and instinct for 'fair play'.

A sense of personal responsibility for the well-being of one's wife and family.

A spirit of patriotism.

The will to make financial provision for old age.

Recognition for the voice of authority, be it authority born of age or position.

An aspiration towards gentlemanly behaviour

An appreciation of good manners, politeness and courtesy.

A respect for the gentle sex.[26]

While Hutber is sensible to take a certain intellectual distance from the letter, he presents in its entirety and it is clear he is broadly sympathetic with its aspirations. These are exactly the same mix of aspiration and nostalgia that Thatcher supported all her life. The grocer's daughter from small-town Grantham, with her visceral reminiscences of toiletry arrangements and her belief in her father's work ethic put her squarely among the aspirational lower middle classes. Her assertiveness and strength of will fitted a certain neurotic uneasiness regarding both 'arrivism' and class-based distinctions of education and upbringing.

The list from Hutber's correspondent fits Thatcher's own aspirations for the country once in power: a return to sensible housekeeping, the importance of home and the values of sincerely held beliefs (the 'true' and radical beliefs of lower-middle-class non-conformist religion: sincere and determined by self-belief), and the more advanced views of a new type of individualism based on a sense of embattlement which could only be defeated by a new-style Victorianism based on self-help and entrepreneurial effort. It was more like Manchester liberalism than traditional Toryism. It would also be only the vaguest of philosophies and a reactionary one at that until mixed with the economic theories of Friedrich Hayek and the Chicago School that made Thatcherism so powerful an ideological tool.

Hutber's correspondent also strikes the same embattled note that sounded in Thatcher's own version of Thatcherism:

> In evil moments one is tempted by the image of a society where militancy on the labour front is countered by the edict 'Work or starve', where individual acts of violence and terror are met by punishments of a primeval character. Evil moods can be swept aside in the cold light of day and what does abide is the deep sense of helplessness, the feeling of utter frustration, as being unable to do anything to improve the situation.[27]

This was exactly the language of the besieged that Thatcher instinctively understood. In facing a society on the brink of apocalyptic destruction by unseen and manipulative hands, Thatcher would effectively bring light and halt decay. It was, in effect, a wartime attitude, but one where the internal enemy was the government, the unions, the Marxists and the intellectual left. The enemy within meant that Thatcher needed to construct a sense of embattlement, of fighting against the odds to survive in a decaying and tired world in need of rejuvenation. No wonder Hutber, in humorous mood, looked to Thatcher to bring the Seventh Cavalry of Conservative fiscal sense before the middle class died out and with it the idea of Britain:

> There is a firm pledge by Mrs Thatcher, the Conservative leader, to repeal [Capital Gains Tax]. The best advice, therefore, is to stay alive till the Conservatives get back. Since this is not really within one's direct control (we all would if we could), it is necessary to take some precautions while waiting for her to gallop to the rescue.[28]

No wonder, too, that Margaret Thatcher carried around Winston Churchill's speeches; nor is it odd that she convinced herself that she had known him. It was somewhat ironic that Thatcher was actually indisposed on the day of Churchill's funeral.

6

BRIAN CROZIER'S SHIELD

Many right-orientated thinkers were obsessed with two things, the Soviet model of the political takeover and the concept of the *coup d'état* and its effects on a country. Their test case was Chile where Salvador Allende had won with a popular mandate even though he was a socialist working towards a constitution with a 'socialist orientation'.[1] He had won 49.7 per cent of the vote in April 1971, having become president in September 1970. It was a greater percentage of the vote than Thatcher was ever to win.

Nevertheless, his economic plans, centrally organised, had started to unravel so much that a military takeover was planned by Augusto Pinochet. The National Truckers' Federation went on strike in October 1972 and its action was the catalyst for the coup that followed after Pinochet was made Commander in Chief of the army. The army took control and Allende committed suicide.

Chile was now seen as a test-bed for the liberal monetary theories of Hayek and Milton Friedman, and as a bulwark against communist infiltration by Alan Walters, NAFF and Thatcher herself. The fact that the Chilean regime was a murderous dictatorship could be ignored by economic free marketeers led by Friedman's Chicago Boys who looked to Chile to provide evidence that market economies without state interference worked!

It was a strange illusion that fascinated those who were generating what was soon to be called Thatcherism. The attack on Allende's regime through Brian Crozier's group and NAFF was oblique but relentless, his use of state mechanisms a constant cause for obloquy. Peregrine Worsthorne, a tepid and snobbish type of Conservative, was really only converted to the Thatcher way of thinking after a visit to Chile in March 1974 to report on the dictatorship for the *Sunday Telegraph*. Worsthorne wrote that there was indeed a dictatorship, but it was not a 'Hitler-type' dictatorship, instead one that was entirely benign:

> All right, a military dictatorship is ugly and repressive. But if a minority British Socialist Government ever sought, by cunning, duplicity, corruption, terror and

foreign arms, to turn this country into a Communist State, I hope and pray our armed forces would intervene to prevent such a calamity as efficiently as the armed forces did in Chile.[2]

Worsthorne had joined all the other right-wing travellers. When Pinochet was arrested in London by the Blair government in October 1998, Thatcher consoled the ageing generalissimo; after all, he had been a loyal friend during the Falkland's War.

Writer Robert Moss too was obsessed with the 'disaster' that was Chile before the dictator. His overriding fear was of a socialist coup in Britain, not organised from without, but the result of the democratic process and from hidden forces waiting in the wings which would take over the government and seize power. Hence Chile became an urgent matter for study.

Moss was, perhaps, the brightest of the liberal market advocates around the Crozier group and was at the centre of the clique. His books were used to put the arguments for market forces and against centrally controlled economies. His definition of capitalism was simple. It was 'economic liberalism', which meant 'economic pluralism' and 'political pluralism', so that, with pluralism and liberalism both in place, centralism would literally be unthinkable.

For Moss, collectivism implied the 'population was composed of mental defectives' and the public sector was merely the inefficient result of central bureaucracy.[3] 'Public ownership' was the substitution of 'the apparatchik for the entrepreneur' and should be replaced with 'popular capitalism', which was so influential an idea in Thatcher's sense of her own mission, as was his sense of the centrality of family life.[4]

The slogan of the Chilean Marxists during the 1970s, 'el pueblo unido jamas sera vencido' ('the people united will never be defeated'), later became the chant of the British miners and their women: the enemy finally unmasked and at home. Maybe this sent Moss doolally, as he would later return to the Antipodes and become a 'shamanic counsellor' and 'dream teacher', transformed from market liberal into psychic novelist and 'dream archaeologist in the multiverse'.

❧

Nigel Lawson was in many ways Thatcher's staunchest ally when it came to the new version of Conservatism through his distaste for 'middle-class guilt' which he shared with Thatcher, Moss and Crozier. He also had picked up Friedrich Hayek's *The Road to Serfdom* in which he, like his contemporaries found a rationale for the market and a reasoned refutation of socialism.

Lawson had first met Brian Crozier in 1972. At the time, Crozier was conducting an 'investigation' into subversion in the unions, and he helped Lawson when he had become the editor of the *Spectator* in 1972 after having written an anti-communist diatribe in the *Times*. With Crozier, Lawson produced a report called *Subversion in*

British Industry, which was sent to leaders of major companies. The paper was influential, and Lawson gained the support of John Whitehorn, director general of the Confederation of British Industry.[5] This important set of people, of which Lawson was a prominent member, then became a 'study group' in which Hayek was discussed. Lawson commented:

> Hayek's development of the concept of a spontaneous natural order provided a strong philosophical underpinning for the market, not least by demonstrating that our understanding of the nature of society and the economy is too partial to admit economic management by the State … above all, Hayek also opened up for the first time since the war the possibility of a morally superior political conception to that of socialism, by elevating private actions above public direction and dismissing 'social justice' as both vague and arbitrary. These were all ideas which, like Margaret Thatcher, I had nursed, without much articulation, since I left Oxford.[6]

Like Thatcher too, Lawson was also a free-market economic 'liberal' populist rather than a dyed-in-the-wool Tory of the old school. In a way, Thatcher was a politician who was beyond politics:

> At a more down-to-earth level, Margaret was unusual, for a Tory leader, in actually warming to the Conservative Party – that is to say, the Party in the country, rather than its members of Parliament. Certainly, that had not occurred for many years. Harold Macmillan had a contempt for the Party. Alec Home tolerated it, Ted Heath loathed it. Margaret genuinely liked it. She felt a communion with it, one which later expanded to embrace the silent majority of the British people as a whole.[7]

Thatcher herself suggested she was 'the rebel head of an Establishment government'.[8] Her first administration certainly seemed as much with a Cabinet filled with six old Etonians, six former Guards officers, five barristers and one lord.[9]

As Prime Minister, Thatcher took time to impose her will as she slowly formed her vision. It took two further elections and the assassination attempt at Brighton to make clear to her what her own brand of Thatcherism looked like. Her final government's incarnation as an almost 'elected dictatorship'[10] meant that Thatcher could at last become what perhaps she had only dreamed of: 'Thatcher was [now] a revolutionary authoritarian, a true apostle of the dictatorship of the bourgeoisie'.[11]

Once in power, Thatcher never fundamentally disagreed with the views of those she had admired in the 1970s, but she modified her public utterances as she continued in office. She had already forged links with Robert Moss (who wrote her 'Iron Lady' speech of 19 January 1976) and was intimate with Brian Crozier and the McWhirters as we have seen, and, during her period in opposition and while she was in power, the group around Crozier believed they could influence Conservative future policy against subversives.

Crozier was to some extent a man who puffed up his own importance, yet it does seem that, for a time, Thatcher flattered him into believing she was listening. They shared almost every ideological bent, including being paranoid about the Labour Party and the unions which they believed had been deeply infiltrated by communist elements directed from Russia and which were on the brink of a coup. Thus Thatcher entertained Crozier's hare-brained scheme to reform MI5. The Labour Party had plans to democratise MI5 by making it more accountable to Parliament, but Crozier wanted to make it more efficient by making it more secret.

During 1976 and 1977, Crozier formed a secret committee called Shield to brief Thatcher on world politics. The central cause of Shield was to fight 'subversion' everywhere, including the Church. The committee consisted of Crozier; Nicholas Elliott, a former intelligence agent; Harry Sporborg of Hambros Bank, who had been in the Special Operations Executive during the Second World War; and the Conservative backbencher Stephen Hastings. The activity was funded by money from the Institute for the Study of Conflict, and two researchers were employed to provide intelligence briefing papers: Peter Shipley and an American who lived in London called Douglas Eden. Thatcher attended meetings, as did some of her senior shadow cabinet, William Whitelaw, Sir Keith Joseph and Lord Peter Carrington. Carrington, however, worked against the group's purpose as a fifth column to undermine the attempts to influence policy towards the unions.

At some point, Thatcher might have realised she was dealing with a possible cabal which wanted to direct her policies, a cabal which had advocated troops on the street and the suspension of parliamentary democracy if Labour won the next election. General Walter Walker even suggested that 'the country might choose rule by the gun in preference to anarchy' and Moss, following what he had learned of Frank Kitson's work in the colonies and Ireland, had even suggested a 'vigilante group to help protect against a Communist takeover'.[12] At any rate, while she kept friendly, once in power, Thatcher ditched any associations with the Shield scheme; the product of a peripheral group whose actions were so hubristic and secretive that even Thatcher was forced to draw back. Crozier remained on the scene, convinced he had the key to Soviet intentions. His researcher Douglas Eden went on to help form the Social Democratic Party.

It is clear that Thatcher always admired the McWhirter brothers, Gouriet, Moss, Hutber, Gorst, Martyn-Martin, Small, Parker-Brown, Alan Sherman, Alan Walters, Keith Joseph, General Walker, Crozier and others throughout her premiership, although each had his own take on the Thatcher revolution and exactly what Thatcherism meant. Once in power, Thatcher would let others lead the witch-hunts.

Foremost among those willing to sniff out traitors was the *Daily Express* journalist Chapman Pincher, who was very closely connected to the security services and had already run some of Colin Wallace's fake stories about subversives. Pincher was, however, aware that Harold Wilson was the subject of a plot as early as 1978, and equally aware that elements inside MI5 seemed to be acting independently. Nevertheless, the person he had received the initial story from, Peter Wright, collaborated with Pincher in his next book, *Their Trade is Treachery* published in 1981. In it, Pincher repeated the accusation originating from Wright that Sir Roger Hollis was a Soviet mole. Thatcher baulked at any investigation of the accusation and there it lay until Wright's own memoir was published.

Pincher, no doubt reinvigorated from working with Wright, did not then return his attention to those out of control on the right; instead he was out to name and shame those 'reds' he perceived under every bed, and, as late as 1985, was continuing the naming war in his book *The Secret Offensive* dedicated to 'the all too few who care enough to give tongue'. Pincher's central thesis regarding the United Kingdom was that Soviet subversives had infiltrated the unions, thus justifying by extension Thatcher's campaign against the miners. Pincher's initial premise was simply those who were 'potentially subversive, should be subject … to being watched, having their telephones tapped and their letters opened'.[13] This surveillance of 'potential' subversives was, of course, not merely subjective and open to the judgement of those doing the bugging and letter-opening, but was also illegal. To Pincher, obviously aware of 'insider' practice, this was a natural and normal way of doing things. Pincher remained an advocate of covert security measures throughout his long career. 'I have made continual inquiries into the surveillance of extreme left-wing trade unionists over many years and am convinced that it is justified and necessary in the national interest.'[14]

Pincher looked back in history for his justification of 'illegal' surveillance. He found that, in 1947, the Joint Intelligence Committee had produced a paper entitled 'The Spread of Communism throughout the World and the Extent of its Direction from Moscow'. There were the findings of the Templar Committee in 1950 and the list of crypto-communists garnered by MI5 in 'Party Piece'. The threat apparently remained throughout the 1960s as communist infiltration into trades unions was Moscow's ace in the hole as far as subversion went. Indeed, Wilson had taken the message seriously and ordered surveillance on militant trade union leaders during the seamen's strike of 1966 and there had been further investigations as late as 1973. Ted Heath had taken no more action than Harold Wilson to stop the rot of illegal surveillance methods.

The Home Office had eventually clarified who was now to be a target as a 'subversive'. Its definition was so broad as to include many whose legitimate rights to protest would now place them on the wrong side of the law: 'Those which threaten the safety or well-being of the State and which are intended to undermine or overthrow Parliamentary democracy by political, industrial or violent means.'[15] Furthermore, there was supposedly a peculiar group called the Three Advisers who gave direction to ministers with regard to those who were felt to threaten the work considered 'vital to the state', although who they were remains a mystery.

Thus the government, and those who served the government, were free to decide who threatened the well-being of the realm. There were no laws to protect the public from such interference as was deemed necessary to enforce conformity for the sake of the 'well-being of the state', an entity entirely imaginary. Now it would be quite legitimate to watch civil servants, trade unionists, anti-nuclear protesters or those whose lifestyle simply offended the intelligence services or those in government. The state was increasingly aligned to the *Conservative* Government's explicit agenda as well as to a quite separate but related agenda followed by those in the upper circles of the bureaucracy: this was the notion of a traditionalist and *conservative* state as symbolised by the 'crown'. Allegiance to the crown, the realm and the state was dictated by the traditions of birth, family and education. By this very definition, most of the population was fair game for any underhand methods of control in the name of 'stability'; a stability notable for being beyond the temporary reach of politicians and voters and therefore, by definition, prey to permanently employed and unaccountable state bureaucrats.

7

KNOWING YOU ARE RIGHT

What were these threats which had evaded the security forces and the vigilante brigade during the late 1970s? There was, for instance, the National Union of Journalists, 'infiltrated' by Marxists and militants who orchestrated strikes and worked to undermine the 'truth', at least that truth as understood by Chapman Pincher and the readers of his newspaper.[1] Indeed, the whole of the newspaper and television industries were supposedly infiltrated and directed by left-wingers. Then there was a long list of unions which were secretly under the cosh of communism. Pincher claimed that 10 per cent of all trade union officials were members of the Communist Party and therefore taking orders directly from Moscow:

> These include figures like Ken Gill, the General Secretary of the Technical, Administrative and Supervisory Section of the Amalgamated Union of Engineering Works (AUEW), Mick McGahey of the National Union of Mineworkers (NUM), James Milne, General Secretary of the Scottish TUC, Terry Marsland, Assistant General Secretary of the Tobacco Workers' Union and Ray Alderson of the Civil and Public Services Association, who are all overt members of the Communist Party ... These include Arthur Scargill, President of the NUM, Ray Buckton, General Secretary of the Associated Society of Locomotive Engineers and Firemen (ASLEF), Jimmy Knapp, General Secretary of the National Union of Railwaymen (NUR), Alan Sapper, General Secretary of the Association of Cinematograph, Television and Allied Technicians, Jim Slater, General Secretary of the National Union of Seamen, Ken Cameron, National Secretary of the Fire Brigades' Union and Campbell Christie, Deputy Secretary of the Society of Civil and Public Servants.[2]

The result was the extraordinary success of the Soviet offensive. The point was, apparently, 'to move the Labour Party increasingly to the left so that in the event of its election to power it can be manipulated in the Soviet interest.'[3]

Although no statement of general policy was published by the Conservatives between 1975 and 1979, it was clear that, in private, Thatcher had not modified her views regarding infiltration by subversives. The publication of *The Right Approach*, a document produced to ameliorate the divisions in the party and unite both wings, remained bland and reserved on Thatcher's *bêtes noires*. There would be no direct confrontation with the unions until the Conservatives could be confident of winning, so *The Right Approach* was conciliatory. As late as 1976, Thatcher still claimed the government was willing to talk to union bosses to provide the 'policies that are needed to save our country'.[4]

This was patently not true, as Thatcher had, from the start, no doubt that union power had to be crushed, and, if the government had to fight shy of confrontation, then the independent groups that she supported could continue to bring legal and propagandistic pressure. Thatcher was, as we have seen, very interested in Crozier's anti-Trotskyist think tank, the Institute for the Study of Conflict, which engaged in exposing left-wing groups, union leaders and radical MPs. She also continued her support for NAFF and Norris McWhirter and only seemed to distance herself from the findings of a secret report called *Stepping Stones* produced by John Hoskyns and Norman Strauss which called for urgent action against the legal and political rights of working people. The strategy urged in *Stepping Stones* was simply to confront the immunities and closed-shop practices of the organised working class. Thatcher at first rejected the plan as too radical and unworkable, but it was the apparent collapse of the government during the Winter of Discontent that persuaded her to embrace the expected conflict.[5]

The agenda was ultimately fuelled by fear both of infiltration by subversives and of communist takeover of industry. These concerns were consistent with a fear of the imminent break-up of the fabric of the United Kingdom. It was, to a certain extent, a paranoid projection. Arthur Scargill would stand in for the straw 'red', as Red Robbo (Derek Robinson) had done at British Leyland until his dismissal in November 1979. For Thatcher, Robinson and his ilk were the enemy personified, Robinson being 'a notorious agitator'. Defeating those like Scargill would become an obsession. In July 1984, Thatcher addressed the backbench 1922 Committee: 'We had to fight the enemy without in the Falklands. We always have to be aware of the enemy within, which is much more difficult to fight and more dangerous to liberty.'[6]

There were, however, a number of 'enemies within' and none would remain silenced. The various enemies were a heady mixture inherited from the 1970s and some new creations of the 1980s. They included over-powerful trade unions abetted by the collapse of the British work ethic through communist infiltration in everything from factories to universities to building sites. There was also the rise of nationalisms threatening the United Kingdom, and left-wing and international revolutionary terrorism (as exemplified by the IRA in Northern Ireland; the Tartan Army in Scotland, Angry Brigade in England and the Palestine Liberation Organisation (PLO) in the Middle East). To this brew was added the continuing threat of the Soviet Union and the nuclear disarmament movement and women's movements, the changing demographics of cities filling with ethnic minorities, the abandonment of Britannia for a European future and even sexual liberalism, including the cultural over-representation of gay people. The malaise had to be halted and reversed, but to do so would embrace actions that were more authoritarian and more coercive than had existed before. It would have to be tough medicine.

Those on the left were also feeling in a beleaguered mood. Enemies, indeed there were, but they too took a paranoid tone, believing not that they had won the war of social and economic attrition of the 1970s, but, indeed, that they had won *some* battles, but were, by 1979, fighting a rearguard action. The sense of defeat was palpable:

It used to be said by many people that 'it could never happen here'. Today there is not the same degree of certainty. The political atmosphere is bristling with the sinister activities of the forces of state repression – the armed forces, the police, the Special Branch and the secret spy services. It means that hard-won basic democratic rights which are cherished by millions of working people and trade unionists are endangered.[7]

Now it was not merely a political fight, but one in which the police and army were actively engaged in destroying working-class gains: 'The class struggles which erupted under the Heath government (1970–74) – Saltley coke depot during the 1972 miners' strike, the Shrewsbury pickets frame-up, the Pentonville dockers, the Industrial Relations Act – brought the police and the army into the arena of Britain's industrial and political life.'[8]

Extreme left-wing groups, such as the Workers' Revolutionary Party, which considered themselves some way to the left of the official Communist Party of Great Britain and considered the International Marxist Group to be revisionists and liberals, spent the 1970s fighting a war of words (for the most part) with Heath's government, and, in the early 1980s, with Thatcher, whom they accused of developing a 'strong state' precisely to destroy working-class gains.

Indeed, the strong state was always a central ideal for Thatcher, despite her desire for smaller government and less interference in personal affairs. This proved to be the greatest contradiction in Thatcher's three administrations. Amid increasing talk of decentralisation, there was an equally increased level of central control. Thatcher's desire to increase home ownership led Lord Denning to exclaim that Section 23 of the 1980 Housing Act was 'a most coercive power ... that enable[d] central government to interfere with a high hand over local authorities'.[9] The Marxist historian Eric Hobsbawm noted in his obituary of Lady Thatcher that:

Increasingly obvious [was the fact] that a government devoted to dismantling the state has inevitably strengthened it, ... Since the dream of an economy and people entirely independent of the Treasury is unreal ... the state must

henceforth – in the interests of withering away – give ever more precise directions about how its funds should and should not be spent … Central power and
command are not diminishing but growing, since 'freedom' cannot be achieved
except by bureaucratic decision.[10]

The need to shrink the state had needed state intervention at every stage, often
of a most brutal type, to create agreement. Instead of Hayek's market-determined
anarchy, there was state control in the name of freedom of choice. Thatcher's centralism was also a matter of angry accusation within the government. Kenneth Baker,
Thatcher's Education Secretary, even suggested that the proposed reforms of the universities which were directed at social utility smacked uncomfortably of 'Leninism'.[11]
Thatcher remained untroubled by the contradiction.

The situation was exacerbated by the bomb at the 1984 Conservative Party conference in Brighton. Thatcher's personal heroism displayed to perfection at that event
nevertheless left her more embattled and isolated. There was no rush to increase
anti-terrorist laws, but, the MP Emma Nicholson remarked that the bomb 'locked
her away in a Nixonian bunker, staffed by overzealous ideological activists and cut
off from the voters she needed to see and hear and touch'.[12]

Thatcher had already felt the chill down her neck from lurking enemies after the
killing of Ross McWhirter when she was given her own police protection in the
figure of Bob Kingston, a Special Branch officer.[13] In her eulogy on Airey Neave,
Thatcher seemed convinced that only a tough individual and tough government
could defeat the powers of totalitarian darkness that seemed to surround her:

[Neave's] long and varied public service began with one of the most famous feats
of the Second World War: his escape from Colditz. He learned much from that
extraordinary experience. The prisons of Nazi Germany taught him all that he
needed to know about the character of totalitarian rule. Airey did not have to
speculate how a brutal police state behaves when freedom falters: he had himself
suffered at the hands of the Gestapo. Nor did he have to read Dostoievsky to
know what it means to be told (falsely) that he was about to be court-martialled
and shot: it had happened to him.[14]

A strong state, for Thatcher, was one that felt itself permanently embattled and one
that would not hesitate to use all its machinery to destroy opposition from within and
without. This credo would effectively be her way of understanding the world, whether
it was in terms of the miners, the Greenham Common women or councillors from
Liverpool. All seemed to connive the victory of external enemies against whom the
'state' – which meant Thatcher's version of government – had to stand firm. In Neave's
obituary, Thatcher also defined her philosophy, one based on the 'individual' and predicated on the thoughts of the eighteenth-century philosopher Edmund Burke, who had

created the basis of modern conservatism. In this model, the first principle of government was to 'reinvigorate not just the economy and industry but the whole body of
voluntary associations, loyalties and activities which gives society its richness and diversity,
and hence its real strength ... a society of this sort is the best one in which to live.'[15]
Thatcher's target was the parlous situation of much of the previous ten years:

> When the State becomes involved in every strike, price or contract affecting a
> nationalised industry, people tend to associate the State with those things rather
> than with its higher traditional and necessary role. Consequently its authority is
> not enhanced, it is diminished.[16]

It was this *diminishment of the authority of the state* that Thatcher and Thatcherism
sought to reverse:

> In our Party we do not ask for a feeble State. On the contrary, we need a strong
> State to preserve both liberty and order, to prevent liberty from crumbling and
> to keep order from hardening into despotism.
> The State has ... certain duties which are incontrovertibly its own: for exam-
> ple – to uphold and maintain the law; to defend the nation against attack from
> without; to safeguard the currency; to guarantee essential services.
> We have frequently argued that the State should be more strongly concerned
> with those matters than it has been.
> But strong government is quite different from total or absolute government.[17]

What then was strong government, but government by the authority of the state
which was tasked with the continuance of the 'British way of life' and those traditions
which sat convivially with the unquestioned authority of those in charge?

> The State also is the custodian of national traditions, institutions and customs
> because they are part of our way of life and our national heritage. They are
> justified not on any basis of abstract logic – few, if any, of them could have been
> constructed that way – but because over the years they have worked and we
> should be cautious before changing or discarding them.[18]

It was precisely because the old Tory elite had been infected with liberalism and had
become 'wet' that tradition (whose guardian was the state) had been betrayed and
fallen into the hands of the 'left'. How the Tories were effectively going to wrest
back control of society and culture would be the key political quetion for the new
Conservatism, but it would require the government to walk a tightrope. Quoting
Anthony Quinton, Thatcher continued, 'What is essential to conservatism is that it
would confer absolute power neither on the individual nor the State ... Law is the

collective and historical element that is needed to control the actions of individuals, whether rulers or subjects, living and acting in the present.'[19]

Nevertheless, it was in the very idea of lawful behaviour, rather than 'law' per se, that meant those tasked with seeing the Thatcher ideology through would be required both to amend laws (against the Greenham Common women, for instance) or obfuscate the activities of those who were meant to uphold the law (such as the army in Northern Ireland or police action in the miners' strike).

Further, though ideal government has to be strong, 'it [was] not charged with the direct control of all the activities of the community',[20] yet this was what became the pragmatic solution, not merely as a perversion of the ideal, but, in the end a course of action that was sanctioned by the ideal itself. 'The Conservative' argued Thatcher, 'unlike the political theorist of idealism [the left) neither identifies the State with society nor absorbs society within the State.'[21] Nevertheless, the only way to defeat the political idealists was to identify the state with the very programme the state was charged with delivering: the emancipation of the individual. Thus, and without a hint of irony, it could be suggested, 'These are the things which *only a government can do* [my emphasis] and which a government must do. Today, many other services – pre-eminently health and education – are the object of Government participation or supervision.'[22]

It was, however, the restructuring of society that came to dominate Thatcher's thinking and government policy, specifically the reconfiguring of the relationship between government and the unions. In short, the Conservatives knew they had to reinvent union thinking, which was supposedly held in the grip of its historical evolution, or destroy the unions once and for all.

Indeed, it was the argument that had arisen over the closed shop, following the Grunwick dispute in 1977 (itself central to the work of the McWhirters), which would create one of many conundrums for the Conservative leader while she developed her ideas in opposition. Keith Joseph had opposed the closed shop while Jim Prior (tasked with its future destruction) had equivocated, aware of the hostility of the unions and many industrial magnates. Thatcher, in America meeting Jimmy Carter, was caught between the two positions: 'We do not think it is right. We are against it … But because I do not like it, and think it is against the freedom of the individual, does not necessarily mean that I can pass legislation about it.'[23]

On the one hand, Thatcher supported Joseph, while on the other, she was aware of the difficulties that had occurred during Heath's time. Her remarks on the Brian Walden television programme *Weekend World* confirmed that she was not about to embark on a confrontation 'of the kind that Ted had [because] it didn't work'. Nevertheless, Walden was persistent and asked, 'If we vote Margaret Thatcher into Number 10 … will we be voting for a disastrous and futile confrontation between the government and the unions?'[24]

In the mid 1970s, no one had yet formulated a solution to the problem of trade union 'abuses', but evident from Walden's question was the fact that the issue was central to the reconfiguration not merely of British industrial relations, but more importantly, to the nature of what it meant to be British.

Thatcher's eulogising made it quite clear that confrontation would be the government's only way out of the impasse brought about by the confrontation of state power and union prestige. In destroying union power and thus rendering union opposition impotent, Thatcher would have been able to 'impose' the notion of individualist 'Conservative' culture, and, by solving an apparently economic problem, she would have defined the British way of life. The solution was as old as socialism and as new as Thatcherism. Each might have had different ends, but both recognised the same problem. By Thatcher's second term, when she had won a 144-seat majority, left-wing intellectual Cassandras were in despair. It was quite clear that the battle would be around the notion of culture. Their predictions would take over ten years to come to fruition and, like Cassandra's, they would centre on war and catastrophe.

8

OPERATION BARMAID

The essence of Britain as a nuclear state was secrecy. What was to be kept secret was power, and power was to be used to fight enemies abroad and, more crucially, at home. Once upon a time, power had been nakedly displayed to deter aggression from all quarters, but since the time of Clement Attlee's government in the post-war period, this policy had been reversed and power came from the holding of as many secrets as possible in a perpetual game of international and national bluff.

The Attlee decision to develop an independent atom bomb was made by a highly secretive group of ministers called GEN 163. This process of secret decision-making, which effectively bypassed the Cabinet and Parliament had become part of government policy and governmental practice. Harold Wilson, discussing nuclear warhead testing during June 1974, rebuked Michael Foot over his over-pushy insistence in getting at the truth behind a previous denial of the testing by Cabinet colleague Jim Callaghan. Wilson's reply spoke for all that could no longer be spoken of in a democracy. 'It has always been the convention of Cabinet that certain things are not discussed in Cabinet ... I could not consult Cabinet because a leak of any kind would have very serious effects for reasons I can't give now.'[1]

By 1979, the year of Thatcher's election, such attitudes gave the Prime Minister carte blanche to ignore colleagues. This meant that in her new style of 'directed' Cabinet, the sort of debate that might be had in a consensual government group was forgotten in the heat of moral certitude. Such a position made the Prime Minister ever more isolated from colleagues who disagreed, which isolated those colleagues and forced them into the intrigues of cabals. Thatcher was never quite free of wets and half-baked Thatcherites who wished to modify her vision. Thus 'handbagging' was the only solution when common ground was slowly removed and extreme positions adopted.

This effectively created paranoia at the very top and a sense of beleaguered-ness, something of which Wilson had been only too well aware. Barbara Castle remembered a conversation with Wilson in which he had wondered out loud about his Cabinet, 'Do you really think there is any one of them I can trust?'[2] Neil Kinnock, with a sense of bravado, but also a certain truthfulness, suggested that by 1986 Thatcher herself '[had] retreated into a fantasy world where all her friends [were] abroad, all her enemies [were] within'.[3]

To accommodate this sense of siege mentality and to reinforce governmental security, Thatcher simply bypassed Cabinet by creating a committee system that appeared to democratise and disseminate information, but that in fact made it more secretive, more difficult to pin down and more effective as a weapon to avoid awkward Cabinet colleagues. Thus the group that decided to adopt the Trident missile system was a very small select committee, just as in Attlee's day. In 1981, Thatcher set up another small group to be chaired by Willie Whitelaw called MISC 62 (known colloquially as the Star Chamber) to resolve budgetary issues. This fitted the style of Thatcher's mode of government, where she preferred to rely on small but trustworthy ad hoc groupings rather than the officially acknowledged committee structure which would involve keeping a strict record of proceedings.[4] Such cobbled-together working parties were the result of fundamental insecurities and, as Neil Kinnock was to point out in 1986 when drafting his own manifesto, 'insecurity imposes its own tyranny'.[5]

At the heart of secrecy was and still is power. It is intoxicating. Barbara Castle, the most powerful female politician before Thatcher, recalled that she enjoyed the 'febrile, exacting and fulfilling world of power' when she was a minister.[6] She imagined that Thatcher would love it no less. Thatcher, Castle decided was 'in love: in love with power, success – and with herself'.[7] With the intoxication of power came the real bonus: control. Whoever held the most secrets held power, and whoever had power had control. While it was the mission of the government to neutralise opposition by whatever means necessary in order to safeguard Britain's return to the world stage; it was the duty of those who opposed the government to find out these secrets and expose them.

The direct connection between secrecy, power and control reached its climax between May 1979, when Thatcher became Prime Minister, and 1989, when the 'old' Cold War ended. Indeed, the three prongs of the nuclear state had never fully been integrated before. During the continuing crisis of the 1980s, which, in the end, amounted to undeclared warfare at home and abroad, Thatcher was in charge of a host of secret policies and activities hidden from parliamentary scrutiny and sometimes even from the government. The secret state and those who wielded power effectively reached further than ever before into the private lives of its citizens.

Occasionally, the forces of state authority were forced to reveal themselves – the police, Special Branch or the SAS making periodic interventions on the streets, in the coalfields, or in the sunny climes of Gibraltar on behalf of law and order – and sometimes the workings of the secret state were exposed by events, as in the scrutiny given to the secret service after the exposure of Sir Anthony Blunt and in the Geoffrey Prime affair and the squabble over unionisation at GCHQ.

Such interventions and such exposure were infrequent and often unconnected in the public mind. This gave leeway to government and protection to the state even in their most perilous days. It effectively hid the secret paths of power and the opportunities for control. In pursuit of freedom, Thatcherism provided the blueprint for the modern surveillance society which is so much taken for granted today.

If Thatcher did not approve of certain actions, perhaps, she could be branded as not Thatcherite enough. Such conflations meant that more pressure might be applied to those who were incalcitrant, and more coercive means used where necessary. In this regard, the sobriquet Iron Lady was a gift from Thatcher's international enemies and confirmed her in the public imagination as Boudicca, Britannia and an imitation Winston Churchill, a position that she hardly challenged as she became more imperious and took to using 'we' on the famous occasion of the birth of her grandchildren.

As the Iron Lady, Thatcher was happy to live up to the title. She said that she 'had to be an Iron Lady' to a rapturous reception from an audience of 2,000 in New York, using the occasion to lecture on the communist menace and the joys of the free market. Her title led her inevitably towards a metamorphosis into Britannia. She occasionally even dallied with military uniform as she did when visiting the UDR on 19 August 1979 after the killing of Lord Mounbatten and the massacre of eighteen soldiers at Warrenpoint. She was more than happy to be photographed with the SAS soldiers who had stormed the Iranian Embassy. Indeed, after the siege, she had gone to Regent's Park Barracks to congratulate the soldiers involved.

At a reception two days after the siege was over, Thatcher was admonished by her permanent secretaries who told her that 'we are the system'. The evening was 'etched into her soul' and demonstrated the 'wet' attitude of the civil servants and politicians who surrounded her and the 'can do' attitude of the army whose sense of duty she shared.[8] Thatcher's moral position was always that of an outsider whose relationship to the system was one in which she was the beleaguered hostage waiting for rescue by a loyal SAS. Later, on 28 September 1986, she would command a Chieftain tank dressed in goggles and Hermès scarf. On that occasion, she had the wit and self-deprecation to poke out her tongue at the cameras.

Thatcher was never a militarist, but Thatcherism was in essence aggressive and authoritarian, and the more Thatcherite Thatcher became, the more she embraced militarism. Thatcherism also gave carte blanche to those wishing to stamp out union disputation, local council activists or the Greenham women who stood in opposition to Conservative policies. The police became more secretive and more authoritarian, turning areas of Britain such as pit villages, Stonehenge and the inner cities into temporary 'miniature police states', and, where necessary, the new authoritarians changed evidence to suit circumstances, as at Hillsborough.

Thatcher had changed her personality and even her media voice in the years between being a junior minister and becoming Prime Minister. She had also embraced the policies of the free market worked out by Friedrich Hayek, Milton

Friedman, Alan Walters, Enoch Powell and Sir Keith Joseph, who all contributed
to the idea of monetarism and therefore the compatible concept of Thatcherism.
The resultant character change in Thatcher during her first premiership appeared
almost theatrical. For Michael Moorcock, a man who knew something of metamorphosis, having been a rock musician, novelist, CND activist, Labour Party member,
Liberal Party worker and anarchist, Thatcher had become of necessity a 'fictional
character'.[9] This Thatcher was 'a sharp-tongued school "marm", a nagging wife,
the shrewish secretary of the local women's institute'.[10] Thatcherism's 'talk of "auton-
omy"' merely acted to [increase] the powers of central government'.[11] Moorcock
was well aware of left-wing paternalism and authoritarianism, well aware of the
shortcomings of the 1970s and the problem of welfare-statism and a disenfranchised
population, but Thatcher was another example of the 'authoritarian personality',[12]
not from the left but from the right, whose emergence at the time of a collapse in
'morale' allowed her party to present her as 'tidying up ... the *apparent* chaos' and
by so doing create an atmosphere which made 'people prey to ... coercion and
control'.[13] The Conservatives had finally learned from Labour about the importance
of the social engineering at the centre of the welfare state and were set on the reconstruction of a failing society and a 'failed' dream.

⁂

The dispute between authoritarian Conservatism and liberalism crystallised around
the sinking of the Argentine cruiser *Generallisimo Belgrano* by the submarine *Conqueror*
on 2 May 1982. A year later, it seemed that the talk of conspiracy and coercion was all
true when, on 24 May 1983, Diana Gould confronted Thatcher during a question-
and-answer session on the BBC's *Nationwide* programme. The programme, presented
by Sue Lawley, was meant to give Thatcher a platform before the upcoming election.
After the usual concerns and the usual appropriate general answers, Gould confronted Thatcher with her knowledge of the Prime Minister's decision to sink the
Belgrano. The implication was clear: the Prime Minister was a war criminal:

> Gould: Mrs Thatcher, why, when the *Belgrano*, the Argentinian battleship,
>   was outside the exclusion zone and actually sailing away from the
>   Falklands, why did you give the orders to sink it?
> Thatcher: But it was not sailing away from the Falklands – It was in an area
>   which was a danger to our ships, and to our people on them.
> Lawley: Outside the exclusion zone, though.
> Thatcher: It was in an area which we had warned, at the end of April, we had
>   given warnings that all ships in those areas, if they represented a
>   danger to our ships, were vulnerable. ...

Yet Diana Gould persisted in her interrogation in a voice both calm and firm, against which Thatcher appeared hectoring and patronising. Thatcher appeared more rattled as the interrogation proceeded, especially as Gould seemed to have specialist knowledge so arcane that to many viewers (especially those looking for the grail that would 'expose' Thatcher) her comments had to have a grain of truth in them:

Gould: But Mrs Thatcher, you started your answer by saying it was not sailing away from the Falklands. It was on a bearing of 280 and it was already west of the Falklands, so, I'm sorry, but I cannot see how you can say it was not sailing away from the Falklands.

Thatcher: When it was sunk.

Gould: When it was sunk.

Thatcher: It was a danger to our ships.

Gould: No, but you have just said at the beginning of your answer that it was not sailing away from the Falklands, and I am asking you to correct that statement.

Thatcher: But it's within an area outside the exclusion zone, which I think is what you are saying …

Gould: No, I am not, Mrs Thatcher.

Lawley: I think we are not arguing about which way it was facing at the time.

The 'lies' of Thatcherism seemed about to unravel as the Prime Minister lost her temper:

Gould: Mrs Thatcher, I am saying that it was on a bearing 280, which is a bearing just north of west. It was already west of the Falklands, and therefore nobody with any imagination can put it sailing other than away from the Falklands.

Thatcher: Mrs – I'm sorry, I forgot your name …

Lawley: Mrs Gould.

Thatcher: Mrs Gould, when the orders were given to sink it, when it was sunk, it was in an area which was a danger to our ships. Now, you accept that, do you?

Gould: No, I don't.

Thatcher: I am sorry, it was. You must accept …

Gould: No, Mrs Thatcher.

This was the type of grilling usually reserved for a court of law, not a cosy discussion on Britain's leading television magazine programme. Diana Gould appeared to be in possession of hard facts; Thatcher merely left with the rhetoric of patriotism, regrets about war casualties and pious platitudes about 'what could not be revealed'. Gould persisted, and by now even Sue Lawley was animated enough to need a theory for the sinking. Gould duly gave it, and so plausibly that it left little room for an answer. Indeed, any answer would have appeared, de facto, to be a 'lie' intended to protect the Prime Minister at the forthcoming election:

Lawley: Let me ask you this, Mrs Gould. What motive are you seeking to attach to Mrs Thatcher and her government in this? Is it inefficiency, lack of communication, or is it a desire for action, a desire for war?

Gould: It is a desire for action, and a lack of communications because, on giving those orders to sink the *Belgrano* when it was actually sailing away from our fleet and away from the Falklands, was in effect sabotaging any possibility of any peace plan succeeding, and Mrs Thatcher had fourteen hours in which to consider the Peruvian peace plan that was being put forward to her. In those fourteen hours those orders could have been rescinded.

Thatcher: One day, all of the facts, in about thirty years time, will be published.

Gould: That is not good enough, Mrs Thatcher. We need …

Thatcher: Would you please let me answer? I lived with the responsibility for a very long time. I answered the question giving the facts, not any-one's opinions, but the facts. Those Peruvian peace proposals, which were only in outline, did not reach London until after the attack on the *Belgrano* – that is fact – I am sorry, that is fact, and I am going to finish – did not reach London until after the attack on the *Belgrano*. Moreover, we went on negotiating for another fortnight after that attack. I think it could only be in Britain that a Prime Minister was accused of sinking an enemy ship that was a danger to our navy, when my main motive was to protect the boys in our navy. That was my main motive, and I am very proud of it. One day all the facts will be revealed, and they will indicate as I have said.

Lawley: Mrs Gould, have you got a new point to make, otherwise I must move on?

Gould: Just one point. I understood that the Peruvian peace plans … were discussed on midnight, May the first. If that outline did not reach London for another fourteen hours …

Lawley: Mrs Thatcher has said that it didn't.

Gould: … I think there must be something very seriously wrong with our communications, and we are living in a nuclear age when we are going to have minutes to make decisions, not hours.

Thatcher: I have indicated what the facts are, and would you accept that I am in a position to know exactly when they reached London? Exactly when the attack was made? I repeat, the job of the Prime Minister is to protect the lives of our boys, on our ships, and that's what I did.

The fury of the Prime Minister after her drubbing was matched by the anger of her husband Dennis who thought the whole affair had been engineered to discredit his wife and that the BBC was, as he suspected, 'a load of Trots and wooftahs'.[14] Paranoia was no less a property of the left as of the right. The argument has raged ever since even though the captain of the *Belgrano* and secret British intercepts suggested the ship was manoeuvring for an attack on the British fleet.

At the time, Tam Dalyell had raised concerns in the House of Commons. He was a maverick, an old Etonian and former trooper in the Scots Greys; the Labour MP for West Lothian who was also the eleventh baronet Sir Thomas Dalyell Loch with a seventeenth-century Scottish baronial home and parkland of 200 acres. He was also Thatcher's most outspoken and tenacious critic. Dalyell accused Thatcher of being a murderer to further her own ends at the forthcoming elections. Offering very detailed information, over a number of years, that could only have come from information at the both the highest level and at operational level (which the MP called his 'deep throats': defence civil servant Clive Ponting and Leading Stoker Simon O'Keefe), Dalyell forensically went through the details of the attack by the submarine HMS *Conqueror*. He had by now the private diary of Lieutenant Narendra Sethia, the supplies officer of the *Conqueror* (which had been given to Dalyell by O'Keefe without Sethia's knowledge). Dalyell also knew that the logbook of the submarine had somehow gone missing.

Dalyell had listened to the questioning on *Nationwide* and drew the same conclusion as its viewers: Thatcher was lying. The point was irrelevant to the election which followed, but it gave an insight into the murky world of undemocratic decisions and undemocratic organisations that lurked behind the democratic process. Walking into the Commons library, Dalyell accosted Alan Clark, junior defence minister, over the allegations. 'Was Thatcher lying?' asked Dalyell, 'Of course she bloody is' replied an insouciant Clark.[15] As late as 2005, the right-wing political journalist Peter Oborne admitted that, 'There is no doubt that Margaret Thatcher lied to the electorate over the sinking of the *Belgrano*'.[16]

The *Belgrano* question muddied the triumph that Thatcher had snatched from the disaster that proved to be GCHQ intelligence gathering. GCHQ had not been able to listen in on Argentinian plans because those plans had been devised in conversation only behind locked doors. The gathering clouds had been on the horizon for years and had become threatening months before. The government chose to ignore the signs. Sir Anthony Williams, the Ambassador in Buenos Aires between 1980 and 1982 recalled:

> I was sending warnings back that things were getting worse. I sent a very much more acute warning when I had a long talk with the Argentine Foreign Minister in September 1981. Then President Viola was displaced by Galtieri. The very hard-line head of the Argentine navy, Admiral Anaya, was a person who believed in a forceful solution. We would draw the attention of London to this time and time again. I suspect the Foreign Office thought that this was a problem which it

could let ride. So many times before it had come to a fairly high–decibel level and had cooled down again. They were by no means convinced that my information was necessarily better than what they were getting through other intelligence sources [Signals Intelligence, the interception of Argentina's diplomatic cypher traffic by GCHQ].[17]

He was correct. Nicanor Mendez, the Argentinian Foreign Minister in 1982, confirmed in 1989 that neither GCHQ nor live agents knew of Galtieri's plans for invasion in advance of the war, something revealed in the subsequent Franks Report into the controversy:

The plan was to climax in a very strong diplomatic offensive at the UN General Assembly, so as to reach the end of the year with maximum momentum. The British Secret Intelligence Service managed to get hold of this plan. I don't know exactly how … Unfortunately the British government took no notice and ignored or misread the plan and failed to understand our urgency.[18]

Things went at such a pace that they caused panic in the Foreign Office and in the government generally, and improvisation replaced planning. Sir Anthony Parsons, Britain's Ambassador to the United Nations in New York, was forced to call an emergency meeting of the Security Council:

The day before the Argentine invasion I was instructed by the Foreign Office to call an emergency meeting of the Security Council to try and take some pre-emptive action. I called my colleagues – other members of the Security Council. They simply couldn't believe it. It is perfectly true it was April the 1st. One or two of them literally thought that I was playing an 'April Fool' joke on them and that I wasn't serious.[19]

Resolution 502, passed on 3 April 1982, called for an immediate cessation of hostilities and the withdrawal of Argentine troops. It also proposed a diplomatic solution to the problem. Nevertheless, so rushed were plans that even the Russians were nonplussed. 'The position of the Soviets was very interesting. They were taken totally by surprise … It was pretty clear to us that they were in a mess.'[20]

It was in this heated atmosphere that the *Belgrano* had been sunk. The leaked information on which Gould and Dalyell hoped to destroy the credibility of the Prime Minister threw Thatcher into a spin, and every avenue was to be pursued to track down the person who had leaked the information. Needless to say, government grinds slowly, and it was two almost years from the first questions to the search for the 'mole'. The search began in earnest during 1984. Michael Heseltine as the Defence Secretary was instructed to leave no stone unturned.

Heseltine had been appointed as Secretary of State for Defence on 6 January 1983 because he had a proven track record of managerialism and cost-cutting and because Thatcher needed him where she could not see him. She disliked him (as 'not of us') and, echoing his mentor Edward Heath, he called her 'that bloody woman'. Heseltine knew nothing of war or strategy and little about the *Belgrano* and the Falklands War. he had not been part of the War Cabinet. His predecessor, John Nott, had created the snare that Heseltine was about to fall in to. The *Belgrano* fiasco was a mixture of military secrecy and bureaucratic incompetence, and Heseltine needed to know what to do fast and who could do it for him. His choice was the senior civil servant charged with briefing ministers on the Falklands.

The secret inquiry had again been prompted by Dalyell, who had refused to forget the affair and had sent Heseltine a nineteen-point letter that he required answering. Clive Ponting, who was head of Section DS5 at the Ministry of Defence, and had worked closely with Thatcher, was given the task of collating information in response to new revelations, now backed by the Labour Party, that had emerged in a book called *The Sinking of the Belgrano* by Desmond Rice and Arthur Gavshon. Ponting's report was intended as a piece of 'disinformation', both to clarify what had actually happened for the government and to put investigators off the scent to avoid, in Heseltine's words, another Watergate and the possible destruction of the government. Ponting's report was nicknamed the 'Crown Jewels'.

Ponting then advised the Secretary of State how to stonewall the questions, but soon became disillusioned by the process of government cover-up. He took the step of writing to Dalyell to advise him as to the specific questions he should be asking. Armed with this information, on 2 May 1984, the second anniversary of the sinking, Dalyell was suspended from Parliament for calling the Prime Minister a liar. Undeterred, Dalyell again sent a letter with a series of questions to Heseltine.

Ponting, meanwhile had realised that he was protected from breaching the Official Secrets Act if he passed information direct to the Foreign Affairs Committee. The letter and the continuing pressure by Dalyell led to a meeting between Thatcher and Heseltine in which it was finally decided to track down Dalyell's source. Ponting was arrested soon afterwards and would later have his day in court. Meanwhile, Dalyell's accusations meant that anyone vaguely attached to the *Belgrano* affair, or even their relatives, might be suspects.

The first to come under suspicion was former commander Robert Green who had been at headquarters when the order to sink the *Belgrano* was given. He had become disillusioned and now was a roofing thatcher on period buildings. Was he the disaffected mole? The problem was that he was the nephew of the anti-nuclear campaigner Hilda Murrell who had included information about the *Belgrano* in a leaflet she had been distributing around her home town of Shrewsbury. This led the investigators to the erroneous conclusion that her nephew had deposited sensitive information at her house which she had copied.

Green was implicated as the 'traitor' who had fed information to Dalyell. But the MP had mistaken Green's intelligence role for an operational one – a disastrous mistake and one that put both Green and his aunt in peril. Both were bugged, burgled and threatened, as was Green's commanding officer. On 21 March 1984, Hilda Murrell was killed, possibly murdered, in a bungled burglary-cum-surveillance-operation, two days after the creation of the 'Crown Jewels'.

If the sources and the missing logbooks were ever to be found, it would be through all sorts of dirty tricks and officially sanctioned burglaries and phone tapping. Dalyell was interviewed by the security services, but would not reveal his sources. The control room logbook for HMS *Conqueror* conveniently went missing on 7 November 1984, the very day Heseltine was required to give evidence to the Select Committee on Foreign Affairs looking into the *Belgrano* sinking. The revelation was made on BBC news that night. As it was unlikely that so important a piece of evidence would be on the mantelpiece as a cosy memento, it was somewhere in the official pipeline. But, where? Lieutenant Sethia – whose diary Dalyell had photocopied – had left the *Conqueror* in July, although the logbook was still in place during October and November 1982. Dalyell concluded:

> I concede that it is probably true that the *Conqueror's* log did not end up at Fleet Headquarters, Northwood. I concede it did not end up as it should have done in the Records Department of Naval Establishment at Hayes, Middlesex. I assert that it is so politically sensitive, not because of what it contains but on account of the political usefulness of its 'disappearance', that it was sent to the Ministry of Defence itself, almost unique among records, and there it remains.[21]

The slowly revealed revelations regarding the course of the *Belgrano* suggested that John Nott (the Defence Secretary), Michael Heseltine, the Conservative press and the Attorney General were determined the truth should not come to light, preferring to divert attention through their ever more hysterical witch-hunt for the supposed mole. It slowly became clear that the cruiser had been on a zigzag course back to base and was no immediate threat. She was sunk before any British servicemen had been wounded or killed; she was sunk before any declaration of war; and she was sunk as the Peruvian peace plan was nearing completion. *Conqueror's* missing logbook looked suspiciously like a blatant cover-up to avoid revealing the truth.

The government took the line that it was those who had revealed their machinations that were the real enemy, and it set about finding the mole. Sethia proved an easy target, especially as an old drinking friend of his called Richard Morley, who also went by the name Daijhi and who claimed to be an East German spy, suggested that Sethia had stolen the logbook as a souvenir. Both Dalyell and Arthur Gavshon, in his book *The Sinking of the Belgrano*, had made liberal use of the diary, and television and newspapers were fighting to get a handle on the story.

Having served his country Narendra Sethia, worked in the West Indies, but there was no escape. He had been betrayed by his pal and inadvertently ill-used by Dalyell and Gavshon looking for clues to the course of the *Belgrano*, and he had been portrayed as a type of traitor by the press. Conveniently for the government, Sethia was hauled before a naval board which accused him of being a homosexual (then illegal in the services) and later visited by Special Branch and vilified in the press. He was for a time forced to work at menial jobs until finally getting a position in a yacht charter business in St Vincent.[22]

What secret was the government so keen to disguise? The sinking of the *Belgrano* certainly, but were there others that might have emerged if things had progressed? For instance, there were the nagging suspicions that nuclear warheads were lost when HMS *Coventry* was sunk and that *Conqueror* was one of five submarines sent to the exclusion zone, two of which were providing protection for a Polaris submarine armed with nuclear warheads, which was strictly against Protocol One of the Treaty of Tlatelolco which banned nuclear weapons from the South Atlantic and which Britain, but not Argentina, had signed.

Why was a Polaris submarine there at all? This was revealed years later by Ali Magoudi, the psychiatrist to President Mitterand. On 7 May 1982, Mitterrand had interrupted a therapy session with Magoudi to answer Thatcher on the telephone:

> I had a difference to settle with the Iron Lady. That Thatcher, what an impossible woman! With her four nuclear submarines in the South Atlantic, she's threatening to unleash an atomic weapon against Argentina if I don't provide her with the secret codes that will make the [Exocet] missiles we sold the Argentines deaf and blind … She's got them now, the codes … one cannot win against the insular syndrome of an unbridled Englishwoman. Provoke a nuclear war for a few islands inhabited by three sheep as hairy as they are freezing! But it's a good job I gave way. Otherwise, I assure you, the Lady's metallic finger would have hit the button.[23]

According to this anecdote, Mitterand, exasperated by Thatcher and fearful of nuclear war, supposedly handed over the codes to the supply of Exocets ordered, but not yet delivered, to Argentina. The story has both the ring of truthfulness and of exaggeration and myth, but it is on record that Thatcher would certainly have ordered the nuclear annihilation of Argentina's military base at Cordoba if the two aircraft carriers with the task force had been sunk. (As a side note, she changed her mind once she was a grandmother. Previously, Callaghan had hoped if he had needed to 'press the button' he would have been dead soon afterwards and not required to face the consequences.)[24]

And so the situation regarding the movements of *Conqueror* and *Belgrano* remained a matter of debate until the journalist Stuart Prebble revealed a last twist. Prior to going into battle, *Conqueror* had been at Faslane, refitting for a final outing against the Soviets. Intelligence had shown that the Russians were ahead in underwater sound-recording equipment called 'towed array', and one of these needed to be secured for the West. *Conqueror* was being fitted with a highly secret pincer device created to allow a submarine to sneak up on an enemy with one of these towed devices and 'chew' it off without being detected. It was one of the last great gambles of the Cold War. The fitting was interrupted by the decision to send *Conqueror* westwards.

Only on her return from the South Atlantic, was *Conqueror* again required to go searching for the elusive towed array machinery. In July 1982, information was obtained that suggested a Polish vessel was operating one of these devices. *Conqueror* put to sea and, in an operation that was as brilliantly conceived as it was executed, managed to cut the device free and recover it without being noticed. Thus not only was the period of the *Belgrano* incident covered in the missing logs, but so was the crucial period of this operation, known as Barmaid, which was part of Project 2000. Was the logbook (actually the logbooks from April to September 1982) missing because of this vital piece of information? What happened to these A3-sized books with old-fashioned cardboard covers? Amazingly and almost certainly they were simply incinerated as they had not been designated 'confidential' or 'top secret' enough to be sent to an archive.

The cross-examination of the Prime Minister by Diana Gould and Tam Dalyell was a consequence of a number of parliamentary questions, leaks and books by people who refused to believe Thatcher's version of events. The indifference of the population to the fate of the *Belgrano's* sailors (exemplified by the notorious 'Gotcha' headline in the *Sun* on 4 May 1982), and the ultimate victory, neutralised the threat of the *Belgrano* conspiracy theorists.

9

THE SHOW TRIALS
OF OLD ENGLAND

The secret crisis of confidence that occurred in 1974 when Clockwork Orange was activated was matched by a peculiarly different crisis inherent in the overconfidence of the government in 1984. The fear of comparing what Thatcher was doing with George Orwell's nightmare vision in *1984* was such that it could not easily be ignored, and the ghost of Orwell's prophetic words had been constantly turned against Labour. The campaign began in 1980.

Thatcher's team of speech-writers quickly saw the need to make their leader into a crusader. Her speeches during 1980 would accentuate the bickering at the Labour Party Conference where the radical views of Tony Benn had convinced his party to lurch to the left and pass a motion backing unilateral nuclear disarmament. The Soviet invasion of Afghanistan, which began on 24 December 1979 and was the catalyst for the final decade of the Cold War, was grinding into bloody disaster and 'proved' that Benn and others were enemies within the state working for Soviet world domination. The 'soft' left, both at home and internationally, was in retreat, and the left hardliners seemed triumphant. Unemployment was also rising and the unions still menaced the government with increased threats of militancy.

This needed to be directly addressed so that Thatcher was not seen in the same light as Heath and that her portrayal was one of unbending sacrifice and dedication whatever the odds. At the Conservative Party Conference on 7 October 1980, Thatcher's speech-writer Ronnie Millar had effectively turned Thatcher's speech from a dull talk on economics into one with which she reaffirmed her drive and determinacy and also the sense of her doggedness in adversity. 'She should give a speech that affirmed the deepest instincts of our people.'[1] The speech was the most famous of her career. 'To those waiting with bated breath for that favourite media catchphrase, the U-turn, I have only one thing to say, "You turn if you want to. The lady's not for turning."'[2]

It ended with a six-minute standing ovation, but not before Thatcher had invoked the horror of a Labour future. 'Let Labour's Orwellian nightmare of the left be the spur for us to dedicate with a new urgency our every ounce of energy and moral strength to rebuild the fortunes of this free nation.'[3] Haunting Thatcher's early premiership was George Orwell who seemed the ghost at the party. Indeed, in invoking Orwell, Ronnie Millar had effectively confirmed Thatcher as a Thatcherite.

In so doing, the sense of what Thatcher was to herself was revealed. Paul Johnson, to whom Thatcher grew close in the 1970s following the publication of his book *Enemies of Society* (another book from the period with a paranoid title), later judged her 'the most ignorant politician of her level that I'd come across'.[4] Thatcher was 'ignorant' in terms of intellectual weight: she garnered opinion that essentially confirmed her own moral and 'visceral' outlook vaguely formed from her own personal past and which lent her the sobriquet of a conviction politician.

Thus, academics of the likes of Sir Michael Howard, Leonard Shapiro, Isaiah Berlin and Robert Conquest were ushered into her presence to give her the 'facts' regarding Soviet aggression.[5] Thatcher spent little time reading about it herself, preferring to rely on gut instinct. This meant that Thatcher was never a politician in the traditional sense. She replaced political sophistication with moral certainty. Paul Johnson, like others who surrounded the Prime Minister, was more zealous and more Thatcherite than Thatcher and so felt that Thatcher was too unregenerate to understand the revolution that took her name.

For Johnson and many other British right-wing intellectuals, Thatcher was the embodiment of expectations which had been formed throughout the 1970s. What such thinkers wanted was the fulfilment of the necessary basic conditions of personal freedom, market forces and the defeat of the 'red' enemy. Thatcherism was, therefore, fully formed in the minds of people such as Ross and Norris McWhirter, Keith Joseph, Alan Walters, Enoch Powell and a string of right-wing thinkers and ex-army generals before Thatcher gave it all a focus. Thatcher herself mixed most happily with moralists rather than politicians whose positions were always going to be contingent. Thus, she was intrigued by the Conservative Philosophy Group that had been set up by Hugh Fraser and Jonathan Aitken and which had an academic flavour lent by Roger Scruton and John Casey.

Thatcher was originally unconvinced of the importance of the group as it had backed her rival, Keith Joseph, for leadership, but she did finally attend a number of meetings while in opposition. Here she was able to meet Enoch Powell. When she was Prime Minister she went to hear Edward Norman, Dean of Peterhouse, Cambridge, talk of the dangers of Sovietism. Norman had argued for a rigidly conservative moral position that must never be compromised. Nuclear weapons for Norman were no different from conventional weapons and they might need to be used to stop the 'philosophical materialism of Soviet Communism'.[6] In searching for a 'Christian justification for capitalism', Thatcher looked for an ethical 'prophet', as she called Norman, who would allow her the certainty that 'choice is the basics of ethics', a claim she later made at the Zurich Economic Society.[7]

The difficulty with this position is that it remains a zero sum game. In the middle of the discussion following Norman's talk, Thatcher could contain herself no longer and, against the opposing views, she apparently shouted out, 'I agree with Dr Norman: we must defend Christian values with the ATOM BOMB [sic]'. Such outbursts in private would define Thatcher's position in public.

In this, Thatcher's religious and moral beliefs never wavered. She always stayed personally committed to what Norman called the 'English sense' and the '[resuscitation of] a world we have lost'.[8] Passionately attached to the Judaeo-Christian tradition, many of Thatcher's closest advisers were Jewish, such as Alfred Sherman, who insisted she stuck to a belief in an 'explicitly Christian' version of 'British Conservatism' and to those Victorian verities of 'benefaction' and 'selflessness' which were part of an older world all but obliterated by socialism, and which stood for 'the living flesh of British culture'. 'Economic choices' also 'had a moral dimension'.[9]

Orwell's vision was cleverly co-opted for the right and was well enough understood by the party and by the electorate to become shorthand for the old-style left-wing and state-directed misery, the revenant that could not be laid. Such was Conservative awareness of the nightmare of potential publicity blunders that Central Office tried the trick when it put out a press release in 1983 to calm fears and dispel growing left-wing comparisons of the government's policies with those of totalitarian South American regimes. The message was couched as if Thatcher herself had personally answered her critics:

> 1983 was an historic year for the Conservative Party. We won a decisive victory at the General Election. Faced with a clear choice, the British people once again rejected State Socialism and supported the ideals of the Conservative Party ... We have stayed right on course. We have kept in tune with the people of this country. And we have remained true to our ideals. Today, no less than when we first came into office, we believe what we say, we say what we believe, and have the courage to see it through. And that is why I am convinced that for Britain at least, George Orwell was wrong.[10]

1984 was to be 'a year of hope and a year of liberty', something Thatcher's speechwriters had anticipated in her speech of 30 December 1983. Conservative policies were an attempt at re-engineering society towards liberal market forces in exactly the same way as the welfare state, with its echoes of 1984, had supposedly suppressed it, and, as such, there was a certain irony about Conservative social control. There was also a directness about this new unleashed and blatant social tampering which was startling, but there was much obfuscation as to the execution of policy. Policy was often blatant and aggressive, good for some, but bad for others.

Yet it is also clear that those opposed to Thatcher saw her policies as motivated by other more 'clandestine' concerns and carried out by agencies that appeared shadowy and unaccountable. Intellectuals, politicians and journalists of the left tried, but failed, to convince the electorate that something was happening behind their backs.

ೕ꘎ಲ

Thatcher was Prime Minister for just over eleven years, and she seems to have kept morally consistent throughout her three premierships with the comments she made on becoming Prime Minister for the first time:

> I know full well the responsibilities that await me as I enter the door of No. 10 and I'll strive unceasingly to try to fulfil the trust and confidence that the British people have placed in me and the things in which I believe. And I would just like to remember some words of St. Francis of Assisi which I think are really just particularly apt at the moment. 'Where there is discord, may we bring harmony. Where there is error, may we bring truth. Where there is doubt, may we bring faith. And where there is despair, may we bring hope.'[11]

In her statement at the door of Number 10, were the first triumphant signs of heart-felt sincerity. Britain had its first 'conviction politician'.

Long before her election victory, Thatcher had got into evangelical habit. In an interview given in 1971 to Terry Coleman of the *Guardian*, Thatcher admitted to being a believing 'Christian and [praying]' which she confided was part of her 'upbringing' and 'background'.[12] To the journalist she was 'an evangelist, … busily evangelising'.[13] Yet alarm bells rang for those of a less evangelical frame of mind that all might not be well and that 'discord' and 'harmony' might need less-than-democratic means to reconcile opposites. The ends slowly came away from the means and sincere faith in policy might need underhand methods to achieve gaols that might be entirely worthy. Even those of a Conservative persuasion have, with hindsight, come to the conclusion that political lies became a necessity in Thatcher's early years and that this cast of mind became entrenched.

Thatcher was 'disingenuous' from the first,[14] making carefully worded statements about rises in VAT in 1979 which she knew were impossible to uphold and later lying to such an extent during the Westland affair that Michael Heseltine was effectively neutralised because she thought that she might be forced to resign. Thatcher might be caught in networks of untruths that all politicians utter, but her moral convictions suggested she should have found these more distasteful than they appeared. Like conviction politicians after her, Thatcher was able to reconcile her morals with her actions. Moreover, her relationship to those who were Thatcherite or who were licensed to act secretly meant that many more potential lies were tolerated for the good of the Thatcherite experiment; Thatcherism could not be ditched as it was the plank upon which all the rest depended.

Tony Blair fought his 1997 campaign on getting rid of Tory sleaze, but his team had learned the lesson of the Thatcher years. Blair, like Thatcher, was always sincere; his problem, like hers, *was to believe his own falsehoods about being sincere*. Blair's government was the fruition of many of the authoritarian policies that Thatcher herself could not implement.

Thatcher found herself in a fix, for to bring about the greater democratisation of British life and to free it from the hind-bound institutional traditionalism that she felt was exemplified by old-school-tie wets she would have to work with the very institutions and personalities that kept the state (rather than the government) running, but which she wished to reform. Thatcher's rather authoritarian manner and her willingness to embrace the politics of power, rather than conciliation, meant that those who served her, or those whose views now flowered under her leadership, might carry out policies or actions that would be, in their view, in the spirit of Thatcherism *sans* Thatcher. Her famous comment in choosing her civil servants – 'Is he one of us?' – might not be merely apocryphal.

This created a problem for Thatcher's style of leadership. No one doubted her fidelity to liberty, but no one could deny her dislike of contrary opinion. This would be the case with any voice shrill enough to command attention for non-Thatcherite views. Thus Thatcherism was caught in a contradiction. On the one hand, it stood for liberty of choice and conscience; and, on the other hand, it had to silence those who opposed that view or had an alternative idea of British liberty. Thatcher's government could support a union such as the Polish Solidarnost, but also General Pinochet's suppression of unions; could fight for liberty in the Soviet Union and suppress those liberties in British coalfields and urban streets. This central contradiction was never truly sorted out.

It was nevertheless, supported by the world of secrecy that surrounded government and the Civil Service. Almost from the beginning, secrecy became the grail of Thatcherite authority and was the basis for her conviction politics and for her everyday pragmatism when faced with a challenge.

State secrecy has a relatively short history in Britain. Although there have always been state secrets and state functionaries, the modern secret state began in the mid-nineteenth century with the appearance of the Criminal Law (Larceny Act) of 1858 which debarred civil servants from giving unauthorised access to state secrets. This was followed by the first Official Secrets Act in 1889, but it was another twenty years before a fully functional state apparatus was set up for intelligence gathering. Thus, between 1909 and 1910, the rudiments of both MI5 and MI6 were put into place. This was itself followed by the Official Secrets Act of 1911 which repealed and replaced its nineteenth-century ancestor. In 1912, the D-Notice Committee was established to vet things that were deemed too sensitive to be made public. Another Official Secrets Act was passed in 1920 to deal with the Bolshevik threat. This Act was replaced in 1939, and so it remained until the 1980s, despite numerous committees on reform and a Reform Bill in 1979. Nevertheless, there remained considerable growth in the intelligence and security sector and greater enforcement of D-notices.

During the 1980s, this ring fence of security measures which Thatcher' government inherited, but also made continual use of and strengthened, was challenged in the courts by four cases which the government failed to suppress and which alerted it to the need for reform of the confidentiality system within both the Civil Service and the intelligence services.

The first case was that of Sarah Tisdall, which went to trial in 1984. The case had its roots in October 1983 when the *Guardian* had published classified information on the government's plans for dealing with the arrival of Cruise missiles. Of two leaked papers, the newspaper chose to publish the one dealing with the methods the Defence Secretary intended to use to handle any bad publicity. When the government went to court to recover the papers, it was able to trace the source to a young woman in the Foreign Office, who confessed to breaching section 2 of the Official Secrets Act. Tisdall's defence was that the leaked documents attempted to keep secret certain attitudes and approaches which by right should have been available for parliamentary scrutiny. At her trial, she was sentenced to six month's imprisonment to make her, in the words of Judge Cantley, an example in 'these days'.

Encouraged by its success, the government's next task was to punish Clive Ponting, the senior civil servant in the Ministry of Defence who had leaked information to Tam Dalyell. Ponting had sent two classified documents to Dalyell which showed that the Foreign Affairs Committee had been misled over the sinking of the *Belgrano*. Ponting was traced and charged again under section 2, but giving information to a Member of Parliament was excluded from the Act and this gave Ponting a get-out-of-jail card apparently unnoticed by the Attorney General's office.

The trial, which began in February 1985 and lasted ten days, was a messy affair which showed that some of Ponting's claims were based on unclassified information that might be freely circulated anyway. Eager to get a conviction, it appeared that Justice McCowan's summing up was another speech by the prosecution. The central concern hinged on the definition of 'the state'. McCowan had suggested to the jury that 'duty in the interest of the state' was synonymous with duty to the incumbent government – carte blanche to anything governments deemed secret. The jury would have nothing of such sophistry and threw out the case which they saw as a purely political prosecution determined by government expediency.

The Ponting trial was a watershed in one important way. The shock of severe deterrent sentencing, as in the case of Tisdall, worked against the government's intentions. Ponting's trial was seen as a 'show trial' by Roy Hattersley and an 'East European style state secret trial' by David Steel.[15] It hinged on the definition of the state and how information was allowed to circulate in a free country.

The definition of the state, let alone its role, had always been comfortably assumed to be understood, and the exact nature of what 'it' was, let alone the parameters of action allowed to those who acted in its behalf, had been long avoided in law because the state had only existed in its present form for little more than seventy years. To the judge in the Ponting case, who took a rigidly conservative and partisan view, the work of the state was synonymous with the requirements of the particular government in power. For the defendant (and in the end the jury), the state consisted of those organs responsible to Parliament and ultimately to the voter, and was to be seen as separate from the partisan requirements of those sitting in governmental power. It was this final decision by the jury which acquitted Ponting and that defined the state as other than the mere executive organs of governmental priorities. The state was a body of organisations that were democratically accountable and might not remain secret simply because a Prime Minister decided as much.

The government was again on the warpath, but was inconsistent in its attitude to certain figures and certain forms of accusation. This was the case with Cathy Massiter. Massiter was a member of MI5 who revealed that there appeared to be a policy in British intelligence to carry out apparently authorised as well as unauthorised surveillance on perfectly legitimate organisations such as trade unions, civil rights organisations and the Campaign for Nuclear Disarmament (CND). The revelations related to activities which began as early as the 1960s, when CND had been deemed as subversive because it was 'communist controlled'. There was some truth in the allegation originally, as John Cox, CND chairman from 1971 to 1977, was a member of the Communist Party of Great Britain.

From 1981 to 1983, however, Massiter was in charge of surveillance of CND (although the surveillance had been downgraded). In 1985, Massiter broke silence and went on a television programme to argue that government surveillance was increasingly becoming 'political'. She also revealed that MI5 had a spy called Harry Newton in CND. Newton reported, with little concrete evidence, that CND was a communist-inspired front; but that was not all. The government suspected the National Council for Civil Liberties as being another front and had surveillance placed on Harriet Harman and Patricia Hewitt. Oddly, Massiter's claims had sufficient veracity to frighten off any prosecution for whistle-blowing; she clearly had damaging evidence of wrongdoing which could be substantiated. She was never challenged or prosecuted.

The government was temporarily nonplussed, but went on its way to bring the further disastrous prosecution of Peter Wright in September 1985. Wright had been a member of MI5 and his memoirs had been published as *Spycatcher*. The government tried to ban publication. Many of the accusations in his book were already known, especially those that related to illegal activity and the accusations against MI5's Roger Hollis, but the book was freely available across the world and might be brought into Britain without prosecution by any tourist.

The government's case was that officers of the intelligence services had a lifelong obligation to keep the secrets they knew, and to do otherwise was a form of treasonable behaviour. The *Spycatcher* trial, with its complex machinations, lasted until 1988, by which time, most Britons who wished to had read the book. This disaster for the government again led to hasty changes to certain provisions in the Official Secrets Act and the creation of a new Act relating to official secrets and those who were tasked with keeping them, which themselves led on to a slew of further legislation.

Reflecting on her service in MI5, Eliza Manningham-Buller (who became director general in 2002) was conscious of the fact that 'security should not damage our most important civil liberties', but conceded that the secret service gathered 'intelligence' – 'information that is deliberately intended to be concealed'.[16] She recalled some years later that:

> The Security Service Act of 1989 was long overdue. The government of Mrs Thatcher was not, at first, convinced of its necessity, but its importance was critical … And of course, all that the Service does must be done strictly within the Intelligence Services Act (1994) and the Regulation of Investigatory Powers Act (2000). When I joined the Service there was no law governing our work and our operations.[17]

Manningham-Buller suggests that the legislation was brought in because Thatcher was queasy about spying on her own people. Yet this was doubly disingenuous: first because Thatcher's governments continued to gather intelligence on those deemed 'the enemies within' – in other words, those who posed a direct threat to the government, government policies or agencies of the state; and second because, at least to some, the legislation was actually a sleight of hand of which the consequences were to free the security services from closer scrutiny, because they now appeared to be under the law:

> Despite the introduction of the Security Service Act in December 1989, the secret services are still far removed from public accountability. Some observers have pointed out that intelligence personnel could, for example, under the powers granted by 'Royal Prerogative', murder their fellow citizens in the interests of national security. It is perhaps also worth mentioning that, if the secret services are indeed involved in actions as sinister as murder, the recent reform of the Official Secrets Act will further secure their anonymity.[18]

To bring in legislation was not altruism or sloppy sentimentality about freedom of opinion or liberty of action, but a move that would appear to hobble the intelligence services with legislation and force them to conform to laws which might then be broken. Nevertheless, the legislation was both the result of and *the cover for* intelligence-gathering operations in areas such as Northern Ireland, and the infiltration of nuclear protests, women's groups, Marxist and Trotskyist 'cells' and others such as unions which were considered threatening.

The gathering of intelligence on most opposition groups has, however, always been denied unless accidentally exposed. 'Intrusion into privacy must be necessary and proportionate to the threat it aims to counter. What is proportionate and who decides? Those are crunch questions … For to secure freedom, within a democracy and within the law, some secrets have to remain.'[19]

Yet, were elements acting outside the law during the 1980s ever to be brought to book by legislation?

10

THE 20 JUNE GROUP

The 'left' was itself fracturing under the onslaught of policies they seemed incapable of opposing. With Michael Foot, the Labour Party had its most principled leader, but also one whose convictions made him unelectable. Foot was a gift to Thatcher, but the Labour Party had little option but to back a person whose anti-nuclear and union credentials seemed impeccable yet were unredeemable in votes.

Foot was already too old and too worn out, appearing too vague and too undistinguished in public and on the media. The left looked to revitalise itself in feminism, anti-imperialism, the politics of identity and of gender choices and cultural studies, but to no avail. Taking its lead from semiotics, left-wing and liberal thinkers (such as Stuart Hall), it took more and more to analysing how Conservatism had captured the field of representation.

The impotence that marked the left was no better illustrated than in Jonathan Miller who was so apoplectic with rage that he was reduced from the suave commentary of an intellectual to a sort of biologistic Hitlerian rant:

> Loathsome, repulsive in almost every way with all her 'odious' suburban gentility and sentimental, saccharine patriotism … Catering to the worst elements of commuter idiocy … Why hate her? It's the same as why the bulk of the human race is hostile to typhoid.[1]

So out of touch were intellectuals of the left that they dreamed their own dreams of *coups d'état*. During 1986, Harold Pinter, John Mortimer, Penny Mortimer and Antonia Fraser formed the 20 June Group, to plot the downfall of Thatcher, just as the 20 July plotters had hoped to bring down Hitler (others who joined included David Hare and Salman Rushdie); the analogy was far-fetched, the ambition ridiculous, the likelihood nil.[2]

From the right of the Labour Party, such vitriol was reserved for their own. If politics was now in the arena of cultural representation, how was it that the pre-eminence of left-wing critics had created no effective political opposition? John Golding, right-wing trade union leader and Labour MP for Newcastle-under-Lyme, was reduced to simple abuse. For Golding, the 'Benn mafia' was merely a 'motley collection from the dark side'.[3]

How then to defend left-wing ideology, embodied in the welfare state and nationalisation, and how to create an argument for the consistency of union rights, let alone remove Thatcher? These became an urgent and often tortured set of questions for those in opposition. These were questions never fully answered, which left the ideological struggle of the unions without an effective counter-narrative to de-unionisation. The rise of non-parliamentary political movements from the 1990s onwards, left-wing and counter-cultural but no longer 'Marxist' (from anarchism to environmentalism), came directly from the disintegration of the left as Thatcherism reconstructed society by co-opting left-wing concepts: 'economic in the last instance' appeared vulgar to sophisticated and orthodox Marxists, but proved highly effective as right-wing ideology.

For her press secretary Bernard Ingham, Margaret Thatcher represented the socialist values of his working-class background in Hebden Bridge. His parents had never used the word 'socialist': it seemed too pretentious. Instead, 'The cause of my father and grandfather could be much more simply expressed: it was to better the lot of ordinary working people like themselves, to equalize opportunity and to curb or eliminate unearned or inherited privilege.'[4] To this end, Thatcher seemed to Ingham to be the embodiment of the saying 'hard work never hurt anyone'. '[Thatcher] mined a rich seam of support among traditional Labour voters ... She restores common-sense values'. Above all, people did not recognise her as a 'Toory' as he put it in his northern dialect.[5]

That these aims had been partially achieved by nineteenth-century collectivism and were a form of primitive communitarianism seemed neither to worry Ingham nor Thatcher. Thatcher, in this sense, was not a Thatcherite, but an old-fashioned type of low-church evangelist. Unlike her party, Thatcher's family virtues stemmed not from privilege or education, but from upbringing and a certain moral and mental mind-scape that she learned to develop and harness as she convinced herself that her background and outlook were as humble as her voters. It was a myth that Ingham and others took for truth, and myth proved harder to break than the facts.

For those of the left, everything hinged on what to make of social change. Thatcher's brilliant claim that there was no such thing as society was made in an interview on 31 October 1987 for *Woman's Own*. The edited interview produced what to many was her most infamous line.

> They're [the left] casting their problem on society. And you know, there's no such thing as society. There are individual men and women, and there are families. And no government can do things except through people. It's our duty to look after ourselves and then, also, to look after our neighbours.[6]

This 'word bite' not only elevated the individual and the family as the basic units of society, but also confirmed that the old sociological ways of discussing social institutions – a way dominated by academics and researchers predominantly socialist in leaning, but also by a generation of historians grounded in sociological models such as Christopher Hill (an un-regenerated Stalinist), Raymond Williams and E.P. Thompson – was effectively silenced for ever. If there was no such thing as society, then left-wing sociology was simply propaganda.

Older-style Marxists were also to suffer from left-positioned Continental Marxism, a post-modern and post-humanist way of looking at politics which was suspicious of all positions and produced powerful critiques of both sides. In doing so, it also robbed the left-wing pragmatists of any moral superiority. Indeed, such philosophy saw pragmatism as part of right-wing and humanist ideology.

The approaches had been developed in France between the 1960s and 1970s by Roland Barthes, Michel Foucault, Jacques Derrida, Gilles Deleuze and Louis Althusser and were now being made available to a wider anglophone readership through a flurry of English translations coming out of the United States. On the whole, these post-Marxist theorists suggested that not only was power culturally based but it was an ephemeral production of language formation, which created narratives of power rather than actual power. Those involved with this newer form of analysis were bereft of the tools to discuss actual governmental policies and the pragmatics of daily decisions regarding the use of power.

When E.P. Thompson fought back over the very real issue of the deployment of Cruise missiles in 1980, he created not a socialist revival, but a new cultural awareness unintended by his own polemic. This new 'communalism' was a mixture of spontaneous self-help anarchist activity around nuclear issues mixed with a large dose of feminist separatism. These conjunctions were resistant to parliamentary protest in the old union/CND models and instead opted for direct civil disobedience learned from America and dedicated no longer to a political party but to general justice. During the 1980s, it was easy to isolate such protest as the work of cranks and it was not until the twenty-first century that such politics would begin to form the new resistance. Effectively, throughout the 1980s, the traditional left had not been defeated by Conservative arguments, but had been silenced by its own introspection.

For the political left, the problem of putting any sort of positive message across seemed to have been stymied by the apparent break-up of class-based antagonisms. The left wing of the Labour Party was under the twin pressures of defeating Thatcherism and defeating rightist tendencies in its own party. The prospect of vanquishing Thatcher by becoming even more introspective would have to be avoided, but how was it to be achieved without a rethink of what the Labour Party stood for? As early as 17 December 1974, Jim Callaghan had surveyed the prospects for Britain in the near future and told colleagues at Chequers that, 'if [he] were a young man, [he] should emigrate'.[7] How was Labour to govern? The party was suffering from inertia and decrepitude. It could be argued that it took itself out of office in 1979 rather than was defeated. The edifice was already crumbling into dust.

When the radical Michael Foot became leader on 10 November 1980, after an exhausted Callaghan had resigned, the Labour Party had taken a turn back to its roots. It would become more left, more pacifist, more unilateralist, vehemently anti-capitalist and anti-European in outlook. It was a form of self-deceiving bravado based on a desperate gamble that Labour ideology of the past would serve the present if presented and implemented correctly. The change of direction was led not only by the remnants of 1970s union militancy and by Trotskyist and communist revolutionary elements who came to convince themselves that the revolution was at hand as Thatcherism squeezed harder, but also by a left wing whose policies adopted by the Labour Party that had become synonymous with Benn, whose own position on the National Executive Council (NEC) had been strengthened as the Party swung leftwards.

As late as 1985, Bennites seemed to believe that a breakthrough by the left might persuade the electorate to abandon Thatcher for a left revolutionary utopia. While Thatcher's supporters revelled in Labour's futile debates and death-wish philosophy, Benn's supporters gathered for the coup they thought was at hand if they could take control of the Labour Party.

On Sunday 5 May 1985, a group of intellectuals, all former advocates of revolution associated with the journal *New Left Review*, met with Benn to devise tactics. The attendees consisted of Ralph Miliband, John Palmer, Perry Anderson, Tariq Ali, Hilary Wainwright, Caroline Benn and Benn himself. Benn recalled:

> Ralph outlined the three elements of the left: the ultra-left (eg the Workers' Revolutionary Party and Militant) and some radical feminists, who were intransigent; the [Roy] Hattersley to [Eric] Hobsbawm left (including Frances Morrell and possibly Ken Livingstone), who lean towards the leadership; and the independent socialist left, the Bennites inside and outside the Labour Party, who wanted socialism without rocking the boat. Ralph wanted to see this last element strengthened.[8]

He said Bennism could be summarised as 'the need for a democratic revolution' in Britain to tackle corporate power and the class structure.[9] But how? What really was Bennism? On 2 April 1981, Benn issued a statement that defined his approach:

> The first priority was to restore full employment during the lifetime of the next Labour Government, by the adoption of the Alternative Economic Strategy. The second to expand and develop housing, health, education, welfare and other essential public services, both to meet people's needs and to create jobs. The third, to strengthen the rights of women, to extend democracy and self-government at all levels of industry, to defend the unions, protect the ethnic communities, to enact a Freedom of Information Bill, and to abolish the House of Lords. The fourth

priority was to adopt a non-nuclear defence policy, to work for European nuclear disarmament and to secure the removal of all US nuclear bases from Britain.[10]

It was the 'how' that stumped the group and paralysed it; not only how to get power in the party, but how to take power from the Conservatives. How might Labour win back power on a socialist ticket? It was answered by two books published in 1986 with radically different approaches to the problem. One was by the left-wing backbencher Eric Heffer called *Labour's Future: Socialist or SDP Mark 2?* and the other by Neil Kinnock, by now leader of the party having wrested power from the more left-wing factions, which was called *Making Our Way: Investing in Britain's Future.*

The left found itself fighting a rear-guard action on two fronts: against Thatcher, and against tendencies in its own party to veer towards the right, as demonstrated when David Owen, Shirley Williams, Roy Jenkins and Bill Rodgers formed the Social Democrats on 28 March 1981. Their statement, the 'Limehouse Declaration' was seen to identify the group as the Labour Party's own enemy within, a clique of traitors. These were the 'gang of four', so named to identify them with the 'cleansing' of reactionary tendencies in China. On the other hand, the 'enemy within' to this right-centre breakaway group were the Bennites, whom the Social Democrats saw as another clique bent on the destruction of Labour principles.

Treated as class traitors, the SDP could be left to sink or swim as far as left-wing ideologues were concerned. Some of those left-wingers, like Eric Heffer and John Palmer, thought that capitalism was the central enemy and that Thatcher was a mere symptom, although she represented 'the worst form of capitalism'. All agreed that there was no sustained attack on capitalist values from the left.[11] Others later saw Neil Kinnock as the enemy – even though he appeared to be supported by Foot – bringing Thatcherism in by the back door. The 'how' posed by Benn's supporters, who were themselves divided, was never satisfactorily answered until Kinnock forcibly and overtly attacked the extreme left of the party at the Party Conference in 1985.

From the extreme left, things seemed no better; the question of how to deal with extreme left-wing entryist tendencies as represented by Militant was no easier to answer than before. And then there were intransigent Liverpool council officials such as Derek Hatton, the uncontrollable opposition of Ken Livingstone and the Greater London Council and the National Union of Miners under Scargill, the epitome of the 'enemy within', all of which marked the slow and painful break-up of a unified (or at least allied) socialist politics.

Eric Heffer, MP for Walton in Liverpool, a one-time junior minister, a member of Labour's NEC and a reluctant Bennite, still held to what could only appear a nostalgic vision which had its origins in the NEC's vision from the Party Conference of Whitsun 1945. The Conference passed a resolution stating that, 'The Labour Party is a socialist Party, and proud of it. Its ultimate purpose at home is the establishment of the Socialist Commonwealth of Great Britain.'[12]

Heffer was happy to see the party purged of dissident elements (but not Militant or the Liverpool councillors) in order to return it to its socialist roots and its adherence to 'revolutionary reformism'.[13] Like Benn, Heffer aligned himself with the class struggle, because 'any socialist worthy of the name identifies … with the workers'.[14] Moreover, Heffer still held to his own revolutionary platform developed in the 1950s. At a meeting of the Socialist Forum movement in July 1957, he had outlined the plans of an organisation called the Socialist Workers' Federation of which he had recently become secretary:

> A revolutionary party is required, not because some comrade thinks it a good idea but because it is an absolute necessity if we are ever to achieve a socialist Britain. Neither the Labour Party nor Communist Party can guide the workers in their struggle for socialism. Therefore as Marxists we must begin anew. To enter the Labour Party is in fact to look for a short cut, assuming that those entering the Labour party retain their socialist beliefs.[15]

It was, of course, all bravado. There was absolutely no mass movement in Britain for revolutionary change except within the imaginations of a handful of impotent fanatics whom the right mistook as having some central role in a radical conspiracy.

Varying degrees of revolutionary socialist fervour mainly represented rogue and peripheral ideologies and ideologues. Nevertheless, in the struggle for possession of party policy, pragmatic considerations were equally important in putting the mainstream party in an ideological conundrum. Thus Tariq Ali's application to join became a matter of hot debate, especially as it appeared that this was a tactic to inveigle the International Marxist Group into mainstream politics. Ali had already announced his own opposition to parliamentary democracy in an interview in the *New Statesman* in which he had declared, 'The state and its institutions cannot be reformed, a Labour government would need to sweep the whole thing aside.'[16] Arthur Scargill was still arguing for rebellion at the Labour Party conference of 1983. Predicting social disintegration if Thatcher won another term of office, he called for extra-parliamentary action by the unions including specific political strikes. As Thatcher's hold on government tightened, so the left's discussions became more intemperate.

The same problem arose with the adoption of Peter Tatchell as candidate in Bermondsey for the by-election of 24 February 1983 after the resignation of right-of-centre Robert Mellish. Tatchell, a gay human rights activist from the age of 16 was vilified in the media and turned into a yet another straw devil. But, Tatchell did not endear himself to the right of the party (John Golding, MP for Newcastle-under-Lyme, declared him to be a 'known homosexual and wild leftie'[17]) nor to the electorate when he suggested in the Livingstone-inspired newsletter *London Labour Briefing* that:

Surely … imaginative and defiant forms of protest are justified in response to the callous policies of this government? Indeed perhaps they are even necessary to motivate and inspire a large-scale popular opposition which can seriously challenge the authority and legitimacy of Tory policy. Such challenges, especially when combined with the industrial might of the trade union movement, are probably the only means by which this government will listen to the voice of the people and be deterred from its monetarist course. Debates and parliamentary divisions are fruitless cosmetic exercises given the Tories' present majority.[18]

It did not help either that the leader Michael Foot strongly believed in parliamentary process. Tatchell lost to the Liberal Simon Hughes, 7,698 votes to 17,017 and his candidature might have helped Labour lose a seat it had held for sixty years. The frustration with parliamentary democracy that Thatcher's style of government created was to have major ramifications for every Prime Minister since.

The 'democratic revolution' as represented by Benn's supporters, or 'revolutionary reformism' as represented by Heffer would both have to support such revolutionary sentiments as expressed by Scargill and Tatchell while at the same time forming a unified opposition within the Labour movement. This unified movement would take power in the Labour Party through a complex set of manoeuvring that included attempts to capture the NEC and the changing of awkward rules governing constituencies. At the same time, those on the left had to sway Conference towards radical policies. This was always going to be an uphill struggle, for, despite the rise of the left of the party, the right and centre still predominated.

Benn, like the French revolutionary Georges-Jacques Danton, before him, believed that he embodied the revolution (and felt he deserved the Deputy Prime Minister's position to prove it), but like Danton he was too timid in action and was tactically defeated when boldness might have won the day. Either way, he would have needed a large swing to secure power, a base he never commanded. He remained instead the conscience of the party, slowly growing into its elder statesman. His rationale for his increasing isolation was a simple one: Benn saw himself as a martyr for socialism.

I have lost successively my seat in the Shadow Cabinet, the deputy leader-ship of the Labour Party, the Chairmanship of the Home Policy Committee last October after Conference, and, this year, my seat in Parliament. Four major setbacks. But the reward is that the Party has, I think, been irreversibly shifted back towards socialism and is more democratic, and that is the most important of all.[19]

❧

The most serious threat to the credibility of the Labour Party, and one which gave credence to the accusations of the right, was the activities of extreme left-wing groups with the loose affiliation that had always represented the party and its aims. If Labour was socialist, it certainly was neither communist nor Trotskyist, but both factions saw a way into power through slow infiltration. Communism was discredited in Labour eyes and did not pose a threat, but British Trotskyism, which had grown after the Second World War, might. Militant was formed in 1964 around its newspaper of the same name and was an offshoot of the Revolutionary Socialist League. It followed the teachings of Marx, Engels, Lenin and Trotsky.

Militant had worked tirelessly to create a power base within the Labour Party, and it was the growing profile of the organisation through the 1980s that was seen to be discrediting 'Labour'. Even the *Daily Mirror*, whose line was socialist even when its owner Robert Maxwell was a friend of Thatcher, highlighted Labour's dilemma.

> Mr Eric Heffer, a member of Labour's NEC, says a media campaign against Trotskyites … is designed to frighten Labour voters and help Mrs Thatcher … Not in the *Mirror* it isn't. This paper has consistently supported the election of democratic socialist governments. It still does. It is the Trotskyites who do not. Mr Ted Grant, leader of their organisation, the Militant tendency, wrote to the editor of the *Mirror* this week: 'We stand for the ideas of Marx, Engels, Lenin and Trotsky …' Fine. That's up to him. But they are not what the Labour Party stands for. If they were, that would really help Mrs Thatcher.[20]

Militant was indeed openly supported by Heffer, who saw it as a force for socialist change in a party whose traitors were decidedly on the right and far more worthy of expulsion. Heffer was concerned with democratic procedure which should allow Militant a place in Labour.

Michael Foot, who would always 'stand by socialism',[21] was always ambiguous about Militant, which he called a 'pestilential disease' as early as 1981, but against which he rarely acted except in fits of anger. In 1981 he moved a motion at the Organisation Committee of the NEC to investigate Militant's activities.

> To obtain from the organisers of Militant Tendency details of the scale of their operation within the Labour party, its funding organisation, full-time staff and international connections; to obtain from all regional organisers of the Labour Party their assessment of these matters in their regions including such places as Bradford, Liverpool, Bermondsey and Swansea and on the state of the party in their regions.[22]

In 1982, an internal inquiry was held which concluded that:

> *Militant* was not just a newspaper, but an organised faction with its own long-term programme, principles and policy, a substantial number of full-time organisers, and its own publishing house. Cambridge Heath Press. It had its own caucuses

in several trade unions, owned the fund-raising company WIR Publications Ltd, which had raised hundreds of thousands of pounds, and had its own international network, too.[23]

Militant had, however, started on a high. Back in the 1970s, it gave credence to the worst right-wing scare stories. It had campaigned on behalf of the rebel Clay Cross councillors, had worked within union disputes and produced an Irish monthly *Militant* calling for an Irish workers' republic. The organisation was also identified with the Revolutionary Socialist League, which was the representative of the Fourth International and which had entered the Labour Party as early as 1953. As late as 1976, the rise of the organisation within the Labour Party was a matter of fierce debate as to its real intentions:

> But a question mark hangs over 'Militant's' success: whether it is less the product of a search by sincere Labour supporters for answers to endemic economic crises and more the result of painstaking entryist work by committed Trotskyists, who by definition owe no allegiance to the mainstream of the party.[24]

The situation remained confused until early in the 1980s when expulsions killed Militant's power base. The organisation was proscribed by the NEC in December 1983 as having its own agenda separate from that of the party. In 1983, the editorial board of *Militant*, consisting of Peter Taaffe, Ted Grant (described by MI5 as a man who looked like a 'tramp' and as though 'he slept under a hedge'),[25] Lyne Walsh, Clare Doyle and Keith Dickinson, were expelled from the party. The group claimed it now had over 4,000 supporters within Labour and indeed the group dominated Liverpool Council between 1983 and 1987.

The whole sorry tale came to a head after the 1987 election when the Conservatives won with a huge 100-seat majority. This was a further disaster for the Labour Party, which had tried to play down its 'loony left' credentials and could not allow itself to side with the breakdown of law and order. Under Kinnock, the party decided not to give credence to illegal opposition to the Scottish poll tax. Militant's calls for non-registration and non-payment by local residents had been met with disdain by the party even though a few MPs had refused to pay and one MEP, Alec Falconer, had been fined.

Militant was at the forefront of the refuseniks approach in Scotland, and the threat of the left putting Labour out of power for another decade was enough for the NEC to expel six Scottish Militant members including Tommy Sheridan, the leader north of the border, his sister Lynn Sheridan and George McNeilage. Tommy Sheridan went on to head the British Anti-Poll Tax Federation, but from now on he was out-side the security of the Labour Party. The subsequent rioting against the tax which broke out in in Trafalgar Square in 1990 highlighted the contradiction that Neil Kinnock faced. Tony Benn suggested, 'The Labour Party [was] more frightened of the anti-poll tax campaign than of the poll tax itself.'[26]

11

SMELLS LIKE
TEEN SPIRITS

The paranoia on the right regarding those on the left was matched by paranoia on the left regarding those on the far left. The fight over the inner city came to epitomise those divisions, and local government became not only the centre of political opposition to Thatcherism, but the experimental ground for right-wing social engineering too.

Much of what came to annoy the Conservatives about local government had its roots in an ignorance of the poorer areas of Britain's inner cities – areas such as those in South London, Bristol, Manchester and Liverpool. Much resentment had accumulated in these areas as unemployment rose. This was not helped by the almost total lack of real knowledge within the government, as well as among the population at large, regarding black British youth culture, often at the centre of unemployment. It led police into greater and greater conflict both with local communities and with the local councillors in areas that traditionally supported Labour.

Flashpoints from police activity and the rise of far-right extremism were ignored or sidelined as peripheral issues that might either be ignored or cured by economic 'trickledown' and assimilation. By 1980, community relations had already reached the point where some police and local organisations had ceased to talk at all. A meeting in central London during that year, organised by ethnic minority groups – including 100 leaders of around fifty black organisations such as those of Indian and Pakistani Britons – called on black people to withdraw support from the police. The conference was indicative of deep distrust.[1] It was no surprise, therefore, to local people that riots broke out in Brixton and Toxteth in 1981, both areas of neglect and poverty; but the riots were a huge shock to the wider community and to national politicians.

The last of the 'ghetto' uprisings of the decade was not on any street, however, but at Strangeways Prison in Manchester during spring 1990, when the worst prison disturbances of the century took place, triggered by overcrowding as well as racism and violence by the authorities. The government had done nothing to alleviate conditions since the prison officers' strike in 1980 when it had been forced to use emergency powers. The prison system had been forgotten and the situation had deteriorated over the previous ten years. A further twenty penal institutions including Dartmoor took part and such were the appalling conditions in prisons that an inquiry under Lord Woolf had to be commissioned. The government considered bringing forward a bill which would make any protest in prison 'mutiny'. On 7 and 8 April, there was coordinated action at all the prisons taking part. At Armley in Leeds, there was a sit-down protest following the arrival of over 100 men from Strangeways. Armley had for several years been infamous as Britain's most overcrowded jail and had an appalling record of suicides among young remand prisoners.

It soon became clear, however, that authority had no intention of punishing its servants. 'While the ball of fire that was Strangeways ricocheted around the prison system, four Armley screws appears in court in Leeds charged with assaulting prisoners and perverting the course of justice. Unlike their victims, they were not remanded in custody but granted unconditional bail.'[2]

The situation in prisons might be ignored, but street violence and disorder was another matter. For Thatcher, inner-city rioters were merely an unruly 'mob'.[3] When Thatcher had visited Toxteth, she concluded that it had all been whipped up by 'left-wing extremists' who had created a 'virtual saturnalia' of criminal violence.[4] The use of petrol bombs in Toxteth and the killing of PC Keith Blakelock at Broadwater Farm four years later suggested the parallels were exactly those of Northern Ireland and created an atmosphere of panic among senior police officers such as Sir David McNee, the Commissioner of the Metropolitan Police. Thatcher recounts that:

> It was something of a shock to contemplate the kind of equipment the British police now required, which included a greater variety of riot shields, more vehicles, long truncheons, and sufficient stocks of rubber bullets and water cannon. They had already received vital protective helmets from the MoD, but these had had to be altered because the visors provided inadequate protection against burning petrol. Afterwards I stressed to Willie [Whitelaw] the urgency of meeting these requirements.[5]

Indeed, the run-down and ethnically mixed 'inner' cities (such as Toxteth in Liverpool, south London's Brixton, Tottenham in north London, Southall in west London or Moss Side in Manchester, or indeed the pit villages of South Yorkshire) were effectively treated as areas no longer to be of any real concern to government. These areas were 'set free' from the national pattern, but had to be 'sealed' against further problems, something undertaken with some success for another thirty years. Thatcher's promise of a plan to revive the inner cities, proposed for the final election battle in the 1990s (which for her never materialised), was to be her government's ultimate attempt to create 'Social Thatcherism'.[6] Even though Thatcher's analysis of these early riots was written over twenty years later, she was still not able to recognise the irony in the role of the government in destroying mining communities and her own lament for a lost community in these inner cities:

> The rioters were invariably young men, whose high animal spirits, usually kept in check by a whole range of social constraints, had on these occasions been unleashed to wreak havoc. What had become of the constraints? A sense of community – including the watchful disapproval of neighbours – is the strongest such barrier. But this sense had been lost in the inner cities for a variety of reasons. Often those neighbourhoods were the artificial creation of local authorities which had uprooted people from genuine communities and decanted them into badly designed and ill-maintained estates where they did not know their new neighbours.[7]

The troubles of the actual inner cities had brewed for some years, but they were felt only to exist in Northern Ireland, somewhere distant and seen only on the news. There were few if any mechanisms in place to deal with communal hostility to the police, who were often believed by minority groups to be the oppressive wing of Thatcherite policy. The police were seen as conservative, authoritarian and racist by turns.

In April 1980, drugs raids at the only black café left in the ethnically mixed area of St Paul's in Bristol sparked rioting that left nineteen police officers injured. This has to be seen against a background of apparently rising 'anarchism' on the streets. Also in April, the Iranian Embassy siege had been resolved by violence and, coincidentally, the coroner's report was delivered on the death of Blair Peach, who had died in anti-Nazi demonstrations at Southall in 1979. The coroner called for much tighter control of the SPG after it emerged that it had acted recklessly. In July of the same year, the Commons Home Affairs Committee investigated 274 deaths in police custody between 1970 and 1980, but astonishingly no evidence was found for any police misdemeanours. This alerted mainly left-wing social workers and investigators who founded INQUEST in 1980 sponsored by the Greater London Council and chaired by Melissa Benn, 'an active feminist and socialist'.[8] Meanwhile, situations across the Irish Sea were rapidly deteriorating. In December, nine policemen died in Ulster.

In 1981, a fire in Deptford killed thirteen people, but the police blamed the event on an accident rather than a potential racist attack. In March, a demonstration against this apparent disregard turned violent as it entered Fleet Street. Coincidentally, marches by the National Front were also banned throughout England for fear of counter-demonstrations of the kind that had seen the death of Blair Peach. In the same month, Operation Swamp '81 began with the unreformed SPG attempting to stop street crime which was on the rise. Stop-and-search operations had risen anyway throughout 1980. There were 1,469 arrests of both black and white youths in London during the period, but this related to approximately 6,000 searches and in Toxteth there were 3,482 people searched in the first four months of the year, of whom only 179 were actually charged. Many complained of being stopped more than once; some began to accept it as a way of life. The Merseyside Police Committee noted a level of 'harassment' in Liverpool and called for greater consideration in procedures. The inner cities were slowly becoming other countries and the youth that roamed them yet another enemy within.

Police brutality in the privacy of snatch-squad vans and the arbitrariness of arrest caused great concern. Brixton police station cells were allegedly smeared with blood, and dreadlocks supposedly cut off as trophies. In April 1981, tension turned into insurrection as black and white youths began three days of uncontrollable street violence after a minor incident grew into a cause célèbre. By May, Labour councils were calling for greater local control and oversight, but this was firmly resisted as yet another left 'plot' to undermine police authority.

In the summer of 1981, there were riots in Peckham and Southall, and police more or less provoked a riot in Toxteth by arresting a black youth for 'stealing' his own bike. Unrest lasted for three days, with a hospital attacked and looted. Having lost control, the police reverted to the first use of CS gas on the mainland and drove Land Rovers into the crowds, which resulted in a death.

The streets of Toxteth appeared ungovernable. Conservatives were convinced that the trouble had been whipped up by left-wing agitators encouraging the 'mobs' from the safety of local council offices. At the same time, there was media hysteria regarding the steep rise in muggings. Then, in July, there was rioting in Moss Side in Manchester where the police station was besieged after racist taunts. There were also disturbances at thirteen other cities which some blamed on 'copycat' rioting, but was rather that the problems were replicated elsewhere.

Margaret Thatcher emphatically rejected conciliatory arguments and some MPs called for guns to be issued. In July, Lord Scarman's report on the Brixton riots found Operation Swamp to have been a 'serious mistake'. It fell on deaf ears (although there was an improvement in day-to-day policing), as did the attempt by John Alderson, chief constable of Devon and Cornwall, to rethink police methods. More, not fewer, authoritarian methods were contemplated and a hard-line attitude adopted as chief constables closed ranks. In September, James Anderton, chief constable of Greater Manchester, even refused to give evidence in the inquiry into the Moss Side riots; he also secretly acquired two machine guns for evaluation without informing the police authority. In the same year, twenty-three RUC officers were killed on duty under the extreme circumstances of a terrorist revolt, but it was the RUC whose methods would slowly come to infiltrate aspects of English police thinking.

∾ↄৎ৯

The most run-down area of Britain was Liverpool, which had been in steep decline, and no one epitomised the contempt in the newspapers and in political circles (of both main parties) so well as its council's eventual deputy leader, Derek Hatton. Hatton was reasonably well educated, articulate and media savvy. He also dressed in designer clothes and sharp suits. Indeed, he was a supposed contradiction, a well-dressed, entrepreneurial left-winger. Hatton became the most famous member of Militant and confirmation of the subversion of the Labour Party. He is known to have commented: 'It's because I believe there are only two alternatives facing mankind: nuclear annihilation, or Socialism. There's no other road left now, as society collapses around our ears.' Such assertions were to be seen as the intemperate, if heartfelt, views of an extreme left-winger (a 'Trot') who couldn't be trusted with power. That, at least, was what the media put out in growingly hysterical tones.[9]

Hatton should have been a good Thatcherite. After all, he dressed like one and acted like one – the northern version of Essex Man (ironically, a Labour jibe at working-class Conservative voters), but he seemed to be still true to those concepts of class division and struggle that were apparently so outdated that even Labour had abandoned them for the sort of identity politics that the Islington literati were comfortable with. In this sense, Hatton was seen as representing an outdated and discredited way of thinking about politics by both major parties. Nevertheless, the news had not reached Liverpool, and that was what made this particular politician so hated and feared in Westminster. He was not eccentric or a maverick, but someone at the heart of the difficult politics of municipal management in the years of Conservative austerity. Like Ken Livingstone, Hatton and his colleagues recognised that it was only at the local level that Conservative politics might be opposed.

Liverpool had been in decline since the devastation of the Second World War, which had not been repaired. The war had reduced a large proportion of the housing stock to rubble and housing conditions had further deteriorated throughout the 1950s. Those forced to live in such conditions became increasingly bitter and this also hardened attitudes in the unions. It was true that Liverpool had had a short renaissance in the middle 1960s, but that had done nothing at all to redistribute wealth or stop factory and dock closures. By 1979, Liverpool's share of Britain's global market was down from 6.15 per cent to only 2.4 per cent, and the rate of factory closures was so alarming that almost 50 per cent of those who had lived in the city sought work elsewhere. It seemed a city in such terminal decline that it might just be left to die. Unemployment among young people was now very high and various schemes to regenerate the city through private business encouraged by the Liberal council had failed.

A decade before the Toxteth riots, Liverpool had already seemed another country, brutal, brutalised and politically half-forgotten (or at least half-ignored). The city council and local unionists represented all that the proto-Thatcherites of the 1970s despised. After Thatcher's election and pledge to cut local spending (code for cutting Labour council spending), attitudes in the city hardened even further. The 'People's March for Jobs' started in the city in May 1981 and the agonised cry of 'Give us a job' by the scouse character Yosser Hughes in Alan Bleasedale's *Boys from the Black*

Stuff was the signature phrase of a generation out of work. To alleviate the sort of decline one might expect after a nuclear attack, Michael Heseltine was appointed Minister for Merseyside and took a real interest between 1981 and 1983. Nevertheless, the money poured into the city from central government seemed to drain into the Mersey and Heseltine was withdrawn by Thatcher.[10]

The far-left in Merseyside was no new thing. Indeed, the likes of Tommy Birchall and Jimmy Dane had given the area a reputation for political toughness since the 1930s. As early as 1955, Walton Labour Party had selected Ted Grant, the founder of Militant, to be its parliamentary candidate. The difference between Militant and other left-wing groups was that Militant was essentially a grass-roots and working-class organisation whose central thesis was class struggle and communal self-help. In a word, it was proletarian in its most old-fashioned and honourable sense. When it was unfashionable even to mention the word in Labour circles, a word that had been effectively deleted from the vocabulary by Thatcherite policies and propaganda, Merseyside clung to its largely white working-class roots. In 1983, for instance, as the rest of the country voted Tory after a swing of 3.9 per cent away from Labour, so Liverpool swung 2.4 per cent towards Labour, removing the last Conservative MP.

The confrontation between the government and Liverpool began almost immediately after the elections of 1979 over local budget setting. The crisis grew through 1981 to 1983. Liverpool councillors were well aware that the situation in the city was such that cuts might finally destabilise the social fabric as had already almost happened during the Toxteth riots of 1981. In July 1983, the council told the government it would not implement cuts. The ensuing crisis found people like Hatton, now deputy leader, in crisis talks with Patrick Jenkin, the Environment Secretary. Jenkin was intransigent, but, after a visit to the slums of Liverpool, he changed his mind.

By now, the media and right-wing politicians of both sides of the House were calling the Liverpudlians hardened Trotskyists and criminally violent, and councillors were threatened with bankruptcy, surcharging and possible jail terms. Further crisis talks included David Sheppard, bishop of Liverpool, and Archbishop Warlock. Neil Kinnock advised compliance with the law to avoid more anti-Labour propaganda, thus further isolating a besieged council.

Budget-setting day on 29 March 1984 seemed to those present like the beginning of a revolution, with huge demonstrations awaiting the result. The result, which did not accord with government wishes, was vindicated when, in the local elections of May 1984, 51 per cent of the electorate turned out and gave Labour 46 per cent of the vote, increasing their councillors by six and neutralising the last of the opposition. Of the fifty-one councillors elected that day, only nine were actual members of Militant. Even a right-wing writer such a Michael Crick had to admit a sneaking admiration for Hatton (who sometimes dressed with a pocket handkerchief), and even Liverpool's remaining Conservatives agreed that something had to be done.[11]

It was a declaration of hostilities fully backed by Liverpool residents. In October 1984, Thatcher finally had to meet those she disliked so much. The council refused to stand in her presence and she was forced to stoop to shake hands. Hatton recalls that, as she was leaving, he cheekily asked her about the imprisonment of shipyard unionists. Thatcher, angry and irritated, replied in her most frosty tones, 'As far as I am concerned, Mr Hatton, if I had any respect for you before today – which I don't think I had – then it would certainly be gone by now.'[12]

In 1985, and faced with rate capping, the council set an illegal 'deficit budget' which committed them to excess spending of £30 million they did not have. The move was backed by forty-nine councillors. With all their apparent bravado, the Liverpool councillors, now more and more represented in the national newspapers and television by Hatton who always seemed to look like a wide-boy, were on a suicide mission. Their legitimate concerns for their city's future had been turned into a left-baiting exercise, in which Neil Kinnock, desperate to rebuild Labour as a legitimate party, would have to play Thatcher's game and name Hatton and his colleagues as the Labour Party's enemies within.

Hatton was expelled from the party in 1986 and prosecuted for corruption in office in 1993. He was found not guilty. With no way back into politics, however, Hatton became a radio presenter and spent a brief time on television before vanishing from public life. He reinvented himself as a real entrepreneur dealing in media representation and property development in Cyprus. According to a *Sunday Telegraph* interview in October 2008, he was now a 'capitalist', having lost interest in politics after his expulsion from the Labour Party.

ے‌‌‌‌‌‌‌‌‌‌‌‌‌‌‌‌

If Hatton was disliked, he might be dismissed; his power base was too far away; but the rise of Ken Livingstone, a Londoner, seemed to confirm the government in its worst fears. Livingstone was the product of a conventional and respectable working-class marriage. His mother had been a dancer and his father a sailor. They settled in south London, where their son was born and named after a favourite uncle, a one-time Blackshirt. Livingstone's upbringing in Tulse Hill included his famous love of reptiles, astronomy, going to the cinema and enjoying the tales of Dan Dare. Yet he was taught by Philip Hobsbawm, the brother of the more famous Eric Hobsbawm, who was both a socialist and Jewish, and he opened Livingstone's eyes to a new world – a world that included George Orwell's *1984*, the most influential book in Livingstone's political education.

After a stint travelling and working as a technician, Livingstone developed a desire to put his political conscience to practical use. He joined the local Labour Party and took his place as a councillor in Lambeth in May 1971. Throughout the 1970s, he and others worked to create Labour policies, but Livingstone also realised that the key to fighting national politics was through local action. He worked his way up and through the Greater London Council (GLC) which, in the late 1970s, was a Conservative stronghold. The council even maintained strong links with MI5.

In May 1981, this changed and Labour came to power under Andrew McIntosh, a market research executive who had beaten Livingstone to the Labour leadership by one vote by relying on right-wing Labour Party activists frightened that Livingstone was too Marxist. In the election, the former Conservative leader, Horace Cutler, had warned against voting in a person who would make London a 'Marxist power-base'.[13] Ironically, Livingstone was opposed to Militant, with whom he was always closely associated in the public's mind: 'I fortunately became politically active after most of this lot had left the Party. I just always operated within the Labour Party and was prepared to work with any left groupings inside it or outside on a series of policy issues.'[14] The problem was that Livingstone was slippery. Writing in *London Labour Briefing* in February 1980, he had defended the role of Militant inside the Labour Party as an element of the 'battles' to make London 'socialist'.[15]

Livingstone had nevertheless seized power from McIntosh by a complex set of manoeuvres (McIntosh was later rewarded with a place in the House of Lords) and was now head of the GLC. It was a brilliant, unscrupulous and risky strategy. The Livingstone coup seemed to unmask Marxist contentions everywhere. Even though Livingstone was a reasonably traditional member of the Labour Party, he would forever be labelled with the extreme left and now he was ensconced in the centre of London. The *Daily Mirror* argued, 'If a small, unelected group can impose its will on a larger, elected one which, in turn, dominates an even bigger group which runs a city, that is not open government, nor democracy. It is deception.'[16] The accusation seemed reasonable, especially as the GLC veered towards outright conflict with the government.

Events and declarations left no doubt that the GLC was to be the centre for Labour's resistance to Thatcherism. In *London Labour Briefing* Livingstone explicitly pledged to use County Hall to topple Thatcher. The national civil defence policy was abandoned by County Hall thereafter, and those participating in the People's March for Jobs (which started in Liverpool) were to be housed in a redundant space once reserved for offices for civil servants. Less cautiously, the GLC also entertained Alice McElwee, the mother of an IRA killer. Livingstone never avoided controversy. He accused the police of a cover-up over the death of Blair Peach at an anti-Nazi rally in Southall and also condemned the SPG. This sort of thing endeared him to no one, including the Labour hierarchy.

Livingstone's swift victory confirmed right-wing ideologues in their worst fears. The prophesies of the 1970s were coming true. The conspiracies of crypto-communists and those Trotyskyist internationalists Militant Tendency seemed to have carried off the very coup that rightist intellectuals and economists had long predicted.

What might Labour do once in government? The GLC seemed a model of left subversion led by a smarmy lower-middle-class 'Trot'. What would happen if Labour was voted in at the next election? There would be the elected leader of Labour, the new Prime Minister, a mere puppet of the unions, crypto-communists and local government activists all under the thumb of Bennites, Scargill or Livingstone. Those of the right rejoiced as their prophesies came true, and enough of the electorate bought the story to ensure that Labour could not win the next three elections.

❧

No one was more horrified by the Livingstone coup than Shirley Porter, the leader of Westminster City Council. Obsessed with 'reds under the bed' and advised by people with a paranoid attitude against anything that veered away from market liberalism, Porter went to work organising the Keep London Free campaign, which recruited a number of those who had advised Thatcher or influenced her philosophical outlook. Alan Sherman attended a secret meeting Porter had organised on 23 October 1982, as did the philosopher Roger Scruton and the author Kingsley Amis. There were also representatives from business too, including Sir Charles Forte and representatives from Cadbury Schweppes, Taylor Woodrow, GEC, Blue Circle, Tate & Lyle, Sainsbury, Allied Breweries, Beechams, Lazards, Ladbrokes and De La Rue.[17] Later, these organisations would raise £200,000 for the organisation Aims of Industry which was dedicated to the abolition of the GLC, for the single reason that Livingston's fiefdom was considered to be of the wrong political persuasion.

Shirley Porter had found a crusade. She wrote to firms asking them for campaign money. She wrote an impassioned letter which suggested her party leader approved of her actions, which indeed she wholeheartedly did:

> I am sure you understand – though many people do not – that we are in a revolutionary situation … regrettably the battle – has so far been won by the left, which is highly organised. The GLC … has spent about £40 million in backing groups, many of them revolutionary. A major campaign is, therefore, being set up … [with] the full support of the Prime Minister … cheques should be sent to me for 'Efficiency in local government' … the Prime Minster will be meeting a dozen of its business supporters … at 10 Downing Street … I hope you will forgive me for being blunt … and you will support us with a sum of at least four figures.[18]

The letter was blatant and crass and was leaked to Livingstone, who made as much mischief with it as possible. Thatcher cancelled her scheduled appearance at the money-raising rally and disowned the operation. Porter continued the fight in Thatcher's absence and as Thatcher's surrogate in local council politics.

Indeed the destruction of the GLC was planned to be the start of the conversion of inner-city boroughs to Conservatism and the cleansing of city halls of left-wing influence. This, it was hoped, would inculcate Thatcherism at the municipal level, where it was not strong, and start the capture of London for Conservatism once and for all. To achieve this required both ruthlessness and, in the end, corruption on a massive scale.

On 6 November 1982, Michael Heseltine began the process and introduced legislation to curb local government spending. Of the £800-million-cut which had been demanded, over £120 million would fall on the fourteen poorest boroughs controlled by Labour. The GLC under the previous Conservative regime had cut its budget, but Heseltine tightened the noose until there were no government grants going to the GLC, which effectively cut another £150 million from the budget, the shortfall having to be found by ratepayers, creating a tax on those locals who dared to vote Labour. It was a peculiar tax on voting, but Thatcher wanted no more of the GLC or its voters, a personal obsession that took hold going into the 1983 election. The policy had little support inside the Conservative Cabinet; Heseltine was 'dismayed' when he heard the plans for abolition, and Tom King was left 'aghast', but Thatcher ploughed on with her plans.

It is interesting to note that in the 1983 election Thatcher gained 42 per cent of the vote, but she never got quite all her own way in Parliament, despite appearances to the contrary. In the first three months of her term, the Commons voted in a Speaker she did not care for, a pay increase which she thought unnecessary and confirmed their opposition to the death penalty, which she supported. Nor were the government's attempts to curb the trade union movement entirely successful. Internal changes in union leadership did favour white-collar workers, but the Trade Union Act of 1984 tried to curb the use of 'political funding'. An overwhelming 80 per cent of union members voted to retain the funds, thus destroying the attempt to cut money and influence in the Labour Party.

Thatcher had no closer ally in local politics than Shirley Porter. Porter was the daughter of Jack Cohen who had built up the Tesco supermarket chain, and she had had an education that fitted her to be the daughter of a millionaire, but little else. At school she complained of anti-Semitism and at home she complained that she was excluded from the family firm. Porter had no focus for her ambitions and the focus she found in local politics stemmed from her failure in national politics.

Like Livingstone, Porter needed a target for her ambitions, and, like Livingstone, she realised the significance of London's municipal politics, so she began her rise in Westminster Council in the housing department. Unlike Livingstone, Porter felt the need to impress the Prime Minister in an almost pathological manner and to do this she had to make Westminster stand out as a beacon of Thatcherite policies. This was a classic case, perhaps, of over-compensation for her failure to impress her father.

Whatever the cause, Porter built an efficient, but highly secretive, machine to further her ambition. It started with cleaning the streets, a cause that certainly seemed to impress many, but it led to the sale of cemeteries under suspicious circumstances and the targeting of the homeless and the poor. Such people were deemed Labour voters and had to be cleared from Westminster. Some were housed in the almost derelict conditions of an asbestos-riddled tower block, while others were shipped off to council accommodation in Barking. Her own officers were aware of the blatant attempt to rig voting in the borough and it was soon openly being called gerrymandering.

Porter was willing to gamble, as she knew exactly what she was doing. Indeed, her rivals in the Conservative Party warned her often enough. It was as brutal as it got. Council minutes of the secret Chairman's Group on 23 September 1986, record her desire to 'determine if more [homeless people] can be exported'. Porter asked officers if they might seek legal advice to see if there was a legal precedent for '*deporting*' the poor.[19]

Porter was someone whose corruption stemmed from the wish to ingratiate herself through approval at the highest level and that meant an honour from the Prime Minister, but Thatcher couldn't stand her, possibly because both were the daughters of grocers, but more likely because Porter was born with a silver spoon in her mouth and was the sort of Thatcherite whom Thatcher despised – one who was without a moral core and who was greedy for power and recognition. Still, Porter was the second most famous woman in politics, a strange mirror image of Thatcher herself:

> The comparisons with Margaret Thatcher began in the press from the moment Shirley Porter took over City Hall. Both were women with centres of power in Westminster both were the daughters of grocers who married successful businessmen a decade senior to themselves, both were viewed as Tory conviction politicians and baiters of the left, both were bossy and strident, both paid regular visits to the hairdresser and carried large handbags.[20]

Porter would surround herself with consultants and visitors who had once been in Conservative inner circles or she employed those who were vehement anti-socialists, like former Trotskyist Roger Rosewell, who were obsessed with communist infiltration into trade unions and local government. Rosewell even told the *Daily Mail*, 'I know this bunch we have found are just the tip of the ice-berg … The Reds are there, burrowing in, biding their time, I know.'[21] Thus, Porter, the arch opportunist, was surrounded by bully boys and yes-men, who gave a respectable veneer to her Wild West version of liberal and market-led politics.

Thatcher was only too aware of what Porter was doing; she met her often enough and was photographed looking approvingly on Porter's 'accomplishments' in Westminster. Porter even sent her a note explaining her gerrymandering:

> We in Westminster are trying to gentrify the City. We must protect our electoral position which is being seriously eroded by the number of homeless that we have been forced to house. We wish to pursue policies for increased home ownership, but how can we achieve this when we are forced to house over 1,500 families a year, 70 per cent of whom are already in receipt of State Benefit? I am afraid that unless something can be done, it will be very difficult for us to keep Westminster Conservative.[22]

Thatcher chose to ignore the note and its implications and so did the Tory Party which Porter was trying to woo.

If Porter hadn't been rumbled, she might have achieved the dirty work that Thatcher knew about and chose to ignore. Thatcher cannot remain untainted by the final scandal, as she too became a victim of the corruption that for the most part she had managed to avoid. Indeed, Porter's actions had brought about the 'greatest act of corruption in the history of British local government' and senior politicians had chosen not to know what was going on because, if her manipulations had succeeded, London would have become forever Conservative. This might have been a price worth paying for absolute power.

It was not until 13 December 2001 that five law lords met and reported regarding the Westminster scandal. They found Porter guilty of 'political corruption', suggesting she had a known 'history of pretence, obfuscation and prevarication'. They also ruled that the misuse of her position was 'a deliberate, blatant and dishonest misuse of public power'.[23]

The law lords who found Porter guilty also had this to say about the effects of her actions: 'That the selective use of municipal powers to obtain party political advantage is political corruption. Political corruption, if unchecked, engenders cynicism about elections, about politicians and their motives, and damages the reputation of democratic government.'[24]

Shirley Porter left the country, going into exile rather than face imprisonment, and pleaded her innocence to the end, finally coming to a deal in which she paid back a fraction of the £40 million surcharge. She got away with not paying, as she had her son 'launder' the many millions she did have, but she *had* succeeded in changing the complexion of the council.

Bereft of a moral compass, Porter never thought she had done anything underhand. She was finally made a Dame by John Major for services to the party and, as Tony Blair later pointed out, she had been rewarded for her actions (all of which were carried out in a sort of open conspiracy that might have been stopped at any time by those involved) with 'the knowledge and approval of the Conservative Party'.[25] Those who supported Porter were so blinded by ideological righteousness that they no longer saw their own moral iniquity.

The GLC was abolished in 1986 through the application of the Local Government Act of 1985. Livingstone was back in power in 1999 when the Greater London Authority was set up. Lady Porter dedicated her life to philanthropy in Israel. Livingstone and Porter met once at a children's function; for Livingstone, her 'brassy personality' and 'pushiness' combined with 'a complete absence of humour' made her 'one of the few people [he had] ever met without one single redeeming feature'.[26]

12

TAKING POT-SHOTS AT ARTHUR

No one epitomised the enemy within so well as Arthur Scargill. Thatcher used the phrase expressly to describe the man, and Thatcherism made a fetish out of his name, the invocation of which became the invocation of a demon. He appeared the perfect illustration of the dictatorial, egocentric and subversive ideologue that had to be defeated. Indeed, in many ways, Scargill was another distorted mirror image of Thatcher herself: self-assured, righteous and motivated by moral conviction.

Scargill had been born in 1938 into the most humble circumstances of all Thatcher's many opponents. He was brought up a mere mile from where he ended up living as President of the National Union of Mineworkers (NUM), in a respectable but grindingly poor family who had settled in Worsbrough Dale near Barnsley. His father's sense of injustice had sent him to the Communist Party of Great Britain, while his mother found solace in Christianity, a faith which Scargill insisted he retained. At 15, Scargill had become a miner at Woolley Colliery and was active in the Young Communist League from which he resigned or, according to his own self-created legend, was 'expelled'. He then made his ideological way to the Labour Party via the Co-operative Party. Colleagues remember that he was a very ill-educated communist whom many believed had never read Marx; but, like others before him, he had understood the message in a visceral way; to some he appeared a syndicalist while to others he was doctrinaire Stalinist, the latter being the image that the media preferred.

Scargill soon began to flex his muscles and slowly but surely rose through the ranks of his union. By the late 1960s, he had realised that he was engaged in a class war with those powerful, intransigent and entrenched forces that had moulded his father's life, but Arthur was intelligent enough to be practical about how to fight his battles. It was in the years leading up to the 1972 miners' strike in which he developed the practical importance of flying pickets. When the strike was called under

Joe Gormley, the Lancashire-born head of the NUM, 280,000 men at 289 collieries struck to a man. There was no need to picket collieries. Scargill was ready to put theory into practice in other industrial sites such as coking stations. At Saltley Gate, the West Midlands Gas Board works near Birmingham, Scargill had led his flying pickets in a confrontation with the police that had ended with no bloodshed and much bonhomie after the chief constable of Birmingham had backed down to avoid greater disturbance and had even loaned Scargill his loudhailer to disperse the crowd, because Scargill's was 'knackered'.[1]

It was a victory that substantially added to the pressure on the government to bring in the three-days-per-week restriction on electricity and ultimately helped to roll back Conservatism. Later, in 1976, Scargill took his miners to the Grunwick lab in north London to confront the owners in a classic flying picket operation, but here the miners had their first taste of fighting the police drafted in from the SPG, men as hard as the miners and more ruthless in their execution of duty. It was a lesson learned.

Scargill was hubristic and bombastic and loved the new luxury of his financial position in the union and his big-car lifestyle. After all, why shouldn't he, he had come from nothing? His reputation secured him the presidency of the union after Joe Gormley retired in 1981. Scargill wasn't universally trusted or admired, but these were desperate times with three million unemployed and many now unemployable. Thatcher seemed as intransigent and bombastic as Scargill and someone equally strong had to be chosen for the coming confrontation; a confrontation that both sides knew was inevitable since Heath's humiliation and Thatcher's election as Prime Minister. As Mick McGahey, the communist leader of the Scottish miners, said of Scargill, 'He may be a bastard, but he's oour [sic] bastard.'[2]

The NUM was a huge organisation that inherited many of its ideas and practices from the nineteenth century. The organisation operated on three levels – national, area and branch – and the structure was broadly similar at each level. The NUM remained a federal union comprising nineteen groups or 'areas', many of which are powerful trade unions in their own right. Fourteen of the areas are geographical: Cumberland, Derbyshire, Durham, Kent, Leicester, Midlands, Northumberland, North Wales, North Western, Nottingham, Scotland, South Derbyshire, South Wales and Yorkshire; and areas are based on occupational divisions: Cokemen, Durham Mechanics, Scottish Enginemen, Colliery Officials and Staffs (COSA), and the Power Group.[3]

At the annual Miners' Conference on 4 July 1983, Scargill outlined his political creed. It was uncompromisingly and overtly aggressive, a retort to the unstated aggression of state power which threatened not only the coal industry but a whole way of life:

We can fight back. A fight back against this government's policies will inevitably take place outside rather than inside parliament … I am not prepared to accept policies proposed by a government elected by a minority of the British electorate. I am not prepared to quietly accept the destruction of the coal-mining industry, nor am I willing to see our social services utterly decimated.

This totally undemocratic government can now easily push through whatever laws it chooses. Faced with possible parliamentary destruction of all that is good and compassionate in our society, extra-parliamentary action will be the only course open to the working class and the Labour movement.[4]

For Ian MacGregor, the chairman of the National Coal Board, this was tantamount to a justification for the government's actions over pit closures. It was, in his words, a declaration of war which would be fought by Scargill's 'storm troopers'. Thus the war of words morphed into the worst industrial confrontation since the general strike and both sides knew it would be to the death.

Nicholas Ridley wrote in the *Economist* that Thatcher knew, even as far back as 1978, that she would face a confrontation with the miners. She knew that it would be ostensibly an industrial dispute, but, in reality, she knew that it might also be a political fight which might overthrow her government.[5] Ridley was also quite clear about the nature of the confrontation. 'It really was closer to a revolution than a strike … it was very much in the nature of a peasants' revolt, or a Luddite assault on new textile machinery, as well as a political attempt to humiliate and perhaps destroy the Government outside the Parliamentary process.'[6]

Scargill and the NUM were always in Thatcher's sights. Since Thatcher's election in 1979 she had plotted to destroy the union that had almost destroyed her own party. By 1981, she was setting up contingency plans if the miners went on strike and developing a policy that would increase Britain's commitment to nuclear energy to such an extent that coal became redundant. Indeed, even after the death of WPC Yvonne Fletcher outside the Libyan Embassy, imports of oil, while ostensibly banned, actually increased.

From the beginning, the government and the police were determined not to have a repeat of 1972 where the police were overwhelmed. Plans were put in place as early as 1981 to make sure that gates stayed open and that adequate policing would ensure a slow drip back to work. The National Reporting Centre at Scotland Yard would coordinate resources and mutual aid while the Association of Chief Police Officers devised strategies for controlling mass pickets. There would be no repeat of the Saltley Gate episode which Thatcher saw as the moment when Ted Heath's government became unviable and the Conservatism policies of the past finally died.

Thatcher's belief in the romance of the secret services, as described by Nigel Lawson came to a head when she realised that police special branches were unable to prove what she thought was a fact, that Scargill was surrounded by a Marxist clique secretly working to bring down Britain. At this point, she demanded greater intelligence and even went so far as to call for a public order intelligence unit which would infiltrate groups which threatened civil order. This was certainly resisted in public, as there was no possible way that the NUM could be considered a subversive organisation, but this did not stop the campaign of surveillance.

By using infiltrators, MI5 intelligence and GCHQ auditing in collaboration with America's NSA, Thatcher was enabled to tighten the grip that the authorities were unable to maintain by using the police alone. Thus, a mixture of GCHQ and NSA snooping was able to search out and close many of the accounts that the NUM had secreted abroad after the sequestration of their funds during the strike. So thorough was the surveillance of NUM union leaders that Mick McGahey's London hotel was bugged as indeed was the fish and chip shop where he and Scargill would meet; and so overloaded did the phone-tapping and bugging systems become that Tinkerbell (as the system was called) actually broke down.[7] The strike would prove a gruelling test for both sides: for the miners, it was a struggle to keep jobs open and communities together, while, for the police, it carried the crucial imperative never to lose control and not to be humiliated again after their poor showings in Toxteth, Brixton and Moss Side during the inner-city riots of 1981.

In the first few days of the strike, it was thought vital to cordon off areas that were still at work. Large numbers of police, many from southern forces or specialists from London's Metropolitan Police descended on North Wales, Leicestershire, Derbyshire, Warwickshire, Derbyshire and South Yorkshire. A massive operation was mounted to ring-fence Nottinghamshire where the strike had its weakest point. The police had sealed Nottinghamshire early on and flooded it with police who were barracked in old military camps. They had also refused entry to the county to men they thought suspicious, and they acted as if the whole thing was a national emergency rather than a strike. Large numbers of police were employed with riot gear, dogs and horses, while roads were blocked and cars turned back from journeys often having had their windscreens smashed or their drivers dragged out for interrogation at the roadside. No major confrontation had yet occurred, but it suggested the attitude that police might adopt.

From the very beginning, a forum of ministers including Peter Walker, Norman Tebbit, Leon Brittan, Nicholas Ridley, George Younger (for Scotland), Sir Michael Havers (the attorney general), Nigel Lawson and Michael Heseltine (Secretary of State for Defence) met with Thatcher in Cabinet Committee Misc 101 to discuss progress. The manner of these discussions and the atmosphere they fostered indirectly affected much of what police chief constables took to be acceptable in a national emergency.[8] What was done, therefore, in the early days, was often dubious and sometimes downright illegal.

Leading the intelligence assault was Stella Rimington. Throughout the strike, Rimington had control of MI5's F2 Section and, as assistant director, she had over-all control of intelligence operations, including those in Northern Ireland, which

seemed to have been pursued with punishing efficiency. To make matters more complicated, F Branch was actually headed by David Ranson, but he had just returned
from Washington and was not yet up to speed with developments. Rimington
therefore made the running. Not only did she have responsibility for trade union
surveillance (F2n), but she also covered surveillance and propaganda for media and
members of parliament (F2r).[9]

During the miners' strike, Rimington supplied information direct to
Downing Street. Most was public order information of no real interest to MI5,
supplemented by hearsay which Thatcher took as truth, believing as she did that
Scargill was part of a communist-led conspiracy. Concurring were Frank Chapple,
the right-wing leader of the Electrical Electronic Telecommunication and
Plumbing Union, who believed Scargill to be a 'Stalinist' and a 'dangerous buffoon',
and Ian MacGregor, Chairman of the National Coal Board, who thought him an
unreconstructed 'Marxist revolutionary – going under the guise of a normal trade
union official'.[10] It was take your pick. Scargill was finally classified as an 'unaffiliated subversive' by MI5, a result that might have been reached simply by having a
coffee with the man himself.[11]

For this work and her work from 1986 in counter-intelligence and from 1988 in
anti-terrorist activities against the IRA, Rimington was promoted to senior deputy
director general. She was seen as a moderniser, but was in fact another careerist,
whose demeanour reminded subordinates of that of her boss – Margaret Thatcher.
Rimington firmly believed in Queen and Country, herself part of a 'crown' service.
Whistle-blower David Shayler believed the organisation remained bureaucratic and
unchanged despite the appointment of Rimington which was actually used as a
smokescreen to avoid the very changes her appointment promised.

Even senior police officers were shocked by the way intelligence circum-
vented the normal legal methods. Rimington was rewarded for the work by being
made, in December 1991, the first *named* director of MI5, portrayed by the media
as a mixture of headmistress, Marks & Spencer shopper and gymkhana mum.
The announcement of Rimington as head of MI5 was part of John Major's policy
of openness. Nevertheless, it was clear that she had been appointed for using both
secret and quite possibly illegal means. Questions in Parliament and Labour Party
protests did not succeed in removing her.

Allied to Rimington and working as an 'alongsider' (the name for freelance agents)
was David Hart. Hart was a millionaire who lived at Claridges and became a central
adviser to both the Prime Minister and Ian MacGregor at the Coal Board. It was
Hart who had actually taken over the anti-communist briefing papers published
by Brian Crozier and it was Hart, the anti-communist, who toured the Midlands
under the name of David Lawrence (as a sly reference to D.H. Lawrence, a miner's
son) attempting to get men back to work. Hart, who was bankrolled by John Paul
Getty II, Sir Hector Laing of United Biscuits and Lord Hanson, devised the tactic

of embroiling the miners' union in long-winded and difficult-to-fight legal cases, thus reducing its fighting fund.[12] At the same time, he ferried around disaffected pit workers whose business was to try to create a situation that brought others onto their side and would possibly break the strike in certain areas.

Hart certainly had an inflated view of his own success, believing that the confrontation at Orgreave colliery was a 'set up' orchestrated by the police and himself. Hart was essentially a peacetime vigilante being driven around the countryside in his Mercedes and running his operation from London's smartest hotel. Ian MacGregor suggested that Hart's role was to find intelligence and report back to the Coal Board. Indeed, MacGregor says 'it was just like in war time'.[13]

Tactics used against the picket lines were often highly aggressive too, putting the lives of ordinary policemen and miners at risk. Baton charges, 'cavalry' charges, surges and snatch squads with men in in full riot gear were used against miners in civvies, who, nevertheless, were themselves ready to lob railings, stones, bottles or bricks against mass police lines. Both sides lived in fear and both sides became more and more reckless. Most often, the police would try to corral the demonstrators against fences. This was a tactic used by the South Yorkshire force which would have tragic consequences at the Hillsborough football stadium, when crowd control was used in the wrong circumstances.

Police constables (with general directives from above but acting independently) decided to ramp up the action and 'punish' the miners. Some of this was achieved by riding through the pit villages vigilante style and frisking, questioning or arresting people at random. For the most part, police were unacquainted with the lifestyle they were policing and the hostility they met, a large number of officers being quite young and unaware of the circumstances of pit life. Many came from the south; most were continuously tired, often coming to the police lines having been drinking heavily the night before to alleviate boredom. The result was at least one very serious sexual assault (never pursued) and frustration at barracks conditions and long hours that quickly boiled over into violence.[14] Such frustrations were easily stirred as the weather became hotter and miners dressed in T-shirts and jeans confronted sweating policemen in full riot gear who couldn't relax. Many officers recorded how terrifying the whole experience had been.

The strike dragged on and slowly turned into Greek tragedy, its climactic event, which has gained an almost mythic status, was the confrontation at Orgreave coking station, which was considered by the miners a vital target to close down. It was here that coal was turned into coke for the steel industry. Close Orgreave and you closed British heavy industry. This was, in effect, Scargill's showdown with Thatcher, and he was bound to lose, for things had dramatically changed since Saltley. The miners did have justification on their side. The union had reached a 'dispensation' with Orgreave's management regarding the amounts of coal to be moved in and out of the works, but this agreement had been secretly broken. Scargill's reaction was an attempt to repeat the success of Saltley, but this time the police were ready and intent on finishing what the chief constable of Birmingham had failed to do.

A mass picket of 18 June 1984 was called for, and around 5,000 to 6,000 pickets were to be bussed in, but on their arrival they were greeted by large numbers of police under the command of assistant chief constable Anthony Clement. One miner recalled:

> Some of the lads who had just arrived at the battleground were astounded by the sight of police with riot shields and crash helmets stretching right across the road and spanning two fields to the right of the entrance, backed up by a four-deep line of police behind each riot shield. In addition there were on left and right snatch squads and further to the right still, 22 mounted police. In the fields to the left, there were 12 police with dogs and police reinforcements stretched as much as 300 yards back from the front line.
>
> By 2.50 there were 4,000 of us confronting this army of police in a scene that reminded me of the film *Zulu*.[15]

This feeling of entering a battlefield was recorded by the police as well.

> Before the horses went in up at Orgreave it was bloody chaos. There were smoke bombs, all sorts of missiles. They were up in a field; blokes that had ripped up bloody palings and they were waving them at us. We should have gone, taken them out, but for some reason we just stood there watching them. I've never seen so many bloody policemen in all my life. On the road we must have been thirty or forty thick.
>
> They had the advantage of higher ground … It was late in the afternoon the horses went through. And when they came back, we all applauded. I've never been in a situation like it. It was great to see them smashing into all them bastards who'd been giving us grief all day. A lot of bobbies were injured. It was as thought somebody thought, 'Right, we're not standing for this crap any more. We'll sort it out.' And that's what they did. It was the greatest thing I ever saw.[16]

The miners were herded into a field and surrounded on three sides, with a railway line making up the fourth side. They were outnumbered. Further clashes on 18 June led to the arrest of Scargill, who was moved to compare the situation to that of 'an actual police state, tantamount to what you are used to seeing in Chile or Bolivia'.[17] The heave-ho at Orgreave left 72 police and 51 picketers hurt; 93 arrests were made, but the lorries went in and out unimpeded and the furnaces kept working. The gates had not been shut.

At the end of the strike, there had been 9,810 arrests from which 5,653 court cases were brought and there were 4,318 convictions. Of these cases, at least 3 were for murder (the number of killed is claimed by some to be 5 and there was at least 1 conviction for murder many years later); 5 miners were accused of threatening to kill, 3 with explosive offences, 20 with railway offences, and 66 with drunkenness. There were 39 cases of assault causing grievous bodily harm, 429 of assault causing actual bodily harm, 360 of assaulting a police officer, and 49 of possessing an offensive weapon. Over 137 men were accused of riot, 1,682 were accused of obstruction of a police officer, and 19 of assault with intent to resist arrest. 509 were accused of unlawful assembly, 21 were charged with affray, and 4,107 with conduct conducive to the breach of the peace under section 5 of the Public Order Act 1936. Criminal damage cases numbered 1,019, and there were 15 cases of arson, 31 of burglary, and 352 of theft. The importance of roads is emphasised in the fact that 640 men were charged with obstruction of the highway and 16 with reckless driving.[18]

As far as the police were concerned, they had spent 40 million hours on policing the strike, with personnel from 42 police forces involved. The average deployment was unprecedented, with between 3,000 and 8,000 police on duty at any one time. Twelve forces found themselves overwhelmed by events and at least 30 came to their aid. There were among the police 1,392 injuries of which 140 were hospital cases and 85 proved serious, but there were no police deaths.

The process of policing was from the start relatively brutal and it brutalised those involved and opened their eyes to the political manipulation that both the miners and the police had undergone. At the end, at least one PC had learned a harsh political lesson:

> The Tories have a reputation for being extremely pro-police. They've been in since I've been a policeman. Quite what another government would do, I don't know ... No question, we were 'Maggie's boys'. I hated that. I hated the feeling we were being used. But they had us by the short and curlies. We had no choice. No choice at all. I like to think the Chief Constables do have independence. We're supposed to be fucking impartial. I don't think we are. Not now. That's the unpleasant truth.[19]

This was a lesson reinforced in the courts which tried the miners en masse under 'instruction' to come down hard. The police, meanwhile, concocted stories which were repeated word for word in police statements. Many of these statements were sheer fabrications in order to get convictions. Some mass trials collapsed even before the prosecution had spoken because the evidence was so weak.

Nevertheless, the South Yorkshire police force under chief constable Peter Wright pushed for exemplary sentences to 'punish' the offenders. So it was that seventy-one miners were charged with riot, an offence rarely used as it has punishments of up to life imprisonment, but which had surfaced in the Brixton riots. 'Riot' was a very serious offence and it worked very well as a scare tactic even though it was notoriously ill-defined and had been since its legal status was confirmed in the eighteenth century. So it remained when Lord Justice Scarman presented his inquiry on the Brixton disorders in 1981. It was the definition that held during the Toxteth riots in the same year and the Broadwater Farm riot in 1985:

> A tumultuous disturbance of the peace by three or more persons assembled together with an Intent mutually to assist one another by force, if necessary, against anyone who opposes them in the execution of a common purpose, and who execute or begin to execute that purpose in a violent manner so as to alarm at least one person of reasonable firmness and courage.[20]

The law was only changed in 1986, to a fractionally broader account:

> The offence is [now] defined by section 1 of the Public Order Act 1986 as being where 12 or more persons who are present together use or threaten unlawful violence for a common purpose and the conduct of them (taken together) is such as would cause a person of reasonable firmness present at the scene to fear for his personal safety. Each of the persons using unlawful violence for a common purpose is guilty of riot. The section continues to indicate that it is immaterial whether the 12 or more use violence or threaten it simultaneously and, beyond that, that the common purpose may be inferred from conduct and that it is an offence which may be committed in private as well as in public places.[21]

One feature of the miners' strike was confirmation of the use of 'special courts' which had operated after the riots in Southall in 1979, again after the inner-city riots in 1981 and even in September 1983 against squatters in Manchester. Such courts were, to an extent, another legacy of events in Ireland where special courts were used to try political prisoners. The political use of trials to criminalise communities was both a breach of judicial practice and an insult to the relatives and friends of those being prosecuted:

> The tendency of special courts to impute collective criminality and deny individual justice is one of the most common complaints levelled against them. Individual justice means that cases must be determined by reference to individual circumstances which are relevant to the issue. The defendant's membership of a class of people, e.g. homeless people, black people, persons who live in a particular area, striking miners, should not be relevant.[22]

The strike also had consequences for the police, who had been able to mobilise what was a national police force, learning crowd control and handling of riotous disorder on the job. Special equipment and training now appeared vital if chaos was to be avoided in the future. A national riot police with dogs and horses, shields and batons was effectively created and given carte blanche to stop traffic, search people and distribute 'justice' without either parliamentary oversight or judicial control. Effectively, the police had shown what it might achieve as an independent arm of the state and crown.

The military tactics adopted by English police forces mimicked that of the RUC in Northern Ireland, but were used against unarmed and perfectly legal strikers. It was an interesting sign of how tactics in crowd control had moved to the mainland from across the Irish Sea. The militarism shown in the language of 'cavalry charges' and 'long shields' and the film *Zulu* might have harked back to a dictionary of colonial terms from the Victorian age, but they were far from mere metaphors.

It was this language borrowed from warfare that denoted the attitude taken by an increasingly beleaguered state, and it was a language that configured the discussions of those inner-city riots that had taken place in 1981 and the eruption of violence at Broadwater Farm in Tottenham on 6 October 1985, where racism and colonial attitudes in policing were confronted by an ethnic uprising which only confirmed the stereotypes. At least some of the police tactics in the Tottenham riots were learned on the streets of Belfast:

> Seeing a person on fire is a dreadful sight. I always think that if it hadn't been for the advent of the plastic bullet, we'd all be lying dead on the ground. Each baton charge used to lose us a quarter of the men. There's thousands of people in a riot. You are limited in the number of charges you can make and you can't run up and down the streets all night.
>
> Those who criticize us have never been standing in a riot. You ask any policeman who was at Broadwater Farm if they'd have used plastic bullets. But they had their baton guns chained in a Land Rover with a key in the guv'nor's pocket. Nobody could use them. One thing people forget: plastic bullets are an intermediate force. If we wanted to kill people, we'd use guns.[23]

The methods of keeping the peace in Ulster, as we have seen, leaked into 'English' policing:

> The problem, in England, is with image. The police in England want to project the image that they're still policemen in normal circumstances. They went out there with absolutely no protection apart from shields. They were taking casualties left, right and centre. I've got an awful lot of sympathy. I can remember, as most of us can, the outbreak of the riots in Derry where policemen were on their feet for days with no shields, their handkerchiefs over their faces for the CS gas! It was a ridiculous situation. We learned, I must say that the Police Authority came to our aid with the training and equipment. Maybe it's the kind of thing

the English police are reluctant to do – and perhaps rightly so. Perhaps they don't want to be seen to be going this far, if they can settle it with normal policing.[24]

It was no coincidence that practices in the RUC filtered into mainland attitudes. Sir Kenneth Newman, who had trained in the Metropolitan Police, was chief constable of the RUC from 1976 to 1980, but had returned to the Met as its commissioner in 1982. He had indeed started far-reaching reforms such as disbanding the SPG and replacing it with the better-trained Tactical Patrol Group on lines learned in a long career of policing the inner cities of Belfast and London. He had also been responsible for replacing the army as the major security force in the province with his own police.

The defeat of the miners was conclusive in defeating the whole of the union movement. The struggle between the last of the nineteenth-century industrial unions (but the most organised of those in the twentieth century) and a contemporary government backed by a modern state apparatus might not have been so easy to predict despite the skewed odds. Nevertheless, internal divisions within the mining community and the refusal of representatives from the National Association of Colliery Overmen, Deputies and Shotfirers to close mines on health and safety grounds, helped seal the fate of the industry against the external onslaught of oil and the nuclear industry. The banning of unions at GCHQ was yet another attempt to close all unions and restrict pay and work negotiations that might return the country to the bad old days of the 1970s, the period of greatest conservative proselytising against unionisation and the closed shop.

At the TUC Congress in September 1985, Arthur Scargill had been marginalised, and Eric Hammond of the electrician's union had led the right-wing union revolution that would prove the new model; class war was officially dead. Hammond had never backed the miners. Union relationships from now on would be based upon cooperation with management, the pragmatics of the market, the acceptance of technological change and individualism. Central to this new understanding were contractual clauses which banned strikes. So was born the new realism which denied union members the one weapon in their arsenal – the right to withdraw labour.

The unions would retreat from political aims and, as NUPE's General Secretary, Tom Sawyer, pointed out, 'become part of the management'.[25] From now on, the right to strike was a last-resort alternative to negotiation in a world where unionised industries were shrinking fast. In 1985, strikes did fall to their lowest level in fifty years, perhaps more through fear of government retribution than because of the new relaxed attitudes in business. Either way, the TUC Conference of 1985 proved the ironic fruition of those Thatcherite ideals expounded while Thatcher was still in opposition: the turkeys had voted for Christmas.

❧

Although he had been defeated, Arthur Scargill wasn't forgotten by Thatcher who warned successive energy ministers to watch their backs. The surveillance and intelligence operations didn't cease either, and Roger Windsor (Chief Financial Officer of the NUM) was used in 1990 by the *Daily Mirror* and by Thames Television's *Cook Report* to stain Scargill's image over monies received from Libya and Russia, supposedly to pay off a non-existent mortgage. Windsor, it was claimed, had been a plant by Stella Rimington. The story was utterly false, but believable enough to create the need of the NUM's executive to initiate an inquiry headed by Gavin Lightman. The inquiry proved nothing regarding the monies, but further blackened Scargill's name.

To cap things off, in the autumn of 1984, someone fired a pistol at Scargill as he left his home. Special Branch contacted Scargill immediately and suggested there was a plot against union leaders including Clive Jenkins, Jack Jones and Hugh Scanlon, and offered him round-the-clock protection. Whether this was an actual plot or one of the first attempts by MI5 to put the frighteners on Scargill by engineering a shooting and suggesting it was a failed assassination attempt is not known, but, instead of using Special Branch officers, Scargill formed a guard of miners at his home from then on.[26] By these sorts of tactics, the intelligence services were able to spread paranoia among those who were being watched and create circumstances under which that paranoia destroyed its victims without them having to intervene. It was this black propaganda war with the miners that Frank Kitson and Colin Wallace would have admired and which was the true legacy of the Irish Troubles.

13

THE GREAT ENDEAVOUR

Enemies within were secretly backed by enemies without. Internal enemies were seen as part of the broader problem of defeating the Soviets, for whom the enemies within were mere pawns of the Russian state strategically placed to undermine the British way of life. On 18 October 1979, Margaret Thatcher delivered the Winston Churchill Memorial Lecture in Luxembourg. Its theme was 'Europe – the Obligations of Liberty' and Thatcher used it as an occasion to lay out in moral and patriotic terms her own ideal of liberty:

> Liberty and tyranny; democracy and absolutism; the tension between rights and obligations, between discipline and licence; these have been constant themes of political debate in Britain since Parliament first challenged the absolute powers of the King. For centuries we British, secure in Shakespeare's 'Fortress built by nature for herself', developed our free institutions undisturbed by invasion and but rarely by revolution. Two World Wars ended that splendid isolation. We learned then the meaning of the words of Edmund Burke, among the greatest of British statesmen and orators: 'When bad men combine, the good must associate; else they will fall, one by one, an unpitied sacrifice in a contemptible struggle.'[1]

Yet there was a word of caution. The enemy was almost at the gates and the remnants of those in the right must remain vigilant. This was a position reinforced by the duplicitous methods employed by the Soviets and their allies during the 1980s, especially highlighted by the murders of Georgi Markov and Vladimir Simeonov in London and of Vladimir Kostov in Paris during August 1978. The growing belief that the Warsaw Pact simply didn't play to the rules and was in essence clandestine and creepingly sinister was finally confirmed at the very height of the 'evil empire' hysteria with the revelations of the defector Oleg Gordievsky, a KGB colonel and British double agent.

Thatcher reiterated her long-held belief that:

> The Soviet armies in Europe are organised and trained for attack. Their military
> strength is growing. The Russians do not publish their intentions. So we must
> judge them by their military capabilities. I doubt whether any Russian leader
> would easily contemplate a repetition of the immense sufferings through which
> his country went less than forty years ago. But it is up to us to ensure that there
> is no doubt in his mind that this —and worse —would now be the price of any
> Soviet adventure. That is what we mean when we talk of maintaining the cred-
> ibility of our defensive forces.[2]

This would remain a *sine qua non* of British policy, but it would also go quite against
something else Thatcher had to say that night, which was her other fear, 'there is
another, more subtle, threat [to security] from within' she argued:

> Even free societies have come to rely too much on central authority. No doubt,
> in an era of social, economic, and technical upheaval, loyalty to family and neigh-
> bourhood would anyway be under pressure. But years of supposing that only
> governments can undertake great endeavours have weakened our capacity for
> private initiative and self-reliance. We shirk the hard business of thinking through
> the moral implications of our actions.[3]

This was nothing if not an untruth because there were some vital areas that the
government could not relinquish to private enterprise and which had of necessity
to remain the prerogative of central authority. These were defence and nuclear armament and nuclear energy.

The 'great endeavour' was in fact nuclear power, which was at the most secret centre
at the heart of government and had been so for earlier generations of politicians, both
on the left and on the right, for Labour and Conservative governments. The question of
nuclear energy and its ultimate purpose and application were never properly discussed
in parliament from the inception of the nuclear programme just after the war right
into the 1980s. Budgets were kept secret or produced in much redacted form and the
governance of nuclear development was a closely guarded secret known only to the
closed agencies who determined policy. Even ministries and secretaries of state were
wrong-footed and faced hostility by a nuclear lobby jealous of its own prerogatives
whose power even included its own police force. The importance of both civilian and
military nuclear power would remain an imperative of central government policy. It is,
perhaps, the only form of energy that can cause a major disaster or end life on the
planet. The government's position was entirely dictated by thirty years of developing
nuclear energy for the twin purposes of creating a sustainable energy source and also
a source of military deterrent aimed at the Soviets.

Thus, Thatcher's government inherited a programme of mixed development it could not abandon and was constantly forced to defend. The defence of nuclear power, in the end, became its *raison d'être*. It also tied Britain closer to the international policies of the United States with regard to western security against the deployment of a new generation of Soviet missiles. At the same time, such military developments suggested a means to undermine the agitators who effectively formed the leadership of the power and mining unions within the fuel and energy industries.

Indeed, what did nuclear power mean for a host of co-joined areas of interest? There were, of course, international circumstances centring on Britain's role in NATO and the determination to develop closer military links with the United States and base Cruise and Pershing missiles in Britain. There was also the decision to drop the tradition of commissioning British-developed nuclear reactors and replace them with an American design. Both strategic changes, one military and one civil but both based on nuclear fuel, would galvanise opposition from new left alliances that replaced the traditional opposition found in Parliament. The secret state was seen to have removed the velvet gloves and had apparently decided to move towards confrontation. This was a fight that gave the left growing confidence, as the logic of the open market could not be displayed in discussions regarding nuclear power.

The fight would be about central authority and its motivations and the limits of democratic decision making. Opponents of nuclear energy hoped wider revelations might be afforded and greater revelations produced about the underhanded and secret machinery of state bureaucracy under Thatcher's direction. This was therefore going to be a confrontation with the forces of the state. It was a confrontation neither side could afford to lose given that the outcome, at least to those who opposed nuclear warhead proliferation and civil nuclear safety, was the potential destruction of life on Earth, or at least the poisoning of millions of civilians from radiation leaks.

Any confrontation regarding a nuclear future would also have serious consequences for the government whose policies towards the militancy of the Soviets and the miners was growing, but whose growing awareness of nuclear annihilation rendered every move void. It was a zero-sum game, with much riding on an outdated view of British engineering prowess and military capability.

This was demonstrated when the country went to war with Argentina. The scramble to get some sort of military coherence, the need for civilian ships as well as the temporary halt to decommissioning aircraft carriers meant that even if Britain won, the country would be a spent force internationally. This international role could only be maintained through the retention of nuclear weapons. Such retention was deeply popular, and the move towards unilateralism taken by the Labour Party was seen as cowardly and defeatist.

The acceptance of Cruise missiles on British soil was never a central issue with the general public and most people felt they would be safer under Thatcher than Michael Foot. Many voters also saw something else: that Thatcher had restored pride in being British. Britain was no longer 'the sick man of Europe', but a world player with the technology to prove it. In effect, there was restored prestige:

> Perceptions that Britain requires a long-range nuclear missile force derive in the last instance not from strategic calculations (although strategic calculations can be adjusted to match) nor even from political calculations (though these can also be adjusted for the sake of compatibility). Rather, they derive from a basic belief that Britain, being *Britain*, with all that means, with all that history, ought naturally to be in on this, the most devastating military instrument … What matters is that Britain has Polaris, and thus, in its own eyes, it has the requisite tinge of greatness.[4]

For those on the left, such talk was anachronistic and harked back to a desire for the market-driven world of the Victorians where Britain was the major power. The retention of nuclear weapons was, therefore, both incredibly dangerous and an impotent symbol of a lost history. 'Neither Polaris nor Trident is really about "defence" at all. The submarines and missiles are there to sustain the self-image of the British state and ruling circles, an attempt to maintain the appearance of being a major world power long after the fact has ended.'[5]

Yet a darker world, unnoticed apparently by voters, something lurked behind the rhetoric of restored pride. This was the encroaching power of the state itself which might need to be deployed against those who used liberty for 'subversive' reasons: liberty could sincerely be invoked to silence 'liberty in action' if it threatened this central tenet of government power: nuclear energy in all its forms. The price of the liberty Thatcher so lauded as her ideal in Luxembourg might, in the end, have to be sacrificed to international and internal security. Protection of the nuclear prestige of Britain was too important to allow purposeful opposition.

What the general population might have objected to (if it had known) was the growing belief in government circles that most of them might have to be sacrificed in a nuclear attack or on the occasion of a major nuclear accident. How did this judgement come about and what were the consequences?

The answer was literally concealed beneath the ground, a secret twilight world of governmental control. This hidden world of mines and tunnels meant new possibilities for the safe storage of weapons and officials. It had begun in a very tentative way in the First World War as protection against Zeppelin raids, but, by the Second World War, the potential of hidden spaces below the surface was recognised as the perfect means of invisibility against air attack. Work on a new network of hidden ammunition dumps had begun as early as 1930 and had accelerated once war seemed imminent. The 1934 government review of the process concluded that the pressure to build faster and larger underground stores was potentially financially crippling. Building went ahead. It also had the unexpected side effect of creating a new 'weapon':

As the technology of destruction has advanced man has burrowed ever deeper, from cave to catacomb to bunker reinforced with iron and concrete, seeking protection for himself and to defend his weapons of war. Out of sight, these boltholes created in themselves a new weapon – *secrecy* - with which to further confound the enemy:[6]

The underground factories and munitions storage facilities were shared out across the army, air force and admiralty and, for the most part, were located at disused mine workings which were then extended into networks of tunnels. These were concentrated at Bradford-on-Avon and Corsham near Bath, which became the Central Ammunition Depot, as well as some workings near Birmingham, and in London along the Thames. The workings and their purpose were given their first public exposure in 1943 in the *Daily Mail* and the *Daily Express*, on 23 November. Both papers pointed out the enormity of Corsham and its invisibility in the landscape and both were amazed and delighted with British ingenuity, a view that would turn to dismay in the 1960s. In 1943, the scheme seemed a welcome morale booster:

Somewhere in England, Monday – A lonely looking policeman is at this very moment stamping his cold feet on a bleak railway siding. There is nothing about him to suggest that he marks the spot where two worlds meet. Yet such is the case. Before him are the familiar scenes of normal life. But behind him slopes a tunnel to the preposterous underworld built as a series of permanent ammunition depots, biggest of their kind, each a lavish Temple of Mars.[7]

For the most part, the extended mines and tunnels played their part in winning the war, but they were prone to landslips and flooding and the possibility of explosion. The RAF munitions tunnels at Fauld exploded on 27 November 1944. The huge blast vaporised the inhabitants of Upper Castle Hayes Farm and their herd of cows who were all living directly above in what was apparently tranquil countryside. It was an omen of what might occur if such facilities were not hedged around with extraordinary protection.

The end of the war saw these various facilities left mothballed or abandoned, but the beginning of nuclear confrontation made them seem attractive and useful again. The hardened concrete shelters and reinforced underground bunkers were part of a pragmatic and apparently practical military ideal going back to 1914. Thus, what accelerated under the various governments of the 1970s and 1980s was not a new policy but the reinstitution of policies that had been going for years. The changes in ideas about warfare from the late 1940s to the late 1980s came to reflect the differing understandings of nuclear war. Would a war be winnable quickly with pre-emptive strikes? Would initial attacks be localised and containable? Would the whole thing inevitably end in mutually assured destruction with nothing left but the wreck of civilisation and death by radiation poisoning? The concept of trying to evacuate or save the majority of the population slowly degenerated into the abandonment of the population and the necessary troglodytic survival of the government. This policy of apparent abandonment of the civilian population came to crisis point during the 1960s and near to the point of implementation in the last and most dangerous stages of the Cold War.

The reinvigoration of underground bunkers was symptomatic of the new international relationships Britain found herself in after the Second World War. For a brief few years, Britain's nuclear capacity allowed its governments to believe that Britain was independent of the United States, but it quickly emerged that the defence of Britain was intimately tied to the fate of continental America.

The withdrawal of France from NATO in 1966 meant that Britain became the front line for the defence of the United States. Through their military presence on British soil, American forces made the need for nuclear provision more urgent, forcing an agenda of armed belligerence on Britain which it need not have embraced except for its mistaken belief in the international prestige accorded to it by its membership of the UN Security Council. Britain's belief that it could act alone in a nuclear crisis evaporated with the very nature of American neurosis over Soviet ideology and 'world domination', fantasies which came to a head in Ronald Reagan's 'Star Wars' (Strategic Defence Initiative) dream.

It was all too easy to misunderstand data and become trigger happy as when, on 9 November 1979, a simulation exercise in America alerted operators to a 'real' attack to which they had to respond. Equally:

> In June 1980, a computer glitch at NORAD Headquarters underneath Cheyenne Mountain announced the arrival of phantom Soviet Missiles over Washington and the Third World War was just the flick of a switch away, across the Atlantic Ocean, four thousand miles away, the runway lights at RAF Fairford flashed on, eighteen KC135 tankers rumbled down the runway *en route* to refuel the retaliatory B52s that were already airborne in a distant western sky and half of Gloucestershire knew within minutes that something was up with the Americans.[8]

There was thus a visible infrastructure of United States airfields in Gloucestershire and East Anglia. As well as numerous RAF stations housing American personnel there was also the early warning station at Fylingdales Moor which was in effect an American protection facility – 'the outermost radar shield that protects the central government of the United States'.[9] This meant that decisions about the military use of Britain's nuclear deterrent were extremely limited, a limitation highlighted with the appearance of Cruise missiles, which were effectively being stationed in 'independent' American bases across Britain and which would be deployed on England's road network.

The problem of keeping American engaged with European defence exercised both Nott and Heseltine. It was not merely the problem of smoothing the way for cruise missiles or nuclear production or even Sikorsky's interest in Westland. central to the strategy was keeping American ground troops, in the shape of the 7th Army, in Bavaria and therefore engaged in any European war from the beginning.

The network of underground facilities, however, expanded in relation to Britain's own sense of futility. Both grew in the wake of predictions regarding even the devastating effects of nuclear warheads designed for limited use in the European theatre of war. If Britain retained the bomb, it had to embrace the power of NATO led by the United States, and if it embraced the idea that it was one of a number of allies, it had to appear at least to be willing to use the bomb, and perhaps not even as a last resort.

Such a decision, most informed people believed, would lead to the destruction of the country's infrastructure and at least half of its population. What would be left would have to be organised. Central government might crumble, but regional 'dictatorships' run from bunkers deep in the earth might rescue some semblance of order from the wreckage. The message was simple: 'better dead than red'. The building of these facilities, essentially anti-communist strongholds whose purpose differed as the threat seemed to change, was the most secret project of every government since the 1950s, but, by the 1980s, one writer calculated it had reached levels of hysteria unequalled in a history of paranoia. In 2002, once the threat had receded, he could still point out:

> Within a fifteen-mile radius of the house in which I live there are some thirty nuclear bunkers, including six underground ROC posts, a UKWMO Sector control bunker, the Emergency National Seat of Government, three military communications bunkers, a Regional War Room from 1955, an underground telephone repeater station, at least eight local authority bunkers and at least three belonging to the pre-privatization water boards, a ROTOR radar station, an underground radar Sector Control Room, and three Civil Defence control bunkers dating from 1957. This pattern is repeated throughout the country.[10]

The crisis that necessitated the beginning of a new phase of bunker construction was the stand-off between the East and the West that developed during 1979 to 1989 and was at its most dangerous prior to the installation of Cruise in England and talk of the evil empire by Ronald Reagan. The Conservatives were pledged to increasing spending on the armed forces by 3 per cent, but quickly realised the economic impossibility of that target and reigned back spending and, on the brink of the Falklands conflict, decided to sell two aircraft carriers.

On the other hand, President Reagan had allowed his Defence Secretary, Caspar Weinberger, to massively increase spending. The new warheads developed for American Trident submarines would necessitate renegotiation over Britain's seaborne nuclear capability. In selling Trident II to Britain to replace Trident I, American negotiators had insisted Britain kept its naval capacity. Although this proved advantageous in the Falklands War, it was another proof of who had the whip hand. The purchase of 105 American AIM9L Sidewinder missiles which had been diverted en route to Germany allowed the United Kingdom to decisively win the Falklands War, yet the reliance on American military know-how meant Britain was again in thrall to US foreign policy even if Thatcher might declare that we had ceased to be a nation 'in retreat'.

Thatcher found a soulmate in Reagan, who had been elected in November 1980, and of whom she remarked that she 'knew that [she] was talking to someone who instinctively felt as [she] did'.[11] From their very first meeting in 1975, Thatcher became Reagan's firm ally, or, in Neil Kinnock's words, his 'poodle'. Either way, once she had allied herself with American interests, the aggressive language, mostly abandoned in the late 1970s, returned and was justified by the language coming from Moscow and the moral position taken by Reagan in his attitude towards an implacable enemy of American freedoms. Thatcher's consistent belief that the issue wasn't what weapons a country accumulated but how they were going to be used, an argument she took to the UN General Assembly in June 1982, seemed moot to say the least.

Thatcher had already committed Britain to receiving Cruise in December 1979, before Reagan was elected, and she was to drive the defence of Europe as a personal crusade with or without Reagan at her side:

> The stage was set for an epic battle over the next several years with protesters and peace movements, generally supported by the churches, in all the recipient countries. To Margaret Thatcher's annoyance, none of these demonstrations was directed at the Soviet Union, which had caused the problem in the first place. In an interview in the Netherlands, she pointed out that the Russians had SS20 targets on every country in Europe. 'Do you really expect us to sit back and do nothing?'[12]

The plan to purchase Trident to replace Polaris had a history going back before Thatcher and had been discussed by diplomats at a meeting in Guadeloupe as early as January 1979. The result was that on 2 June 1980, Thatcher formally agreed to buy Trident. The decision was not announced to Parliament until 15 July. In August 1981, Caspar Weinberger told Thatcher that the United States would upgrade to Trident IID5, a move, if widely known, would have created public disquiet and parliamentary questions. The total cost was £7.5 billion, 3 per cent of the defence budget, which was considered a bargain.

Moves in Europe seemed to justify the purchase. On 13 December 1981 the government of General Jaruzelski declared martial law in Poland in order to curb Solidarity. The villain was seen as Russia, and Reagan called for sanctions. At this,

Thatcher baulked, but she needed American support for the war in the Falklands. When Reagan came to Britain on a state visit in 1982, he reiterated that the economic crisis which had threatened the political order was not the introduction of free markets in the West, but the knowledge of the free world in the East. Thatcher and Reagan's joint belief (the 'Reagan doctrine') that communism would be assigned to the 'ash-heap' of history (a phrase borrowed from Trotsky) was greeted by disbelief on the left. The *Guardian* reflected on Reagan's 'wishful thinking, bordering on the delusional'. Reagan and Thatcher's reasonable belief in the triumph of ideas over ideology had strength, but it belied the question of why Britain needed to protect itself with greater weaponry if ideas would destroy totalitarian regimes. Thatcher was convinced that nuclear brinkmanship underpinned the battle of ideas.

Such thoughts were themselves based on the mistaken belief that war was predicated on the breakdown of Soviet power, exactly what Thatcher and Reagan desired. In this scenario, the end of communism as a world power would be the end of Britain as any power at all. This seemed confirmed when America pointed out that the Strategic Arms Limitation Talks (SALT I) had not restricted nuclear arms proliferation and that the Soviets were developing weaponry outside the SALT remit. (The United States withdrew from SALT II in 1986.)

On 8 March 1983, Reagan made his most inflammatory speech, calling Russia the 'evil empire', a phrase borrowed from Hollywood, as was his poker bluff regarding his Strategic Defence (Star Wars) Initiative – a delusional fantasy of monumental proportions decried even by Thatcher's own advisors but attractive to the Prime Minister who wanted to know more 'as a scientist'. In February 1985, Thatcher addressed both houses of congress and, using Churchill's rhetoric, defended the 'shield' of nuclear weaponry. Foreign Secretary Geoffrey Howe, unhappy with the Prime Minister's hawkish attitude, suggested in a speech to the Royal United Services Institute, that there was 'no advantage in a new Maginot line … in space'.[13]

For this gaff in protocol, Thatcher had to personally apologise to Reagan and his staff, who nevertheless still left her hungry to know quite what Star Wars was. It was such a secret that Thatcher actually did not know what Reagan was talking about and probingly asked Bud McFarlane, the National Security Adviser, 'Are you keeping SDI under appropriate restraint, adhering to the ABM [anti-ballistic missile] treaty and so forth?'[14] She did not get any further in finding out if SDI was all a fairy story.

In November 1983, NATO conducted war games which had so alarmed the Soviet Union that it thought a strike was imminent. It was only then, if official records are to be believed, that Thatcher decided to engage with Soviet politicians. It was supposedly a Road to Damascus moment in which the Iron Lady became the conciliatory mediator. In the narrative that followed, her subsequent support for Mikhail Gorbachev helped to bring the evil empire to an end without bloodshed. In this scenario, the uncompromising attitude Thatcher brought to bear on East–West relations was a decisive factor in bringing Soviet disarmament. Thus Lord Renwick, Thatcher's one-time ambassador to Washington concludes:

> When the missiles were deployed in Britain and elsewhere, the Russians walked out of the negotiations, as we had expected they would. In due course they were back, also as expected. By this time, Gorbachev had taken over the leadership in Moscow. The Russians suddenly accepted what had been so confidently predicted to be non-negotiable – that is, a real measure of nuclear disarmament. The INF Treaty, signed in 1987, resulted in the elimination of this entire category of nuclear weapons on both the western and Soviet sides, and the removal of the missiles from Greenham Common. Mrs Thatcher and Reagan had reason to feel that this was a turning point in the Cold War – or rather the beginning of its end.[15]

Yet it seems clear that the coming to power of Gorbachev and the crippling cost of defending the USSR against Western aggression had as much to do with the final days of Cold War antagonism. Bringing Western Europe to the brink of nuclear catastrophe in pursuit of a principle hardly seemed a price worth paying.

There were by the 1980s, anyway, enough secret facilities and bunkers for early warning systems, central government headquarters (at Corsham), regional seats of government (the network already complete by 1962), local authority bunkers, essential industry bunkers and, most secret of all, the Post Office communication system. These had been built across a period from 1948 to 1962 and upgraded from 1979 onwards. Alongside these facilities were supposedly structures for civil defence above ground. Most of these facilities were filled in, abandoned or sold off once the Cold War ended and the emphasis changed to electronic warfare (EW). What security did such burrowing offer?

In 1962, an organisation known as Spies for Peace first exposed information about these secret bunkers and the fact that the general population would be left to its fate in the event of a nuclear war:

> This pamphlet is about a small group of people who have accepted thermonuclear war as a probability, and are consciously and carefully planning for it.
>
> They are above the Army, the Police, the Ministries or Civil Defence. They are based in fourteen secret headquarters, each ruled by a Regional Commissioner with absolute power over millions of people. In the whole of Britain only about 5,000 men and women are involved: these chosen few are out shadow military government.
>
> Their headquarters are called Regional Seats of Government. Our story mainly concerns RSG-6 [Reading], which will rule much of Southern England. The people in RSG-6 are professors, top civil servants, air marshals and policemen. They are quietly waiting for the day the bomb drops, for that will be the day they take over.[16]

By 1968, the charade of civil defence had been abandoned and, by the time of the publicity surrounding publication of the *Protect and Survive* booklet and the Thatcher government's stark admission that war might be imminent, it was clear the civilian population would have to be abandoned to its fate. The Home Defence Planning Assumptions of 1973 made it clear that governmental security was all that was at stake. This remained the position throughout Thatcher's premiership, most acutely during the agreement to station the latest technology from the United States in Britain following the Soviet invasion of Afghanistan and the apparent aggressive positioning of new-generation weapons in the Warsaw Pact.

To counter this apparent ratcheting up of the Cold War, the Thatcher government had a number of options apart from the use of conventional weapons. These choices were nuclear weapons, chemical weapons and the 'offensive' use of civil defence. Each choice had a relatively long history that was not of Conservative making, but was, for the most part, remodelled in the bizarre fantasies of the last decade of the Cold War. The non-conventional options had had to be handled in almost absolute secrecy, indeed they were treated as if they didn't actually exist. Each had to be upgraded in the vacuum of the secret state where new and stranger weapons were being constructed in laboratories, ranging from the use of computer chips to mind-altering experiments.

It slowly emerged through the 1970s that new chemical and biological weapons, which had been developed in Britain and the United States, were being tested in the passes and mountain ranges of the Hindu Kush to devastating effect. Psychochemicals and Blue-X gas were tested and clouds of a dirty yellow substance that caused horrific injuries were reported from 1980 onwards. This 'yellow rain' seemed to be 'a burning agent, a nerve agent and a bleeding agent' and seemed to be derived from a fungal poison.[17] While the Carter administration had sought to avoid calling attention to its own use of such weapons, Reagan's team actively sought to revive military interest. While Congress blocked Reagan's attempt to revive research into toxins in warfare, this was not the whole picture.

Indeed, predictions of the 'Third World War', such as that by General Sir John Hackett and his colleagues, identified the use of chemical weapons alongside conventional and nuclear deployment. In the paranoid atmosphere of the times, Hackett's book became a bestseller. Hackett saw the use of chemical weapons as a possible Soviet first strike which was only to be deterred by the fear of retaliation. In his estimation, the Soviet Union was unlikely to deploy chemical weapons even though it appeared to be ahead in development. The fantasy ignored the potential disaster for civilians of downwind drift, the same problem as with radiation from a nuclear explosion. In this scenario, therefore, war would be devastating but limited, at least at first. The book was important in offering a glimpse into military thinking; limited war of the conventional type might, after all, prevail. For critics this was simple blimpishness, and the general's opinions 'represent[ed] a dated concept of ground warfare being waged as it was forty years ago by ... Hans Guderian, the brilliant German tank corps commander, who made a deep impression on the Soviet Union, as he did on nearly everyone in the early stages of World War II'.[18] Nevertheless, preparations for chemical attack had to be taken into account and the use of chemicals was to be seen as only a 'defensive' measure':

> In the midst of such confusion, in the absence of a clear-cut policy, it was agreed only that NATO should have its own 'limited offensive capability' to carry out a chemical counterattack – just enough to discourage Moscow from introducing chemicals. This was labelled a 'credible retaliatory threat', meaning that any use of chemicals by Moscow would risk immediate chemical reprisal, cancelling any advantage. [19]

The world of chemical warfare had long been considered too dirty and repugnant to outlast its general use in the First World War. Britain disposed of its chemical weaponry after the Second World War and closed its nerve gas plant in Nancekuke (RAF Portreath) in Cornwall in 1955. Britain could still rely on the United States or ship over chemical weapons, effectively, a cost-cutting exercise. Nevertheless, the main chemical and biological weapons facility, the Chemical Defence Establishment at Porton Down, which had been founded in 1916, continued to be the world's leading laboratory for chemical weapons and micro-biological adaptations until overtaken by facilities in the United States. In 1981, Britain had bulk supplies of over 100kg of sarin and other poisons and these were actually supplied to police in Northern Ireland.[20]

British policy towards the development of such weapons was driven partly by fear and partly by a hope that such poisons were too terrible to ever use even in an emergency. In 1970, Denis Healey had told the House of Commons that, although NATO had such weapons, it would never use them:

> NATO as a whole has chemical weapons available to it because the United States maintains an offensive chemical capability. However, I believe that both the former and the present government in Britain were right not to stockpile offensive chemical weapons in the United Kingdom. If the House really considers the situation, I believe that it will recognise that it is almost inconceivable that enemy forces would use chemical weapons against NATO forces except in circumstances of a mass invasion – in which event even more terrible weapons would surely come into play.[21]

To have weapons that could never be used was a peculiar cleft stick that might be useful to the Soviets to beat the West if they were using toxins in Afghanistan. A few months before the Soviet invasion, however, Defence Secretary Francis Pym had categorically stated to the House of Commons that the armed forces were not to be supplied with chemical weapons. Yet, after the invasion in June 1980, Thatcher confirmed that she had had talks with Harold Brown, the US Defence Secretary, concerning Russian intentions in regard of toxic warfare. Thatcher appeared to give her approval for the American establishment of such weapons which might jointly be developed. War games in 1980, however, showed the unpreparedness of American troops to face such warfare. In front of television cameras, soldiers fumbled with gas masks, taking too long to put them on their faces. They might not have known that the Soviet Union now had gas that could penetrate a mask anyway.[22]

Would the Cruise missiles which Thatcher had agreed should be based in Britain be equipped with the same weaponry? The answer came in 1979, when Philip Goodhart, parliamentary under-secretary for defence for the army, was evasive and cautious. In a written reply to Frank Allaun MP, Goodhart chose his words carefully. 'There has never been any suggestion that the 160 cruise missiles to be based in the UK as part of NATO's modernisation of its long-range theatre nuclear forces should have chemical warheads.'[23] The answer, as with all such answers, was couched in the present tense so that it might be changed when the biennial review came around.

In January 1981, John Nott, who had replaced Francis Pym as Defence Secretary, had to fight off MPs' questions regarding chemical warheads coming to Britain with Cruise. This was not a mere fantasy: American bombers based at USAAF Lakenheath in Suffolk and Upper Heyford in Oxfordshire were capable of delivering a 'spray-bomb' which could be fitted to F-4s and F-111s. Some days after Nott assured the House, Reagan announced that he would be trying to get budgetary approval for a new toxin plant at Pine Bluff in Arkansas. In attempting to create a new arms race in biological weaponry, Reagan was gambling on the development of a new generation of airborne weapons, the so-called 'binaries'. Porton Down and its American equivalent at Fort Detrick continued with joint projects despite apparent government assurances to the contrary right through the 1980s.

In 1981 Amoretta Hoeber, deputy assistant secretary for the US army, told Reuters news agency that the Defence Board was pushing for British acceptance of these weapons as West Germany had refused. Much of this toxic arsenal was being developed as tactical weaponry. Europe might expect to be destroyed by tactical chemical weapons, and this was a more likely scenario than nuclear holocaust. In 1982, the Labour Party Conference voted by a two-thirds majority to oppose the build-up of chemical and biological weapons. This was whistling in the wind, but it suggested the way the wind might blow, because two years later Reagan's plans were again blocked by Congress.

14

A MANUAL OF BASIC TRAINING

One non-nuclear option for a deterrent weapon was the use of civil defence. Civil defence had made sense in an age of total warfare caused by aerial attack on civilians which, however brutal, was predicated on the survival of the majority of the population and the continuance of government. Winston Churchill had, to a large extent, remained in London during the war, and the Blitz had not destroyed sufficient infrastructure to end resistance. The original *Protect and Survive* handbook was published in 1950 as a 'manual of basic training' for the likes of a gas attack, including how to deal with casualties and what to do if you needed to make emergency equipment. A second volume, 'Pamphlet 6', dealt with nuclear war and its after-effects. The advice of the pamphlet was more optimistic than realistic, giving some hope of recovery.

> The high initial intensity, however, will fall very quickly and allow rescue parties, fire fighters and other Civil Defence workers to enter contaminated areas and carry out essential work normally without any special protective clothing though the time they stay there may have to be limited in accordance with certain maximum permissible radiation dose, which is now being investigated and will be announced in due course.
>
> … It is, however, satisfactory to know that in the design of shelters protection against the lethal results of radioactivity is a practical proposition.
>
> … Delayed radiation risks are not considered likely to be serious with air burst atomic bombs. If experienced they will be mainly due to the agency of fission products and, more rarely, of induced radioactivity; a remote possibility may arise from the employment by an enemy of certain radioactive by-products.[1]

The advice was helpfully illustrated with pictures of explosions and devastated cities. It was meant to reassure and to offer practical advice in a paralysing situation.

The problem of civil defence was taken for granted by successive governments. It took money and resources and was highly secret, but it was never really believed in and was simply abandoned at the end of the 1960s when things seemed to have reached the stalemate known as détente.[2]

e⁓ɔɕ⁓ɔ

By the early 1970s, the threat of war seemed distant; but, in 1974, local government was to be reorganised and so, therefore, were the contingency plans for local government control in time of war. Little of significance happened, but this changed when Thatcher came to power in 1979, becoming an acute problem once Thatcher and Reagan had embarked on their gamble to oppose the Soviet Union once and for all. In 1980, there was a review of 'civil preparedness for home defence' and, following this, an upgrading of vital services such as 'the United Kingdom Warning and Monitoring System', the 'wartime' broadcasting service and the army's green goddess fire engines. A current version of *Protect and Survive* was available to local authorities, the police, fire services and so on, but was not known publically until a series of articles in the *Times* during January 1980 which had been preceded by a letters campaign from concerned readers. The last straw of confidentiality was broken by the *Times* on 19 January 1980. It was finally publically acknowledged by Leon Brittan in a parliamentary answer which forced more general publication and distribution of the pamphlet in May 1980. CND illegally reproduced the pamphlet and distributed it, and it was again reprinted in November 1981 by the Home Office with a rationale.

The instructions and their accompanying short information films were designed to show what might be done at home in the event of a nuclear strike, but they were tantamount to an admission that it would be a case of everyone for themselves. The pamphlet was followed in 1981 by two further publications showing how to construct a domestic nuclear shelter and technical advice on the maintenance of such spaces. Nevertheless, despite growing disquiet, underground building projects continued apace as did plans to evacuate artworks to underground caverns. There were no plans to evacuate the population, however; cities would have to be abandoned at the first signs of war, and government, local authority, some academics and scientists would have to be spirited away – effectively a doomsday scenario.

By 1980, the opponents of nuclear proliferation were again finding a voice. They found it in the 'socialist' historian E.P.Thompson, who went to work writing a rejoinder to *Protect and Survive* after reading a letter to the *Times* on 30 January. The letter was from Michael Howard, Chichele Professor of the History of War at Oxford.

Howard was a staunch supporter of Thatcher, but had written his letter after a parliamentary debate on 24 January had infuriated him. The issue was the significance of civil defence to overall defence policy. Howard seemed to accept the likelihood of nuclear war and of an initial strike followed by a later attack. Civil defence was needed between the first and second attacks. It was Howard's implication that civil defence should be such that it would reassure the population regarding survival, a position inherited from the Attlee era when it was believed that the survival of the population was actually a means of deterrence. In other words, why attack if you could not disrupt the organisation of the country and its ability to resist? Thus the government was being merely tardy in telling the public and preparing for the worst. Howard seemed to believe in the possibility of civil defence as another deterrent to go alongside the use of the 164 Cruise missiles soon to be delivered to British bases. Such means would ensure Britain's retention of an 'independent deterrent'.[3]

It was this letter that galvanised E.P. Thompson into writing *Protest and Survive*, the most influential radical political pamphlet since the days of Tom Paine in the eighteenth century, and one designed for the 'most dangerous decade in human history'. Its influence galvanised opposition to NATO's aims, both internationally and nationally, and revitalised the peace movement. CND's flagging numbers steadily rose and the pamphlet gave a clear political focus to the women's movement: 'gum boots should be taken' prophesised Thompson. Although quite mistaken (and old fashioned) in believing that academics at Oxford and Cambridge might provide an intellectual focus for protest, Thompson did predict a new style of protest politics that has lasted into the twenty-first century.

> A final, and important, consideration is that this European work *need not wait upon governments*, nor should it all be routed through centralised organisations. What is required, and what is now immediately possible and practicable, is a lateral strategy … We must act as if we are already citizens of Europe.[4]

Thompson's aim was simply to analyse Howard's letter and show the futility of its speculations in the light of nuclear destruction and the misinformation that he considered had emanated from both the Conservative government and its Labour predecessor, for 'when we come to hard information, the air is very much fouled up'.[5] Indeed, there was an air of 'mendacious rhetoric' which seemed to 'stink'.[6] There was no doubt in Thompson's mind that the public had been 'made dull and stupid by a diet of Official Information' designed to take its mind off the fact that 'if war commences, everything is lost'.[7]

Thompson recognised the 'evils' of the Soviet Bloc. He was clear about the Soviet mentality too.

> If you press me for my own view, then I would hazard that the Russian state is now the most dangerous in relation to its own people and to the people of its client states. The rulers of Russia are police-minded and security-minded people, imprisoned within their own ideology, accustomed to meet argument with repression and tanks. But the basic postures of the Soviet Union seem to me, still, to be those of siege and aggressive defence; and even the brutal and botching intervention in Afghanistan appears to have followed upon sensitivity as to United States and Chinese strategies.[8]

Yet Thompson was also clear on who the real enemy might be. The United States seemed to be 'more dangerous and provocative' and it had dragged European NATO allies and Britain towards a war that was the result of American posturing represented as a reply to Soviet aggression.

> The entire 'debate' in Britain was conducted in the press and television on the basis of letting the people believe that there was a massive build-up of Soviet SS-20s and Backfire bombers, all aimed at 'NATO', (but with the United States, the dominant power in NATO, removed from the equation), and that NATO's programme of nuclear weapon 'modernisation' was a tardy and inadequate response to this. Nothing at all was mentioned, in the general press, as to this little addition to the Western sum ('2,000 or 3,000 missiles') as part of a huge strategic triad.[9]

In fact, NATO's modernisation programme, taken together with that of the United States, was one of *menace*.[10] What was the purpose of all this hot air about civil defence, asked Thompson, if it wasn't to create fear in the population and trick it into submission to government policies?

> For the country – that is, this country – must now not only be made to bear a burden of heavy expense, loss of civil liberties … but also the expectation, as a definite and imminent possibility, of actual nuclear devastation … Hence it becomes necessary to create not only 'the idea of a threat from without' but also of a threat *from within:* 'political turbulence'. And it is necessary to inflame these new expectations by raising voluntary defence corps, auxiliary services, digging even deeper bunkers for the personnel of the State, distributing leaflets, holding lectures in halls and churches, laying down two-weeks supplies of emergency rations, promoting in the private sector the manufacture of Whitelaw Shelters and radiation-proof 'Imperm' blinds and patent Anti-Fall-Out pastilles and 'Breetheesy' masks, and getting the Women's Institutes to work out recipes for broiling radio-active frogs. And it is also necessary to supplement all this by beating up an internal civil-war or class-war psychosis, by unmasking traitors, by threatening journalists under the Official Secrets Acts, by tampering with juries and tapping telephones, and generally by closing up people's minds and mouths.[11]

The challenge that Thompson laid down to Thatcher was essentially to turn everyone into a subversive 'enemy within', wear the badge with honour and thereby defeat the government's plans, hence:

> Whether they are permanently sited at these spots, or dragged around on mobile platforms in 'emergency' to subsidiary bases (as at Fairford or Greenham Common), we can be sure that there will be a permanent infra-structure of buildings and

communications devices, wire and ferocious guard dogs. It should be easy to find out what is going on. As a matter of course, in a question of national survival, any responsible and patriotic citizen should pass his knowledge of these matters on, whether they call it an 'official secret' or not. How can a question which may decide whether one's children live or not be anyone's official secret?[12]

In order to take things beyond the continued defeats of the Campaign for Nuclear Disarmament (CND), Thompson, a lapsed member, had already formed an international organisation called European Nuclear Disarmament. The campaigns that Thompson envisaged and which were inspired by Thompson and Bruce Kent, then general secretary of CND, were organised around non-violent direct action and appealed to those who were members of small local CND organisations who felt impotent. CND was considered by many such local groups as being 'a defunct organization'.[13] Such small beginnings were inspired by the efforts of the women's movement in the United States and by the Three Mile Island nuclear scare, but were soon encouraged by Kent, who was also able to revive CND's membership to around 9,000. Thus by 1980, there was a growing and vociferous grass-roots organisation about to take on the government.

The Greenham women had also helped to revive the fortunes of CND. Since the early 1960s, CND had dallied with both the Communist Party of Great Britain and the World Council of Peace, a Soviet organisation. This had made it suspect to many who opposed nuclear weapons but were not persuaded that dalliance with a corrupting influence was a good idea. Yet this did not dent the organisation as much as its ineffectual marches and rallies and its increasingly hind-bound administration, which was strangling itself with bureaucracy even as early as the mid-1960s. The activist Peggy Duff recalled the frustrations of organisational work:

> Like most organizations in a so-called free society, CND spawned an incredible number of committees, groups, regional councils, specialist sections, *ad hoc* committees, planning groups. The number was not always directly related to its vitality. They tended to increase as its impact lessened. During those seven years from 1958 to 1965 I must have sat through thousands of such meetings, long in to the night.[14]

The fortunes of CND revived with the growing power of robust physical activism. By March 1981, there were 16,500 national members, up from a moribund couple of thousand, and total membership was 200,000. The Greenham women were now coordinating national activities with CND and were invited to speak at CND rallies. On 24 October 1981, Ann Pettitt accepted an invitation to address a 250,000-strong CND rally in Hyde Park and, although there had been prominent women in CND, such as April Carr, Peggy Duff, Sheila Oakes and Olive Gibbs, their contribution to the movement had been largely unrecognised until then. In November 1981, the CND chair was taken by Joan Ruddock as part of a revival of direction at the top of the organisation.

Inspired by E.P. Thompson's zeal, Ann Pettitt decided she must act. Likening the newly constructed wire around the American airbases to that which surrounded Auschwitz-Birkenau, she did not consider the bases were there to protect the West, but rather they were enclaves designed for extermination. This time, the inmates were outside the wire. She also realised that Thatcher was as ideological as her opponents and that reasoned argument would not stop the proliferation of weaponry about to arrive in England.

Pettitt was the daughter of 'leftie' parents who had brought her up as a free-thinking teenager who had graduated to the squatting movement in the 1970s and had wound up eking out a living on a farm in Wales. She had gone through the ideological spectrum of the left, from Stalinist to Trotskyist to anarchist and feminist. She was a mother by the time she became aware of the prospect of nuclear war and quite rightly she feared she would not be able to cope if 'any harm came to [her] children'.[15] She was already committed to leafleting on behalf of a 'nuclear free zone' in West Wales (an idea which eventually sprang up in almost every Labour borough), but it hardly seemed enough. It was in May 1981, having read Thompson's pamphlet, that she decided to walk from her home in Llanpumdaint in Dyfed to Greenham in Newbury, Berkshire to protest the siting of missiles. Pettitt was the coordinator of the Carmarthen Anti-Nuclear Campaign. At this stage, men were welcomed, but the feeling of the marchers was to restrict the protesters to those with a uniquely female perspective:

> But we felt that women felt differently about war and violence than did men ... Of course this is not universally true, and the then new Prime Minister, Mrs Thatcher, was to challenge the notion that women in power would be any more compassionate than men ... Women were far more concerned about nuclear weapons than were most men, and this concern was both a gut instinct about a weapon that goes on killing silently and invisibly, through generations as yet unborn, and a robust common sense about a weapon too utterly horrific ever to be any use in legitimate warfare ... In the growing anti-Cold-War movement, if women did have a distinct voice saying new things in our unique, female, way, that voice was not being heard.[16]

The marchers were inspired partly by the actions of women in the United States and partly by their own anger and sense of purpose. On 26 August, Pettitt and three others headed from Cardiff to Greenham Common. They were joined on the way by a few dozen more. It was a march in the tradition of the Blanketeers of the nineteenth century and the Jarrow marchers of the 1930s. On the way, thoughts of needing to camp became a reality and the idea of direct action was formulated. Eunice Stallard suggested buying chains and doing what women had done in the past – chain themselves to the railings. The response from her colleagues was cautious as none was a 'battle-hardened activist'.[17] On 5 September, the first of many disruptive plans was activated.

At first, the police presence was non-existent – they thought the protesters were the cleaning women – and even when things became much more serious, police activity and arrests were kept to a minimum and the use of by-laws and magistrates were more effective in harassing the women who chose to stay in camp. The government was in difficulties as to how to respond, 'because such an attempt could easily backfire in a rash of anti-Thatcher publicity'.[18] 'If nuclear missiles were necessary to defend Western freedoms, then those freedoms must be seen to be upheld – including the freedom to demonstrate.'[19]

Things developed with the arrival of the Reading Women for Peace who chose to use the 'feminist' tactic of keening, an uncanny and particularly feminine form of wailing for the dead. It suggested a change in approach. Camps were soon formed and the Greenham fence decorated with the symbols of life, the women's movement and the anti-nuclear lobby. It was a newspaper man from the *Sun* who first brought the Greenham women to the public's attention. A rally by CND was organised for October in Hyde Park to highlight the cause as the women's struggle came to be 'sponsored' by CND activists such as John Cox, who first named their encampment the 'Peace Camp'.

The Greenham camp was becoming like a rock festival and indeed, in 1981, Glastonbury coordinated its festival with CND, and, like festival goers, those at the camp were forced to put up with rain and mud and inordinate mess. By now, the campers were all women and the protest was heading in directions that were decidedly new to the political arena. The first major effort was, however, similar to the Yippee attempt to make the Pentagon vanish. Indeed, Barbara Doris, who suggested the copycat tactic, came from the United States. The women surrounded the camp in an 'embrace' on 12 December 1982.

The Embrace the Base action was symbolic of solidarity in adversity, but changed nothing. The women were simply ignored. By now, the protesters were divided as to their real aims. Was this an anti-nuclear protest or an affirmation of women's identity, or both? The women invented their own protest art, spinning webs and talking of goddesses, spinsterhood and witches. It all came to seem a slightly unhinged theatrical experience. The camp continued in defiance of government plans, but was now irrelevant. Cruise would come. In 1985, Michael Heseltine (borrowing a flak jacket against the cold) visited one of the bases at Molesworth at the head of a police raid. It achieved nothing itself except publicity. There seemed to be an impasse.

Throughout the Cruise missile 'crisis', CND and others tried to keep pressure on government. There were rallies in Westminster in June 1980 and May 1983 and a peace camp in January 1982; a camp at Trafalgar Square in October 1980; rallies in Hyde Park in June 1980, October 1981 and June 1982; a blockade of the Royal Ordnance Factory in March 1983; a 'peace chain' formed around Aldermaston in April 1983 in which 70,000 people took part; a picket of the Russian Embassy during June 1983; protests against the visit of Caspar Weinberger in October 1981; a march along the Embankment in May 1983; a 'Stop the City' demonstration in

September 1983 preceded by a 'die-in' at the Bank of England in June 1982; and there were eighteen separate peace camps by the summer of 1982.

Things were no longer clear. Large demonstrations to close Greenham were defeated, but a core of protesters had been turned into full-time subversives and would not give in easily. The nature of subversion had changed too. While Pettitt and others communicated and met with the peace movement in Russia, Thatcher kept on winning elections and, by 1983, the ideological struggles in the camp were directed towards such stuff as whether women were 'mimmin', 'womyn' or 'wombyn' and whether separatist lesbianism was the only solution to male aggression. For Pettitt:

> One woman in particular had a reputation as the most 'hard-line' of the anti-men tendency. She was American, and with her near-shaven head, militaristic style of dressing, an emaciated body and an expression of intense severity, she seemed to embody everything scary the public had come to stick in between the two words 'Greenham' and 'women'.[20]

What was achieved? One supporter writing in 1983 suggested that although 'people's resistance to the nuclear threat [was] growing ... the Peace Movement [was] almost invisible'.[21] The multiplicity of protests and demonstrations had not penetrated the general population. Indeed, Thatcher was again voted in with a huge majority in May 1983, and again, those fighting for unilateral disarmament had to question what they were doing wrong.

For many female supporters, the actual cause had changed direction. It was no longer bombs that were to be feared, but men! Zoe Fairbairns put the case in an article in 1983 called 'Taking it Personally'. Fairbairns was clear that 'patriachy' was to blame and that the presence of Thatcher was simply the willing co-option of yet another woman to the cause of men's wars. 'It is not necessary to declare Margaret Thatcher a (dis)honorary male in order to identify the war movement as a predominantly male phenomenon; all she proves is that women are allowed to join, and we knew that anyway.'[22] Her solution was the rise of women-only spheres of action – a 'spinsterhood' against war:

> As women they call patriarchy's bluff. A woman's place is in the home, women are the nurturers of life. And so the women of Greenham Common make homes and nurture life right there, a few feet away from men preparing to destroy both. You women are so emotional. You take everything so personally. Exactly.
>
> The webs of wool in the woods, round the bases, the courts, the prisons, have many symbolic meanings. It helps to have read *Gyn/Ecology* by Mary Daly (Women's Press, 1979). From the looks of things, the policemen with the clipboards and wellies, puzzling over the tangled-up women in the mud, have not read it. (Cartoon question marks hovering over their heads would not look out of

place.) Mary Daly traces the original meaning of Spinster – not, as now, a woman defined by the fact that she has not been had by a husband, but a woman with an honourable and marketable skill and consequently no need of a husband: a woman whose occupation is to spin.[23]

Nevertheless, this played into the hands of those who chose to demonise female protest-ers, something too often helped along by the stridency and peculiarity of those separatist women involved. It also created two, separate, gendered spheres of activity, one of which was seen as divisive and pushy. In the autumn of 1983, and again in the spring of 1984, CND came close to a split and the cost of avoiding the destruction of the organisation was that when Cruise arrived there were no nationally prepared demonstrations.

The brilliant Cruise Watch scheme, however, did strike a chord with those frus-trated with the lack of success. Protesters would monitor Cruise manoeuvres and disrupt traffic from the bases. From now on, action would of necessity be decen-tralised and local, but that would rob CND of a national profile. By the time of the 1987 election, the steam had run out of campaigning and getting nowhere. Although two million leaflets were distributed in May 1988, opposition effectively collapsed from exhaustion, lack of success and the public turning to other interests in the wake of Russia's new spirit of Glasnost.

15

OVER THE RAINBOW

A quite different path towards emancipation was taken by the women of the coal-fields once the strike began. At the beginning, these women were quite unlike those at Greenham and the other bases. They were traditional working-class women, married and most with children, whose realm was the home while their men worked down the pit. The villages they came from were solid working-class and old-fashioned Labour; their lifestyles were those of their parents and, on the whole, were conservative and inward looking.

The strike and the government's reaction changed all that. The strike had been sparked by the surprise announcement in March 1984 that Cortonwood Colliery in South Yorkshire was to close. The pit itself had had millions of pounds spent on renewing its infrastructure. It was also just down the road from where Arthur Scargill lived, so the closure notice was tantamount to a declaration of war. The pit would eventually be bulldozed in 1985, as men started to drift back to work and an industry of 170 collieries and 180,000 men, the last vestiges of the industrial revolution, were erased, and a way of life consigned to oblivion. By 1987, the area had been re-landscaped.

Yet something had happened in that year of the strike that could not be foreseen. Women who had been born to wed and have families now saw their men in battles with the police, many of whom came from the south of England and were therefore seen as colonial interlopers. Wives and girlfriends came together and formed Women Against Pit Closure in Barnsley in defence of the South Yorkshire coal industry. They were already well aware of the stakes, not just for the economic well-being of their areas, but for the symbolic and real effects on communities. Their campaign song summed up their plight as well as their determination:

> We are women, we are strong,
> We are fighting for our lives
> Side by side with our men
> Who work the nation's mines,
> United by the struggle,
> United by the past,
> And it's Here we go! Here we Go!
> For the women of the working class.[1]

Other groups soon followed, and, against the original opposition of their own men (who were deeply traditionalist in regard to the roles of men and women), they began to set up soup kitchens and networks of support. They also began to realise there was a bigger world out there as they mixed with gay and lesbian supporters as well as anti-nuclear women. Effectively, there had grown up from grass roots a new communal political opposition. Thatcher had succeeded in creating the most unlikely of enemies within.

The Cortonwood Comeback soup kitchen founded by Denise Fitzpatrick was probably the last to close. Like many others, the strike created opportunities, but also intolerable pressures on married life:

> Roles have changed in many households. Bastions of male chauvinism have met fresh challenges between the washing-up bowl and the collecting bucket. Marriages have been cemented by greater communication and understanding of common aims. Or cracked under the strain. The most timid have turned orator at meetings and rallies. Some have shared platforms with politicians and learned more of politics. Some have joined the Labour party and earned the right to criticise. Many have ventured from their communities for the first time and dared the dragons of new experience for the cause. And through such courage, and participation, and solidarity, and strong bonding kinship they have found new strengths. A new collective power that was unforeseen and cannot be relinquished.[2]

Circumstances had created new bonds and possibilities. Women went on flying-picket duty and fought police. Women were attacked like their menfolk, with a number sustaining injuries from baton charges. Betty Cook recalled the mayhem at Woolley Edge soup kitchen as police seemed both intent on causing a riot and arresting her son Glyn:

> One morning at Woolley Edge, police were really really heavy; all sorts of things had gone on. They had smashed all the lads' car windscreens. We had got back to the picket caravan and were serving soup, and this guy came in and he was in

his fifties. All of a sudden they just laid into him. He'd done nothing. I ran out screaming and shouting. You know when the Nazis used to wear their jackboots? These policemen had jackboots on like the motorcycle police do, and all I could think of was Nazi Germany, and I was screaming, 'Leave him alone! Leave him alone!' They told me to shut up or else I'd get some, and I'm saying, 'You try it – you do it and it will be the last thing you do!' … I thought, 'Right, I'll go back a few feet and take a running jump and jump up at 'em.' So there I was, and they were holding the line and I am thumping them on their noses and on their chins, shouting, 'He's mine, you're not having him!'[3]

Cook finally had her kneecap broken by a policeman at another stand-off at Woolley.

The activation of large numbers of women was of major significance in giving them an insight into the pragmatics of political power. Interestingly, only seven woman ever served in a Thatcher Cabinet between 1979 and 1990, but the activities of ordinary women educated them in the harsh and sharp end of politics. Here they were first introduced to the police as 'oppressors', the illegal withholding or delay of various benefits at DHSS offices across the country, judges who meted out revenge, and prisons that were political jails, proving for many that there were direct parallels with Northern Ireland and the H-block struggles:

The announced closure of Corton Wood was a political act, the struggle which followed was a political struggle, and the police, the judiciary and the prisons have all been used in a *'special' political way. It is this which determines the miners* in prison *as political prisoners;* from the beginning they have been dealt with in a different and *special* way.[5]

❧

Another important political conjunction occurred as if by serendipity when the anti-nuclear movement found allies in the older alternative-lifestyle community that had thrived since the 1960s and that had turned into the squatting and ecological movements of the 1970s. The lifestyle adapted by the protesters fitted into the mould of what had come before and created a new political conjunction.

The people that became known as New Age Travellers originated in the free festivals and lifestyle experiments of the 1960s. The movement had its origins in meetings at Stonehenge, at Windsor and the Phun City Festival on the Isle of Wight. In 1971, dairy farmer Michael Eavis decided that music was as much fun as farming and the Glastonbury Fayre began. The Windsor Free Festival was more political and billed itself as the Rent Strike: The People's Free Festival, taking as its theme social change and lifestyle choices. Sid Rawle, one of its founders and so-called King of the Hippies, voiced the new mood:

We have to find out how all us individuals in the world can have enough space to live in love and harmony, enough to be self sufficient and be ourselves, and how to give everyone else this space. That is the Vision of Albion, that is the vision of the rainbow people … All over the world there are still other people who do remember what their roots are, people who are still in touch with their tribal history. What lies deep in their systems must also lie deep in our own system. We have to learn to find it again.[6]

This was an important statement giving the free festivals an alternative take on conformist and capitalist culture and replacing traditional left-wing politics with anarchist ideas of social justice. Alongside Phil Russell (known as Wally Hope) and others, Rawle was forging a new idea of politics which would accord with the Greenham women's view of their own activities: lifestyle was now the realm of political action.

The first proper Stonehenge Festival took place in 1974, but, from the beginning, the police were willing to break things up by force and did so when opportunity arose. Meanwhile, Russell had been diagnosed as schizophrenic and been hospitalised, but had later died in such mysterious circumstances that some festival-goers were beginning to think that they were the target of Special Branch surveillance. The festivals at Stonehenge continued, however, into the 1980s, by which time the older hippy elements had morphed into something different. This new movement was not merely into drugs and music but was becoming radicalised. Could such a movement threaten the establishment?

Entirely unlicensed, unpoliced and free from the profit motivation that drives modern-day commercial festivals, it was one of the great people-led social experiments of modern times. The festival existed in sharp contrast to the vacuous modern political rhetoric about 'community', for despite its many foibles, it was a genuine example of people working through the realities of the word.[7]

The whole nature of protest and lifestyle merged in the migratory pageants of thousands of young people unwilling to toe the line and disgusted with monetarist principles:

Travelling took on a meaning borrowed and amended from the social and economic nomadism of the Gypsy peoples of the world. It gradually dawned on a growing number of festival goers that the glimpses of an alternative lifestyle, which the festivals of the late sixties and first half of the seventies had offered, could be turned into a full-time reality. A bus, bender, tipi or truck were cheaper to obtain than the sedentary life and so-called 'security' offered by a house or flat. And these new homes allowed their occupants to move relatively easily from venue to venue. The first wave of these 'new travellers' had grown up with a loosely defined hippy lifestyle of marijuana, Hawkwind and indigenous third world clothing. They were the traders, stage builders and sometime performers of the festivals. And, shock, horror – some may even have traded in drugs! Add to them a 'new wave' of anti-Thatcher town and city kids nurtured on 1976–78 anarcho-punk, and you have some idea of the melting pot that brewed up the traveller culture that was to become the most despised scapegoat of successive Conservative governments.[8]

By 1981, the traveller movement had matured sufficiently to align itself with those at Greenham Common and elsewhere and its rolling carnival of buses and lorries would travel to offer support for the protests. The first Peace Convoy went from Stonehenge to Greenham in 1981, and a second, larger convoy went during the Falklands War. By 1983, the mixture of festival and protest at Stonehenge attracted 30,000 people and finally, with the miners' strike in full flow, class-war demonstrations held to 'stop the city' and with the memory of Toxteth, Brixton and Moss Side, the celebrations were getting more ugly and confrontational. During 1984, the police broke up festivals at Boscombe Down Airfield and at Nostell Priory in Yorkshire, following violence from travellers who had hijacked a peaceful animal rights protest.

Animal rights and alternative medicine had already come to Thatcher's notice during the 1970s. The nascent movement, which was supported by a general consensus of the left and of intellectuals, was exactly what made Thatcher wary and uncomfortable. Such New Age thinking would get no shrift from Thatcher as Prime Minister, something that had originated when she was Minister of Education and Science under Ted Heath. Then, she had condemned the whole movement in a speech on 18 July 1973.[9] At Boscombe Down, for instance, the police, frustrated with protesters, had lost control of the peace convoy which was, 'cut up by riot vans, boarded, attacked and trashed by a squad of Special Branch police'.[10]

It was only the beginning, and at Nostell Priory, police fresh from fighting miners at Orgreave were sent to the festival to deliver a 'message', which they did with unabashed savagery and the Zulu-style shield-thumping they had employed years before in Brixton, arresting along the way almost all of the 360 campers who were herded into military jails only to be prosecuted on trumped-up charges. Many accused the police of beating them up in their cells, exactly the same accusation that had been levied at police during the Brixton riots. One protester remembered:

It came to my turn to hand myself in. As I did, these two bobbies took hold of me and cuffed me up with two lots of cuffs, and quite smartly marched me away down the field. As they marched me down I looked to the right at my home. I had a Pilot Showman's trailer, and the contents were literally flying out of the windows that they'd broken. They were supposedly looking for drugs but they were systematically smashing up every home in the place. In fact, the trailer next to me, the inside was a total and utter wreck. There was nothing left.[11]

The Rainbow Peace Camp at Molesworth was evicted in February 1985 in the largest ever peacetime army mobilisation.

War was declared by the time the travellers had decided to celebrate at Stonehenge on 1 June 1985. Police from Wiltshire, Hampshire, the Thames Valley, Avon and Somerset, Gloucester and Dorset, as well as military police, had again set up roadblocks as they had during the miners' strike and prepared to 'ambush' the convoy of 140 vehicles and 450 people as it trundled down the various A-roads leading to the site. In Falklands fashion, the police had declared the area an 'exclusion zone'. There were 1,300 officers fully equipped with riot gear; 8 miles away, they sprung their trap in what became known as the Battle of the Beanfield.

Stonehenge became the alternative society's front line, just as Electric Parade in Brixton and Broadwater Farm Estate in Tottenham formed the front line for disaffected young people and Afro-Caribbeans. Those arrested would later sue the police for false imprisonment, but for now there was little to be done. One male protester recalled:

> There were hundreds of colourfully painted vehicles, which stretched back as far as I could see. The slow convoy, not travelling more than 20 to 30 miles an hour, was followed by a police helicopter above us. The first encounter with the police was when they blocked the road with a few tons of gravel, so we turned off just before the roadblock. We travelled down the narrow road for a mile and then turned onto the A303, the main London to Exeter road, which passes Stonehenge. The road was blocked with two lorries full of gravel, and behind them police. I thought, 'This must be the edge of the exclusion zone.'[12]

Another female Traveller recounted:

> The police began attacking the leading vehicles, smashing windows and arresting the occupants, which caused everyone else to break through the fence into the neighbouring field. At the same time as the front vehicles were being trashed, the police also attacked from the rear, smashing up the last coach in the line. Up to this point, no one had done anything to break any laws or to provoke the police in any way.[13]

The insurrection of the inner cities saw its rural equivalent in the trashing of convoys of New Age travellers. These too were the 'enemy within' and those who had battled the miners were well suited to contain this latest threat, itself the inheritor of the long-quiescent anarchistic legacy of the squatter movement of the 1970s. The Greenham Common women and those at the Beanfield, however, created a new politics that sought social justice rather than political power, a movement that would define cultural struggle in the twenty-first century.

Perhaps the episode with the highest profile up to this point in the confrontation between anti-nuclear protesters and the nuclear testing authorities was the sinking of the *Rainbow Warrior* by French operatives as it lay at anchor in Auckland harbour on 10 July 1985. *Rainbow Warrior* was the flagship of Greenpeace's British division. The French secret service (DGSE) exploded two underwater mines and sank the boat with the loss of one life. Greenpeace had intended to sail the boat into a French test zone in the South Pacific. They took succour from the stance of New Zealand's Prime Minister, David Lange, who had declared the country nuclear-free and withdrawn from the weekly London meetings of the Joint Allied Intelligence Committee. The French believed that Greenpeace had been infiltrated by Soviet agents and that earlier in the year *Rainbow Warrior* had visited Vanuatu, which was governed by Father Walter Lini, who had good relations with Libya, Cuba and Russia.

The French operation was a disaster on every level and the bombers were arrested and charged by the New Zealand government. Of course, both French and British intelligence were anxiously watching events and when things went awry it took little effort to throw the blame at the British secret service. An inflatable Zodiac dinghy had indeed been bought in a private purchase in Brent, north London by the French agent Eric Adreinne, who had stayed at the Vanderbilt Hotel at the end of May 1985. The vendor himself was apparently a former MI6 operative. This might have been a decoy to throw the scent off the real perpetrators. Perhaps it was, as claimed, British revenge for French Exocet sales to Argentina. Thatcher was livid, and Sir Geoffrey Howe, then Foreign Secretary, considered the accusations 'patently absurd'.[14] Others in the DGSE claimed that it was a French double agent working for Britain who had double-crossed his compatriots.

❧

The most worrying episode was not to do with nuclear weapons at all, but it had far reaching implications nevertheless. On the evening of 14 April 1986, FI-II American fighter bombers took off from Upper Heyford and Fairford. Their target was Libya, a retaliatory raid for a terrorist bombing against United States soldiers attending the La Belle disco in Berlin on 5 April. So horrified were other European nations at this unilateral action that France, Spain and Portugal closed their air space. The attack on Libya was code-named 'Operation El Dorado Canyon' (part of 'Operation Prairie Fire'). Twenty-four F-111s from Tactical Fighter Wing at Lakenheath were joined by twenty-eight KC10 and KC135 transport and refuelling planes from Fairford and Mildenhall as well as five EF111 electronic counter-measure planes from Upper Heyford, all of which then rendezvoused with the Sixth Fleet.

In Britain a full Cabinet meeting followed in which Thatcher justified her acquiescence in the action. It was bitterly opposed by Norman Tebbit, John Biffen and Douglas Hurd, who all disagreed with Thatcher for almost the first time in open rebellion. Thatcher was herself 'appalled' by reports of civilian casualties.

Thatcher justified the action in her statement to the Commons of 15 April in which she explained that Libya was a terrorist state and moreover one that had organised the shooting of WPC Yvonne Fletcher in St James's Square. There had been little time to make a decision, she told the Commons, and so she had reluctantly agreed to these extraordinary measures. . This was an apparent improvement on strategic diplomatic objectives, as the Americans had long pursued a policy of uni-lateral decision-making. Was this so? The US *News and World Report* on 12 May 1986 carried a story by William Broyles Jr to the effect that the United States was looking for an excuse for a confrontation to test new weaponry including 'smart' bombs, and *Aviation Weekly* of 21 April wondered if it was an exercise to test the planes in readiness for war in the Mediterranean. This was all hearsay, but what was not hearsay was the fact that Thatcher had given permission for foreign planes to take off from British bases and use British airspace on a non-NATO mission, something con-sidered strictly taboo and guaranteed to cement or ruin Anglo-American relations. It also became clear that Thatcher's claim that she had little or no time to make her decision was suspect. What was a possible motive?

It was the Falklands. During the war there had been negotiations between Argentina and Libya which Whitehall had temporarily swallowed. After the death of Yvonne Fletcher outside the Libyan Embassy, which itself was becoming sufficiently suspect to lead some to believe it a set-up by MI5, there need not be any excuse for final revenge.

The implications for the deployment of nuclear weapons were huge. It was quite clear that American bombers could take off from British bases loaded with nuclear weapons without consulting the British government. As early as Clement Attlee's post-war premiership, the British understanding of any 'special relationship' or any agreement as to American deployment of weaponry on British soil had been torn up by then US Secretary of State, Dean Acheson. Of the gentleman's 'agreement', Acheson, with some irony said, 'we had to unachieve that'.[15]

If this frosty warning had been forgotten, it was repeated in the *Times* interview on 7 March 1983 when Gene La Roque, director of the Centre for Defence Information told the paper:

> I cannot see how the interests of the Nato nations can be well served by comfort-ing deceptions about who controls nuclear weapons. I favour close cooperation within Nato and an effective defence for all Nato members. But we must face facts. American nuclear weapons are American nuclear weapons, whether they are located in the United States, at sea, or in Europe.
>
> The American nuclear weapons in Europe, and those that are to come, are totally under the control of the US Government. They will be used only if and when the US Government decides to do so. No prior understandings or arrangements about consultation will alter this fact. No member of Nato has a veto power over American nuclear weapons.[16]

In case Britain's humiliating position was not clear enough, Gerry Northam pointed out in the *Listener* on 15 May 1986, 'It may be impolitic to say so, but the fact of the 1952 "joint decision" agreement is that the United States President would make the decision, and the British Prime Minister would make it a joint decision.'[17]

☙ ⟿ ❧

In 1986, while American bombers went off from British airfields, the government had decided to adapt the civil defence organisation towards plans for civilian use, always believing sabotage from within was as likely as destruction from without. That year, it passed the Civil Protection in Peacetime Act which recruited 30,000 worried people to its ranks and in many ways attracted those who might have belonged to one of the freedom associations of the 1970s. As the estimate of volunteers needed in London alone was nearer 50,000, the exercise was futile, and, as some pointed out, if London were hit it would cease to exist so no volunteers would be needed! By 1990, civil defence planning was actually even greater than before. Indeed, the Conservatives had plans for building a huge government bunker under the Ministry of Defence as late as the second half of the 1980s. The PINDAR bunker was commissioned as a base for central government in the capital on 7 December 1992 and revealed to the Commons in April 1994 by Jeremy Handley, Secretary of State for the Armed Forces:

> The purpose of the PINDAR joint operations centre is to provide the Government with a protected crisis management facility. It became operational on 7 December 1992. A number of plans exist for the use of PINDAR and the centre is manned by a permanent staff, which is augmented in times of crisis. There are a number of categories of personnel allocated space in PIDAR, including Ministers, senior military and civilian personnel, plus service and civilian operational and support staff. It would be inappropriate to give any more detailed information than this as it would relate to operational capability.[18]

Interestingly, in the case of a nuclear attack Thatcher would have been taken to the bunker at Kelvedon Hatch, Essex (RGHQ 5.1), from whence she would have broadcast to what remained of the nation and continued to run the government. Should the bunker have been hit by a Russian bomb and the survivors trapped inside, Cabinet members were to take the cyanide tablets with which they had been issued.

The PINDAR bunker was Thatcher's last grand gesture in the emergency that she and Reagan had helped manufacture. It was also symbolic of Thatcher that her last great building project should imitate that of Winston Churchill's own wartime bunker.

Nevertheless, the bubble burst with Glasnost and the threat began to evaporate. With the end of the Warsaw Pact and the old Soviet Union, the bunkers and facilities started to look less and less meaningful. By July 1991, all work on underground facilities and civil defence planning had stopped. The air-raid sirens that had been regularly tested during the 1980s went silent. It was the end of the longest and costliest 'non-war' in British history; but it was the beginning of new networks of self-help activists unaligned to the left or the right of politics which proved the true legacy of the end of the Cold War in Britain.

16

WHITE NOISE

Throughout the Cold War, both NATO and the Eastern Bloc had looked for an alternative to the idea of mutually assured destruction (MAD) and so had begun experimenting with weapons other than nuclear warheads. Plans to implement the Strategic Defence Initiative needed huge investment in electronics and computers, and a number of programmes were begun in the early 1980s designed to enhance nuclear capability by 'masking' preparations and deceiving an enemy before an aggressive strike.

Complex computer modelling would provide information that might hobble an enemy long enough to create disorder in the chain of command and by so doing destroy its forces piecemeal. In the next conflict, it was argued, control of the battlefield would rely on accurate computer forecasting, warning systems and jamming devices as well as the development of more sophisticated ways of destroying enemy personnel without resorting to nuclear strikes. Such developments would connect field operations to headquarters staff through linked programmes and satellite communication. This was the new-style EW that might avoid nuclear meltdown. Alongside EW, there was renewed interest in psyops, something first experimented with in the 1950s, used by Colin Wallace's team in Ireland in the 1970s and certainly revived in the 1980s in the United States. This went along with technological interest in the possibilities of pilotless drone aircraft and stealth bombers.

EW had proved its worth early on when Israel had been equipped with technology that allowed pilots and seamen to predict attacks and electronically block enemy decisions, and had been used again with success against an attack by an Argentine submarine during the Falklands War. EW was also at the heart of Reagan's Star Wars SDI policy and was the subject of huge armament contracts which were intended to speed the process of development. Much of the work was being done in Britain and was worth millions of pounds. The companies were often US subsidiaries. The developments were seen to be at least four to five years ahead of Soviet ones and were the subject of intense secrecy.

The work was coordinated through an elaborate network of secret and semi-secret companies linked to both the American and British governments. Thus the intelligence services of both countries were joined by intelligence filtering through GCHQ in Cheltenham, which was itself linked to developments in both the Ministry of Defence and government defence contractors. Under the MOD were at least four sub-divisions working on aspects of the SDI agenda and the technological require-ments of new weapons and platforms. These were the Royal Armament Research and Development Establishment (RARDE), Royal Military College of Science, Royal Signals and Radar Establishment (RSRE) and Aeroplane and Armament Experimental Establishment (A and AEE). Complementing and overlapping with their organisations were the military development companies which formed part of the American corporation GEC, such as Marconi, Easams and Micro Scope, Plessey and ICL, as well as companies directly linked to the British government such as British Telecom and British Aerospace.

All were charged with the task of creating complex deception systems that would confuse and defeat the enemy (the Warsaw Pact countries). However, these systems could not be activated in reality for fear of alerting the opposition, so they had to be tested through simulation and it was the sophistication of such simulations that would determine the success of what had been developed. To get this information was vital to the Soviets if they were to maintain any balance of weaponry, but they lagged behind. As such, the war against spies and subversives would take on an unex-pected urgency. The fear of the weakest link became a real priority and everybody seemed to be looking over their shoulder, especially:

> In the light of a supposed onslaught by what former Civil Lord of the Admiralty Sir Charles Orr-Ewing once described as 'thousands of Russians … all trained to detect weakness in character, weakness for drink, blondes, drugs and homosexuality' … [One] GCHQ employee said that when he left he had to sign several forms which in effect declared his knowledge null and void.[1]

Take, for instance, the complex relationship between GEC's Computer Applications Group which was at the forefront of data collaboration with Micro Scope, a com-munications company later bought by GEC. The two were cooperating on Uniter, a communications network to link RAF and United States bases throughout the UK. The system was designed to withstand nuclear attack and was due to come into use in 1991. Uniter would form the basis of the system Improved UK Air Defence Ground Environment (IUKADGE), an early-warning system which itself would not come into use until the twenty-first century.

IUKADGE was a vast project requiring the expertise of more than just GEC. Marconi, Plessey, American Aerospace and Hughes were all involved. At the heart of the system was the development of the command and control networks known as C3 (Command, Control and Communications) and its adjunct C3i (Command, Control, Communications and intelligence). GEC Computer Application Group general manager Rupert Soames, the son of Lord Soames and grandson of Winston Churchill, warned a conference in 1989 of the dangers of employing unreliable staff in such a security-conscious area. It was a speech that combined blatant snobbery regarding old-fashioned retainers with utter contempt for the middle-class wage-owners he actually employed; these were people one simply couldn't trust:

> To my mind the worst threat from those who wish to spy or make money is in the potential to pervert members of staff, and we have to recognize that the types of people who are handling our information and our money have changed. Twenty years ago, the accounts department or document registry was run by loyal clerks who had been with the company or the department for thirty years and intended to stay there until retirement – the sort of people who were the incorruptible backbone of every organization.
>
> Today, the people who have the opportunity to steal are often highly mobile, ambitious, self-confident and fiscally imprudent young people. How many of your programmers have been with you for more than five years? How many intend to be with you for another five years? How many of them want to drive sports cars? How many of them have small families and large mortgages.[2]

The odds stacked against employees in the security industries and in GCHQ seemed to be very high:

> What if [the intelligence employee] was not prepared to erase from his mind what he knew? What if he wanted to leave Britain for a country which was beyond the scope of the Official Secrets Act? And what if the security services suspected him of being disaffected or even subversive, a potential security risk? I would rather not think of the consequences.[3]

The circumstances seemed insurmountable and the dangers of working on top-secret projects quite stark once it became known that twenty-five workers in the EW industry had died in mysterious circumstances. It seemed to confirm the paranoia of those who suspected that MI5, MI6, the army or Special Branch ran dirty operations. It would be this paranoia that would create one of the major conspiracy theories of the period and uncover abuses that would seem to confirm the conspiracies had basis even if the conclusions were false.

Then there were the unexplained 'suicides'. Between the mid 1970s and the late 1980s, at least twenty-five specialist computer analysts working on classified projects in British EW establishments died in mysterious circumstances. This might not be strange in an industry where at least 14,000 people were employed by the Ministry of Defence alone, but what singles them out is not merely the odd circumstances of each death but the apparent fact that the deceased had all been either working on underwater surveillance techniques or analysing data on the development of the American Star Wars programme.

The deaths included Vimal Dajibhai who drove from Middlesex to the Clifton Suspension Bridge in Bristol on 4 August 1984 and who threw himself 245ft over for no apparent reason and who might have had a syringe puncture mark on his buttock. Although he did not drink, a bottle of wine was found in his car. Arshad Sharif also went from London to Bristol. He 'killed himself' by attaching a rope to a tree and to his neck and then driving off. Arshad didn't like smoking but three partially smoked cigars were found in his car. Their presence has never been explained. There then followed a succession of other unexplained deaths.

In 1987, another Asian man, Avtar Singh-Gida, vanished from his home only to turn up miles away having suffered a form of mental 'fugue'. Oddly, Bristol police working on the two Bristol deaths hinted that they knew what had happened to Singh-Gida, but kept silent.[4] These deaths and disappearances were part of a pattern that included the 'suicides' of Peter Peapell, who died by inhaling carbon monoxide, John Brittan, who died in an odd traffic accident, Trevor Knight, a Marconi worker who was found asphyxiated in his car, and, in 1988, the gruesome deaths of Peter Ferry, who had apparently wired his own teeth to the mains, and Alistair Beckham, who had also been connected to the electricity supply. Those who knew the victims say they were not 'suicidal types' and were reasonably happy people. Others died by suffocation from cling film or by turning their cars into oncoming traffic, such as Stuart Gooding, who died on 10 April 1987.

One particular death stands out. It was that of Jonathan Wash, a 29-year-old systems engineer, working on a project called System X. His death, on 19 November 1985, took place amid a spate of suicides that month. He had been employed by the British Telecom Technology Executive at Martlesham, which has strong connections to GCHQ, and, at the time of his death, he was in Abidjan in the Ivory Coast, working on a communications assessment. It was a leap from the balcony of his hotel that caused his death. Like Colonel Kurtz in Joseph Conrad's *Heart of Darkness*, he seemed to have gone insane.

Wash had left a strange set of messages scratched on his bedroom wall which included such enigmatic comments as, 'If there is a god, He knows the truth Haynes [his British colleague] British tele-consultant wants Wash dead or mad' and 'Abidjan, asylum or death, no chance of reaching England'.[5] The mystery deepened when it was seen by the post-mortem doctor that there were marks consistent with a struggle. Wash's possessions were also found one room above the balcony from which he fell. Despite evidence to the contrary, Home Office Minister Douglas Hogg dismissed the allegations of foul play and effectively closed the case in November 1986.

Were all these people suicidal or temporarily insane, or did they have sexual or other secrets to hide that they couldn't live with? Or were their deaths part of a conspiracy to hide top secret work? Were they part of an experiment themselves, or did their deaths simply create an accidental pattern?

The only woman to die in such mysterious circumstances was also a worker in the communications industry. Shani Warren was found on Saturday 18 April 1987 by physiotherapist Marjorie Allen when she was out walking her dog near Taplow Lake. Warren's body had been dumped in the water and had been there since the previous day, Good Friday. She was dressed in jeans and a T-shirt with a quilted gilet, but she was also gagged and had a noose around her neck; her ankles had been tied together with a tow rope and her wrists were tied behind her back. Strangely, she was still wearing her high heels, and seemed to have 'hopped' to her death in only eighteen inches of water. The papers dubbed her the Lady in the Lake. Her car appeared to have been rifled too and objects strewn around so much that the police suggested that 'someone had been looking for something'.[6]

Was Warren caught up in the circumstances that had killed the others? She was not highly placed or working on a secret project, but she was working for Micro Scope and the company won a contract for IUKADGE soon after her death. To all intents and purposes, Warren was a well-adjusted and lively person. The coroner's report recorded she had not been sexually assaulted and there was no sign of injury, although this judgement was to be seriously challenged by evidence which came to light later. The Home Office pathologist, Dr Benjamin Davies concluded suicide, but added that it was 'a very bizarre case'. He was later struck off, but reinstated, adding to suspicions of a conspiracy. The police now suddenly changed their tune and began a murder inquiry. A request for help from the BBC programme *Crimewatch* took things no further, however. A smear campaign had begun with hints that Shani might have been terrified of catching Aids, suggesting she was more than a little promiscuous. There was no proof and the Home Office clung to its suicide verdict although the police now had witnesses to a man lurking around the investigation site.

There the investigation seemed to halt, but it was not the end of the matter. Warren's family insisted that she had been murdered and that she had no suicidal tendencies. They were ignored. There was perhaps a simple and terrible reason. The police 'knew' all along that she had been killed, and had even changed their investigation. Why? In 1982, a woman was raped in Bradford and in 1983, another woman suffered a horrific attack in Leeds. The two attacks seemed similar:

West Yorkshire police rapidly realised the two offences were linked and set up an incident room to catch the rapist. They ran an extensive inquiry, knocked on 14,153 front doors, but got nowhere. With both rapes, police gathered numerous swabs, body hairs and other evidence from the victims and their cars but, when they failed to find their attacker, even though they knew it was highly likely that the serial rapist was still at work, they simply threw out the lot. The first woman had produced a photo-fit of her attacker, but the police lost it.[7]

West Yorkshire Police had already blundered over the Yorkshire Ripper and the police were to do so again in spectacular fashion now. In 1985 linked attacks took place in Doncaster and in April 1987 Warren was indeed killed. The attacks continued up to 1998, when Clive Barwell was finally identified as one of Britain's worst serial rapists. Amazingly, he had already been imprisoned for sixteen years for armed robbery, but had been able to continue the attacks when he had been let out on licence, apparently a model prisoner. He was finally arrested on 20 March 1998.

Shani Warren's case is significant in a number of possible ways in regard to possible EW deaths. The interest by this time in such deaths had to be squashed quickly and efficiently. It is not inconceivable that the Home Office collaborated in a cover up, including misinformation and incorrect procedures in order to put amateur investigators and journalists off the scent. The Home Office pathologist's comments were misleading and problematic. Warren might indeed have been sexually assaulted and police comments regarding her fear of Aids were wilfully misleading. There can be little doubt either that the police did not want observers to note the incompetence of their investigation into this and similar murderous rape attacks where information had been lost and crime scenes incompetently searched.

Added to this, the finger of suspicion pointed at EW connections which might reveal things that were highly secret. Either way, although the accusations of murder by some shadowy force of government assassins were to prove bogus, it was certain that there had been a level of conspiracy and silence authorised by Home Office personnel and acquiesced in by West Yorkshire police, as a matter of pre-emptive precaution. This endorsed rather than refuted conspiracy theories relating to other alleged victims.

Suspicions of foul play in high-security companies by the authorities in the 1980s were, however, partially confirmed when a man called Joe Vialls rang *Computer News* magazine in March 1987. Editor Tony Collins suspected Vialls was just another reader of 'questionable sanity'.[8] Nevertheless, the two men met. Joe felt disorientated as if a vague threat lay over him following employment at an American oil plant in India that used highly secret drilling equipment much sought after by the Soviets, who had been nosing around the site. The site had to be protected against industrial sabotage, but the rig *was* finally sabotaged – probably by the Americans to prevent Soviet attempts to infiltrate it.

It started, Vialls suggested, with threatening phone calls and calls in the dead of night so that it was difficult to concentrate in the morning. At the same time, Vialls noticed 'unusual sounds emanating from his [hotel] telephone'. These he recorded:

In the morning I played it back and was considerably alarmed to find an electronic noise on the tape, impossible to describe in writing, which seemed at
the time to keep pace with the sound of my breathing. As I gradually fell asleep,
so the electronic noise (or pulse) also slowed down … maintaining exactly the
same rate as the breathing itself. This tape I carefully packed away.[9]

Vialls too, it appeared, had had a 'fugue' and found himself the victim of an inex-
plicable and near-fatal accident. Back in Britain, the former RAF engineer took
the tape to be analysed. At the same time he 'dreamed' that he was going to have a
car accident. The next day the prophetic dream came true. The uncanniness of the
experience frightened Vialls, not because of the premonition but because the crash
seemed 'wrong'. He reported the accident to Suffolk police, but the notes were
mislaid and he even had difficulty getting his tape back. When he did, it appeared
to have been tampered with. By this time, Vialls felt that there was some conspiracy
regarding his life and so he was encouraged by his wife to visit Special Branch, but
achieved nothing.

The crux of Vialls's accusations was strange, but plausible. He felt he had been
subject, through the telephone, to some sort of hypnosis which had induced a temporary 'paranoid confusional state' and a feeling of 'unreality'. Had Vialls been got at
in a way that was untraceable – a remote-control form of self-induced destruction?
The question might have formed the basis of merely a fantastic conspiracy theory
with no substance, but for the fact that it had been known since the mid-1980s that
there were strange experiments in parapsychology and psychology being funded
by private enterprise and by the Pentagon. These were first exposed in America by
journalist Ron McCrea in 1984 in his book *Mind Wars*, where both parapsychological
and new forms of psychological warfare were detailed. McCrea showed that both
Carter and Reagan were fascinated by the new experiments in 'psi' as it was called
and that Uri Geller had performed for Carter in the 1970s.

The Pentagon, fearful of Russian intentions and believing that Russia was ahead in
mind-directed warfare, had funded parapsychological experiments and psychological innovations. Most were exposed as hokum, the paraphernalia of parapsychology
dreamed up by clairvoyants and hucksters to fleece the government, and all were
dropped as disastrous failures, but not before mind-defence machinery had been
installed in nuclear bunkers.

Needless to say, nothing worked or at least was ever proven to work. Nevertheless,
a side development of these experiments and installations suggested newer forms of
warfare which might prove effective in situations where information needed extract-
ing or where the enemy needed to be silenced. Alongside talk of parapsychology
was the very real possibility of more effective means of mind control. 'The use of
telepathic hypnosis also [held] great potential. This capability could allow agents to
be deeply planted with no conscious knowledge of their programming.'[10]

Such weapons would prove perhaps most effective protecting the new range of electronic weaponry being developed. As early as 1977, the American navy was funding experiments at Stanford University into extremely low-frequency radio waves, or EFL. It was believed that certain frequencies could generate mind control. Its implications were far reaching and pertinent to the deaths in the EW indus-try. 'Because the human brain generates electrical signals in the same frequencies, scientists speculate[d] that transmitting strong signals in these frequencies might interfere with the natural brain activity of persons in the target area, produc-ing effects ranging from hypertension to sudden death.'[11] Interestingly, by 1984, McCrea noted that 'research on the effects of ELF on the human brain [were] well-funded and highly classified'.[12]

Meanwhile, Joe Vialls was referred to specialists attached to the Medical Foundation for the Care of Torture Victims based at the National Temperance Hospital in London. Vialls was judged 'normal' and with a 'stable personality' by Professor Haward from the Foundation and by others who looked at his profile. Was Vialls influenced by hypnotic suggestion or drug manipulation? Many of the scientists who had died had become progressively paranoid, had lost confidence just before their deaths, had committed suicide in unusual circumstances and/or had suffered periods of absence that could not be explained.

According to Barbara Honegger, who worked in the US Department of Policy Development, Reagan was well informed on parapsychology and wanted to fund projects that went further:

Initial results coming out of laboratories in the United States and Canada that certain amplitude and frequency combinations of external electromagnetic radia-tion in the brain-wave frequency range [were] capable of bypassing the external sensory mechanism of organisms, including humans, and directly stimulating higher level neuronal structures in the brain. This electronic stimulation [was] known to produce mental changes at a distance, including hallucinations in various sensory modalities, particularly auditory.[13]

The covert world of hypnosis and drug-induced hallucinations which were being developed as part of psyops was first brought to the British public's attention by Peter Watson of the *Sunday Times* in 1980. However, it had been around a long time. One form was already commercially available in the United States in the mid- to late 1970s. It was called the Psychological Stress Evaluator and had been developed for the CIA and army marketed through Dektor Counterintelligence.[14]

Frank Kitson certainly used forms of psychological warfare during his period in Northern Ireland in 1970 to 1972. The history of brainwashing was well known, but new forms of influence were becoming, perhaps, so subtle that they could not be detected. They were, in fact, auto-destruct methods which meant there could be an assassination without the presence of an assassin. Years before, Dr Frank Olson had surreptitiously been given LSD by the CIA in an experiment to see what might occur. He threw himself from a tenth-floor window. Peter Wright, that arch conspiracy theorist at the centre of the secret state, even hinted at the use of car crashes by the security services in *Spycatcher*. Perhaps those members of EW development who were seen as homosexual, sexually deviant or simply too weak to cope were weeded out by a new form of warfare designed to protect the interests of the SDI programme? 'In EW, the enemy need only discover its weakest link.'[15]

Mind-altering warfare was curiously in tune with the aims of Thatcherism and Reaganism, being predicated on the notion that they were fundamentally *democratic* in their values. Such values endorsed the idea that the power of faith and individualism could destroy any obstacle, including Moscow. The advocates of these new forms of warfare represented the idea:

> The American faith in self-help and the self-made man is the faith in the practical power of positive religion … The American faith in the power of positive thinking is a democratic faith, the faith in the potential of the ordinary man. If anything, that faith actually rejects special talent or genius.[16]

Moreover, the power of the ordinary person was also to be the power of the masses. The most extreme form of such mysticism was the US army's First Earth Battalion which was the product of California and the brainchild of Lieutenant Colonel Jim Channon, who, in 1979, started to organise an 'elite' force of zen warriors. Their creed was that anything might be overcome with 'love' and 'will'. This eccentric religious cult within the American army had adherents at the highest levels of command.

It might have been ironic to know that the webs spun by the peace women to keep out Cruise were similar to the language of webs and nets being spun by theoreticians of future war. One 'tribal elder' of the First Earth Battalion, Colonel Mike Malone, in a talk at the Army War College in 1982, actually invoked the language of Christian parable to explain the importance of the new army philosophy and its relevance to the little men of democracy:

> I am one of the tribal elders … my name is 'The Mullet Man'. I am known as the one who casts nets. And I try to tell people that of all those who cast nets, most should be concerned with the catching, but some, at least, should focus more on the casting than the catching. I live with, fish for, and push the cause of the mullet, because he is a 'low-class' fish. He is simple. He is honest. He moves around in great formations and columns. He does damn near all the work. But he is also noble.[17]

It might seem to be even more perverse that the language and style of the Greenham women and the actions and lifestyle of the New Age travelling community with their peace convoys trundling around the country presented a mirror image of the language and lifestyle of the very soldiers they opposed. The new United States warriors used single self-chosen names, imitated Native American culture and lived on a frugal diet of vegetarian meals and nuts; they too wished to embrace the mystical and the esoteric. There seemed to be warriors for peace everywhere, the New Age peace protesters and green activists might have been shocked to learn their opponents had adopted their culture wholesale and had also 'dropped out'. Thatcherism might have deplored the laxity of the 1960s, but the spirit of Haight-Ashbury and Stonehenge was the spectre in the American war machine.

❧

A note of caution: Since the 1990s, the interest in psychological warfare has become wilder and wackier, and self-help groups have sprung up for those who feel they are victims of state surveillance. In the case of those alleged psyops murders I have outlined, a great deal of caution has to be exercised, especially with regard to those who feel they have been affected by such activities, but who seem, by all accounts to be paranoid schizophrenics whose fears, picked up through reading or watching news that seems to directly affect them, are regularly noted by psychiatrists.

One such person was Darrim Daoud, who claimed he was half British and half Iraqi, a 34-year-old who was found dead on railway lines near Crawley. It is claimed he was killed on 15 November 2011 to silence him because of what he knew regarding psyops. Daoud believed he was the victim of a campaign which had been initiated by the secret services (for whatever purposes). He died the day after uploading a video cataloguing his concerns on YouTube, and after not having slept for 133 hours and apparently having being burned on the face by some invisible 'weapon' planted in his home:

> The two types of harassment that Darrim alleged were organised stalking, and torture inflicted from a distance by the deployment of non-lethal directed energy weapons, often called electronic harassment. Darrim conducted an online survey of people who reported either of these two types of abuse, discovering that over 80% of those who reported either type of abuse, reported both types.[18]

The website dedicated to Daoud's claims seems to be administered by John Allman of the Beulah Baruch ministry, and those who support Daoud believe themselves to have been wilfully excluded from giving vital evidence at his inquest and that there is some unexplained cover-up by the authorities. On 24 April 2014, Allman posted the following diatribe against homosexuality:

Nobody who says that there is no such thing as a 'gay cure', cannot have given homophobia a serious try yet. Choosing homophobia, working on one's homophobia, and in time perfecting one's homophobia, cures and prevents one from choosing homosexual behaviour – either from choosing that behaviour for the first time, or from choosing it.[19]

Others who support the Daoud case for electronic surveillance also believe they are deliberately 'bounced' from certain websites which might contain sensitive information. A blog from April 2014 sets the tone regarding a form of attack known as 'gang stalking', now called Internet trolling, which consists of 'organised harassment and the targeting of an individual person for purposes of revenge or jealousy or even malicious amusement', but might also be used to keep people quiet. 'It's a psychological attack that can completely destroy a person's life, while leaving little or no evidence to incriminate the perpetrators.' Targets are often women, sometimes minorities, and certainly might include individuals that appear dangerous such as dissidents or whistle-blowers:[20]

> Many gang stalking targets complain that their internet is interfered with ... attempts to log in to various sites, supposedly those containing enlightening information, were diverted and substitute pages sent to the enquirer instead. This seems ... highly plausible. [Having] also noticed the delay in accessing sites ... the blogger noticed that particular sites [he?] had trouble accessing [and] when [he] finally managed to access [them], the information was outdated, going back from 6 months to 2 years – even though the sites were current.[21]

Such is the imaginative power that has accumulated from pysops operations that many people believe they are the target of their own household appliances. Thus Mike Corley, aka Boleslaw Tadeusz Szocik, believes that he is the victim of an MI5 assassination plot and that television presenters talk about him and to him in coded language and that his microwave oven is used to listen to his conversations. He has posted on the Internet information about his paranoia since 1995. Indeed, Tadeusz has become a Usernet celebrity for his weird, amusing and paranoid postings which are both bizarre and seductive. Corley has been banned from posting through Google for his abuse of Usernet, and has been similarly bounced from most ISPs in England. In the past, his posts were relatively easy to filter out due to his similar subject lines and email address. However, at the start of 2008 he began a series of posts that avoided filters through sporgery (flooding sites with spam-forgeries to make the information look like others have sent it) and by slightly varying his subject line of 'MI-5 Persecution'.[22]

17

THE INTELLIGENCE
OF SLEEPING DOGS

At the heart of the security state was GCHQ (General Communications Headquarters) in Cheltenham with its outstations around the world. When Tam Dalyell mentioned it in the Commons, it was virtually unknown to the public and its work was absolutely confidential. Few knew its secrets, but a window was briefly opened on its affairs with the 'ABC' spy trial in 1978. Secrecy soon re-enveloped the place and interest waned. GCHQ had grown out of the wartime codebreaking which had gone on at Bletchley Park. The government's Code and Cypher School became GCHQ after the war, moving into its new base near Cheltenham in 1953 and, although it occasionally flexed its muscles (over Suez for instance), it became an adjunct of American foreign policy working closely with its American counterpart, the NSA. Despite all attempts to peer into this world of signals traffic, GCHQ remained a place apart in the English landscape, known by the few who dared to enquire and closed to all but its workforce.

Thatcher's premiership was part of a long process of intimacy with the United States which has never truly cooled, but in the last instance she fooled herself that she was Reagan's conscience or could actually influence American foreign policy to any great extent. The United States had bases across Britain, and the NSA maintained through the RAF three bases at Edzell, Menwith Hill and RAF Chicksands as well as having permanent NSA staff in its embassy. This proved a two-way process of accommodation so that during the Falklands War, Britain was able to utilise American satellite information which was in turn tied to British ground stations at RAF Oakhanger in Hampshire and the island of Diego Garcia in the Indian Ocean. Anyway, the relationship was one of stewardship rather than ownership, and Blackbird spy planes operated independently for years from RAF Mildenhall in Suffolk and RAF Akrotiri in Cyprus unless specifically refused when they threatened British interests, as during the Yom Kippur War when Britain did not want to spoil Anglo-Arab relations.[1] The significance of American involvement in British intelligence affairs is incalculable.

It was in the nature of the intelligence world that personal secrets and activities might be winked at if they remained discreet or could be profitably controlled. The secrecy surrounding GCHQ also inadvertently gave protection to those working inside the organisation and therefore to their personal activities. Once inside GCHQ, the employee was meant to be trustworthy, having jumped all the hurdles. If they weren't, then they might act in a way whereby they would assume a type of immunity from further scrutiny. This was the case with Geoffrey Prime, the man responsible for the most serious breaches of secrecy during the 1960s and 1970s. The Prime affair was especially painful as Thatcher had revealed to the Commons the identity of the fourth man in the Cambridge spy ring in a speech in 1979 and probably felt that was the end of the embarrassment. Prime was arrested just three years later and proved a much more serious criminal.

Sir Anthony Blunt's exposure was meant, after all, to be the end of the long-standing hunt for the remainder of the Cambridge spy network. Blunt confessed and had been granted immunity two decades before (after suspicions aroused in the 1950s). Even the Queen had been informed, but the whole affair was hushed up, in part by Harold Macmillan as exposure seemed to serve no real purpose and might damage both the government and the monarchy.

Such inertia had conveniently allowed Blunt off the hook and given him carte blanche to continue his life almost as before. Renewed interest in 1979 following a new book and articles in *Private Eye* had led to further speculation and this finally led Thatcher to make a statement in the Commons on 15 November 1979, which followed an arranged question regarding security from Labour back-bencher Ted Leadbitter.

Thatcher had been advised by Michael Hanley, head of MI5, to let sleeping dogs lie, but she had been insulted by such an idea. To Thatcher, a traitor was a traitor, and an upper-class homosexual traitor stunk of the old-school-tie cronyism she abhorred and which was made worse by the fact that Blunt's friends and colleagues were all in high enough positions in society to want to cushion the blow when it fell. Even the Cabinet Secretary Sir Robert Armstrong didn't want to create waves as they might be unprofitable to the establishment.

Blunt's exposure simply opened the lid on speculation about intelligence and there was loose talk of much larger networks of traitors fuelled by the speculations of a Northern Irish writer called Robin Bryans (who wrote under the name Robert Harbison) that Blunt's career had been long and illustrious and protected by the security services for over thirty years, because Blunt had been part of a homosexual and paedophilic ring which had included Lord Louis Mountbatten and the Kincora Boys' Home and which linked the royal family to sexual deviance and murder on both sides of the Irish border. Mountbatten's murder was, in this scenario, the direct result of MI5 connivance not IRA hatred. The stories, still repeated in hard-core conspiracy publications today, have never been proven.[2]

The boil had been lanced it seemed, but the consequent panic following Prime's subsequent exposure meant that everyone who opposed the government's plans was now subject to the same surveillance as that placed on a real traitor. This was especially so with the protesters at CND who came under the watchful eye of a new Ministry of Defence unit, DS19. Prime had worked at GCHQ for fourteen years, but he had a secret life as a spy for the Soviet Union and as a paedophile.

Geoffrey Prime was not a 'toff' like the Cambridge spy-ring members, but he was decidedly not 'one of us' either. A difficult upbringing in Staffordshire, in a less-than-tolerant Catholic family, had nevertheless resulted in good language O levels, but a dead-end job. During his national service, Prime had wanted to be a radio operator, but had ended up in stores. His luck changed when his talent for languages was recognised and he was packed off to learn Russian. He found himself at university taking advanced Russian and then taught himself Swahili during operations in Kenya. Here he was introduced to colonial exploitation and began an interest in communism. He was not vetted until 1966 even though he was working on Russian codes in Berlin. It was at that time that he made contact with the Soviet authorities in East Berlin. Prime next secretly visited East Berlin at the same time as applying to GCHQ. The job he gained at GCHQ was as a translator in the London Processing Group. Work was easy and spying easier. He met his handlers regularly, but was never rumbled and soon had a job in Vienna. In 1976 he arrived in Cheltenham as a linguist.

Meanwhile, Prime had met and married Helen Organ, but the marriage failed, partly through her suspicions about his activities. When she reported those suspicions to her husband's female vetting officer, nothing was done, the two women finding that they hated each other. Prime remarried, left GCHQ, and tried to make it as a wine salesman and then a taxi driver, mostly driving GCHQ personnel around. While he had worked at GCHQ, however, Prime had continued to hand over sensitive material. This accelerated when he found himself in Berlin in 1980 and 1981.

Prime seemed to have got hold of GCHQ's most secret secret, the latest 'SIGINT' information from space research and information on VHF, UHF and microwave transmissions. At the same time, others in the United States were also spying for the Russians in this new area. Prime's most serious handover of information was regarding the tracking systems used to watch Soviet submarines and the attempts to capture Soviet listening devices then being put into practical form aboard HMS *Conqueror*. Interestingly, the unthinking racism of this secret intelligence gathering by which the radio transmissions of submarines could be tracked (and which might have been part of Project 2000) was its name: Project Sambo. It was the very expression of the racism Prime had found in Kenya.

As a spy, Prime might never have been caught. Instead, he was arrested as, of all things, a serial child molester, which he had carried out with the same cunning and planning as his more traitorous activities. Prime would stalk young children and visit their homes when their families were out and, posing as a plumber or builder and calling himself Mr Brookes or Mr Williams, would attack the children. Latterly, he had taken to wearing a mask and carrying a knife, just in case. He had been finally cornered after leaving his car where it could be seen. In his house were 2,287 files detailing local girls.

When Prime was arrested he confessed to his second wife Rhona and told her about his espionage. Rhona said later, 'It came as a total shock – I knew nothing about it. I don't know how he led his triple life.'[3] Finally, on 23 May 1982, Rhona told the police about Prime's other secret. Detective Chief Superintendent David Cole was now in charge of the operation, but was stymied by not being allowed to investigate the case because he had no security clearance. Special Branch would have to be called in under Detective Chief Inspector Peter Picken. Cole was inquisitive:

'What goes on at this GCHQ place, Pete?'
The reply was brief and to the point.
'No one really knows apart from the security services and a few in the government.'[4]

The secret Prime had confessed to his wife took weeks to actually uncover. On 10 November 1982, Prime was sentenced to thirty-eight years in prison, thirty-five of which were for offences under section 1 of the Official Secrets Act 1911 and only three for his sex offences. The press was not allowed to report on the trial which was conducted on camera. Prime was only released from prison in March 2001.

❧

Prime was not the only one working for the Russians, yet he was at least secretive when it came to his criminal pursuits. This was not the case with Michael Bettaney, who worked for MI5 and was caught while attempting to hand over secret documents to General Guk at the Soviet Embassy in London. Unfortunately, Guk worked with Oleg Gordievsky, who was a double agent, and Bettaney was arrested. He was sentenced to twenty-three years in prison under offences defined by section 1 of the Official Secrets Act 1911. Bettaney had been vetted twice and passed as loyal, despite the fact that when once arrested for drunkenness he had shouted 'I'm a spy,' and despite his long-time admiration for Adolf Hitler. He was kept on and trusted with sensitive material. The journalist Paul Foot considered Bettaney 'off his rocker' and 'living proof that there [was] no limit to the insecurity, lunacy and chaos into which a bunch of entirely irresponsible men [sic] with vast powers and megalomaniac intentions [could] lead us'.[5]

In 1992, Michael Smith was arrested and charged with four offences under the same section of the Official Secrets Act for 'communicating material to another for purposes prejudicial to the safety or interests of the state'. Smith had been recruited by Viktor Oshchenko in 1975 and had been active until 1979. His value was in giving

Russia information on the XN-715 radar fuse for the British WE177 freefall nuclear bomb. Smith had obtained the information while working for GEC although he had also worked on top-secret technology at EMI. After Oshchenko defected, Smith was arrested, although he pleaded that he had been set up. The documents that he was alleged to have leaked are still shrouded in secrecy.

❧ ⁂ ❧

The greatest gaff of all with regard to security was Thatcher's own insistence that those working at GCHQ be de-unionised. Anyone of Irish extraction had already been banned for years, as GCHQ was exempt from the relevant sections of the Race Relations Act.[6] Before the row erupted, GCHQ was a little-known entity and certainly one that asked not to be the centre of attention even though it was a surveillance centre of industrial proportions. Thatcher's nagging made it so in 1984 during the aftermath of the *Belgrano* rumours and the 'Crown Jewels' affair. Thatcher was furious and looked around for scapegoats and government organisations not wholly loyal. One place they might be located was in the unions long embedded at GCHQ and which had actually been working there for years, but were now under the uncomfortable spotlight as the enemies within. The context of the union ban was not merely the *Belgrano* incident, but also the miners' strike and the Wapping printing dispute. The decision, which was mainly down to Thatcher's caprice, was announced in January 1984. GCHQ had always had unions, and communist infiltration was always going to be an issue, although a sexual pervert like Prime had slipped through without much trouble.

There had even been strikes before, such as the five-day strike in September 1969 and a one-day stoppage in February 1973, but nothing since and the workforce of 7,500 was contented and loyal. Nonetheless, there was another major strike in 1979 which was unconcluded by 1981 and coincided with the heating up of the Cold War and the Soviet invasion of Afghanistan, the hostage crisis in Iran, the invasion of Poland and Soviet military exercises.[7] At the centre of the dispute, were the radio operators and their new SIGINT equipment. Things seemed to go wrong, with poor intelligence and technical breakdowns. The Americans were fearful that their allies, who were also their subordinates and taking radio signals from the NSA satellites beaming to RAF Menwith Hill in Yorkshire, were going to the dogs.

Brian Tovey, who took over as director of GCHQ in 1979, considered that the TUC would target GCHQ 'as a damned good hit', and he told his counterpart Bobby Inman in the NSA that he intended to get unions banned. Inman considered this 'marvellous news' as the Americans had always pressed hard to get British unions barred from security work.[8] Jim Prior, Secretary of State for Northern Ireland, recalled that America had been 'very much upset' by the decision to strike. The pressure for de-unionisation came direct from the NSA. Tovey even apologised to Inman for GCHQ'S inefficiency.[9] Thatcher's decision to ban the unions was therefore wholly directed to American needs and was taken because of perceived American pressure; both Lord Carrington as Foreign Secretary and Francis Pym as his successor objected. Thatcher allegedly misrepresented the objections to create a greater sense of government unity.[10]

Thatcher had played a purely diplomatic card to appease the head of the NSA and please Reagan, but she also wanted to introduce the American use of the polygraph after the debacle with Geoffrey Prime and others whom she no longer trusted. Deputy director of the NSA, Benson Buffham, had even come to Britain to exert extra pressure. MI5 was to undertake a fourteen-week programme of training. The polygraph was to be used to protect against 'hostile penetration' and Sir Robert Armstrong argued the case for its use within the Civil Service. Nevertheless, the Royal Commission on Criminal Justice Procedure had concluded that at least 25 per cent of polygraph readings might be wrong – too high a rate to proceed. Even in the NSA, four traitors had passed the test. The government's hesitations and Geoffey Howe's doubts before he had to announce the ban on unions to Parliament were answered by Bernard Ingham's bluff demand for de-unionisation expressing his 'ability to articulate the Prime Minister's prejudices more crisply even than she could herself'.[11]

John Nott, perhaps smarting from his demotion after the Falklands War, suggested in the Commons that operational effectiveness of GCHQ had never been affected by the strikes, but William Waldegrave, a junior minister in the Foreign Office, was put up on Radio 4's *Today* programme to argue that there had been constant disruption, which was untrue. The decision remained arbitrary and directed from abroad. It was divisive and pointless, but it proved Britain's loyalty to the United States, which was paramount. The unions took immediate action, the result of which was a court decision that the ban was unlawful. Last-minute and hasty toing and froing from GCHQ by Howe and work in the Court of Appeal got the ruling overturned. The whole thing went next to the Lords to be debated by five law lords. They upheld the decision of the Court of Appeal.[12]

By 1986, the government finally turned its attention to recalcitrant union members. The resultant pressure proved disastrous.[13] A brain drain from GCHQ began, with scientists, mathematicians, cryptographers and computer scientists seeking lucrative jobs in the private sector. Indeed, 50 per cent of its best computer officers left between 1984 and 1985, compared with 1983, when the rate was nil. These were being offered jobs by GEC, Plessey, Racal and Marconi at interviews held at the Golden Valley Hotel made famous as in ATV's soap opera *Crossroads*. Even Brian Tovey jumped ship and secured a job as a consultant for Plessey.[14] Gareth Morris, the last trade unionist, was sacked on 2 March 1989. The polygraph, seen as unreliable and next to useless, had been forgotten years before. Richard J. Aldrich, the authority on GCHQ, concludes that 'Thatcher's approach was incompetent' and that moreover, the sight of striking senior civil servants marching in protest down Cheltenham high street, arm in arm with members of the NUM summed up Thatcher's miscalculations with regard to the nature of intelligence work.[15] By the end, 'Almost every aspect of the work and location of GCHQ was rehearsed again and again in the press. Our most secret service had become almost the most public.'[16]

GCHQ now proved a rich ground for investigators, but the government had become overly cautious and decidedly jumpy. A casualty of such secrecy was investigative journalist Duncan Campbell who had been commissioned to produce a report on the disastrous Zircon satellite programme which had so far been kept secret partially because of the fact that it didn't work and costs had spiralled. The story as it emerged was that, for some years, Britain had been trying to get intelligence spy satellites that might free them from the monopoly of the United States. The whole affair had been kept from the Cabinet and the costs kept secret. The programme of development had emerged in the 1970s from a need to arm Polaris with an accurate propulsion unit which would allow Moscow to be brought into range. This project was code-named Chevaline and it grew into Zircon which was intended to reinvent GCHQ and make it the major player in European intelligence gathering. The project was, however, turning into an expensive shambles.

This was what Campbell was to expose in his documentary scheduled for transmission in February 1987. Instead, in January, Scottish Special Branch raided the BBC studios in Edinburgh looking for the tapes. The raid was in essence a 'fishing trip' to make the BBC toe the line, directed not by the Scottish police, but by the Metropolitan police in London. The raid was undertaken with a warrant deemed unlawful in Scottish law, but this made no difference to the operation. Ironically, the provisions set out in the original warrant covered only English law and did not hold in Scotland.

Who had authorised such a high-level operation? Tam Dalyell sniffed conspiracy yet again and he was probably correct in his assumption that the source was Downing Street itself.[18] It certainly appeared that the Secretary of State for Scotland, Malcolm Rifkind, was well aware of the warrant by 30 January. Bernard Ingham told the press that the operation was quite unknown to the Prime Minister and she had first heard of it on 31 January. Dalyell called this denial 'egregious' at the least, believing instead that Thatcher had chosen not to know![19] Roy Jenkins, SDP MP in Glasgow, called the affair the work of a 'second-rate police state'. Whoever actually authorised the raid was never established, but the implications were clear: don't produce media programmes like this one again.

Seven BBC employees, including the assistant director general and the controller of the BBC in Scotland, had been questioned at length about the BBC's internal documents. Each interrogation lasted an average of five hours. In early March, BBC Scotland's public oversight body, the Broadcasting Council for Scotland, urged the corporation to take action to defend its staff against such continued 'harassment' by the police.[20]

18

THOSE HEAVY PEOPLE

If intelligence gathering had to be kept classified, so did Britain's new role as arms supplier to the world. Indeed, so important became the trade, especially to the Middle East, that it became the most guarded secret of all.

Those who were intent on finding conspiracy at the highest level had unwitting cooperation from the Foreign Office, especially when the Foreign Office was at the centre of a massive military trade deal with Saudi Arabia. On the night of 19/20 May 1979, a young nurse called Helen Smith, who had been recruited by the private Baksh Hospital in Jeddah, Saudi Arabia, fell from a balcony after a boozy sex party at a flat owned by a Dr Richard Arnot and his wife Penny. Helen's father, Ron Smith, wanting to understand more about his daughter's death and to find out what the outcome of the Saudi autopsy had been, travelled to Saudi on 25 May. But, from the beginning, British Embassy staff were cagey and defensive.

Ron Smith knew that Helen's was not the only body recovered, for a man's body had been impaled on railings at the same time, also having fallen from a great height. There had been no autopsy on either body due to the peculiarities of Saudi procedure which required immediate family assent. Smith gave his, but the family of Dutchman Johannes Otten did not and his body was flown back to Holland in a sealed coffin and cremated. The original circumstances of the death of the two victims was strange and unresolved after numerous different accounts emerged of how the bodies were discovered.

Helen's father pursued the case, on the understanding that the Saudis were conducting a murder inquiry. They were also conducting an inquiry into the apparent use of illegal alcohol and the fact, as it emerged, that Arnot had possibly conspired in his wife's adultery on the night of the murder with New Zealander Timothy Hayter. Both the Arnots had been arrested. By December, it was clear that the inquiry was over and that foul play was not suspected. The two victims had perhaps simply tumbled over the balcony. By now it seemed the Foreign Office and Saudi Ministry of the Interior had washed their hands of the case. Why?

As Helen tumbled, so did the Callaghan government and with it a change in foreign policy. The Thatcher government, though friendly to individual Jewish entrepreneurs was turning hostile to Israel, suspecting, rightly, that there was business to be made in Saudi Arabia. In February 1979, the Queen had started what would become policy, travelling to Saudi on a state visit. This had reassured the Saudis, but their hold on power had been temporarily shaken by the Shi'ite insurrection that had been backed by Ayatollah Khomeini and that had captured the Grand Mosque in Mecca in November 1979.

In watching the threat from Iran to the Middle East, Britain saw an opportunity, and a trade delegation was dispatched to Riyadh under John Nott, then Secretary of State for Trade, following instructions from COMET, the Committee for Middle East Trade. The trade talks were mainly on 'defence', with emphasis on electronic surveillance. A trade union shop steward from Marconi accompanied the businessmen to sell the deal through the British press. Foreign Secretary Lord Carrington followed on 14 January 1980.

On 13 February 1980, it was announced that Britain had secured £100 million worth of business. This was quite a coup, for, although arms trading had traditionally been a European preserve, America had spotted a gap in the market in the Middle East following the Arab-Israeli War of 1973. Far from Russia expanding arms sales as it had done since 1955, the West (here the Americans) realised commercial opportunities following the diplomacy of Richard Nixon, the quiescence of Russian arms diplomacy in the region and the retreat from the Gulf by Britain. For the moment, therefore, no one in in British diplomatic circles or arms manufacture wished to rock the boat and both the Saudis and the Foreign Office soon let it be known that there was 'no question of any criminal responsibility for the deaths' in Jeddah, thus reversing a previous Saudi police investigation into possible murder.[1]

Things would not go smoothly for anyone, however. On 24 March 1980, sentence was passed on the Arnots and Hayter. Adultery was a more serious crime than murder in Saudi Arabia and the sentences reflected this:

> Mr Arnot was sentenced to a year in prison and to thirty lashes. Tim Hayter to eighty lashes … The most shocking sentence of all, however, was that handed down to Penny Arnot. Like Tim Hayter, she was sentenced to eighty lashes of the cane, the flogging to be carried out in public.[2]

The British revulsion at the sentences had to be smoothed over and the Arnots merely expelled, but, on 9 April, the programme *Death of a Princess* was televised. Its focus was the execution for adultery of Princess Misha'al. The programme incensed the ageing King Khaled who threatened to call off all trade deals and start an oil embargo. The British government had to grovel. Lord Carrington, weak at the thought of loss of trade, concluded, 'We may need to ask [the Saudis] to be more understanding of our way of life.'[3]

Although things were soon patched up and even the Arnots were released without punishment, Helen Smith's father was left more frustrated with the deliberate way he had been obstructed by the embassy in Jeddah and the mandarins in the Foreign Office. Just after the programme aired, Smith travelled to Holland to explain his concerns to the Otten family. These concerns were new to them, and it was also the first time that Otten's name was linked to Helen Smith in the papers. On 17 June, Smith finally flew to Jeddah to collect his daughter's body. Here he was delayed and harassed by Saudi secret service agents apparently tipped off by the embassy regarding alleged illegal photographs. He was later released and flew back on the plane following his daughter's body. The Arnots returned to Britain on 8 August 1980.

Through numerous autopsies and one coroner's inquest and a huge amount of obstruction from ministers and the Foreign Office, Smith, a former policeman, finally established that his daughter had sustained injuries not compatible with the fall she was said to have had. An autopsy carried out by three pathologists established that she may have been hit with a blunt instrument and dumped unconscious where she was found. Her body also showed signs of violent sexual activity. Nevertheless, at the final coroner's inquest which began on 16 August 1982, the jury could not decide what had happened. They brought in an open verdict. Helen Smith's body was not cremated until 9 November 2009 and Ron Smith died on 15 April 2011 without ever knowing what really happened to his daughter.

So, what occurred remains a mystery. It might have been that she was raped and killed by others at the party and her body dumped. It might have been that Otten was trying to protect her and was thrown over the balcony at 3.10 a.m. It might have been that British Embassy staff were at the party and serious diplomatic repercussions would have followed which would have threatened an arms deal. It might just have been that Saudi royalty or those attached to the royal household were present. No one talked and no one admitted anything. Yet at the heart of this double 'murder' seemed to be a very murky world of arms diplomacy in which people of no consequence might be ignored or lied about with impunity.

It was hardly surprising that the Foreign Office didn't want to rock the boat. Between 1980 and 1990, Britain became the fourth largest exporter of weapons after the United States, Russia and France. Arms exports rose from £1,070 million in 1980 to £1,980 million by 1990. By 1986, Britain was the second largest exporter, with most of its sales going to the Saudis. In the mid 1980s the Third World, including the Middle East, represented more than 50 per cent of all exports. It was the golden goose of economic recovery.[4] The export of arms to the Middle East became the central plank of Britain's foreign policy during the terms of the Conservative government from Thatcher to Major.

Once one apparent cover-up has taken place, then every suspicious instance afterwards will be regarded with the deepest scepticism. In a way, it all began with the 'accidental' death of Helen Smith. Her case is one that suggests diplomacy cannot be disrupted by unacceptable facts. Indeed, so outrageous were the official falsehoods and carefully worded obfuscations that the case and the way it was so badly handled by officials still had resonance in the 1990s and was taken into account when Princess Diana died in circumstances that suggested more official obfuscations.

～♋～

Middle Eastern affairs were becoming more important as tensions between Arabs and Israelis started to affect world politics. Countries such as Iran, Iraq, Syria and Lebanon seemed inherently unstable and the Palestinian question appeared intractable; most of the arms sold from Britain were destined for Saudi Arabia (indeed as late as 2005 'around 40 per cent' of all staff in the Defence Export Services Organisation – part of the Ministry of Defence – were working on Saudi contracts; their names redacted from the ministry directory); and new banking institutions had appeared which joined many of these countries to Pakistan.[5]

This then was the complex mix which ended up with an attempted assassination outside the Dorchester on 3 June 1982. Shlomo Argov, the Israeli Ambassador, had been gunned down as he left a dinner. He had been severely wounded in the head. His would-be killers – Hussein Ghassan Said, Marwan al-Banna and Nawaf al-Rosan – approached Argov as he got into his car after the reception. Said had pulled the trigger. Once Argov was dead, the men were meant to assassinate Nabil Ramlawi, the London representative of the PLO. The assassins were terrorists working for Abu Nidal, a displaced Palestinian who had become frustrated with the PLO and Yasser Arafat and gone on to form a more violent splinter group. The actual attack might have been ordered by Iraqi intelligence (Nawaf al-Rosan was an Iraqi intelligence officer) in order to destabilise the PLO and create friction with Israel. One gunman was wounded and captured while the other two were tracked down and arrested.

The attempted killing was too much for the Israelis, who mistakenly blamed the PLO. Operation Peace for Galilee followed on 6 June, Arafat being temporarily dislodged from Lebanon:

> The then Israeli defence minister Ariel Sharon had a pretext for his long-planned campaign to eliminate the Palestine Liberation Organisation and its headquarters in the Lebanese capital, Beirut. In his memoirs, Sharon admits that the Dorchester ambush was 'merely the spark that lit the fuse'.
>
> The next day, Israeli forces bombed PLO arms depots in Lebanon, Palestinian forces retaliated with cross-border Katyusha rocket salvos, and, barely 48 hours later, Israel launched its ill-fated Operation Peace for Galilee. At first, the invasion

routed the enemy. But before long, Israelis were fighting in the streets of Beirut itself; and, as civilian casualties mounted, international opprobrium grew.[6]

Abu Nidal had organised his finances through Credit and Commerce International (BCCI), a major international bank set up in 1972 by Agha Hasan Abedi, a Pakistani. Its headquarters were in Karachi, but it had branches all over the world, including in London. BCCI was created with capital from Abu Dhabi, the United Arab Emirates and even the Bank of America. The whole thing was a set-up to avoid too-close scrutiny and, in effect, acted as a no-questions-asked money-laundering organisation used conveniently by any country wishing to carry out covert operations or aid people otherwise deemed *personae non gratae*. The Soviet Union, Britain and the United States used the bank's facilities and could count on its discretion.

But the bank was soon infiltrated by both MI5 and the CIA. MI5 ran two agents inside the London operation, an operation first made public through the *Sunday Times*. The paper leaked the contents of the Sandstorm Report, the name of the secret inquiry carried out in March 1991 by Price Waterhouse on the insistence of the Bank of England. The report named Sloane Street branch manager, Ghassan Qassem as the main link to MI5, but there was also allegedly another unnamed British link. Qassem dealt with an Iraqi called Samir Najmeddin or Najmedeen who set up accounts to allow arms deals with Iraq. The investigation into the bank's affairs brought a certain closure, for, as we shall see, exposing links with Iraq would come to embroil ministers in the greatest scandal of the Thatcher years.

The BCCI case seemed shut and the Lebanon war a disaster manipulated by foreign politicians and foreign terrorists, now safely locked up or out of the country and silenced. Nevertheless, on the transfer of the terrorists between prisons, some nagging doubts surfaced in Israeli newspapers regarding British collusion in the attack on the ambassador. On 8 July 1999, Lord Alton of Liverpool put a written question to the government regarding one report. He asked, 'whether the allegations contained in the Israeli newspaper *Ha'aretz* of 11 June that MI5 had prior knowledge of the attempted assassination on 3 June 1982 of the then Israeli Ambassador to the United Kingdom, Mr Shlomo Argov, are correct?'[7] Lord Williams of Mostyn answered for the government in the usual bland manner required to silence questioners. 'It has been the policy of successive governments,' he said, 'not to comment on the operations of the security and intelligence agencies. In line with that policy, I do not propose to comment on the newspaper's allegations.' Ironically, British interests were directly threatened by Abu Nidal two years later when he planned to assassinate the Queen on a state visit to Kuwait on 14 June 1984. The plot was foiled by David Spedding, later head of MI6.[8]

Nidal was interviewed three years after the plot to assassinate Argov by *Der Spiegel*. In the interview, Nidal appeared to revel in his protean persona:

What Arafat says about me doesn't bother me. Not only he, but also a whole list of Arab and world politicians claim that I am an agent of the Zionists or the CIA. Others state that I am a mercenary of the French secret service and of the Soviet KGB. The latest rumor is that I am an agent of Khomeini. During a certain period they said we were spies for the Iraqi regime. Now they say we are Syrian agents … I will tell you something. Many psychologists and sociologists in the Soviet bloc tried to investigate this man Abu Nidal. They wanted to find a weak point in his character. The result was zero.[9]

Abu Nidal was found dead in his home in Baghdad on 16 August, 2002, either having committed suicide or having been murdered by Iraqi intelligence who were interrogating him for links with Kuwaiti and Egyptian intelligence and even possible contacts with the CIA.

Was the Dorchester assassination attempt on Argov avoidable, and, if so, why didn't MI5 warn the ambassador in time? It was certainly true that MI5 and MI6 had been watching developments around Nidal's financial transactions and it was also clear that the Foreign Office did not appreciate Argov's criticisms of its attitude. That the two sets of events coincided may have been very convenient for someone. Better to ignore warnings and not alert the ambassador rather than blow the cover for an operation? Whatever the case, British hands were not as clean as they might have been, and British interests in the region, especially those involving arms might quietly be forgotten.

⋰⋱

A second assassination target (this time successfully murdered) was Roberto Calvi, the chairman of Banco Ambrosiano, the Vatican's own banking institution, who was found hanged from scaffolding under Blackfriars Bridge on the morning of 18 June 1982. He had been missing since 15 June after coming to London on 11 June. The City of London police saw the death as another rather unpleasant suicide, especially as it was realised that Calvi was deep into money laundering and illegal money transfers which could not be accounted for and which linked him directly to organised crime and secretive Italian freemasons. Suicide, it was suggested, might have been a quick way out of his problems. His organisation was also deep in unrepayable debt.

However, there were complications, and two coroner's inquests could not resolve the discrepancies in the evidence. Speculation was rife as to how Calvi had died and an accusatory finger was soon pointing towards Italian mobsters or even Argentinian assassins linked to the Junta. How did Calvi figure in British intelligence operations? The case proved a fantastical distraction during the last days of the Falklands War. Yet, there was one link which connected Calvi to the war which had begun on 2 April with the launch of the Argentinian Operation Rosario to 'recover' the Malvinas and which had caught GCHQ completely unawares as Argentinian plans had been conducted by word of mouth, and so bypassed electronic methods of surveillance.

The British task force sent to defend the Falklands had met with an accurate and deadly response in the form of French Exocet-39 missiles launched by air and by land. The Argentine army and air force only had five missiles between them and their personnel were untrained as to their effectiveness when launched from their Super Etendard fighters. The attacks were able to inflict terrible casualties and sink ships despite the fact that the Exocets did not always detonate; HMS *Sheffield* and the *Atlantic Conveyor* were both hit as was HMS *Glamorgan*. To find the remaining Exocets became a priority for the task force and Operation Mikado was launched to seek out and destroy the last missiles.

The operation was designed by Peter de la Billière, then director of the SAS. De la Billière had had a very distinguished career. He had fought in post-colonial wars in Aden and Borneo, won the Military Cross in 1959 and 1966 and gained a DSO in 1976. He was appointed director in 1978 and in that capacity oversaw the Iranian Embassy siege in 1979. The plan now was to land fifty-five SAS men directly on the airbase at Rio Grande and seek out and destroy the Exocets; the SAS men afterwards escaping to Chile. The British had no idea if the missiles were on the base nor how well defended it was.

Operation Plum Duff was to be a reconnaissance on the night of 17–18 May, but it proved to be a disaster as the Argentines had prior warning and good communications. A helicopter was ditched and set on fire during the preliminary operation. The SAS men from the reconnaissance were rounded up by the Chilean police. They would later be released, but the failure to locate the remaining Exocet missiles obviously left the task force vulnerable and potentially open to defeat. Whatever happened in operational terms, there were no more jet attacks as Argentine airfields were secretly attacked and disabled; the attack on HMS *Glamorgan* was from a land-launched Exocet. What the British could not be sure of was how many Exocets were left, although a count suggested that there remained one unaccounted for.

With more Exocets, the Argentinians might inflict unsustainable damage on the supporting fleet, and the Argentinians were actively seeking to purchase more. Roberto Calvi stood to recoup his lost millions and rectify his dubious accounts if he could supply Argentina with more Exocets, especially as the French had embargoed any exports of arms to Argentina, although they had a promissory note for delivery that had been suspended after the EEC had imposed sanctions on Argentina. The embargo did not cover Banco Ambrosiana, however, and Calvi was looking to sashay his way around the sanctions. Indeed, it might even be patriotic to help Britain's enemies as so many Italians lived in Argentina and Italy was supportive of the Argentine regime. How was Calvi, who had a complex plan to 'sell' the missiles to Peru, going to finalise his deal and get the missiles to Argentina? Calvi intended to cover his movements with the elaborate banking deals he had previously secured.

It had begun in 1977, when Calvi had created Ambrosiano Group Banco Commercial, which had its headquarters in Nicaragua. In 1979, when the Somoza family had all but lost control of Nicaragua, Calvi liquidated the bank and placed the remaining assets in Banco Ambrosiano Andino. Many of these assets were from the Argentine government. In January 1982, a further sum was placed in Banco Andino. However, the money from the Argentine government had evaporated through bad deals. The Argentinians were not aware of this as war became imminent. At the same time, Calvi was part of a huge banking consortium which included the Midland Bank in London, many of whose foreign transactions were allegedly run by or monitored by one or more of the British security agencies.[10]

Calvi's timing was disastrous. Indeed, he arrived in London with a briefcase full of the necessary paperwork on the very day the Argentinian government surrendered. He had flown into Heathrow with his bodyguard under the name Gian Roberto Calvino and, despite MI6 attention focused on his bank, came into the country unnoticed by MI5 or Special Branch. His intention was to transfer the money earned from General Galtieri, which was apparently on its way to secret French accounts. To complete the deal for more Exocets, Calvi had intended to make various payment transfers to secure the necessary funds, and that would involve the cooperation of the Midland Bank which may or may not have been under instructions to allow the transaction for intelligence purposes. At the same time, Calvi was embroiled in massive deception and fraud which could only be resolved by the successful deal that he contemplated. It looked like the last shake of the dice for both sides. Calvi actually arrived too late to make the necessary bank transfers.

If the British had indeed murdered him because of his closeness to a deal over more Exocets, it might therefore be convenient for the British simply to close ranks and deny wrongdoing by presenting the neutral evidence of the two inquests (July 1982 and June 1983). The spotlight could then fall on Calvi's more sinister and more interesting connections with the Vatican and organised crime and secret societies such as P2 and even our 'allies' in Chile:

> As for Chile, Stella Rimington [in MI5] was aware through GCHQ and other sources that General Pinochet was 'sleeping half the night in one bed and the other half in another'. The photographic evidence of Pinochet's duplicity was apparently shown to Thatcher on his visit … but she refused to accept the evidence.[11]

Giovanni Di Stephano, who originated this particular conspiracy story, concluded that:

> The decision by the British Security Services to murder Calvi was taken on 16 June 1982 and carried out on 17 June 1982. The British could, without any problem, delay or defray money transfers from a British bank in London, but could they risk that Calvi would send some secret message to another bank in another country or simply that he would escape Britain and find another way of

making payment for Argentina for military hardware that had been pre-ordered and paid for and Calvi was holding the money?[12]

Di Stephano's conclusion, essentially unsubstantiated except by his own logic, directly implicates both Thatcher and the heads of MI5 and Special Branch in Calvi's death because 'the order came from the highest level. Only a handful was chosen to know and the deed was carried out on 17 June 1982. Calvi was killed by "State Order".' Yet what is a 'state order'? Is the conspiracy simply the problematic confluence of coincidence and probability? Indeed, 'Once speculation starts on a subject like this, it soon mushrooms into an ever-increasing array of unsubstantiated allegations.'[13]

What is more likely to have happened in those last days is more interesting. MI6 was desperate to stop Calvi getting shipments of Exocets agreed and, as we have seen, Midland Bank had a large share of the consortium which Calvi headed. Yet, a high proportion of the boards in the City of London were filled with former MI6 officers. This network of former secret intelligence officers and the City of London's merchant banks created a unique synergy where 'the Friends' would rally to protect Britain's economic well-being. Moreover, many of MI6's most important retired officers were Catholic (unlike at GCHQ) and themselves members of the Knights of Malta, the most senior organisation for Catholic laity. (According to Peter Wright, MI5 was equally controlled by masonic connections.[14]) It would have been a pleasant meeting at some exclusive London club that could have reversed Calvi's fortunes and left him isolated and prey to Argentinian, Italian, Freemason or Mafia assassins.[15]

☙⁓Ꮆ⁓Ꭷ

The end of another actor in the saga, Robert Maxwell, would prove even more complicated and the explanations more convoluted. Like Calvi, Maxwell was proud of his humble background, distrustful of those around him who he thought sneered at his origins (and religion), highly secretive and conspiratorial and imbued with a megalomaniac ego. For both Calvi and Maxwell, the belief that they were as important as the institutions they dealt with would be their downfall.

Maxwell was a strange mixture of egotist and sentimentalist; he was a liar and absolutely sincere in equal measures. He was always a foreigner despite his Scottish-style name, which was taken, apparently, from a make of coffee. In fact, he was born Abraham Lieb Hoch on 10 June 1923 in Slatinsky Doly, a border town that is now in Ukraine. Called Lev at home, when he joined the British army, having been in the Free Czech forces, he changed his name to Du Maurier (after the cigarettes) and only later to Robert Maxwell. He won a military cross in the Second World War but never trusted the British establishment, which to him was snobbish, lazy and anti-Semitic. As an outsider, he liked Thatcher and agreed with her line over trade unions and her stand over the miners' strike. He would frequently telephone her to tell her what the headlines were to be the next day in the *Daily Mirror*, the paper being among his many assets. Yet he had no compunction in placing his allegiance to Israel above any that he might owe to Britain, first because he had lost his family in the Holocaust, and second, because his real allegiances were to the East, especially Bulgaria, East Germany and Russia.

Maxwell was no Russian agent, but he was a Russophile and a lover of Bulgaria in ways that were not to be expected from his adopted name. More importantly, he was obsessed with getting the remaining Jews out of Russia and to safety in Israel (he succeeded in helping 300,000 out), a wholly honourable passion which, nevertheless, went with a megalomaniac belief that he was a statesman of extraordinary brilliance, above national factions and border disputes. Through his connections, he had worked with international intelligence services, the governments and even mafiosi of many countries and seemed to think that he was essentially untouchable. Using this network he helped to market a highly secret piece of software called Enhanced Promis, a tracking device of real significance in the intelligence world. However, the form he took to market was knowingly compromised by an embedded Israeli Trojan Horse that allowed Israel to track its enemies (Osama Bin Laden even obtained an uncorrupted version later on). This made Maxwell powerful, rich and dangerous.

For many years, Maxwell had been well known to the intelligence services. He had worked in military intelligence and was a linguist. This might prove useful to other British intelligence agencies. Maxwell was approached by MI6, but did not join. Indeed, MI6 might have helped him get going, for it was the intelligence services which connived to help him after the war when he was able to finance a travel agency called Marshall's which was a front for secret MI6 travel to the Soviet Bloc.

At that time, the British needed agents in Russia and people the Russians might entertain in their scientific community. Maxwell might do the trick, and more money allowed him to merge the German Maxwell-Springer publishing company with Butterworth Press which itself sometimes acted as an MI6 front. In 1954, Maxwell travelled to Russia and put forward the idea of publishing translated Russian scientific papers which meant he then had access to Russia and its secrets, something he ruthlessly exploited and which was exploited by the East too as Maxwell had to produce a number of propaganda works which, however, sold few copies, if any. Thus Maxwell started on his life as an international go-between, the classic Jewish 'fixer'. Yet he was no patsy. On the contrary, he had built up connections and created a vast, complex and arcane business empire backed up by political connections. According to writers Thomas Gordon and Martin Dillon, 'Over the years there had also been reports that Maxwell had been approached by both MI5 and MI6 to pass on information he had gleaned from his visits to the Soviet Union. But, if that was true, he had never shared it with anyone.'[16]

Not surprisingly, Maxwell was always referred to as 'Maxwell the spy' by the KGB, but this smear could be bypassed as Maxwell frequently dealt with members of the Soviet Presidium.[17] This meant that no one trusted him. Mossad certainly did not, nor did the British, whose MI5 and MI6 kept closer watch on him as his career blossomed. MI6 had watched Maxwell for years as he dealt with senior members of the KGB, the East German Stasi and Mossad, while MI5 monitored his dealings with the financial markets in London. He was implicated in the 1986 Iran-Contra affair (Irangate), and money laundering too, all of which might have passed muster if he hadn't become caught up in intrigues around the 1991 failed coup to oust Gorbachev while at the same time his financial empire was under the deepest scrutiny.

Maxwell was wanted by just about everyone now. This might have led to one too many questions being asked. In 1998, Bogomil Bonev, the Bulgarian Minister of the Interior claimed that 'Money from the pension funds of the British millionaire Maxwell, the Central Committee of the Communist Party and secret services were used to fund [Maxwell's] Multi-Group.'[18]

What was certain was that Maxwell went on a trip on his yacht *Lady Ghislaine*, possibly to make a deal with Russia or others to buy his silence and save his companies. But late on 4 November or early on 5 November 1991, Maxwell mysteriously vanished from the deck in circumstances which appeared to rule out suicide. If the motive was murder, there were several possible explanations. To some there was no doubt. Stanislav Sorokin of the KGB suggested, 'I think it was a contract killing performed very professionally to look like suicide'.[19] The crew was new and led by a British captain who, it seemed, was not above suspicion. Mossad, too, could have silenced Maxwell before he revealed any secrets.

Thus, his last hours were sketched out in *The Assassination of Robert Maxwell* by Gordon Thomas and Martin Dillon in which they speculate that a Mossad assassination squad had boarded the ship:

> The two frogmen came on deck. One carried a waterproof pouch. From it he removed an already loaded syringe. Both men wore rubber-soled shoes. They reached Maxwell in a few strides. The [agent-assassin] with the syringe plunged the needle into Maxwell's neck, just behind his right ear. The substance was a lethal nerve agent. It had been developed at the Institute for Biological Research in Tel Aviv.[20]

Yet other possible scenarios emerged too. The *Financial Times* revealed on 15 June 1992 that it was the British who were keeping the closest watch on Maxwell and that the Joint Intelligence Committee (JIC) was privy to a secret report on his activities. Robert Robinson, a former administrator for the JIC, confirmed that GCHQ, which had been keeping tabs on Maxwell since 1989, had monitored Maxwell's faxes and telephone calls from his yacht and that Thatcher had been informed of his activities, as had representatives of the Bank of England. This would have shown up financial irregularities of enormous proportions, but also suggested perhaps that Maxwell was a lifetime 'communist' with allegiance only to Israel. He would therefore have been the perfect example of an enemy within who needed to be ditched as quickly as possible. It was certainly believed, after his death, that Maxwell had been a permanently paid informer for MI6.[21]

Was the murder a British affair after all? As long ago as the 1950s, Sir Dick White, head of MI6, had explicitly forbidden assassination plots (when were these ever authorised?),[22] and, during intelligence gathering before the first Gulf War, Thatcher herself had banned the use of torture in gathering intelligence.[23] Nevertheless, we know that the army in Northern Ireland and later in Iraq tortured prisoners and that the government was complicit in rendition procedures which allowed others to torture prisoners. We also know that the state was not beyond secret assassination committees and deadly SAS attacks in Ireland. There is nothing to suggest, therefore, that the British state was above murder, just that it might hide its involvement and deny the existence of its subcontractors.

An investigation into Maxwell's death by *Paris-Match* suggested these British connections had more to them than mere interest. Its journalist Jacques-Maris Bourget interviewed the yacht captain Gus Rankin after the incident and received this enigmatic response: "'[Maxwell's] well off where he is," he replied. Behind him, a chorus of sailors, hired in New York that spring, laughed.'[24]

What did it mean? Rankin, it emerged, had previously been involved with rogue elements from the CIA who had been gun-running to Libya. Nevertheless, the next revelation was of greater significance. Bourget claimed he had overheard a telephone conversation in English by one of the *Lady Ghislaine*'s crew. He noted the words carefully. ALthough the conversation wa sin French it ended in an odd Anglicism:

'*Nous avons accompli notre boulot. «L'autre» a un peu fait le con, mais tout est arrangé maintenant … N'ayez pas peur. Ici, c'est le bordel, comme en Afrique. Les Espagnols font en disent n'importe quoi. Ils sont un peu collants, mais pas vraiment efficaces. N'ayez crainte. Tous les feux sont au vert. Au revoir, sir.'* ('We've done our job. The "other one" pissed about a bit, but everything's fixed now … Don't worry. It's a shambles here, like in Africa. The Spaniards do and say any old thing. They stick to you a bit, but they're not really effective. Never fear. All lights are green. Goodbye, sir.')[25]

The caller is identified by Bourget as a member of the crew of the *Lady Ghislaine*. If this was true, the members of the crew were a subcontracted group of MI6 and CIA whose agents murdered Maxwell, in his cabin, faked the logbook and evidence and dumped him overboard. Ironically, the investigation into what might be retrieved by his creditors, especially the plundered pension fund, was headed by Sir John Cuckney, former MI5 officer, intimately involved in the arms-for-Iraq scandal and a one-time director of Midland Bank.

More bizarrely, on 5 November 1991, Arthur Scargill was telephoned anony-mously by someone who had knowledge of Maxwell's death. Scargill was told that he had forty-five minutes to do something about any miners' pension funds tied up in the Mirror Group. Scargill was convinced that the call was a genuine one from someone in authority in the intelligence services. The call might have been sympa-thetic, as Maxwell's line in the *Daily Mirror* had been consistently hostile to Scargill, and the disinformation spread by Maxwell had been at the centre of the Libyan and Russian money smears investigated by Gavin Lightman. Perhaps the fact that the NUM still had funds tied up in Maxwell's organisation was the real scandal. Whatever the case, forty-five minutes later the millionaire's death was publically announced.

19

THE FAT CONTROLLER

When Iraq finally went to war with Kuwait in 1990, that which had been left dead and forgotten rose to haunt the political establishment. The circumstances of Britain's relationship with Saddam Hussein's regime proved a major scandal which exposed the underhand world of military exports during Thatcher's last years in office.

Although most people think of Thatcher's economic revolution in terms of turning a civilian economy around, from the early 1980s onwards, the economic 'miracle' had become deeply militarised. Although trading with the Middle East and with the Saudis had begun before her premiership, it was in Thatcher's own time that opportunities in the Middle East, and by extension Malaysia and the Far East, widened and broadened to such an extent that a large section of the economy depended upon their success.

The government's involvement with the Middle East found an opportunity to blossom after September 1980 when Iraq invaded Khuzestan as a prelude to a full-scale war with Iran. This militarised economy was entirely based on the illegal transference of knowledge and hardware to Iraq and Iran, and, when the war came to an end on 20 August 1988, to Iraq only.

The story of arms for Iraq was complicated and obscure and had begun when the dreams of a Middle Eastern dictator coincided with the ambitions of a Canadian artillery expert: Saddam Hussein and Gerald Bull were made for each other. Born in Ontario, Bull had become fascinated with armaments during his wartime school years, and this grew into a lifelong interest in aeronautics and ballistics. While the West was developing intercontinental ballistic missiles, Bull became engrossed with artillery, especially artillery that might launch satellites or fire warheads that could be cheaply deployed to shoot down missiles. Rising through the military ranks, he eventually became, in effect, the foremost expert on the subject. Not only did Bull want to develop a supergun capable of launching missiles, he was also trying to develop a guided missile system as the ammunition.

Bull helped to develop a greater range for naval shells in the Vietnam War, but finally left the military and become an international arms dealer. He set up a company to work, theoretically, on his big idea of a gun with extreme trajectory. It was now that Bull entered the murky and dangerous waters of international arms trading and development, setting up a secure compound on the Canadian side of the American border so that he might exploit the laws concerning both countries' export bans. Bull was happy to deal with the highest payer, which might include Israel, to which there was no ban on exports, or South Africa, to which there was. Although the American government connived at South African exports, Bull fell foul of the rules and went to prison in 1980.

He felt he had been unfairly treated, and he drifted towards countries which had become pariahs like himself. Bull was always a contradiction. Oddly, for an arms dealer, he had never fired a gun and, although a rabid anti-communist, he happily worked with the Chinese. His disillusion with the West drew him eastwards and into murkier waters still. His work with South Africans, Chinese and Israelis earned him thick files in customs and intelligence agencies around the world.

Nevertheless, Bull seemed oblivious and pursued his dream of a satellite-launching big gun. In November 1987, he had his break when Baghdad invited him for a meeting. This had been the result of a long gestation. In September 1980, Iraqi forces had invaded Iran and the secret supply of weapons to Iran (which became the Irangate scandal) and to Saddam Hussein had begun. Saddam wanted to dominate the Middle East and to defeat Israel in order for Iraq to become the leading country in the region. The key was new and greater weaponry.

So far, Bull was uninvolved with whatever deals were going on at either side. Reagan's Operation Staunch was designed to strangle supplies to Iran and favour Iraq and in so doing promote Iraq's relationship with the West and secure the supply of oil. At this point, Amir Saadi, a diplomat working for Hussein Kamil, Saddam's son-in-law, contacted Bull. Bull must have known what he was getting into, especially as he had excellent relations with Israel, but his company needed the work, so he went to Iraq to begin work on a supergun to launch 'satellites'. Kamil had already infiltrated the British armaments industry by 1987 when he purchased the Technology Development Group (TDG), a company that pretended to be wholly British but was in fact run entirely by Iraqis. TDG then acquired Matrix Churchill which manufactured precision lathes. MI6 watched as things developed.

Bull started on Project Baghdad in 1988 with a relatively modest budget and high hopes. The expertise in tubular engineering would be supplied by Britain. The work was highly confidential, but the specifications for 'pipework' for the 'oil industry' were so evidently specific to a piece of artillery that the whole thing was an open secret. It was dangerous ground, as all the major Western countries had signed up to the Missile Technology Control Regime which banned exports of missiles and components to those countries considered potential threats. This included Iraq, but not Israel, which fuelled Bull's sense of personal injustice, especially as he actually liked the Iraqi regime he was working for and found Iraqis polite and friendly (which, interestingly, was quite unlike the British experience).

So, Bull went about distributing contracts for components in the UK by advertising for bids. He received a number, even though the companies were aware that this smelled fishy. In 1988 'pipes' were being produced by Walter Somers, a Birmingham company which usually produced tank barrels and was a Ministry of Defence supplier. Suspecting the specifications were incorrect, Walter Somers applied for an export licence and was told that one was not needed. People in authority were starting to turn a blind eye even though Sir Hall Miller, the local MP, had supplied the information on the true use of the pipes to intelligence and named Bull as the contractee. Another company, Sheffield Forgemasters, was also involved, subdividing the work between Forgemasters Engineering and River Don Castings. It too knew that it was a gun barrel being produced and it too was given the go-ahead by the Department for Trade and Industry. Another company, DESTEC, based in Lincoln provided experts but it wasn't until DARCHEM Composite Structures Ltd was asked to quote for the production of high-tech carbon fibre 'drill' equipment that it was blatantly obvious that what was being developed was missile-cone technology.

Iraq was still at war with Iran; the ban on exports specifically banned trade with the two warring factions, but no one cared. Trade was encouraged if it was discreet. Anyway, Bull had let the Americans, British and Israeli intelligence services in on the project in September 1988. They had even visited his offices for talks. This extraordinary situation could not last for ever, especially as Bull had begun development of his missile armament system. This could mean only one thing, and the cover story of a gun to shoot satellites into space would no longer be plausible. Bull's apartment was regularly broken into as a warning to back off. He wasn't sure of the agents and the warnings were not persuasive enough as he came nearer his goal. His phone had been tapped for years and his baggage regularly searched. This would now be the case with his suppliers too.

Filament winding control machines and associated technology was prohibited for export by the Missile Technology Control Regime, so Bull became the focus of even more attention from Mossad, the CIA, and MI6 which was reporting back to the Foreign Office. Indeed the Foreign Office knew but kept mum about the connections Bull had created, his plans and his British suppliers. It was watching Bull through an agent planted in his office – probably a female, probably a secretary; the person was referred to as 'the asset'. Meanwhile, and against American advice, Bull was left to carry on and was even encouraged in his plans.

Like many who work at the very edge of the legitimate, Gerald Bull was someone whose realisation of his mortality came too late. The last clue was an odd long black hair left on his bed, a peculiarly uncanny warning. On 9 April 1990, Bull returned as usual to his apartment. He was shot at close range with five bullets. Two days later, a shipment of boxes containing barrel components were seized at Teeside docks. British customs had acted on advice from MI6 fed to them by Mossad.

Bull was probably assassinated by Mossad agents who might have informed the CIA in advance. Bull was too valuable to British interests, but when his fate had been sealed by others MI6 may well have turned a blind eye to a situation it was happy to leave to the Israelis. There was, however, blood on everyone's hands. Both intelligence services might have had other reasons to be watching Bull. On 14 December 1993, Sir Nicholas Bonsor MP had replied to an enquiry from Gerald James (one of the willing 'victims' in the secret trade in arms) regarding Bull's involvement in clandestine operations in Northern Ireland. Neither James nor Bonsor was able to substantiate the rumour.

The complexity of British arms dealings during the 1980s is partially due to ambivalence and a large dose of ministerial cynicism as to who received military aid once money started to flow. It was soon acknowledged that arms deals might plug the deficit lost in other trading. During 1981, Margaret Thatcher began a policy of multimillion-pound government-to-government deals, many of them brokered by her son Mark. The first of these was with Oman to build a 'university' but actually secretly to build missile silos.

Some months later, an old fireworks company called Astra, which had dealt in explosives, acquired Gerald James as its chairman and began its rise up the arms trade through initial help from the British Ambassador to the United States. By 1983, Astra was being mentored by the British Embassy in Washington although many of the deals being brokered contravened British guidelines and US Congressional limitations on sales to Iran and Iraq. In the same year, James was advised by the British Embassy to move his London offices and, encouraged by the ambassador in Washington, James had indeed moved the Head Office of Astra Holdings Limited to offices above Mappin and Webb in Regent Street, London. Here he found himself opposite the offices of no less than Brian Crozier and Robert Moss.

Crozier and Moss had been bankrolled in the early 1980s by Sir James Goldsmith and the Goldsmith Foundation to the tune of many hundreds of thousands of pounds.[1] Crozier seems to have continued his relationship with intelligence, or at least right-wing factions within intelligence circles. During 1990, it seems that Crozier was still up to his right-wing meddling, as he would help to orchestrate the attempt to frame Arthur Scargill in relation to the monies allegedly received from Libya and Russia. Indeed, Crozier had been in touch with George Miller, editor of the *Soviet London Review*. This was a channel for CIA money and linked with the People's Labour Alliance which worked inside and outside the Soviet Union to undermine its government. In this regard, Crozier had helped manipulate information coming out of the People's Labour Alliance which allegedly worked on behalf of the Union of Democratic Miners led by Uri Butchenko, but had, in fact, a background of Nazi collaboration which even MI6 thought too dangerous to be involved with.[2] Crozier, it seemed, was still in the thick of it, even if officially denied access to the Prime Minister following the Shield fiasco in the 1970s.

It was in the mid 1980s that the British relationship with Chile, which had been so useful during the Falklands War, became central to military diplomacy and under-the-counter trading. The contacts with Chile were a secret guarded for many years and help to explain Thatcher's close friendship with General Pinochet. Ignoring Chile's appalling record on human rights, the British government began to encourage arrangements for British arms sales to be filtered through the arms dealer Carlos Cardoen as if they were exports to the Chilean regime. They were, in fact, exports to Iraq. It was not a good idea to investigate too closely.

The journalist Jonathan Moyles did just that in 1990, and was found dead in his hotel room in Santiago after an interview with Cardoen. Moyles's body was discovered stuffed into a 5ft wardrobe hanging by a shirt from a clothes rail. His head had been covered with a pillowcase and he was wearing two pairs of underpants and covered in a towel and polythene bag. The newspapers and others put forward a theory, which had presumably originated with British intelligence, that Moyles had died in some sort of weird self-inflicted sexual activity. In point of fact, evidence suggests that such arrangements might have been there to stem the flow of bodily fluids, thereby delaying discovery.[3]

The apparently illegal thread of arms sales to Iraq had started to unravel after Geoffrey Howe had drawn up guidelines in 1984 to limit the sale of lethal weapons to both Iran and Iraq during the war, although these guidelines were so weak as to prove useless, especially when military components could be shipped out under the guise of non-military or agricultural usage. This trade became so profitable that the government then brokered another partially secret deal called the 'Jordan defence package', again using Jordan as a secret conduit to Iraq. By October 1985, the situation had deteriorated so badly in the Middle East that the secret ministerial guidelines that the government had created in 1984 had finally to be publicly announced to Parliament.

None of this stopped the flow of arms to Iraq and, in 1986, Alan Clark, the minister responsible in the Department of Trade and Industry visited Baghdad to promote British industry. In the same year, Thatcher signed the first part of the Al-Yamamah arms deal with Saudi Arabia worth £60 billion, a huge improvement in business relationships since those prior to Helen Smith's death. Saudi Arabia too was to act again as a partial conduit into Iraq.

In October 1986, Stephan Kock joined Astra as a non-executive director on the recommendation of Midland Bank's secret defence department, the Midland International Trades Services, a department partially run by MI6. At almost the same time, Mark Gutteridge, export manager for Matrix Churchill, was recruited by MI5 as an intelligence source for information regarding exports to Iraq. In the following year, Iraqis bought into both Astra and Matrix Churchill while the front was kept up that these were both entirely British companies. Meanwhile, Clark at the DTI was authorising larger and larger credits for Iraq. Of the £200 million credits put aside in shares, 200,000 were purchased by Clark in the name of his mistress, Valerie Harkess.

By 1987, trade with Iran had ceased and the Iranians were preparing to withdraw from the British scene. In 1988, Thatcher signed the second part of the Al-Yamamah deal, and Gerald Bull travelled to Baghdad to finalise arrangements for the supergun. Again, Clark was advising members of the Machine Tools Technology Association to emphasise the peaceful nature of what was being exported even though, among those in the know, it was clear that all exports were essentially military ones being sent to a war zone. On 22 June 1988, Westland Helicopters contacted Astra to put in a bid to add weapons to the helicopters being exported to Saudi Arabia. These helicopters were actually bound for Iraq. At roughly the same time, Forgemasters of Sheffield was discussing export licences for parts of the supergun.

Part of this complex set of undercover deals and money laundering processes was the supply of substances which Iraq could use for poison gas purposes. On 19 July 1988, the Iraqi air force bombed Kurdish villages using hydrogen cyanide and mustard gas, components for which had been supplied with government knowledge by British manufacturers. It was certainly the case that Britain exported sufficient quantities of chemicals to produce Iraq's poison gas industry: hydrogen cyanide, tabun, sarin and sulphuric mustard gas were manufactured at the Muthanna gasworks in Bagdhad. Nash Engineering of Cheshire sent Saddam Hussein's war machine a chlorine compressor for a water purification plant in 1986, but the order had more sinister applications: sodium sulphide was sent in 1988 before the export of such chemicals was banned. By this time, Britain had acted as an entrepôt for other countries to avoid the ban on noxious substances. Components of Saddam's weapons of mass destruction were first manufactured and exported by Britain with the full knowledge of the Department of Trade and Industry.[4]

While poison gas components, weapon and radar systems and supergun tubes were being supplied, they might have been defended as part of our anti-Soviet crusade. Nevertheless, once the Iraq-Iran War had finished on 20th August 1988, there was no need to continue the trade. Indeed the Conservative government then looked around for other areas of the world to sell arms to and soon discovered that Malaysia would be a profitable target. A very large aid packet to build a hydroelectric dam at Pergau was again used to hide a massive arms deal.

In 1989, William Waldegrave at the Foreign and Commonwealth Office, Alan Clark at the DTI and Lord Trefgarne at the Ministry of Defence were still approving licences for Matrix Churchill to export to Iraq. By now, the web of companies, deals and individuals was so complex that it was even beyond the understanding of the various chairmen of the businesses subcontracting for the work. Despite the execution of the *Observer* journalist Farzad Bazoft by the Iraqi government as a spy after he had stumbled across Matrix Churchill machinery at the Al Qa'qaa site, the British government merely reprimanded the Iraqis and continued with their weapons transactions. This increased in intensity after a trade visit to Baghdad in 1989.

Trade activity came to a head on 28 March 1990, when forty 'nuclear' capacitors being shipped from the United States by a company called Euromac were seized at Heathrow Airport. Within a few days, defence journalist Jonathan Moyles had been assassinated in Santiago and Gerald Bull had been assassinated in Brussels.

By April 1990, Britain was exporting £450 million of military hardware to Iraq, which was second only to Saudi Arabia in military importation. Iraq's ill-timed invasion of Kuwait, planned for 2 August 1990, was unknown to the security community until April at the earliest that same year – a delay in decision-making of four vital months in which everyone in power turned a blind eye as the profits rolled in. The invasion was the end of the road, and toleration and encouragement turned to sour disapproval. Thus, by 2 August 1990, Iraq had reneged on her debts to Britain and America. Even while the invasion continued, forty-two wagons carrying shells and anti-tank missiles were being shipped via the Hull docks to Jordan en route to Iraq. The growing crisis threatened to sweep the Conservative Party into history and it was certainly this rather than simple inertia that finally led to a tearful Thatcher resigning in 1990.

❧

The whole arms-for-Iraq affair was riddled with spies and intelligence agents. In Matrix Churchill alone, Paul Henderson, the managing director, and Mark Gutteridge, the export manager, were working for MI6 and MI5. Gutteridge, who had worked for MI6 before, was re-employed in 1986 as an MI5 agent being run by 'Michael Ford'. Paul Henderson was working with a man called 'Balsam' from MI6. Both might have had contact with an MI5 handler called by them the Fat Controller and there appears to have been another MI5 agent involved who called himself Ian Eacott.

Why were MI6 and MI5 so interested in the activities of Matrix Churchill? Originally, there certainly had been the desire to learn as much as possible about Soviet military supplies in the region. The attempt by MI6 to find out as much as possible about Sovbloc activities had rapidly wound down with the end of the Cold War. This left MI6 without a clear rationale, so, searching for things on which to gather intelligence, they had increasingly turned to watching activities in the Middle East. The easiest method to do this was simply to infiltrate Matrix Churchill which was entirely Iraqi owned, but British managed. When members of the company were arrested for exporting prohibited machinery, it was soon clear that the intelligence operation was riddled with holes and that the agencies involved felt quite free to contradict elected ministers. For instance, on 13 July 1992, the Cabinet Office 'Gun Group' had circulated a paper which stated, 'Ministers have allowed the supply of some Matrix Churchill machine tools ... for ad hoc reasons of an intelligence nature.'[5] This was corrected by MI6 who wished it to be known that intelligence sources never influenced ministers. 'Our understanding of the situation,' the MI6 reply to the document stated, 'is somewhat different.'[6]

The Secret Intelligence Service may well have been aware that the decision to allow exports with a military application to continue had been taken at a secret Foreign Office meeting on 19 July 1990.[7] Worse still was the fact that both Henderson and Gutteridge would be able to name their handlers and provide detailed information on MI6 penetration if they were ever brought to court.

Nevertheless, Henderson, and his colleagues Trevor Abraham and Peter Allen, were formerly charged by Customs on 17 February 1991 with breaking export regulations. Consequently, when they did appear at the Old Bailey on 12 October 1992, their defence was able to show, despite the plethora of Public Interest Immunity Notices taken out by ministers such as Malcolm Rifkind and Michael Heseltine and the fact that most of the documents released for the defence case were blacked out and the fact that the various anonymous MI6 and MI5 handlers appeared often 'in camera' and behind screens, that the government had lied. It soon emerged that the firm had been advised by the government and that at least one director was working directly with MI6. The trial collapsed in 1992, when Alan Clark admitted under oath that he had been 'economical with the *actualité*'.[8]

Clark, like his two colleagues, was a strange mixture of aristocrat and sharpster. The son of Sir Kenneth Clark the art historian, Clark junior had inherited Saltwood Castle where he would greet guests with his dog Eva Braun and talk about dealing with the officials of 'bongo bongo land'. Although Clark junior was also a serious historian who did not take the authority of the establishment at face value, he came to exemplify the mixture of cocksure elite brashness and low business ethics which characterised much of Thatcherite entrepreneurialism after its initial flush. His brash self-confidence was exemplified by his dismissive interpretation of Geoffrey Howe's guidelines intended to stop the flow of military equipment. Clark simply interpreted them as irrelevant.

Others close to government also ignored guidelines and were placed in positions of authority precisely to see that the guidelines were ignored with impunity. Stephan Kock joins the complex thread of military transactions as a shadow and exits as a shade. His real name is not known for sure and rumours have circulated since he first made news that he originated from the same town as Robert Maxwell. With apparent close connections both to Thatcher and to the intelligence services, Kock was a mystery in the 1980s and has remained so thereafter. He first came to public notice when he was suggested as a partner for Gerald James in Astra Holdings. He had originally been put forward by a man called Roger Unwin who apparently knew him through Midland Bank, which was now offering Astra very large loans amounting to many millions against their business.

Kock may very well have had been the head of Group 13, which apparently worked with the Foreign Office and conducted clandestine operations using personnel from the SAS as well as private security companies. He certainly seemed to be very well placed and to have sufficient contacts in the CIA, MI6 and MI5 as well as the banking community to be able to negotiate himself in and out of public view whenever he wished. Kock certainly worked with the Ministry of Defence and had strong connections with the SAS, admitting on 28th January 1994, when interviewed by *Channel 4 News*, that he had been involved in some way with Thatcher's Malaysian dam project.

Kock had emerged in the 1970s from the peculiar triangulation of white Rhodesian and apartheid South African politics. He certainly considered that 'Africa [was his] parish'.[9] Apparently involved with the Rhodesian air force, he seems to have seen service in the C Squadron of the SAS made up of the many Rhodesian volunteers fighting communists in Malaysia. As he had previously served as a political secretary to the Rhodesian Prime Minister Sir Edgar Whitehead, it might have been that he was an intelligence liaison officer, rather than an active SAS member. Gerald James claims that Kock gained his place on Astra's board in order to effect a coup which would allow the government more control of one of the few large independent arms manufacturers. Whatever Kock's mysterious background and activities, he seems also to have been a braggart, a drunk and prone to violence, shooting at people and threatening James.

Kock, however, seems merely to have been the creature of Sir John Cuckney, who had created the Special Defence Unit at Midland Bank and who had strong connections both to the Joint Intelligence Committee and to the Cabinet, having been in MI5 for ten years. Sir John's activities seem to have been central to the entire 'arms for Iraq' conspiracy. Cuckney had been Chairman of International Military Services between 1974 and 1975 and a director of Midland Bank, the commercial funder of the British arms trade, between 1978 and 1988. He was Chairman of Westland when the Al-Yamamah contracts were signed, having been at Lazards merchant bank previously. When at Westland, he held meetings at Lazards. He was also Deputy Chairman of the TI Group when it sold Matrix Churchill in 1987 to the Iraqis, and he was Chairman of 3i, which was Astra's main institutional shareholder. Thus Sir John Cuckney linked all the companies involved in the controversy.[10]

20

ZEUS AND THE ANGLIAN SATANIC CHURCH

Regardless of new developments in warfare, or who might buy them, nuclear war still seemed central to British government policy for much of the 1980s, and the civilian development of nuclear power was intimately tied into its military value; plants were set up as much to produce military by-products such as uranium or plutonium for bombs as they were for electricity. The first reactor was at Calder Hall in Cumbria. It was for civilian development, but was based on a military model designed to produce plutonium. Plutonium production was seen as useful long before thoughts of cheap electricity and heating for homes. The nuclear power industry was therefore closely tied to martial aims and, as such, was also considered officially secret by government and vital to British prestige. Its facilities were closely guarded and its technology deliberately made to appear magical to the public and Parliament alike. This meant a small army of technical experts had a stranglehold on Britain's energy resources which were hemmed in by official red tape and official silence.

Two reports from the Second World War started things off and both had come from the secret MAUD (Military Application of Uranium Detonation) committee. One was *On the Use of Uranium for a Bomb* and the other was *On the Use of Uranium as a Source of Power.* The decision to go nuclear was top secret too. Only Churchill, his adviser Lord Cherwell and the chiefs of staff were in on the decision. The Cabinet was left uninformed and the Deputy Prime Minister kept in the dark. Britain exploded its first bomb on 3 October 1952 and the civilian wheels began to turn in 1955 when the government ordered the first peacetime nuclear power stations. This too was a secretive affair. Then, in 1957, the government ordered three times as many reactors, drunk on the fact that they were based on British technological know-how; the future would be created by British science and nuclear energy looked like British science fiction. This gave the scientists immense power, as they appeared to be the guardians of the future.

The first debate on nuclear issues was not until February 1961, by which time hundreds of millions of pounds had already been spent without any parliamentary overview and with much of it wasted on failed projects:

The A[tomic] E[nergy] A[gency] were ... a uniquely powerful organization. They were given control over an enormous growing industry, charged with the production, use and disposal of all nuclear power and radioactive substances. Research and training were also their responsibility, as was experimental work to make better nuclear assemblies for nuclear weapons. They were also charged with advising the Government on health and safety, and on international atomic energy matters. And in addition, the new body was given the right to employ special constables, a concession granted to very few organizations outside the Crown. The only limitation was that they would not actually develop or product nuclear weapons 'except in accordance with arrangements made with the Ministry of Supply'. This apart ... here was a type of organization without precedent.[1]

This led MP Maurice Edelman to recognise that UKAEA had 'to a great extent been removed from public scrutiny'.[2] The nuclear industry was, in effect, a law unto itself with its own self-contained organisational structure, its own budget and even its very own police force.

By 1983 to 84, the organisation was complex and consisted of the Central Electricity Generating Board (later known as Powergen), the AEA and British Nuclear Fuels, with the responsibility for security resting with the UKAEA Constabulary which policed 'the UKAEA and British Nuclear Fuel establishments in the United Kingdom'.[3] Interestingly, these bodies were fed by a series of other organisations which were often at odds with each other during the period and especially during the controversial Sizewell B Inquiry. Nevertheless, taken together, they represented the most powerful set of institutions in Britain and were monitored as such.

The UKAEA police could act independently of other police forces, Special Branch and MI5, but were supposed to liaise closely with them. It was partly their duty to monitor dissent, a job apparently sometimes subcontracted to private investigation agencies. Gary Murray, a private investigator who had worked closely with Britain's intelligence agencies and had turned from gamekeeper to poacher, concluded that 'without doubt the nuclear industry [was] one of the most powerful and dangerous organisations in the world'.[4]

Information on these very secretive bodies remained restricted until the 1980s, and millions of pounds were spent on projects whose budgets hadn't been approved by Parliament, the electorate or even the minister in charge. Thus, the history of nuclear fuel had been shrouded in mystery, its facilities kept as one of the most important secrets of the post-war period, its experimental facilities and prognostications not made public, its personnel completely protected by a wall of obfuscation that none could penetrate. The rationale for all this money and development was simple – the elimination of coal as a fuel for power stations which would vanish as nuclear energy became cheaper and cheaper. Thus the belief that a coal shortage would cripple industry, a problem which had worried all governments from the time of Attlee, would be answered by a breakthrough in clean energy produced from nuclear power stations. The building programme, backed by the independent development of British nuclear science, would also provide the solution to the problem of oil shortages, something which worried politicians after Suez in 1956 and the Arab-Israeli war of 1973.

Throughout the 1960s and 1970s, the Coal Board had to continuously fight a rearguard action to protect the coalfields. In the 1950s and again in the 1960s, scientists predicted that electricity produced from nuclear power would only be as competitive as coal by the 1980s. This was still unproven in 1984 when the coal unions were finally challenged and defeated, leading to victory for the nuclear lobby. The problem was that nuclear energy was never to become as cheap as coal or oil energy and that no one could agree on the correct prognosis for British fuel consumption. There were too many official bodies fighting their corner for resources.

If the men in white coats were to replace miners then an economic argument would have to be made out. It never was. Neither were the arguments relating to safety resolved, nor the costs finalised, nor the best form of nuclear plant concluded. The industry up to and throughout the 1980s was in turmoil, with millions pledged and lost on long-term projects whose predictions for completion within time limits (often of twenty years from contract) were never as expected.

More significantly, the plans for new reactors were, until the 1980s, always couched in economic terms as if there were no social costs. Yet the social impact of nuclear energy would dominate the discussions and protests of the 1980s. Throughout the 1950s and right up until the late 1970s, the public remained euphoric about this new clean source of energy. There were no public debates and no protests for the industry to combat. This changed with two factors. The first was the relatively worrying safety record of British reactors and the decision to install American reactors despite near disaster at Three Mile Island; the second was the problem of 'disposing' of nuclear waste products. The impetus for protest again came from America, but was enthusiastically taken up in Britain where, for the first time, ordinary voices were demanding to be heard. Protest would pose a massive security risk, or so the authorities thought, and protesters became the targets of the security services, particularly Special Branch.

Special Branch was not the only one operating clandestine investigators. The nuclear industry was especially nervous and used private investigation companies to ferret out opposition secrets and infiltrate protest groups. One such, employed during the hearings at the Sizewell B Inquiry (which ran for 340 days), was Zeus Security Consultants based in Bury St Edmonds, Suffolk. It was run by a former military intelligence officer, Peter Hamilton, a man who had warned previously against 'domestic subversion' from the unions and who had written *The Handbook of Security*. In his early days, he had spied for the Economic League, creating registers of blacklisted workers. Now Zeus used local knowledge and set up phony protest groups in an entrapment operation.

Hamilton was a member of the Institute of Professional Investigators and was someone who claimed to have been used by 'all kinds [up] to government'.[5] Hamilton was hired in January 1983 as the hearings into Sizewell B began. However, he subcontracted the work to Contingency Services based in Colchester and run by Victor Norris (who also went under the name of Adrian Hampson). The remit was 'to ascertain identities of principal objectors at the Sizewell atomic station [inquiry] at Snape Maltings. If possible, obtain list of objectors, their connections with media, political leanings, etc.'[6]

Norris was, on the face of it, a peculiar choice for such delicate work. He was exposed by Paul Foot in the *Mirror* and by Gerry Gable investigating for *Searchlight*, both as a Satanist who had founded the Anglian Satanic Church and a Nazi, founder of the 5000 Group and the Salvo Society. He also ran AH Services named after Adolf Hitler. In 1969, he had been sent to prison for six years for child offences. Nonetheless, he landed the job of keeping an eye on proceedings and he proved his worth to his unnamed client. He correctly identified the main five pressure groups and names to watch and then went on to identify other groups and individuals. He also claimed that Friends of the Earth had been infiltrated by the 'extreme left' and suggested one objector was a professional nuisance. It was all accurate, but hardly revelatory. His persistence was at least valuable enough to keep his retainer and also to remain ignored by Special Branch, which denied the existence of private investigators.

Norris might have been an obnoxious individual, but he might have been sufficiently dextrous and unquestioning to carry out work that could be denied by the security services. The intelligence services might also prefer a convicted criminal as an operative as he would be easy to discredit if things went wrong. Norris claimed he was a specialist in 'delicate work' who employed 'good imitation lefties', but, more revealingly if true, he also claimed that he undertook work, 'that the Home Office don't want their own people [MI5 and Special Branch] to do'. All these hints were revealed in an *Observer* article published on 27 January 1985. This was virtually the first suggestion anywhere that MI5 might have been using intermediaries for the sort of dirty work it had to avoid undertaking itself.

Norris was able to obtain information on the following groups and individuals: Greenpeace; Friends of the Earth; CND; the Stop Sizewell B Association; the Anti-Nuclear Campaign; the Anti-Nuclear Campaign, Sheffield; the Cornish Anti-Nuclear Alliance; the Welsh Anti-Nuclear Alliance; the East Anglian Alliance; the Town and Country Planning Association; the Council for the Protection of Rural England; the East Anglia Trade Union Campaign; the Ecology Party; the European Group for Ecological Action; the NUM; the Socialist Environmental Resources Association; and the Suffolk Preservation Society. He also watched individuals. The surveillance might have been immoral, but, amazingly, although these individuals were simply acting within their democratic rights, it was not illegal. Taps and perhaps other surveillance were carried out on Mr P. Medhurst, Mr G. Searle, and Mr P. Bunyard, the Chief Executive of South

Yorkshire County Council; Mrs M. Sierakowski of the Ipswich Constituency Labour party; Mrs I.M. Webb of Ipswich and District Friends of the Earth; Mr M. Blackmore of the Socialist Environmental Resources Association; Mr R. Jarrett of the Campaign for Nuclear Disarmament; Mr R.R. Grey of Wansbeck District Council; Mr L. Daly of the National Union of Mineworkers; Mr D. Somervell of SCRAM; Mr C. Sweet of the Centre for Energy Studies, South Bank Polytechnic; Mr M. Barnes of the Electricity Consumers Council; Professor J.W. Jeffery of the Department of Crystallography, Birkbeck College; Mr D. Lowry of the Energy Research Group, Open University; Mr G. Stoner, an individual objector; Mr D. Hall of the Town and Country Planning Association; Mr G. Hancock of Portskewett Action Group; Mr J. Popham of the Suffolk Preservation Society; Mrs K. Miller of the Scottish Conservation Society; Mr C. Conroy of Friends of the Earth; Mr R. Grove-White of the Council for the Protection of Rural England; Mr H. Richards, a Welsh Anti-Nuclear Alliance representative; Mr G. Pritchard, a Cornish Anti-Nuclear Alliance representative; Mr Birch of the National Union of Public Employees and Mr J.E. Lodge of Northumberland County Council, among others, some of whom remain unidentified.[7]

As the list was being compiled, there was, however, a strange twist which would have repercussions. This was the death of a man called Barrie Peachman. Peachman was an intermediary between Hamilton and Norris and ran his own agency called the Sapphire Investigations Bureau in Acle, Norfolk. Peachman filtered Norris's information to Hamilton, suggesting it was Norris who carried out the actual surveillance operations. Soon afterwards, Peachman seems to have ceased acting as filter, and Norris was now working alone and reporting to Hamilton. Just after handing the contract from Hamilton over to Norris on 17 April 1984, Peachman shot himself, supposedly over his mistress and colleague Shirley Smith, but possibly over something more sinister as, before he died, he confided his fear that, 'he was against the wall' and that 'people were out to get him'.[8]

Zeus used parallel investigations to secure its information and double-check its validity. Hamilton also used David Coughlan, an electronics expert in tapping and surveillance. Coughlan was, by his own admission, well versed in working for government agencies. Coughlan had originally been trained by the SAS electronics unit and carried out illegal operations during 1983 against 'all kinds of people' who opposed the nuclear industry. His equipment had been supplied by Zeus but obtained, according to Coughlan, from other sources. The implication was again that MI5 was somehow involved either with or independently of the interested parties in the nuclear industry and that the assumption that one or more nuclear lobby agencies had commissioned Zeus might not have been the whole picture. In 1987, long after the operation to secure a positive result at Sizewell, Coughlan found himself on the wrong side of the law when he went to prison for tapping the telephone of Gerard Hoareau, the leader of the Seychelles resistance group who was assassinated in 1985. Such private agencies operated in very murky waters.

The surveillance operation was apparently a huge success and if somebody had to suffer it was better that Peachman was eliminated rather than Norris, who was a ruthless and efficient operator, or Hamilton, who ran the overall strategy and had connections all the way to Thatcher. Unlike the shady criminal types contracted by Hamilton, those working directly with him had immaculate pedigrees. There was a major general and the prominent banker Sir Dallas Bernard, named as the managing director of Peter Hamilton Security Consultants Ltd. Sir Dallas in turn, was linked to Robert Armstrong, godfather to Sir Dallas's daughter, one-time head of the Civil Service and the cabinet secretary privy to the discussions of the Joint Intelligence Committee. Bernard and Armstrong were also linked by their charity work. Thus the alliance of banking, industrial management, security and Whitehall was sealed.

The rewards came relatively quickly for some of Thatcher's allies. In 1988, Lord Chalfont was closely connected to both Zeus Consultants (as chairman or possibly 'general consultant') and Peter Hamilton Security Consultants. Yet he was appointed deputy chairman of the Independent Broadcasting Authority. Chalfont was also implicated in nuclear-waste-dumping activities, again linked to Hamilton.

Paddy Ashdown, himself a former member of the Special Boat Service, smelled a rat and wrote to the Prime Minister on 25 January 1989. Here he laid out a case against Chalfont's appointment, and accused Thatcher of wilful misjudgement and possible knowing collusion:

> Lord Chalfont has since joined a number of other directors of Zeus as a director of Securipol Limited, incorporated on 16 January 1986. Securipol shares a registered office and directors with Ensec Limited whose purpose is the undersea dumping of nuclear waste. Some prominent Conservatives are Directors of Ensec. The objects of Securipol, as stated in the Articles of Association, are almost identical to those of Zeus …
>
> Did you know of Lord Chalfont's involvement in Zeus Security Consultants and Securipol when he was appointed to the Independent Broadcasting Authority? If not, will you now reconsider this appointment?
> If you did know of Lord Chalfont's past and present connections, do you consider that it is appropriate for someone with these long standing and close links to be charged, as Deputy Chairman of the IBA, with the task of effectively mediating between commercial broadcasters and the Government of the day?
> I ask you especially to bear in mind conflicts which could involve on the one hand national or citizen security and on the other the freedom of broadcasting.
> Let me be clear. It is your judgement I am questioning in this affair.[9]

The main focus of the new public awareness of nuclear fuel was on aspects of safety. Yet the enormity of the government's original commitment to nuclear energy and its problems was not going to sink into public consciousness for another two decades despite all sorts of safety issues, many of which, however, were hushed up. The problems went back to the beginning of development. In 1955, there was a decision to build six military reactors to produce plutonium. On 7 October 1957, there was an uncontrollable fire at Windscale near Calder Hall. The fire dramatically highlighted the terrible danger of civilian nuclear energy, as the procedure for dousing the inferno, which had engulfed 150 fuel channels that became molten metal, had not been tried before. The use of carbon dioxide to quell the flames worked – there was no explosion at the plant, but it had been a close-run thing. The local paper, the *Whitehaven News*, revealed that there had been 'no real warning ... to the public ... despite the presence of radioactive dust'.[10] The Milk Marketing Board put an interdict on milk from an area of 500 square-miles around the plant.

Then, on 26 September 1973, alarms began ringing at Windscale again. Gas had contaminated the plant and thirty-five workers were affected by radiation. A report blamed inadequate monitoring. There were further leaks into the River Calder in May 1975 and these took some months to stop. Locals reported high levels of cancer in the area and alleged that leukaemia levels were ten times higher than the national average. Plutonium had also been reported to be in houses in Cumbria and as far away as Scotland. An inquiry was held in 1977 at which two Special Branch officers were in permanent attendance to watch for alleged troublemakers.

In October 1977, Hunterston B near Glasgow leaked contaminated seawater into the Clyde, but the worst disaster so far came in America on 28 March 1978 with a partial meltdown at Three Mile Island in Pennsylvania. It opened up a debate in the UK over nuclear energy that could not be postponed or silenced. Then, even as the government contemplated an American-designed reactor at Sizewell in Suffolk, another disaster hit Windscale (now called Sellafield). There had been further intermittent leaks from the plant since 1981, but, in the autumn of 1983, around 650m^3 of active nuclear waste was mistakenly dumped in the Irish Sea. Greenpeace divers were contaminated and waste was washing ashore. The Irish Sea was renamed the Plutonium Sea.[11] Reports on the incident put nuclear safety in people's minds and alerted them to the uncomfortable fact the peaceful civilian nuclear energy was just as dangerous as the military variety.

Since the Windscale Inquiry in 1977, there had been undiminished attention on nuclear energy and its economic and social costs. Opposition was becoming vociferous too. The inquiry into Sizewell B, which began sitting in January 1983, followed the appointment of Sir Frank Layfield to head the proceedings on 22 July 1981. The Sizewell B decision would be decisive for the British nuclear industry. For the first time, the government was actively pursuing an American-built Pressurised Water Reactor rather than a British design. The effect would be the end of an independent British atomic development programme. There was also the long-standing relationship between reactors and nuclear warfare development. Sizewell was no exception. Not only might it be useful in the future to sell plutonium to Pakistan, South Africa,

South Korea or Iran, but the US capacity to make plutonium was not sufficient and might need augmenting from Britain.

Tony Benn, who had been Energy Secretary in 1975 and had spent much time on nuclear issues and was often kept in the dark about developments, attended the inquiry and was forthright about the implications. 'In plain language,' he told Frank Layfield, 'every British nuclear power station [had] become a nuclear bomb factory for the USA.'[12] This was not mere bravado. The reactor at Chapelcross in Scotland produced tritium, the 'key explosive' in the hydrogen bomb.[13] Elsewhere, the radiochemical production arm of the Atomic Weapons Research Establishment, which researched the medical uses of radioisotopes, was sold off in 1982 to be reinvented as Amersham International, the very first of the Thatcher government's many privatisations.

The fear of nuclear meltdown also continued to be a question of doubt, something apparently unresolved in the minds of many experts who gave evidence. For instance, the Nuclear Installations Inspectorate, in charge of monitoring safety, noted that the American design had faults, but was happy to issue the required certificate of safety on the proviso that safety would be improved 'once construction had started'. It was hardly reassuring, especially as twenty-seven faults were listed.[14] There was even discussion of plans to evacuate London in the case of a major disaster during fuel transportation.

The Sizewell inquiry would prove one of the longest and costliest in English history, with many objections now being put by 'lay' organisations and unaffiliated individuals opposed to the nuclear industry in terms of its safety record. For the most part, objections were led by the experts at Friends of the Earth and others from the Greater London Council, the National Coal Board, the NUM and the Council for the Protection of Rural England (CPRE). There were also concerned individuals, and the government seemed wary of confrontation and prying eyes on the scale it had suffered at Greenham Common. It is also interesting to note that very few women attended the inquiry and all who did attended in their private capacity as citizens, the first and virtually only appearance of a woman being that of Nicola Pilkington from Durham. As we shall see, however, the importance of the opposition of women to nuclear dumping would have resonance as the inquiry proceeded.

The Layfield inquiry was branded by opponents as a sham; the odds stacked deliberately against protesters:

> The running of the inquiry was also of concern. The Department of Energy decided from the start that it would not provide objectors with public money to allow them to participate at no cost to themselves. The imbalance of resources between the CEGB, on the one hand, and the protest groups, on the other, was one of the most striking features of the inquiry. The length of the proceedings only added to the problem. That ... opponents ... managed to put up such a well-argued and persistent case is remarkable.[15]

The odds might also have had political implications. There was much lobbying by the Central Electricity Generating Board (CEGB) for overall control of projects. The CEGB employed 50,000 workers in 1982 (but never had a woman on its board) while the UKAEA had over 14,000 people on its books of whom 3,000 were scientists. The new arrangements for the nuclear industry meant that the building of new plants was to be under the guidance of the CEGB, giving immense power to the one set of state-owned organisations that Thatcher had difficulty in uncoupling, as had all her political predecessors.

The power unions were also decidedly tame, having swung to the right after the crisis of 1973. The opponent with the most to lose was the NUM, which represented the coalfields that supplied most of the CEGB's power stations. The National Coal Board employed large numbers of men, 266,000 in 1982 to 83, but the industry was slowly being rolled back. The social implications of the handover to nuclear-driven energy were huge. The miners too were represented at the inquiry, but they would finally need to be sacrificed, a policy decided upon as early as 1945 under a Labour government fearful of running out of mineral fuel:

> One of the key arguments for Sizewell B is 'fuel diversity', the CEGB's proposal that Sizewell B would ensure the reduction of the CEGB's dependence upon its now dominant fuel, coal, by adding to its burn of uranium instead … main fear about coal is fear of British miners and their bargaining power; this fear is perennial at the Treasury.[16]

The inquiry was also attended by the security services police. Indeed, one journalist who gave evidence remembered, 'The day I appeared there, I asked almost the only people in the auditorium what they thought so far, and got only an embarrassed silence for reply. They turned out to be the Special Branch.'[17]

Special Branch was there because of a spurious worry regarding the nature of protesters who were now all lumped together as potential terrorists. As early as 1974, it was realised that certain unique difficulties with plutonium might attract extremist elements. The Royal Commission on Environmental Pollution which met under the chairmanship of Lord Flowers that year concluded that it was 'entirely credible that plutonium in required amounts could be made into a crude but effective weapon … the threat to explode such a weapon unless certain conditions were met would constitute nuclear blackmail, and would present any Government with an appalling dilemma'.[18] This gave the green light to the monitoring of dissenting groups. Thus, not only even more heavy secrecy would have to surround nuclear plants and those who worked there but, 'Those activities might include the use of informers, infiltrators, wiretapping, checking on bank accounts and the opening of mail. To track down miscreants, the authorities might need the use of general search warrants, at present illegal.'[19] The tentacles of power were to find a number of unsuspecting victims.

21

VOODOO HISTORIES

The secrecy surrounding every move by the nuclear industry effectively gave carte blanche to the security services to spy on whomever they wished in the future and this, in turn, has had a dramatic effect on those searching for governmental conspiracies and investigating the activities of state-sponsored private surveillance. 'Nuclear decision-making seems to be an extreme form of the characteristic features of British government decision-making – that is, secrecy, concealment, deception and forfeiture of trust.'[1]

The deaths of Hilda Murrell in England and William McCrea in Scotland (see Chapter 23) suggested the intensity of surveillance and concealment surrounding the debate around nuclear power. The murderer of Hilda Murrell was caught and jailed, but foul play was called by many who watched the case unfold. In a straightforward way, the mystery of Hilda Murrell's death was answered and the case resolved. For some, the story is where 'fictional conspiracy theories coalesced with real life suspicions' and reveals much that is wrong with the conspiratorial view of history. Ultimately, 'far from being an agent of the 'secret state', her murderer was 'a sixteen-year-old builder's labourer'.[2] The 1980s were paranoid times and to some extent there were paranoid responses. Some therefore see the case as yet another 'voodoo history', a product of the hot-house nature of the times and of the almost mythic sense of self-deception of those in opposition to the power of the Thatcherite state.

The conspiracy theories, in this instance, seem to have faded away, for the obvious reason, one suspects, that their moment has passed. The particular set of demons that haunted the mid-1908s – the nuclear state with its thuggish minions – has vanished to be replaced by others. But at the same time Hilda Murrell had been a powerful symbol. She had represented an ideal that the embattled campaigners of the period had of themselves. Politically defeated, marginalised even, they had an existence in their own minds that was simultaneously heroic and doomed. If they were unsuccessful, it wasn't due to any deficiency in their cause or their actions, nor was it down to the fact that the majority of British … people simply disagreed with them. It was explained, instead, by the strength and ruthlessness of the forces they were up against.[3]

The ideological context of Murrell's death and the duplicitous actions of the secret state at the time of her murder mean that fictional conspiracy theory and actual conspiracy are difficult to separate. In turn, this highlights the very core of perceived state deception and *actual* state deception described. One reinforces the other in endlessly complex ways that destroy fact and fiction by merging them.

There are indeed few facts regarding the death of Murrell, but much has been made of what circumstantial evidence there is. Hilda appeared a typically conservative WI-type living a quiet life in her house called Ravenscroft in the suburbs of Shrewsbury and her holiday home in Wales, but she was certainly not the type to bake cakes and sing 'Jerusalem'. At 78, she seemed feisty. Murrell had worked in horticulture much of her life and had a rose named after her. She walked, kept a nature diary and was interested in preserving the countryside. She belonged to the Council for the Protection of Rural England (CPRE) and the Soil Association, but she had also become very interested in the politics of nuclear waste. To this end, she belonged to CND, the Shropshire Anti-Nuclear Alliance, the Shropshire Peace Alliance – whose secretary was Laurence Otter – and to Ecoropa, the European ecological action group run by Gerard Morgan-Grenville. When she died, Murrell had prepared and allegedly had accepted a paper for presentation at the Sizewell B Inquiry.

On the morning of 21 March 1984, Murrell drove her white Renault 5 into town to do some shopping. She went home and called on a neighbour, which was the last time she was seen alive. The rest is almost all speculation. She was meant to go to lunch with friends, but failed to turn up, although a witness swore she saw Murrell's car speeding along a local road at the same time, even having to swerve their car to avoid a collision. It seemed to the witness as though a woman was slumped in the passenger seat. The man driving seemed to be 'staring as if he'd lost control'.[4]

At 1.15 p.m., local farmer Ian Scott came across Murrell's white car abandoned near his land, but failed to see a body although the area was relatively open. Two boys even stole the car tax disc, but there was seemingly no sign of Murrell nor had any alarm been raised. The friends who had awaited her arrival finally notified the police as did the farmer regarding the abandoned car. The police traced the car to Murrell and visited her house and (for reasons never explained) a local sex counsellor from whom they wished to know if any sexual predators with hang-ups regarding older women lived in the area. They had found no body yet.

The police finally found Hilda's body on 24 March in the copse where Scott had walked some days before, but seen nothing, and from where he had reported the abandoned Renault. On the same day, police visited Ravenscroft and found little of interest, although a neighbour who entered after the police left the unsecured house, found evidence of a disturbance. The house was peculiarly untidy, and when the neighbour went to phone the police he found that the telephone had been disabled. There was also a broken bannister rail and a picture had fallen off the wall. Later, microphones were found attached to the walls for unexplained reasons.

Murrell's body had now been examined by a police surgeon who reported:

> She [was] wearing a thigh-length, thick woollen brown overcoat. Her right arm [was] extended in front of her, her left arm alongside her body; her shrivelled white legs [were] slightly bent and mostly exposed, with severe abrasions and redness on the knees. Only the coat and an underslip cover the top of her thighs; one thick brown stocking [was] crumpled around her left ankles; she [was] not wearing knickers. Items of clothing [were] scattered nearby: the other stocking, a green skirt and cream suspender belt, but no knickers. The clear cuts on each hand [were] roughly an inch long, but there [was] no blood visible on the hands. They look[ed] like classic defence wounds from a knife attack. There [was] complete rigor mortis and the body [was] stone cold with hypostasis in the legs, mainly around the knees. There [was] dried red blood near the right eye and temple, and three small stab wounds in the abdomen area. A blood-stained handkerchief and the keys to her car [were] in her right coat pocket.[5]

Murrell had died not of her injuries, but of hypothermia, having lain unnoticed for several hours. The case fell within the jurisdiction of the West Mercia Police then headed by one Detective Chief Superintendent David Cole who had investigated the spy Geoffrey Prime. Cole took original control of the investigation, but seemed to get nowhere. The police concluded it was all rather 'bizarre'.

There was now to be a strange turn in events. Murrell's nephew was Robert Green, former personal staff officer to the assistant chief of naval staff and someone who had been present when the order to sink the *Belgrano* had been issued. He was now retired and working as a rural thatcher. Nevertheless, Green knew that his aunt was going to testify at the Sizewell Inquiry. She had spoken of a paper which he hoped to locate. Gerard Morgan-Grenville of Ecoropa spoke to Green on 2 April 1984 and told him that Murrell had said to him, 'If they don't get me first, I want the world to know that at least one old woman has seen through their lies.' Morgan-Grenville had never heard her speak like that. For the first time, she sounded 'rather desperate'.[6] Murrell had told others too that she was 'walking on dangerous ground'.[7] She certainly believed that some time ago, an intruder had rifled her papers on Sizewell, which she was keen to deposit with a third person for safekeeping, and neighbours saw a succession of unfamiliar people and strange cars outside her house or in the street days before she died.

At the same time, the *Belgrano* Inquest was heating up and Tam Dalyell was on the snoop for any information that might show Thatcher to be the liar he suspected she was. In November 1984, journalist Judith Cook wrote an article for the *New*

Statesman probing the Murrell case. In the article, which coincided with the inquest, she made the link between Murrell and Green. Dalyell, acting as a bloodhound, had delivered his letter containing the allegations regarding the *Belgrano* to Michael Heseltine two days before Murrell's body was discovered. The article made him put two and two together and come out with five. Green, he concluded, was the person who had leaked the *Belgrano's* position and direction to his aunt, whose knowledge had been her death warrant.

Dalyell's conclusions were based on incorrect logic and were to prove false. Green insisted he was a patriot and that he would not have acted as a traitor. He refused to cooperate with the MP or the police, so the investigation returned again to the nuclear issue.

Did Murrell have any real evidence regarding nuclear waste, as she was, after all, a mere amateur? Green was arrested in connection with the murder and Judith Cook felt she was now under surveillance too and was interviewed alongside Graham Smith, whose own book on the case had just been published. It was said by his publisher that Jeffrey Archer, then Conservative Party chairman, had tried to get the book banned or pulped. The case had now become big news; further articles appeared and there was even a BBC *Crimewatch* reconstruction. Former deputy chief constable John Stalker (by then a television personality) was commissioned by the programme-makers to undertake an investigation. Meanwhile, Green, who had been let off the hook, admitted to feeling that he had been under surveillance since leaving naval command.

A paranoid atmosphere hung over everything. Murrell's cottage in Wales caught fire. It might have been the actions of the revived Welsh defence movement Mudiad Amddiffyn Cymru, which had been burning incomer holiday homes since 1979 and might inadvertently have stumbled into a murder case, or it might have been the work of a professional covering their tracks, as the police actually concluded. Who would such a professional be? The answer came from the private investigator Gary Murray whose information pointed to a bungled burglary by private agencies paid for by the nuclear industry. He named Zeus as the possible link to the murderers and either Barrie Peachman or the sinister Victor Norris as being somehow involved, the various activities seen around Murrell's house being part of an initial surveillance operation and later a deception plan following her death. Murrell's neighbour Jill Finch believed that her Renault was driven at speed precisely to *attract attention* so that the slumped woman *would* be noticed. In other words, it was a decoy.

Things seemed horribly sinister to those involved. Robert Green was quite convinced his aunt had been murdered and he had more evidence towards his theory when he met Trina Guthrie, a friend of Murrell's. Guthrie was an anthropologist who had worked with the Naga tribe in India. She heard of research that a prison inmate was conducting in the same area. Her visit led to a meeting once the prisoner had been released. He revealed more than mere anthropology, as Guthrie was told that he had overheard a conversation suggesting who the killers were. They were Peter Sanderson, Malcolm Tyerman, a depressive serving sixteen years in Rampton for armed robbery, David Gricewith, who had died after 'accidentally shooting himself' during a police chase, and a woman called Helga who was Gricewith's girlfriend. This 'team' had been run by an MI5 agent to burgle Murrell's house in search of documents (although Murrell's name did not appear on Victor Norris's initial list of nuclear surveillance targets).

The gang had been hired by 'Ceres' to search for incriminating documents to do with the *Belgrano*. They had tortured Murrell and sexually assaulted her and she had been taken to 'America' to be worked over by a further specialist team. This all seems most unlikely, but, America, as it turned out, was not the country, but a section of an old US bomber base now converted into the Atcham Industrial Estate, a strange location, perhaps, for a safe house or interrogation centre. Interestingly, Murrell's alleged torture, by simulated drowning with wet towels, sounds very much like the treatment meted out to IRA internees.

Was any of this even vaguely true, or had paranoia taken over? It certainly appeared to be nonsense when Andrew George, a sixteen-year-old petty criminal in 1984, was arrested and convicted of the murder in May 2005. Prints and DNA from semen seemed to put George in Murrell's home and, he was too young to have a driving licence, which suggested why the car was so erratically driven. The conviction did not convince those who had taken an interest in the case.

Peculiar occurrences continued to frighten Murrell's colleagues and friends, and suspicions continued of an intelligence conspiracy which had used private operatives for dirty work which had gone wrong. In 2011, Green again reviewed the evidence. The foreword to his book was provided by no less than the civil liberties barrister Michael Mansfield. Mansfield's conclusion was that, if there was a cover-up it should be investigated. More significantly, he too felt the conviction was unsafe. 'I doubt anyone will imagine that the whole exercise from house to car, to lane, to field, to copse in broad daylight was accomplished by a slightly-built 16-year-old who had merely been looking for cash.'[8]

Murrell's death was the most extreme example of harassment. Nevertheless, it was not the only example of resilient women being harassed, frightened, burgled or beaten up who fitted a pattern of being on their own in unfamiliar territory, living in isolated homes or simply divorced or single parents. Their vulnerability certainly seemed to make them easy prey; their stories taken together are powerful testimony to the lengths that the intelligence services, Special Branch or malicious policemen would go to in order to menace legitimate protest; taken in isolation their stories represent mere hearsay, precisely what those doing such intimidation wanted.

Madeline Haigh was chair of the West Midlands branch of CND and was put under surveillance by Special Branch in 1980. She had come to their notice through letters written to the local press. After a letter professing her anti-nuclear sentiments appeared in the newspaper, she was visited by police officers apparently wishing to question her about a mail-order fraud linked to her address. The phone rang early on various mornings and cut off when answered. Cars were seen outside her isolated home with men appearing to watch her. Haigh became secretive and took documents around with her while at the same time she complained to the European Commission for Human Rights. Amazingly, in this case, the chief constable of the West Midlands was forced to admit Haigh had been under Special Branch investigation.

In 1983, Domini Hamilton, another anti-nuclear campaigner who was involved with Cruise Watch, found that her telephone frequently misdialled, irritating in itself, but suspicious in her circumstances. This experience was replicated for another campaigner, Carol Lewton, whose calls were interrupted by a man's voice which shouted, 'Oi' before the phone went dead. This was also peculiar enough, but 'She also had the fairly common, and unnerving, experience of dialling a number and hearing not a ringing tone but people moving about in a room.'[9]

Dr Di McDonald was a Cruise protester who monitored traffic to and from Greenham as part of Cruise Watch. In June 1984, she became subject to a campaign of harassment and intimidation. In one incident, she went to a telephone box in Newbury, but was prevented from using the phone by a policeman who stood in her way. On being repeatedly told the number was engaged, she finally made her call to find that indeed it was engaged. This strange incident was followed by the usual home surveillance by men in cars.

The same often happened at Greenham Common and other sites where women protested. This was probably the work of rogue elements having a 'bit of fun', but still left the women deeply troubled if not traumatised. Jane Powell and Hazel Rennie, having spent twelve uneventful months at Greenham, were suddenly attacked on 10 April 1985 by two men who viciously beat them. Powell thought the attack was not for theft, fun or sexual enjoyment, but was a premeditated exercise in sadism:

My overwhelming impression at the time was that the man attacking me got nothing from it. There was no sign of anger or hatred, no indication he was getting something out of his system. At the time of the attack one of my preoccupations was that the man was not enjoying himself, he was just doing his job. Thinking about the events afterwards, I cannot work out their brief. If they wanted to kill us they failed and botched the job, although they had plenty of time. On the other hand, if they simply wanted to scare us, they only narrowly escaped murdering us.[10]

Having suffered horrendous injury, Powell talked to an RAF officer of her acquaintance, but got nothing from him about the attack. Nevertheless, she later received an anonymous letter suggesting that MI5 went through protesters' rubbish and that she was under special investigation, almost certainly by private investigators contracted by the intelligence service.

In the same year, Dora Russell, the 91-year-old wife of philosopher Bertrand Russell found herself under suspicion. Russell claimed that one night she was dragged from her bed and beaten in an attempt to find her 'papers' by a secret service burglar. Despite her age, there seems no reason to believe she hallucinated the incident or invented it to discredit those in favour of nuclear fuel and weaponry.

The most worrying case involved Pat Davis, the estranged wife of Chief Petty Officer Danny Davis who was stationed on HMS *Resolution*. The tale began in 1985. Mrs Davis had given birth in the 1970s to children with birth defects and blamed these on radiation leaks in her husband's submarine, something hinted at by other submariners whose children had been born with disabling problems, also blamed on possible random radiation leakage. This was rigorously denied by the navy, but information given to a Yorkshire Television documentary led to the programme sending Gary Murray to investigate.

His investigations coincided with strange and persistent telephone calls to Mrs Davis by a man with a Scottish accent stating, 'We will kill you,' which were later expanded by a man with an English accent. Always the message was the same: 'We will make you a very dead woman.' Davis was followed as she walked down the road and threatened, as were her children. On one occasion, a witness to one of the phone calls was arrested. Davis recorded further messages; her home was broken into and her tape recorder was wiped. Then, in May 1986, she was attacked in her home by two 'military types'. She then fled to Éire in 1991, where she claimed she was followed and again beaten. Whether Davis is, in the end, a fantasist or not became moot when it was proved that leakage had occurred on submarines when their hulls had been accidentally damaged and further evidence showed that nuclear leaks and deliberate nuclear spillage had occurred in Scottish waters during the 1970s. Not until the 1990s were proper health and safety regulations applied to submarine repair.

22

FRIENDS IN THE NORTH

Nuclear energy and nuclear weapons proved a highly fissile combination. It was no different in Scotland except that the protests were combined with a mixture of nationalism not evident south of the border. It would be the hatred of Thatcherism, combined with the significance of nationalism and opposition to nuclear energy and NATO, that would prove so potent in the north.

Although Scotland had a proud military history within the British army, it also had a strong anti-militaristic, pacifist and non-conformist tradition that had begun asserting itself through a resurgent Scottish independence movement. This movement was itself a parallel development to a more active militaristic independence movement that had appeared in the 1970s which aligned itself with Irish and Welsh nationalist traditions and especially with the IRA.

This militancy had not always been strong, and, although there had been an independence movement of some sort since the late nineteenth century, Scots people as a whole were firmly integrated into the United Kingdom, but resented being ignored in decision processes and this slowly became an issue of national prestige. In 1886, the Scots founded a Scottish Home Rule Association on the lines of Irish home rule, but Scotland's political system was wholly absorbed within Westminster and the appointment of a Scottish Secretary earlier in 1885 seemed to offset the issue.

Nevertheless, 'home rulers' were never entirely silent. In 1951, the University of Aberdeen inaugurated the Blackwell Prize for an essay in English. In 1952, Arthur Turner won it with an essay on Scottish home rule in which he voiced the current Scottish discontentment. 'Discontent with the existing relations of Scotland and England is probably more widespread at the present time in Scotland than at any period since the years immediately succeeding the Union of 1707.'[1] For this essayist, the discontentment started on day one of the union. 'It is, of course, a familiar story how, in the decade after 1707, Scottish interests and Scottish prejudices were so stubbornly ignored, or flagrantly flouted, by Scotland's partner in the Union, that the Scots bitterly rued the bargain they had just made.'[2]

This disinterest in Scottish affairs was momentarily disturbed by the rise of Scottish nationalism in the late 1960s and early 1970s, but it seemed to recede, to the relief of the Cabinet, when the Common Market referendum showed the nationalists out of step with the voters. Thus, at a meeting at Chequers on 16 June 1975, devolution would be shelved as government policy to everyone's satisfaction.[3] This brought to a head Scottish fears and frustrations and left the Scottish radicals with few options, making them dangerously revolutionary, intransigent and aggressive.

The revival of Scottish hopes in the late 1960s, grew from the murky world of Scottish frustration in disaffected groups and the presence, early on, of agents provocateurs. The re-emergence of the IRA during the period helped to create an imitative atmosphere and a sense of possibility. Things began in 1968, when the Scottish National Party (SNP) took the largest share of the vote in municipal elections and a sense of an independent Scottish future emerged. This sense of destiny was greatly increased when Ted Heath committed the Conservatives to Scottish devolution in May 1968 at the Scottish Conservative Conference. The 'Perth Declaration' came as a surprise. Thatcher was 'never happy with the policy'.[4] Indeed, she concluded that, 'there was little enthusiasm for it among English Tories'; the irony seemed lost on her.[5] Heath nevertheless ordered Alec Douglas-Home to investigate the possibilities, but, once he was in office the policy vanished without trace. Later, the Kilbrandon Royal Commission proposed a plan for devolution, but it too was soon dropped.

The policy was revived after the government's defeat, but the Conservatives polled even less well in the next election with many, including a number of Thatcher's parliamentary friends, blaming the policy for diminishing the Scottish vote. When Thatcher came to power she was therefore presented with a dilemma. 'The Scottish party itself was deeply split, with the critics of devolution representing much grassroots opinion pitted against the left-leaning Scottish party leadership of people like Alick Buchanan-Smith, Malcolm Rifkind and George Younger.'[6] It was something Thatcher could not deal with immediately, but it was quite clear where she stood. 'This was the situation which I inherited as Leader. Ted had impaled the Party on an extremely painful hook from which it would be my unenviable task to set it free. As an instinctive Unionist, I disliked the devolution commitment.'[7]

Thus, although Thatcher set up a devolution group under William Whitelaw, she had no real interest in changing things; the group was there merely as window dressing. Bringing in power sharing, which had 'failed' in Northern Ireland, was suggested to prevent the Conservatives being annihilated in Scotland, but again, Thatcher 'would not budge'.[8] Nevertheless, she still supported devolution in principle (but wilfully opposed it in practice), a point she made in May 1975 at the Scottish Party Conference held in Dundee. A series of meetings with English and Scottish backbenchers convinced Thatcher to withdraw any support, especially as those who did support devolution appeared to be flirting with the worst excesses of Labour. Thatcher recalled, 'Alick Buchanan-Smith and Malcolm Rifkind, getting ever more out of touch, were flirting with the idea of a separate Scottish executive. That went yet further beyond the Home proposals and took us well into Labour territory.'[9]

Thus, Thatcher had decided, more or less, to ignore the issue by the time the Labour government's White Paper proposing directly elected assemblies for both Scotland and Wales was published. By this time anyway, Thatcher's position was crystal clear. 'I could not support an Assembly – none of us could support an Assembly – if we thought it was likely to jeopardize the Union. The Perth speech was well received, but of course it did not resolve the Party dispute.'[10]

Thatcher took legal advice and looked carefully at the voting statistics. From these, she confirmed her opposition to any constitutional change. Her victory at a subsequent meeting of 2 December 1976 was acrimonious and still left a large minority in favour of devolution. Her triumph was proof of Tory traitors and left-wing appeasers and a warning to be wary in the future as well as to listen to backbenchers rather than the Shadow Cabinet. 'I had no illusion that this could be done without some resignations. I wanted to minimize them, but not at the expense of failing to lance the devolution boil.'[11]

Warned that the Conservatives were committing 'electoral suicide' in Scotland by Robert Carr, one of the founders of the Tory Reform Group, Thatcher surrounded herself with men of 'robust patriotism' like Teddy Taylor who became Shadow Scottish Secretary. The Lib-Lab pact that intervened as the devolution bill progressed only hardened Thatcher's stance on the union, but she could no longer rely on the Ulster Unionists, who were disaffected, nor on Enoch Powell to rally them to the cause. The Scottish question was effectively Thatcher's first defeat while still in opposition.

At this point, the twin concerns of semi-independent nationalism and the significance of the *concentration of Britain's nuclear deterrent in Scottish waters* were not apparent in Conservative debates. It was a simple question of Scotland breaking away from the union and a feeling that SNP members were pernicious traitors to the United Kingdom (expressed as essentially 'English', by Thatcher and the Tory backbenches).

Part of the pact between the Liberals and the Labour Party had been predicated on the success of the Scotland and Wales Bill which had been defeated in 1977. The bill had been replaced by an act offering a referendum. The SNP had eleven seats at the time and the condition for its continuing support was devolution:

The condition of their support for the government was two-pronged. First, they required legislation allowing for a directly elected Scottish Chamber; second, they demanded that the Prime Minister ensured that the assent of the Scottish electorate was procured by his own wholehearted commitment. The second point was vital: no excuses would be accepted if the referendum failed. In due course, on 1 March 1979, the referendum did fail and in due course again, on 28 March the Scottish National Party voted to bring the government down.[12]

✐↝᷒᷒↜✐

On 1 March 1979, the referendum in Scotland had actually proved there was little enthusiasm for change: 'Devolution was dead: [Thatcher] did not mourn it.'[13] Indeed, by the 1983 election, the SNP was effectively wiped out. Thatcher had played the politician throughout the 'crisis'. 'I will retreat,' she said to a colleague, 'but I do not want to bang the drums too loudly.'[14] This time, Tam Dalyell, Thatcher's most implacable enemy, was also her most careful and diplomatic supporter when it came to opposing devolution.[15] The issue ended in confused deals and confusion generally. It all seemed finished, which was hardly surprising as Thatcher would never wear 'tartan camouflage', her party being seen as fundamentally 'Unionist'.[16]

For the SNP, it was time to regroup; for the devolutionists, it was a time to be silent. Yet there were other groups who did not wish the issue to go away and who were prepared to fight for its success. Extremist Scottish attitudes had hardened throughout the 1970s in parallel with developments in Ireland. Indeed, since the 1930s, Ireland had been the model for Scottish armed resistance to English rule. A radical minority of the 1320 Club (founded to promote Scottish culture and named after the Declaration of Arbroath) decided to go one step further and found the Army of the Provisional Government (APG). The direct threat to the government was Scottish opposition to nuclear weapons. CND was very popular in Scotland and the government feared there might be a terrorist campaign around nuclear sites. To counter the threat of activists sabotaging installations there were army manoeuvres in 1975, 1977 and 1978 – the SAS and commandos playing war games outside Edinburgh Airport. Indeed, the threat to NATO installations in Scotland had been recognised in the early 1950s and, at the height of trouble during the 1980s, there was regular phone tapping of potential troublemakers.

The 1320 Club had plans for a 'provisional government' on the lines of the IRA. There was a to be cabinet and full hierarchy as well as an armed forces committee whose job it was to create an army. This farcical organisation was to be divided into a highland brigade, a lowland brigade, an armoured formation and a parachute battalion as well as a full headquarters staff. The pipe dream was had by only a handful of activists few of whom even had a weapon. Once the plans for the APG were in place, its organisers broke away from the 1320 Club to pursue their 'war'.

This began with bank robberies. John Gillian, a photographer, John Stewart, a bank clerk, and William Murray, a quality surveyor, formed one of the APG's cells or *schiltroms* (named after the medieval military formations of pikemen) and were willing to rob for independence. Their plans were big, as they wanted to take their small army and capture Fort William, Ullapool or Oban in a symbolic occupation which would be defeated by the British government but which would so outrage the Scots that they would rise up and throw out the English as the Irish had been galvanised after the Dublin rising of 1916. Proclamations of the Provisional Government would be read as soon as the towns were seized and a general rising precipitated. On April Fools' Day 1971, the three conspirators were captured in a hotel after carrying out several bank raids.

Matt Lygate, a tailor's cutter and a committed Marxist whose grandparents were Irish, was also a dedicated republican who first engaged in communist propaganda while living in New Zealand. Having returned to Scotland, Lygate joined the Committee to Defeat Revisionism for Communist Unity, a far-left organisation. He intended to form a 'revolutionary elite', joining home-grown ideas of revolution to those of Maoism and the struggle in Ireland. With a few other conspirators he formed the John Maclean Society in 1968. The Workers' Party of Scotland (WPS) expanded and eventually went in for its own bank robberies, striking on 7 May, 21 October, 19 November and 17 December 1971. On the last occasion a bank employee was wounded by a shotgun.

Six months later (March 1972), these men too were in court, betrayed by a colleague. Lygate was quite open about keeping guns and engaging in guerrilla tactics. In the end, he dismissed his defence and made an impassioned speech from the dock which Lord Dunpark was unable to shut up. The judge listened impassively as Lygate finished on a threat, 'I would like to say that in the future a day will come when the roles of this court will be reversed, when the workers will sit on the bench and those people who have judged me now will be judged themselves.' Dunpark replied insouciantly, 'I don't look forward to those days with any longing I must say.'[17] The judge then handed down sentences that ranged from twenty-four to twenty-six years. Lygate received twenty-four years. As he left the dock, he shouted, 'Long live the workers of Scotland.' His trial caused a sensation, being seen as a patently unfair case of class discrimination, and campaigning had him released after thirteen years: he was a 'wee political man' in Lenin cap and jeans.

In 1974, Idi Amin, the President of Uganda, declared himself in favour of an independent Scotland and pledged himself to the Provisional Government. This odd state of affairs followed the emergence of William Anderson, a one-time army sergeant who was living in Aberdeen and deeply disapproved of the English use of Scottish oil. Soon he had a group around him discussing the possibility of bombing English towns on the lines of the Provisional IRA.

Anderson had hidden 109 sticks of dynamite and 50 detonators. He wanted to join the APG, but was already unknowingly involved with a Special Branch agent called Colin Boyd. A meeting of the Scottish Republican Club in Aberdeen helped the campaign along and recruited more people. Eventually, alongside William Bell, a fanatical Anglophobe, Anderson staged a publicity stunt with journalists to announce 'tartan terrorism' by the Tartan Army and Scottish National Liberation

Army. A wholly fictitious secret set of organisations was announced, and Amin, rather bizarrely, rallied to the cause on Ugandan radio. More bank raids followed, but Boyd had shopped the lot and most of the perpetrators were rounded up in 1975. Anderson was given a ten-year jail term.

The shadowy force known as the Tartan Army had originally emerged during 1972 (and might have been a complete fiction, a creation of Special Branch or a number of illicit organisations). Its activities did not come to an end until 31 May 1976, when fourteen people were tried. Detonators and dynamite were stolen and William Wallace's two-handed sword was taken from its museum home. When devolution was not forthcoming, Wendy Wood, leader of the Scottish Patriots, had gone on hunger strike as a protest. She was by this time an elderly woman and her strike was backed by bombing campaigns at Dounreay Nuclear Reactor, ICI and BP's Grangemouth refinery. A decision by the government to write a Green Paper on devolution halted the hunger strike and stopped the bombs.

Although the Tartan Army consisted of fewer than fifty members, it began a violent bombing campaign almost immediately and was certainly sufficient to bring large numbers of police into the case. The police breakthrough came with the arrest of David Sharkey in 1973 for the stabbing of a seaman at a party. When questioned, it became clear that Sharkey was deeply involved with the Tartan Army. Further arrests did not follow until 1976, however. One of the men was Donald Currie, a maintenance engineer from Clackmannanshire who also added to Sharkey's tale of tartan terror. In the end, the case collapsed with everybody accused walking free as the idea of the Tartan Army seemed more and more to be the fevered brainchild of Currie himself.

Despite the efforts of Special Branch and MI5 and the dismissal of tartan terrorism as a fiction, bombings of pipelines, offices and pylons continued, often the work of teenage activists, as with the campaign of 1974 to 1975. Much of the activity centred on Glasgow where there was a large population whose origins were Irish and sympathetic organisations linked to Sinn Fein had existed for years. The Scottish Worker's Republican Party, for instance, reformed as a Trotskyist organisation in 1973 and immediately split when the Scottish Citizen's Army of the Republic was created as a cell to kidnap politicians. Scottish Republican Clubs remained underground because of political surveillance and because their worlds often overlapped with organised crime, as similar clubs had done in Ireland.

Again, robbery was the method of 'expropriation' and again the perpetrators were hunted down and put on trial. In June 1976, the Stanley Green trial opened in Glasgow. Green, a typewriter-maker, was accused, alongside others, of robbing a sub-post office. The usual prison sentences followed. Finally, the loose alliance of left-wing republican movements coalesced as the Scottish Republican Socialist Party, but with most of the leaders in jail things looked like they might quieten down. But it was not to be quiet. A bomb factory exploded during 1980, suggesting activities had recommenced. This time the main culprit was Peter Wardlaw, who had created the Socialist Republican League. Wardlaw was a 'professional revolutionary' according to the police when he was arrested. A deserter from the British army, who would not serve in Northern Ireland, Wardlaw planned his campaign with care and precision, and he and other members of the republican movement were in regular contact with Irish and Welsh independence fighters.

Their first bank raid on 24 October 1979 did not go well and they escaped with only £978. Their plans to blow up the temporary Scottish Assembly building (the Royal High School on Calton Hill) also failed. Another raid, this time on a post office van, netted £100,000 and Wardlaw had the money for his army. The next raid was intended to target Explosives & Chemical Products Limited, in order to gain dynamite and prove to the Provisional IRA that the Army of the Scottish People meant business. This success decided the little army to try to blow up the Scottish Assembly building again on the anniversary of the Battle of Bannockburn. The bomb, however, exploded in the terrorists' flat and led to their arrest. It was all over for the Army of the Scottish People.

In spring 1983, another declaration of war was delivered in *Firinn Albannach*, the official magazine of Siol nan Gaidheal. This was from an organisation called Arm nan Gaidheal (the Army of the Gaels), the military arm of Siol nan Gaidheal, which was dedicated to a highland-style independence and which carried out actions between November 1982 and March 1983 against the 'colonial lackeys' of the English. This group had masonic connections to the Grand Priory in Scotland and the Order of the Templars (reformed in Scotland in 1972). It was Jacobite and monarchical in orientation and championed Prince Michael's 'claim' to the Scottish throne. On demonstrations their members wore full highland dress including the sgian dubh and claymore, despite their being illegal in public places. Their drum core was dressed in black military uniform with a Nazi-style symbol and *Saorsa* (Freedom) on their banner. Disrupting SNP meetings with Nazi songs, they also vied for attention with the 1320 Club which, under MacDonald Douglas, was now calling for civil disobedience with the aim of 'complete independence'. Their first bomb was planted at the Assembly Rooms in Edinburgh and further bombs followed, but all to no avail because of the actions of a police spy. Scottish right-wing Jacobite romanticism came to a halt.

Yet another organisation took its chances when the Scottish National Liberation Army tried to blow up Margaret Thatcher when she came to speak at the Scottish Conservative Conference in Perth. The device, a 6lb radio-controlled bomb, would have killed many, including the Prime Minister. A message, relayed to the BBC by a contact stated, 'It would have been a turning point in British politics.'[18] While the first public reaction would have been shock and revulsion, the assassination would have awakened the political conscience of Scotland in the long term, or so it was believed. Once victory was secured, a 'socialist republic' was to be announced.

23

THE RED ESCORT COMES TO THE HIGHLANDS

Thatcherism as espoused by Mrs Thatcher never took off in Scotland. Despite the fact that, 'in Education, Housing and Health the common themes of [Thatcher's] policies were the extension of choice, the dispersal of power and the encouragement of responsibility.'[1] Scotland should have been an ideal place for the Thatcher experiment, with its long tradition of enlightenment philosophy and its 'invention' of the theory of market forces and individualism, but it was always recalcitrant. Why? Thatcher's answer was predictable. 'But on top of decline in Scotland's heavy industry came socialism – intended as a cure, but itself developing quite new strains of social and economic disease, not least militant trade unionism.'[2] The decline in Scotland's industrial base and the poverty of some of its regions had not improved swiftly enough to allow the Thatcher revolution to take hold or to stop the decline in Conservatism north of the border before the 1987 election.

The question was why the Conservative vote had declined from the 1950s, and was it simply down to economics? Thatcher explained the decline by reference to changes in social demographics:

> It was certainly possible – even plausible – to point to changes in social and religious attitudes to explain this decline. The old Glaswegian Orange foundations of Unionist support which had in earlier decades between so important had irreparably crumbled. Moreover, whereas in the past it might have been possible for the Conservatives in Scotland to rely on a mixture of deference, tradition and paternalism to see them through, this was just no longer an option – and none the worse for that.[3]

Yet this was not enough of an explanation. There had to be an underlying cause, so deep as to be irremovable. Thatcher found the grail in the very fabric of Scottish consciousness, which was one of 'dependency' which even went to the very heart of socialist government. It seemed to prove everything she had fought for and yet the Scots remained intransigent. 'Half Scotland's population were living in highly subsidized local authority housing compared with about a quarter in England. In short, the conditions of dependency were strongly present.'[4]

Everything had been conceded to the 'socialists', even the policies of the Scottish Office. Things changed as Thatcher rearranged her Cabinet to defeat Scottish socialism, but the old devolutionists in the party were preparing for their revenge. By 1990, Malcolm Rifkind had emerged as the Conservative white knight of devolution.

The endless defeats for Scottish Conservatism were recognised as what they were – a distrust of Thatcher herself, something she freely acknowledged:

> Some part of this unpopularity must be attributed to the national question on which the Tories are seen as an English party and on which I myself was apparently seen as a quintessential English figure ... About the second point I could – and I can – do nothing. I am what I am and I have no intention of wearing tartan camouflage. Nor do I think that most Scots would like me, or any English politician, the better for doing so. The Tory Party is not, of course, an English party but a Unionist one.[5]

The appearance of Scottish revolutionary politics was predicated upon the disinterest in Whitehall as to Scottish feelings and objections to nuclear energy being based in Scotland. Successive governments simply took no account of Scottish interests and this led inevitably to friction. Debates surrounding the deployment of Polaris, an American missile system, had begun as early as 1959 when the chief of naval operations in the United States approached the Royal Navy for a suitable base in Britain. The chosen site was Faslane, on the Clyde, near Glasgow. The site was controversial because of its proximity to the city and because the government was fearful of disruption. Harold Macmillan, remembering the 1930s, talked of a 'large number of agitators' in the area.[6]

Not wishing to annoy the Americans, Macmillan put aside his qualms when Eisenhower assured him that no 'control' or use of the weapons would occur without British permission. Suitably reassured, Macmillan agreed, and Polaris was based at Holy Loch in March 1961 (finally closed in March 1992). The process of updating and deployment accelerated after Thatcher was elected. In July 1980, the government announced a plan to update the nuclear fleet with Trident C4 missiles.

Worries long dormant in Scotland began to resurface over the cavalier way the country was treated. Were the protests of the 1970s justified and were the Scots merely the colonial vassals of English Conservative politicians as many suspected? The evidence seemed to suggest their hunches were correct:

> Despite the controversy over devolution in the late 1970s, the possibility of future Scottish independence [did] not appear to have been mentioned in discussions of alternative locations [for nuclear weaponry] ... It [was] also evident that the

prospect of Scottish independence seldom if ever troubled the decisions that led to these commitments.[7]

The imposition of the poll tax in Scotland during 1989 would confirm the government's apparent contempt for Scottish opinion and reaffirm once and for all the diehard opposition to nuclear weaponry. In this case, the best way to get Scotland disentangled from the rest of Britain was to declare Scotland a nuclear-free zone, a policy which would bring the country into direct conflict with both Whitehall and Washington.

There were six nuclear plants in Scotland, including at Dounreay and at Chapelcross, which were capable of producing components for warheads, and Britain's nuclear fleet was based in Scotland anyway. The SNP, which stood alone as the party of disarmament, declared in its election manifesto for 1983 that:

> Scotland is covered with nuclear bases and military installations, making us a number one target in the event of nuclear war. Nuclear weapons have been placed on our soil by both Labour and Conservative governments, without the consent of the Scottish people … A Scottish government will

> - cancel the Trident nuclear programme …;
> - remove all nuclear weapons and foreign nuclear establishments from Scottish soil and territorial waters;
> - promote nuclear disarmament by seeking agreement … to the creation of nuclear-free zones in Europe;
> - divert resources to strong and efficient conventional forces.[8]

Indeed the party, with its non-conformist and pacifist base, had always stood firmly for a nuclear-free Scotland. As early as December 1976, the party had declared in its statement of defence policy that an independent Scotland would pursue a policy whereby:

> all Nuclear Weapon Bases and nuclear weapons on Scottish land, waters or airspace, will be required to remove these … Scotland will also sign the Nuclear Weapons Non-Proliferation Treaty [sic], and will ban any manufacture of nuclear weapons on Scottish soil. Scotland will seek the co-operation of neighbouring non-nuclear states: Iceland, Norway, Sweden, Finland and Denmark to initiate consultations with the USA and other NATO allies and with the USSR on the establishment of a nuclear-free zone in the North Sea/North East Atlantic and Scottish territorial waters.[9]

In 1982, the Presbyterian Church also unanimously voted against nuclear weaponry. It was this atmosphere of hostility to English and American intentions that created one of Scotland's most enduring murder mysteries.

At 6.30 in the evening of 5 April 1985, the Scottish nationalist and nuclear cam-paigner Willie McCrea (sometimes spelled MacCrea) set out from his Glasgow flat to drive along the A87 for a short break at his holiday cottage in Dornie, Kintail. He was discovered some hours later by two Australian tourists, barely alive and covered with blood, but sitting in his car with his 'hands folded in his lap'. The door of his car was jammed. A passing car was flagged down which coincidentally contained a doctor and an old acquaintance of McCrea, David Coutts, a Dundee SNP councillor.

Rushed to hospital, but only cleaned up six hours later, McCrea's was found to have a bullet wound in the forehead. The bullet had lodged in his brain. A small 0.22-calibre revolver was discovered later alongside McCrea's smashed watch and a neatly piled set of ripped-up documents, some way from the site of the crash.

Two years after McCrea's death, Hamish Watt, a former MP for the SNP, offered fur-ther evidence to the *Aberdeen Press and Journal* that two bullets had been fired, or at least this was what he had been told by an attendant nurse at the Aberdeen Royal Infirmary who had been present when the wounds were examined. The mysterious nurse upon whom the evidence rests as to the two bullet wounds gave two interviews to Scottish newspapers. The first was to the *Sunday Post* on 16 June 1985 and the second to the *Aberdeen Press and Journal* on 7 April 1990. In both cases, and for whatever reasons, 'she' chose to remain anonymous, and so the evidence remains merely hearsay.

Everyone agreed that McCrea was brain-dead by the time his car came to a halt. He either shot himself while the vehicle was moving, shot himself when the car was halted or was shot either when the car was halted or moving. Moreover, a group of walkers on the afternoon of 6 April reported that they had themselves been shot at near the crash site by a man who appeared to drive a red Ford Escort, the shots seemingly as if to warn them off.

Thus there were apparent inconsistencies from the beginning. For McCrea to have shot himself at the correct angle of entry required that his arm be outside the car window, but both arms were in his lap. To add to the difficulties, there were no fin-gerprints on the gun, despite McCrea's not wearing gloves. The day after the incident, McCrea's life-support machine was switched off and any first-hand testimony was lost.

The initial investigation appeared either deliberately botched or incompetent. The main police enquiries started the next day, but the car was removed from the scene before even the gun was found. Indeed, the gun was eventually found in a burn, but not until the day after and not until a number of policemen had already looked in the area. McCrea's vehicle was actually moved so quickly that the police could not even properly identify the site of the accident, and two car-removal firms had claimed that they had picked up the vehicle. Two sites now existed, one where the official memorial cairn would be later erected, and one a mile away. Witnesses placed the halted vehicle near the road but sufficiently far off it to need binoculars to see it clearly; the police believed the car had rolled, suggesting how the gun had been displaced, while others said the car was not moving at speed. The car was not forensically searched. Debris was found at both sites! The pile of neatly torn-up papers and McCrea's smashed wristwatch (and possibly a credit card) were only finally found the next day. The cigarettes he habitually carried and a bottle of whisky he had purchased were, nevertheless, missing and never recovered, as were the two briefcases he carried because he considered that they contained information too precious to leave at home. Important evidence seemed to have been lost and the site was contaminated to such an extent that further investigation seemed pointless. Indeed, soon after the incident, someone had gone through McCrea's pockets and searched the car.

The crime scene was treated with the sort of disregard that might have accompanied a petty theft, but this was no ordinary John Doe. After all, McCrea was heavily involved with investigating NATO activity in Scotland and nuclear dumping off Dounreay. He was a well-known activist whose investigations might have thrown a spanner in the works of government policy or corporate enterprise. Unlike Hilda Murrell, McCrea was a very public figure, having been in intelligence and having had the legal training to help create Israel's maritime laws; he was also one-time Vice Chairman of the SNP and a vociferous opponent of the 'establishment' in both Scotland and England. McCrea had, therefore, apparent reason to be cautious. As a fierce opponent of the strategy of nuclear power, and waste, in Scotland, he had spoken at the Mullwharcher Inquiry on waste-dumping in 1980 and was intending to present evidence at the Dounreay Inquiry. He had defeated the nuclear lobby over plans regarding dangerous waste dumping and he had taken an interest in the death of Hilda Murrell. He had told friends, just as Murrell had told hers, that he had some evidence that would clinch things. 'I've got them,' he had told his friends.

Before his death, the police were also investigating McCrea, and Strathclyde Special Branch would watch his house. McCrea even knew the police by their first names. He claimed his post was opened, he was regularly followed and his phone was tapped. His holiday home in Kintail was also burgled, but, he said, 'They didn't get what they were looking for.'[10] Before his death, his Glasgow flat had also been burgled in suspicious circumstances. All his papers were destroyed in the burglaries or 'vanished'.

Others felt themselves touched by the circumstances of the case. John McGill was an old school friend of McRea's, a colleague in the SNP and Scotland-UN (now United Nations Association Scotland), founded by McGill. McRea worked with McGill as a political legal advisor. McGill remains convinced that McRea was murdered during a period of intense harassment for those working both for Scottish independence and a nuclear-free Scotland. Surveillance had become noticeable during the inquiry at Ayr into a proposed nuclear site for waste material (imported from Japan) to be built in the nearby hills at Mullwharcher. The inquiry found against the Atomic Energy Authority (AEA), but the result was that Special Branch attention became focussed on the two friends. According to McGill, the police arrived at the inquiry in three black Rover cars and all appeared to be armed.

Soon after the inquiry, McGill's Saab was hit by a bullet (I'd been shot at') as he drove along the A77 just north of Fenwick on the way to his office. The police carried out forensic tests and suggested it was a stray bullet from a 'deer hunter', but McGill insists it was in too populated an area for such an incident. The forensic report appeared to have been filed, but the requests to make it available to both McGill and McRea were ignored. On Sunday 7 April, McGill read about the death of his friend. He made enquiries which seemed to confirm that McRea had been killed by two bullets to behind the ears and the gun found 40ft from the dead man. This, McGill concluded, was 'the classic SAS kill'. Although he offers no evidence to support the claim, nor evidence as to how he was informed of the nature of the injuries, apart from what he had gleaned in the *Sunday Post* (16 June 1985), he remains certain that this was 'state-sponsored murder'. Why?

McRea was looking forward to going to McGill's daughter's wedding the next week and he showed no signs of suicide; rather he was buoyed up by the 'political' news he had just received. According to McGill, McRea had obtained evidence that 'they're [the AEA] going to bury the stuff [nuclear waste] where the sand never dries'. This may refer to out at sea dumping, but McGill still thinks it was a rather enigmatic reference to Applecross, where the waste might be stored in an area out of bounds to the public because it is near the site of a NATO naval base. This would have been highly illegal and just might explain any extreme measures to shut opponents up. The question remains, however, as to the nature and perpetrators of the kill. Were they private investigators gone too far into illegality, an SAS squad acting as they did on Gibraltar, or was McRea's death merely a tragic suicide with the gunshot evidence a tissue of confusions?

If there were indeed two entry wounds as alleged, then how might they have been administered? Unlike Hilda Murrell, who was found dead in the woods, McCrea died in his car, apparently while driving. There are a number of scenarios we could imagine: a hidden assassin in the back seat could have killed the driver, but would have been seriously injured when the car crashed; more likely McCrea may have been flagged down by two strangers and then shot from behind by one of them, his car being shunted over the hill into the position it was found. Presumably the car was not in motion when the incident occurred, but this cannot be proven. The gun could then have been dumped after being wiped with the expectation that anyone finding the crash might conclude he had stopped and taken his own life with one shot (the other being simply a mistake at the hospital) – but apparently McCrea did not own a pistol.

John McGill confirmed to the author that an investigation into McRea's death was undertaken by the SNP executive, but agrees that 'what happened to it is a mystery'. The archives of the SNP are housed at the National Library of Scotland, but so far the librarians have not been able to locate the missing reports and investigation into the McRea case. Were they simply binned in an act of negligence?

As the *Scottish Daily Record* commented in 2007, when reviewing the unsolved mystery, 'Willie McCrea was nobody's fool … he knew he was being followed by shadowy figures.' An open verdict was returned by the coroner's court, but the evidence suggested to journalists, politicians and investigators that foul play was involved. McCrea's home was not the only place to be rifled at the time. The offices of the Scottish Campaign to Resist Atomic Menace (SCRAM) was also burgled and set alight. SCRAM had also been part of the Sizewell Inquiry secret investigations.

In 2005, a retired policeman and one-time private investigator admitted being employed by an unknown source to watch McCrea despite official denials by the Scottish Solicitor General. It was only after the suspicious death of David Kelly in 2003 that the case was returned for re-examination and a number of explanations offered for McCrea's 'suicide', including alcoholism and depression, closet homosexuality, connections to a drug dealer or involvement with sabotage as a member or associate of Siol nan Gaidheal. He had associated with two militants, Adam Bowling and David Dinsmore, to whom he lent his office. It was further claimed by militant nationalists that McCrea had been involved in planning the letter-bombing of Glasgow City Council which was meant to coincide with the visit of Princess Diana, and in the planting of bombs near the Coalport military base on the nuclear convoy route. Both Bowling and Dinsmore had fled to Ireland and were arrested in Dublin. In other words, McRea was a terrorist. None of the allegations has ever been proven.

⁓⊃Ɠ⊂⌐

There certainly seems considerable overlap between the cases of Hilda Murrell and Willie McCrea. These similarities were first clearly outlined by Gary Murray when he started working for Yorkshire Television to investigate the Murrell case. For a start there was a red (or maroon) Ford Escort observed at each scene, a minor fact until other considerations are taken into account.

Both victims, for instance, had been the subject of activities apparently of interest to MI5, Special Branch or the atomic energy police; both had apparently had their post opened and their homes bugged or phones tampered with; both were about to appear at public hearings dealing with nuclear issues; both were passionate anti-nuclear campaigners under surveillance by the security services and/or private investigators; both had their properties (home and holiday) broken into and set on fire. Interestingly, the two activists were supposedly in possession of something specific about the nuclear industry and in both cases there were anomalies concerning their 'papers'. In each case, witnesses were overlooked or ignored by police investigators, the scenes of crime had been contaminated and evidence sidelined and the cases wound up prematurely and declared suicide or misadventure. Both Murrell and McCrea died in or near their own cars and in both cases the death scene was a quiet country spot. After the event, associates and friends who attempted to pursue the cases became victims themselves of burglary and/or acts of violence, damage to their property or prolonged and sinister harassment.

The cases of Murrell and McCrea remain 'open', despite continuous official denials of foul play and even though someone went to jail for Murrell's murder. What might be the motives for murder? These remain obscure in both cases. In Murrell's case, she was murdered by a teenage burglar; McCrea is supposed to have committed suicide. Both deaths have therefore been solved, but serious questions remain.

Is it likely that both were murdered by the same operatives and the murders covered up to look like murder in one case by a ham-fisted sexually predatory burglar and suicide caused by depression in the other? It is true that McCrea was a member of the Scottish branch of the Voluntary Euthanasia Society, and it is also true that he might have been drinking and that if he was caught for a second time drunk-driving it might end his career. Would that have meant that he made a split-second decision to take the gun and fire? If he had, he chose a poor way of causing his death as such a gun would likely cause injury rather than death. (It is estimated that McCrea was in a coma for eight hours before he was found.)

The answers to these puzzles are difficult to find. After all, both deaths involve people who were seen as subversives and who thought of themselves as 'radicals'. Both deaths revolve around supposed revelations regarding nuclear waste. However, the evidence for earth-shattering revelations looks weak, despite both hinting that they had secret and damning evidence – but for what?

Could Hilda Murrell have been killed because she had information regarding operations in the Falklands? That would hardly have been necessary, as Thatcher's 'interrogator' Diana Gould died peacefully in 2011, and even those journalists and police officers investigating assassinations in Northern Ireland were 'merely' discredited (even though Colin Wallace was framed for murder). Could Murrell, for instance, have known about *nuclear deployment*, let alone intention, in the Falklands or even the highly secret Operation Barmaid? This might indeed be a reason to silence her. If so, the only connection could have been with her nephew who seemed perfectly content to keep the secrets that came his way and who might have had no knowledge of such operations. How then did these two die?

The obvious answer is that they died as the official record relates and that puts an end to speculation. That seems to wash with no one! Perhaps Murrell was murdered during two coincidental burglaries, one by a teenager after swag, another by a private company of investigators working in and for the nuclear industry. The coincidence of events might have triggered unforeseen and fatal circumstances. The same team, if it existed, might have been under instructions to eradicate McCrea too (for whatever reason) and chose two shots to the head to be sure. The distance at which the pistol was found was suspicious and McCrea was not known to own a gun. These two deaths represent the tip of an iceberg on the mainland of Britain, the origins of which were centred on Northern Ireland where murder of the government's opponents seemed to have not only been condoned, but encouraged.

24

THE HOODED MEN

Nowhere was Thatcher more intransigent and ruthless and nowhere so unsuccessful in her dealings with difficult and militarised situations than in Northern Ireland. She had indeed taken on a dreadful mess with intolerance on both sides as her only guide. Yet Thatcher had an uncompromising attitude to people she considered terrorists and murderers (as did most voters) and every bomb outrage strengthened her resolve and showed left-wingers such as Ken Livingstone, who supported the efforts of those he considered freedom fighters, to be dangerous collaborators. In public, Thatcher considered those involved in the struggle as merely criminals. Plagiarising Gertrude Stein, she insisted that, 'murder [was] murder, a crime [was] a crime', but her own government secretly kept channels open.

Neither diplomacy nor bullets had much effect on events, and the hardening of attitudes through the 1980s suggested that Thatcher's ruthlessness might prove her undermining. It had all begun long before she was Prime Minister. Those convicted of paramilitary activities were treated as ordinary prisoners until 1972, but 'special category' status was accorded to IRA prisoners after a short hunger strike. Nevertheless, in 1976 this was revoked and paramilitaries were recriminalised in order to depoliticise their struggle. This started a wave of assassinations of prison officers in revenge. Then, on 14 September 1976, Kieran Nugent began the 'blanket protest' in which prisoners went naked or wore only blankets. By March 1978, the situation had deteriorated such that prisoners refused to leave their cells and were demanding internal showers. This was refused by the prison authorities and the consequent violence led to the prisoners escalating their protest where excrement was smeared on walls. The cells quickly filled with maggots and stank so badly that visitors vomited.

By the middle of 1979, there were between 250 and 300 prisoners involved in dirty protests. By February 1980, the women prisoners at Armagh had joined in too. In January 1980, those involved had issued a statement of demands which included the right not to wear a prison uniform; the right not to do prison work; the right of free association with other prisoners, and to organise educational and recreational pursuits; the right to one visit, one letter and one parcel per week; full restoration of remission lost through the protest. These demands, tantamount to returning to the situation in late 1972, were rejected both by the British government and by the European Commission on Human Rights which considered the protests self-inflicted and self-serving. Thus the pressure was again ramped up and, on 27 October 1980, a number of prisoners began a hunger strike. This seemed to harden the government's position and was called off, but it was followed by another strike on 1 March 1981, when Bobby Sands (Roibeárd Gearóid Ó Seachnasaigh) refused food.

The hunger strikes adopted the tactics of the suffragettes and Mohandas Gandhi and replicated the Irish tradition of 'procedure by fasting' as a form of protest. It also brought to mind the 'blood sacrifice' of those who had died during the Easter Rising in 1916. Information regarding inhuman treatment of prisoners had leaked out throughout the 1970s, but no one was willing to believe convicted terrorists. The European Commission on Human Rights had, however, previously condemned the government for employing inhuman and degrading treatment in prisons including the use of torture. Hunger strikes were the prisoners' means of countering British propaganda and black operations not exposed until Colin Wallace and Fred Holroyd spoke up.

Bobby Sands had already spent almost four and a half years in one of the H-blocks at Long Kesh (also known as the Maze prison). He was an elected MP, but proscribed from taking his seat. He was also a Catholic republican socialist. As he languished in his prison cell, he secretly wrote poetry and mused on the situation, smuggling out scraps of toilet tissue and bits of paper. His main demand was to be able to wear ordinary clothes and be accorded the status of a prisoner of war in a colonial struggle. This, of course, would have given the IRA kudos as freedom fighters and patriots no different from those in other decolonised countries, and it also would have suggested that British rule was imperialistic.

Sands was not well educated, but he was literate and articulate and he thought about his political situation, a situation that once resolved would leave all Ulstermen and Ulsterwomen of any religion to heal their differences. He thought about his comrades as 'guerrilla fighters' who had been driven 'insane' by 'people who oppress, torture and imprison'.[1] Sands himself claimed to have been 'starved, beaten and tortured'.[2]

I have watched my own body and the bodies of my comrades degenerate to pure white shells of skin and bone. Our stomachs are bloated out by white bread – the mainstay of our inedible diet – eyes that once held a glimmer now stare insanely and seemingly at nothing. Sunken faces, long matted hair and untamed beards complete the naked ghost-like skeletal figures of what are referred to as 'blanket men of H-Block' … We wish to be treated 'not as ordinary prisoners' for we are not criminals. We admit no crime unless, that is, the love of one's people and country is a crime. We resist the attempt to criminalise us … I am a political prisoner because I am a casualty of a perennial war that is being fought between the oppressed Irish people and an alien, oppressive, unwanted regime that refuses to withdraw from our land.[3]

Sands died from hunger, weighing less than 7 stone, as did nine other men later. He was 27 years old and was a revolutionary hero to those in countries who harboured a hatred of Britain. There was even a street named after him in Tehran. A partial concession for what Sands sought was finally granted by the Secretary of State for Northern Ireland, Jim Prior, on 5 October 1981, when it was conceded that imprisoned paramilitaries might wear their own clothes.

Bobby Sands had, however, accused the British Government of torture, and that seemed to go beyond the pale even in Ireland. He, of course, had been allowed to torture himself. Nevertheless, the British government was willing to countenance applied torture by interrogators if it had the required outcome.

❧❦❧

From the government of Macmillan in the 1950s, through to the twenty-first century, every British government has denied the use of torture to gain information. Even Peter Wright, happy to dish the dirt wherever he could, had to concede that 'the CIA …[used] methods of imprisonment and physical pressure which would never have been tolerated in MI5'.[4]

Thatcher expressly forbade the use of torture, but, in Northern Ireland, there had been consistent claims of methods of interrogation little different from torture. The accusations came from those men on the dirty protests as well as from the INLA killers of Airey Neave. Of course, no civilian intelligence officer in MI5 or MI6 need ever have been involved as there were army, RUC Special Branch and private agencies who might be employed to carry out work that the security services could truthfully deny.

Since the secret interrogation of Nazi officers during the Second World War, Britain had a record of interrogation methods which bordered on the definition of torture. The post-war application of such techniques went back to a meeting at the Ritz-Carlton Hotel in Montreal on 30 May 1951. Of those present, Sir Henry Thomas Tizard represented British interests. He was there to discuss 'brainwashing' techniques which were being developed by both Canada and America. Britain had experimented already with 'truth drugs' in its battle against insurgents in Malaya. The experimentation with drugs such as sodium amytal continued after the conflict. There was also experimentation with LSD.

By 1959, the War Office had established a top-secret organisation called A19 employing psychological techniques, including sensory deprivation, and experiments that had been tried since 1956 and which were designed to monitor states of isolation and perceptual isolation. The experiments were so secret that all records were 'lost'. By 1960, there was considerable information on interrogation techniques and those designed to send the victim insane if required (something of which we have seen was revealed when those involved in EW died in mysterious circumstances). In 1963, the CIA actually codified its practices in its Kubark *Counterintelligence Interrogation Manual* which remained secret for thirty years thereafter.

By 1971, the techniques described in the manual were established as British inter-rogation techniques as well. The various methods were a mixture of isolation, sensory deprivation, exhaustion, humiliation and the ability to make the victim self-harm. These were collectively known as the 'five techniques', and included such accessories as 'hooding', being subjected to intolerable white noise, and incessant 'wall standing' in painful postures.

Thus it was when private Robert Curtis was the first soldier killed in Northern Ireland, on 6 February 1971, that army intelligence already had a full range of ways to get information under duress. Beginning with internment without trial, the gov-ernment tightened its grasp on security. The army opposed the move, but Sir Dick White, then head of MI6 after years of being head of MI5, saw internment as a way of further experimenting with the five techniques. From now on, certain prisoners would be selected for special treatment. Of the hundreds rounded up under Operation Demetrius (9–10 August 1971) a few were taken away by the RUC in another manoeu-vre code-named Operation Calaba. The subsequent tales of torture enraged republicans.

Operation Demetrius was able to net 337 of the 464 men on wanted lists. There were no Protestants. Of 1,981 suspects detained over the next eighteen months only 107 were Protestant and of the rest, twelve were sent for the five techniques treatment. One victim was Paddy Joe McClean, selected because he was a civil rights leader and from Omagh. Another was Joe Clarke, a 19-year-old mechanic. He recalled that, on arrest:

> After being hooded I was led to the helicopter and I was thrown bodily in. On being put into the 'copter, the handcuffs were removed and were applied to the back of the hood to tighten it around the head. The helicopter took off and a journey which I would estimate to have taken about an hour began. We were taken from the 'copter and led into a building and eventually into a room where I was made to stand in a search position against a wall – fully stretched, hands as far apart as humanly possible and feet as far from the wall as possible. Back rigid and head held up. Not allowed to relax any of the joints at all. If [there was] any relaxation of limbs – arms, elbow joints, legs, knee joints – someone came along and grabbed the limb in a rough manner and put it back into position.[5]

The 'hooded men' were supposedly held at the Palace Barracks at Holyfield near Belfast. They were actually held at Ballykelly airfield, so secret a location it was withheld from both government and European Court of Human Rights inquiries. The torture was not stopped when government stepped in either. An investigation by Lord Parker was set up only to establish whether such ill-treatment should continue not whether the treatment was illegal in the first place. No one was to be blamed for its use. A 'minority report' by Lord Gardiner nevertheless found the techniques to be illegal under 'Article 5 of the Universal Declaration of Human Rights; Articles 7 and 10 of the International Covenant on Civil and Political Rights; Article 3 of each of the four Geneva Conventions; and Article 3 of the European Convention on Human Rights'.[6] Gardiner concluded:

> If it is to be made legal to employ methods not now legal against a man whom the police believe to have, but who may not have, information which the police desire to obtain, I, like many of our witnesses, have searched for, but have been unable to find, either in logic or in morals, any limit to the degree of ill-treatment to be legalised. The only logical limit to the degree of ill-treatment to be legalised would appear to be whatever degree of ill-treatment proves to be necessary to get the information out of him, which would include, if necessary, extreme torture.[7]

No one was listening, least of all the RUC. The bombing campaign underway intensified. In only five months following the implementation of Operation Demetrius, 143 people were killed, including 46 in the security services. On 29 June 1972, the Joint Intelligence Committee sent revised guidelines on interrogation to all the relevant bodies. The five techniques were publically and officially banned, but a *second, highly secret part* to the official document was circulated to only a very few in the know and allowed the continuance of torture techniques by the intelligence services. This second part remained a state secret until 2008. There had been 304 bombs. The torture continued. In 1976, the European Court of Human Rights found the government guilty of 'torture'. The government finally reacted.

Both Heath and Thatcher were aware of the second part of the JIC's directive, but did nothing to restrict or stop its practical implications. While the army started to respect the new guidelines, the RUC simply seemed to have ignored them. By the mid 1970s, the IRA, however, had been reduced to a rump partially through the use of rough-and-ready RUC interrogations. The use of torture, in a way that was approved of by the government and carried out by RUC regional crime squads, meant that by 1978, the death toll had halved since 1976. The means seemed to have justified the ends. Illegal torture went on into the 1980s, never quite stopping the Republicans. The Special Branch in the RUC seemed untouchable and those who opposed it soon fell foul of smears and intimidation.

There was a campaign against Robert Irwin, a Protestant and the secretary of the Association of Police Surgeons, after interrogations had increased in order to counter the 1978 IRA offensive. When Thatcher won the 1979 election, it was still business as usual at police headquarters at Castlereagh. The techniques used in interrogation only slowed down at Castlereagh in 1989 after the appointment of Sir John Hermon as chief constable and his successor Hugh Annersley, who finally banned the practice in the 1990s.

After the death of Airey Neave, Thatcher had become more aware of the difference between intelligence gathered by soldiers and that by policemen, especially following the disaster at Warrenpoint in which six paratroopers were killed. In order to make some sense of intelligence operations, she brought out of retirement Sir Maurice Oldfield and appointed him as security coordinator, his job being to knock heads together. In this regard, Oldfield would be employed to make sure the various intelligence agencies and their contacts and sources of information were coordinated in such a way as to eliminate duplication, something that had dogged intelligence work for a considerable number of years.

As well as the appointment of 'Jack' Hermon as chief constable of the RUC, 1980 saw a new commanding officer of the British army in Northern Ireland appointed. Lieutenant General Sir Richard Lawson was largely a political choice to assuage Irish sensibilities. He hit it off with Hermon and agreed that there should be 'police primacy' in all intelligence work. This was repeated by Brigadier Maurice Tugwell in his influential paper *Trends in Low Intensity Conflict*, produced in 1981. This decision effectively made Oldfield's intervention irrelevant, but it also confirmed the centrality of the RUC Special Branch and its dubious methods.

Unlike British police forces, the RUC had a long and complex history of being involved in Protestant, unionist and loyalist politics as well as having connections with paramilitary groups. Thus it was associated with groups such as the Ulster Defence Association (UDA), which had been formed in 1970 and was involved with sectarian killings for which it used the cover name of the Ulster Freedom Fighters. It was also intertwined with the UDR, also created in 1970, a mainly Protestant organisation which had evolved from the B Specials, and which was a locally recruited regiment of the British army.

Members of the RUC might also be members of the UDR and secret members of the Ulster Volunteer Force (UVF), originally formed on 1 January 1913 and reorganised as the Ulster Special Constabulary before being reformed again in 1966 in its present guise. This group had been declared illegal on 28 June 1966 but was relegalised on 14 May 1974. The UVF sometimes called itself the Protestant Action Force and was part of a wider group called the Ulster Loyalist Combined Coordinating Committee, which comprised the UDA, the UVF (the Red Hand Commando) and other Protestant volunteer organisations.

Many of these organisations were interconnected through family, business and other links to the RUC itself, and RUC officers might indeed be secret members of these other organisations. Senior policemen in the RUC, including those in Special Branch, were connected to Orange lodges and networks of businesses and politicians. Unlike other British police forces, the RUC was also a Protestant organisation and a fully armed force of a military disposition with access to armaments such as sub-machine guns.

The UVF was certainly as well armed as the IRA, but unlike the IRA it did not have to look far to acquire its weaponry. Sten guns, grenades and revolvers were easily acquired through a pattern of contacts in the British army, the UDR and the RUC. The weapons which circulated among the murder gangs throughout the 1970s had largely been acquired by 1973. These included grenades, which had often come back as souvenirs from conflicts in Aden, Oman and Borneo or had been stolen from military depots such as that of HMS *Ark Royal*. This last was almost certainly the work of an Irish ex-serviceman known to the RUC but neither arrested nor interviewed. Indeed, by August 1973, a British army internal briefing paper on 'Subversion in the UDR' suggested that almost all the weapons in loyalist hands were those gained through 'collusion'.[8] Despite the fact that, by 1972, the British and security forces were well aware of the origin of loyalist weapons, and despite the fact that there was a huge push against the IRA whose members were being imprisoned without trial, there were no actions at all taken against UDA members or even the UVF, who were simply considered thugs rather than political terrorists.

In order to cover their tracks, meetings of senior officers were convened under a veil of secrecy. These meetings were called 'Chinese parliaments', the name given to a process whereby a decision was made without the identification of an author. In such a way, cover stories could be concocted.[9] So serious had become the situation that, in 1984, the deputy chief constable of Manchester, John Stalker, was invited by Jack Hermon to take a team to Northern Ireland in order to undertake an independent enquiry into police corruption and specifically into three sets of murders. The first had occurred on 11 November 1982 when Eugene Toman, Sean Burns and Gervais McKerr had been shot by an RUC anti-terrorist unit in Lergan. The second had occurred two weeks later on 24 November, when two more youths, Michael Tighe and Martin McCauley, were shot. The final incident had happened on 12 December when Seamus Grew and Roddey Carroll were shot in Armagh City. Because all the murders had happened close together and all of the murder victims were unarmed it was felt that there might be a deliberate plot to terrorise Catholic individuals.

Stalker and his team arrived in Belfast on 24 May 1984, with an investigative remit to see if there was any evidence of attempting to pervert the cause of justice by members of the RUC. Over the next two years, Stalker's team uncovered a story of murder, collusion and cover-ups. It soon became 'obvious' that Stalker 'could not trust anyone'.[10] His suspicions grew when he felt that his team was blocked at every effort to get at the truth whatever that might have been. Confirmation that there might be a 'judicially endorsed "shoot to kill"' policy surfaced when the policemen accused of one of the shootings were acquitted by Lord Justice Gibson who then went on to dismiss the victims and their fate with the remark that they had met 'the final court of justice'.[11]

Inexplicably, once Stalker had returned to Manchester and was preparing his investigative material for his final report, he became embroiled in accusations of impropriety with a criminal called Kevin Taylor. Stalker certainly felt that he had uncovered a vicious network of authorised killing which led directly to the RUC Special Branch and its senior officers. He believed his sudden dismissal from the case had been a frame-up originating from rumours that Jack Hermon and James

Anderton, the chief constable of Greater Manchester, were not merely linked by friendship but also by shadowy Orange lodge and Masonic connections.

Stalker, therefore, might have been sent to Ireland as part of a smokescreen and a whitewash and had been a 'patsy' all along. Once he came too near to what he believed to be the truth, he was recalled and framed. Thatcher, who must have been briefed on the whole situation, refused to comment about Stalker's 'suspension' or the enquiry that he had undertaken when she was questioned by Seamus Mallon MP in the Commons on 10 June 1986.[12] By the time Stalker had submitted his interim report, he had already gone beyond his remit and his officers had begun to identify some of the culprits who might have been involved with the murders. These included two senior serving RUC Special Branch officers and at least one that had retired.[13]

The rumours of a shoot-to-kill policy in Northern Ireland went back to the appearance of the SAS in Ulster. Elements of the regiment had originally been sent by Harold Wilson on 7 January 1976 to combat a rapidly deteriorating situation. The regiment's organisation was so secret that the SAS put around a rumour that Wilson had assumed he had signed deployment orders for 500 troops when he had actually only agreed to send five. In the event, a significant part of the regiment was to be redeployed to Belfast from training tribesmen in Dhofar, and as soon as possible. The first eleven soldiers flew to Belfast and moved to Armagh (the most troubled region) to carry out intelligence assessment and reconnaissance. In April, a full squadron plus logistic support had also arrived. A White Paper dated 8 January had actually approved an eighty-five strong unit to arrive as a 'spearhead' battalion.[14] This large concentration of specialist troops had been sent alongside 420 regular soldiers to finally deal with IRA insurgency.

So effective was the threat of their appearance that the IRA had been claiming success against the regiment since 1974. The actual deployment of the regiment (which never numbered more than forty or fifty men throughout the period, although WIlson was meant to have sent an initial force of 150), soon gave rise to the rumour that they had been sent as government assassins. This was never the case, as specialist troops had originally gone to provide intelligence enhancement for the regular army and RUC and the regiment was only supposed, where possible, to snatch belligerents from either side of the border.

Nevertheless, the actions of the regiment eventually gave rise to the belief in a shoot-to-kill policy as casualties mounted. Although no actual policy ever existed, casualties were high among those the regiment were meant to detain. Throughout the 1970s and 1980s, the regiment was engaged in covert operations which culminated in the shoot-out at Loughgall in County Tyrone on 8 May 1987 when eight members of the IRA's East Tyrone Active Service Unit were ambushed and killed while they attempted to blow up a police station. The IRA had suffered its biggest defeat since 1921, but one bystander had died, two policemen had been wounded and half the police station was rubble. Using the SAS was always a high-profile gamble and collateral damage always a possibility.

25

ZULU DELTA 576

The deployment of the SAS in Ulster had given the RUC an incentive to rethink its own command and information structures. The police, jealous of their prerogatives, had nevertheless accepted the necessary assistance of MI6 and MI5 and the British army. Yet, when the SAS was deployed, the RUC had become fearful of its position as the paramount peace-keeping organisation and began to create an intelligence unit with the same structure as the army and as a direct rival to military operations. To this effect, the RUC established a new unit called E4A which would gather covert intelligence on behalf of the uniformed RUC police and would especially complement RUC Special Branch. As part of E4A a special support unit (SSU), which was also known as the HQ Mobile Support Unit, was created as an armed 'active measures' organisation.[1] To complicate matters further, anti-terrorist operations were coordinated by the Tasking and Coordinating Group (TCG) based at Gough Barracks in Armagh.

The TCG was under the operational control of Special Branch. Special Branch ran undercover surveillance operations and gathered intelligence directly from informers. These informants included covert army operatives in loyalist ranks who were assessed and then passed on, possibly through coordination with military intelligence and MI5. This produced dangerous duplications which allowed the RUC to further replicate the role of the SAS. The deputy chief constable, Michael McAtamney, stated that the men in the SSU, for instance, were capable of 'firepower, speed and aggression' and were trained by the SAS to 'eliminate' threats. The use of elimination techniques was to be interpreted as widely as possible as the struggle against the IRA intensified. This interpretation of the various guidelines and policies dealing with fatal shootings by armed officers was so wide in fact that it was believed by many that the RUC had indeed secretly embraced a shoot-to-kill policy for a number of years and certainly well before Stalker had come calling.

Thatcher's insouciance in the face of criminality as she saw it had achieved nothing but the deaths of yet more Irish 'martyrs' whose demand for national and personal freedom was, after all, at the very heart of her own belief system; freedoms she would happily extend to those fighting the colonialism of the Warsaw Pact. It was too little too late and republicans harboured long and deep and dark resentments and planned for terrible retribution.

෴

It was in the early hours of 12 October 1984, and the Grand Hotel in Brighton was silent. Most people had gone to bed early in anticipation of the Prime Minister's speech the next day at the annual party conference. Mrs Thatcher had stayed up later than expected, perhaps buoyed up by a whisky, polishing her speech. At 2.54 a.m., the bomb exploded. It had been placed under the bath in room 629 and consisted of 20 pounds of gelignite wrapped in cling film to avoid being detected by the sniffer dogs. It was not a particularly big bomb, but it would do the job. It had been planted long before by a Provisional IRA team led by Patrick Magee who had stayed at the hotel under the name of Roy Walsh.

The explosion demolished the middle of the Victorian hotel and killed five people and injured thirty-one. For a moment, those who by now had grown to hate the iron lady actually hoped she too was dead somewhere in the rubble. The musician Morrissey mused about her possible death, as did writer John O'Farrell. A strange alliance of ill-wishers held their breath, but Thatcher, busy at her speech, had escaped unscathed. Getting dressed, she went to Brighton police station and then busied herself with the wounded; the Churchillian mantle had finally descended on her shoulders and, if she could not go to war personally (with the Argentinians, the miners or the IRA), war had finally come to her.

Nevertheless the Brighton Bomb proved a watershed of a kind. Thatcher who considered 'Ulster … as British as Finchley', was persuaded by her Cabinet secretary, Sir Robert Armstrong, that enough was enough. In this regard, although Thatcher outwardly continued to protest the Britishness of Ulster, she was now willing to meet Garret FitzGerald, the Irish Taoiseach, to discuss power sharing. This led to the Anglo-Irish Agreement which, in practice, compromised British sovereignty but was sold to the public as if it did not.

Not surprisingly, Protestants across Ulster were horrified to such an extent that half of the adult Protestant population went to hear Ian Paisley denounce the agreement at Belfast City Hall. These fiercely patriotic Irishmen and women burned an effigy of Thatcher. Even one of her closest supporters, the Unionist MP Enoch Powell, spoke of her 'treason'. The agreement effectively alienated Ulstermen from the British Government for the first time since 1913. Loyalists now began to prepare resistance not only to the IRA but also to the British Government which was now classed as an occupation force compelling ultimate union. The result was a Doomsday policy thought up by a new clique of loyalists in which Protestants would effectively declare unilateral independence and fight *on behalf* of their crown loyalties for an independent Ulster.

To achieve this, they formed a number of groupings very similar to those of the Provisional IRA. These were essentially reformations of the groups that had been active in the 1970s. On 2 October 1991, working on a tip-off, Sean McPhilemy of Box Productions broadcast his documentary on what was to become known as *The Committee* for Channel 4's *Dispatches* series. This referred to a secret organisation called the Ulster Loyalist Central Coordinating Committee run by a man called William Abernethy, a manager at the head office of the Ulster Bank, a sub-division of the Westminster Bank.

Abernethy, in turn, coordinated intelligence activities through the head of Special Branch at the RUC, assistant chief constable Trevor Forbes. The 'Committee' had emerged in mid-1989 and included a network of RUC and other intelligence groups which seemed to go as high as the RUC chief constable Sir Hugh Annesley. All these groups together essentially represented 'Ulster Resistance' whose members had been running assassinations and robberies since 1972. Included among its operatives were Billy Wright (King Rat) and Robin Jackson (the Jackal). In June 1987, for instance, a number of Ulster Resistance Groups including the UDA and the UVF robbed a bank in Portadown of £300,000 to buy weapons from South Africa and Israel.

So worrying became the activities of this group, whose murderous progress marked the last stages of the conflict, that John Stevens, deputy chief constable of the Metropolitan Police, was asked to investigate by the head of the RUC. He reported his findings in 1990. Indeed there were three Stevens Inquiries into Ulster corruption, but it was not until his report of 2003 that the suggested widespread misdoings. Just like Stalker, Stevens did find activities of a nefarious kind, and a number of loyalists were indicted. Nevertheless, Stevens did not find any 'institutional' problem with the RUC as a whole, at least in 1990. Thus the Stevens Inquiry was effectively able to neutralise the Stalker investigation regarding shoot-to-kill policies. It remains ironic that these groups of often disaffected and criminal loyalists, who Thatcher was well aware of from the beginning, were able to continue their activities aided and abetted by the intelligence services, the army and the RUC throughout the 1980s and finally to turn their ire upon the very government whose support had kept them afloat for so long.

As early as 1976, Irish affairs were meant to be reported differently from other news. When the then Labour Party Northern Ireland Secretary Roy Mason had been invited to speak at the opening of the BBC's new Belfast Studio he was expected to offer the usual after-dinner anodyne clichés. Instead he suggested, 'The BBC was disloyal, supported the rebels, purveyed their propaganda and refused to accept the advice of the Northern Ireland office on what news to carry.'[2]

What Mason began, Thatcher finished. Her prickly temperament towards television journalism was soothed only by those who would do her bidding, for which she turned to the *Sunday Times* and the *Sun* (both papers now contaminated with stories fed to them from the intelligence services) and it was their sort of believable 'journalistic fiction' that soothed her ire, as it would be remembered long after the 'truth' came out; truth which was soon forgotten in the greater lie that had preceded it.

By the 1980s, Irish affairs were on the television every night and Thatcher was getting more wary of people she could not control and who appeared to refuse to accept her point of view, especially with regard to Irish politics. Politicians have always needed and hated the media. Tony Benn thought the BBC full of Tories. While Thatcher had to put up with a belligerent media, she would do all she could to gag what was unpalatable to her particular sense of rightness. Television journalists were a specific *bête noire* and would continue to irritate her and her husband Denis throughout her terms of office. To Denis, after the *Belgrano* fiasco on *Newsnight*, in which his wife had had to grit her teeth because she was dealing with a voter before an election, the BBC was famously awash with 'Trots and wooftahs'.

This was despite the fact that, on the whole, non-BBC, independent documentary makers and independent television had created most of the controversial programmes. Nevertheless, programmes that allowed 'terrorists' a forum were always seen as unpatriotic and traitorous by Thatcher who expected journalists to take a loyal position in regard to the government's actions in the 'war' in Northern Ireland, even though it could never be admitted that there was a war. The problems really started with a BBC interview with the INLA assassins of Airey Neave. The broadcast, made by Roger Bolton and his team, coincided with the IRA atrocities at Warrenpoint and the murder of Lord Mountbatten.

Neave's widow objected after the programme was broadcast despite its excellent ratings with ordinary viewers. Although really no different from any other grieving widow, she expected special treatment. Then Thatcher picked up the story. One source near the Prime Minister suggested her sensitivity to the issue of Neave's death:

> She was desperately affected by … Neave's death, desperately. And in a way this affected her whole thoughts on broadcasting coverage of Northern Ireland.
> She had a mystical view of what he would do in Ireland, that he had actually been killed by the INLA because they thought he was going to do things in Ireland which would have been so successful it would have done a great deal of damage.[3]

Norman Tebbit had long argued that BBC journalists were simply lefties pretending to be impartial. Journalists argued, on the other hand, that freedom of the press was central to democratic thinking and that following the government's line was not unpatriotic but totalitarian, precisely what went on in the Soviet Union; but this cut no ice. During his period as the Chairman of the Governors of the BBC, George Howard had even been mauled by the Conservative Media Committee, which didn't trust his organisation, and he had been accused of being a 'traitor'.[4]

Thatcher even asked Home Office officials what could be done to silence these sorts of programmes. Hence in 1979, all television journalists were tarred with the same brush. Thatcher had been able to control the media during the Falklands War by filtering news broadcasts through a civil servant and by restricting access to war zone information to Max Hastings, whom she could trust, but her lack of control of intelligence leaks, especially after the Gibraltar incident in 1988, made her increasingly jittery.

By 1988, Roger Bolton had moved to Thames Television and there he began to piece together the story of the killing of three IRA members by the SAS on Gibraltar. The programme was to be called *Death on the Rock* and it would look at evidence that the IRA terrorists, Mairéad Farrell, Sean Savage and Danny McCann, had been targets in the type of shoot-to-kill attacks investigated by John Stalker. It had emerged that the three had been unarmed, with none of the bomb equipment suggested, and that there had been a witness to the shooting in the head of Danny McCann as he lay unarmed and on the ground. The SAS appeared to have targeted and then assassinated their victims with bloody efficiency, and with the connivance of Spanish police, in an attack copied from Israeli methods for dealing with suspected bombers. Bolton concluded that there were serious unanswered questions. After all:

> It would be a naïve politician who decided to deploy the SAS and did not expect shooting to take place. And when the shooting starts it continues until all signs of human life are totally eradicated. Mrs Thatcher and the members of the secret Cabinet committee which took the decision to deploy the SAS knew this … You have to take a long time to make up your mind because you know the SAS are trained to shoot first and ask questions afterwards, because they are at risk themselves, and you are putting them into a wartime situation.[5]

If indeed this was the case, then, by implication, this was the first time a British Prime Minister had been caught authorising a death squad.

Operation Flavius had been carefully planned and coordinated with the police in Gibraltar and with MI5. The SAS teams had made sure they had the IRA suspects under surveillance and were waiting for the police force to hand over temporary control to the military. The accidental turning on of the police siren in Inspector Louis Revagliatte's car alerted the terrorists to what they thought might be an attempt to arrest them. The story as it emerged at the inquest from the soldiers involved was that they had attempted to shout their warnings before shooting, but, in each case, it had appeared that the targets looked as if they were about to detonate a bomb from a remote-control device and therefore there was only sufficient time to stop them in their tracks; the split-timing decision was to shoot and kill. When the news broke in Britain in the late afternoon of Sunday 6 March, it seemed to confirm in the minds of many opposed to British policies in Northern Ireland that this was another example of the shoot-to-kill policy that had apparently been in force for a number of years.

Death on the Rock and the subsequent BBC Northern Ireland programme that followed suggested that British soldiers were under instructions to kill terrorists on sight and were not answerable to the law. As in so many cases of this sort throughout the period, the evidence is muddied by the recollections and statements of alleged witnesses. Kenneth Asquez, the star witness of the programme had withdrawn his statement not long afterwards, saying that he had 'made this up', presumably to get some celebrity attention.[6] He had originally given a short, handwritten statement to a local retired soldier, but he had refused to sign what was effectively a draft. As for the other star witness, Carmen Proetta had repeatedly said that she too had seen cold-bloodied assassinations, but later when questioned she had also become more equivocal, saying that she simply didn't know what had actually occurred.

Much soul searching and double checking went on before the programme was broadcast, but, when it was, there was a frenzy of right-wing newspapermen ready to attack the veracity of the story, especially as witnesses at the subsequent inquest changed their stories or were libelled in the papers. Bernard Ingham was on the warpath, and speaking on the record he wished to 'remind the media of their responsibilities'.[7] The inquest on the programme demanded by the government was headed by Lord Windlesham, a dyed-in-the-wool Tory grandee, but, amazingly, he found the programme fair and reasonable, which did not enamour him to those who had employed him. Windlesham concluded, 'The programme makers were experienced, painstaking and persistent. They did not bribe, bully or misrepresent those who took part. The programme was trenchant and avoided triviality. Those who made it were acting in good faith and without ulterior motives.'[8] It was all to no avail, for, at about the same time, the Home Secretary announced that there would now be a ban on sound transmission of interviews with Sinn Fein or the IRA.

A fateful revenge of sorts followed on 2 June 1994, when an air crash wiped out much of the British intelligence infrastructure in Northern Ireland. Official silence shrouded the event in a fog of misinformation. The circumstances of the crash of the Chinook military helicopter Zulu Delta 576 on a lonely hillside on the Mull of Kintyre on that Thursday have never been fully explained. The flight had taken off from Aldergrove near Belfast with twenty-five senior intelligence and army officials and was headed for Fort George in Scotland for a few days of talks and golf. There were four crew and two pilots, Flight Lieutenants Jonathan Tapper and Richard Cook. At around 6 p.m., the flight apparently crashed into a hill on the very tip of the Mull. The BBC announced the crash at 7.26 p.m. There were no survivors.

Once it was known who was on board, the incident soon drew out conspiracy theorists who wrongly surmised that an attack or sabotage had brought the helicopter down. There was a suggestion that the IRA had used one of their newly acquired missiles to down the craft or that those on board who had been intimately involved with the 'dirty'

intelligence and assassination war fought in the previous decade had somehow been sac-
rificed by the British to appease republicans and speed the peace process. Those on board
were Richard Allen, Christopher Biles, Dennis Bunting, Desmond Conroy, Richard
Cook, Martin Dalton, Philip Davidson, Stephen Davidson, John Deverell, Christopher
Dockerty, John Fitzsimons, Graham Forbes, Robert Foster, Richard Gregory-Smith,
William Gwilliam, Kevin Hardie, John Haynes, Anthony Hornby, Anne MacDonald
(or James), Kevin Magee, Michael Maltby, Maurice Neilly, John Phoenix, Roy Pugh,
Stephen Rickard, Gary Sparks, Jonathan Tapper, John Tobias and George Williams:[9]

> Dark rumours abound. The loss of ten senior RUC intelligence officers, nine
> army intelligence officers and six MI5 officers on the eve of the 1994 IRA ces-
> sation was, for some, propitious … Some loyalists believe that the intelligence
> officers were deliberately 'taken out' for 'knowing too much' about the people
> the government would have to deal with in a post-conflict Ulster.[10]

Nevertheless, the rumours were, perhaps, less credible and less terrible than the likely
scenario.

The MOD had decided in the mid-1980s to upgrade its Chinook helicopter fleet
and so had begun shipping helicopters back to Boeing in Philadelphia in the summer
of 1988 to be refitted. In a money-saving exercise, the MOD had decided not to fit
voice recorders or black box recorders. This move would, of course, prevent much
useful information being retrieved from the crash site.

One particularly important piece of new technology was a FADEC software
package to monitor and control fuel to the blades. There are many FADEC systems,
but this particular one was being sold by Textron-Lycoming and the contract had
been awarded before sufficient checks had been made to confirm that the system
was as efficient and as safe as proposed. Ground trials of the system at Wilmington
showed there was a design fault which caused the motors to accelerate and which
might cause the rotor blades to fly off. Finding the fault delayed delivery until 1993.
The Ministry of Defence and the chiefs of the RAF were left annoyed and embarrassed. The software had latent errors which might prove disastrous. Nevertheless,
the MOD took delivery and started to do its own tests at Boscombe Down. The RAF
then took delivery but complaints from senior pilots suggested problems. Some even
wanted to retain the older marque.

After the crash, the usual investigation began. An RAF three-man board of inquiry
found that a probable systems error had caused the crash. It rejected the idea that
the pilots had made a fatal and irreversible decision at the last minute. As there were
no witnesses, black box or voice recorder, it was felt that that system error was to
blame. The most senior RAF hierarchy overturned the board decision with no
recourse to appeal. Air vice-marshals John Day and William Wrattan found instead
that the pilots had been grossly negligent and had, in fact, caused an unnecessary

crash amounting to a case of civilian manslaughter. Day began his report in conciliatory mood. He found:

> That the crew, faced with the expected deteriorating weather, consciously elected
> to make a climb on a track over high ground and in so doing used a speed and
> power combination that is unrecognisable as a Chinook technique. I find this
> difficult to believe; such actions would go against all the crew's instincts and
> training.[11]

Yet, by the end, he had concluded:

> In carrying out that mission, Flt Lt Tapper, as captain of the aircraft in peacetime,
> had an overriding duty to ensure the safety of the aircraft, its crew and the
> passengers. While there may, arguably, be some mitigating circumstances, I am
> regrettably drawn to the conclusion that he failed in that duty.[12]

This might have brought the whole thing to a conclusion. It would certainly get the
air vice-Marshals (one of whom had hopes of the most senior position in the RAF)
out of a sticky hole in which they might have to explain why someone authorised so
many senior officials to travel together in a helicopter with a potential flaw, known as
a 'FADEC runaway': an acceleration combined with a steep climb with unrespond-
ing instruments. Such a machine was a flying coffin and there was enough evidence
to have suggested caution.

  While English law inhibited further enquiry, Scottish law did not. Under the Fatal
Accidents and Sudden Deaths Inquiry (Scotland) Act, the whole affair could be
re-examined. Thus in 1996, a court was convened under Sheriff Sir Stephen Young.
The inquiry was thorough and even SAS pilots were called to give testimony. Flight
Lieutenants 'J' and 'K' suggested that there might be a fault with the improperly
tested aircraft after all:

> We were certainly uncomfortable with being told that the test pilots [at
> Boscombe Down] were not flying the aircraft anymore because they were uncer-
> tain of its operability, and the line pilots were continuing to fly it. It did seem
> slightly the wrong way round. It was an uncomfortable position … [There was]
> an apparent lack of knowledge at higher level as to what was likely to happen
> to aircraft systems in any given set of circumstances, and I mean specifically the
> Fadec-related problems.[13]

This effectively acquitted the two pilots of any provable error.

  The findings of the Scottish inquiry were ignored, but then the freedom of information opportunities afforded by John Major's new policy of 'open government'

meant that new facts began to emerge. The first was that the problem of 'runaway' had been known about since 1989 and the MOD had sued Textron for negligence in both the software and the testing of the various systems. The fact that the MOD had been actively pursuing the manufacturers was not however passed on either to Malcolm Rifkind in 1995 when he was Minister for Defence, nor to John Reid, when he was Defence Minister and testified to the Commons Defence Committee in 1998. Such testimony was interpreted as simply a smokescreen for civil servants and the RAF higher command (who it emerged were fearful of those below questioning orders). Indeed there had been eight serious incidents with Chinooks, and fifty-six design faults found in the software were found by the MOD's consultants. Neither Reid nor Rifkind were well informed on the issue. They had simply been ignored by those in the department whom they led.

Reports and inquiries by both the House of Lords and the House of Commons castigated careless RAF thinking. Evidence grew through 1997 and 1998 and it was suggested as late as 2000 that the air vice-marshals had 'misdirected themselves' (a phrase borrowed from the American diplomatic parlance of 'mis-speaking') and that technical evidence from both the United States and Britain suggested systems failure related to metal dust particles in the software itself. *Computer Weekly* even put the case for a one-off occurrence that might not be replicable under test conditions.

> A computer failure brought down the London Stock Exchange for nearly an entire day, and the bug that brought down the system has not been identified because it has not been possible to replicate the exact problem. The inability to identify the bug is despite the forensic skills of some of the most expert software specialists in the USA and the UK.[14]

Did this make an impact on RAF thinking or the MOD's position? It did not. John Day, expecting any minute to become chief of air staff, even threatened to resign if his verdict was challenged by the Lords' committee.[15]

Such was the concern in Parliament, that the whole affair was manoeuvred into neutral ground. The original problem had occurred through cost-cutting and negligence in the Thatcher era; it had been compounded by obstruction and intransigence, and by deeply conservative and traditional elements in the higher command of the armed forces whose elementary foolishness in putting so many important personnel in one possibly faulty helicopter had to be disguised. The crash was not merely the worst accident in peacetime suffered by the RAF, it proved a strategic disaster, 'temporarily confounding ... an anti-Provisional IRA campaign'.[16]

Blame had to be pushed down the ranks.

> The *only* people who found the pilots guilty of gross negligence (i.e manslaughter), were the two Air Marshals, one of whom (ACM Wratten) had never flown

a Chinook in his life. That leaves just one man, AVM Day, who could reasonably claim to be an expert on the Chinook. Even so, his experience was on the Mark 1, which, of course, was not equipped with Fadec.[17]

The worries over the morals of past decisions finally turned to the immediate concerns over a miscarriage of justice. The process was already two decades old. In 2014, the RAF operated the largest fleet of Chinook support helicopters after the United States army. There were thirty-four HC2s, six HC2As and eight HC3s, but the HC3 had yet to enter operational service because as early as 2004 the Mark 3 Chinooks were deemed un-airworthy and instead were cannibalised for use in Iraq and Afghanistan.

Finally, there was grudging restitution and justice. The case would not go away, and in 2010, a review by Lord Philip concluded with the same judgement as Sheriff Stephens. The verdict was accepted by Liam Fox who announced in the Commons in July 2011 that '[he] hope[d] that this report, and the action I have taken in response to it, will bring an end to this very sad chapter by removing the stain on the reputations of the two pilots'.

Such cases remained as testament to the conspiratorial bureaucracy of the Ministry of Defence, the defence industry and those in charge of Britain's armed forces. It was a world where conspiracy theory finally met prosaic fact. In some cases, the prosaic facts were more worrying than the fantasy. Disasters gestated for many years before happening. Long after Thatcher and many of her less scrupulous ministers were gone, a deadly legacy of Ministry of Defence cost-cutting, initiated by John Knott from before the Falklands War, still survived.

26

THE OLD IRON WOMAN

Edward Heath and James Callaghan were not confrontational politicians, but both had no choice but to fight battles not of their choosing, and both lost. During the summer of 1973, Joe Gormley had sat in the garden of 10 Downing Street chatting pay policy over a cup of tea with Heath and Sir William Armstrong. 'Well, Joe,' asked Heath, 'What are the chances this year?'[1] Arthur Scargill and Margaret Thatcher never had such a cosy tête-à-tête; they never met, in fact. Thatcher had a militaristic attitude to life which drove her agenda, a root and branch attitude which brooked no debate and she had a combative personality which she employed in increasing vehemence as her premiership went on. In her first term Thatcher was tied to the more moderate policies of her Cabinet; the Falklands victory released Thatcher to become more forceful and confident. Indeed, it was after the Falklands War and her second election victory that she started to become the Prime Minister envisioned by the McWhirter brothers, but also by Brian Crozier and Airey Neave or any one of the economic or security ideologues or active senior military commanders who had blazed the trail before the woman had come to match the hour of their need.

Market-led economic reform was only a symptom of Thatcherism, philosophically based as it was on the conflict between communalism (represented as 'statism' or direction from a centralised bureaucracy) and liberal individualism. This was not really a pragmatician's politics (despite Thatcher's early caution) but an apocalyptic fight to the death with unidentified enemies who emerged as if called up by magic throughout the period of Thatcher's premiership. From the GLC to the miners, Thatcher identified straw enemies who were forced to become real enemies in the self-fulfilling prophesy of reborn Conservatism. Thatcher was most at home posing with the SAS, driving tanks or taking an inordinate interest in the security services and GCHQ. Ironically, the Prime Minister was most effective when she felt beleaguered, which gave her a feeling of strength rather than weakening her resolve, as it had done to Wilson and Callaghan. When she was absolutely dominant, however, as after 1987, her hectoring, bullying and petty-mindedness showed her to disadvantage and made her appear weak and doctrinaire without purpose.

The spirit of the woman and the spirit of the age were summed up for many people by two graphic novels, poignant and acidic in turns. Both were the creations of illustrator Raymond Briggs. *The Tin-Pot Foreign General and the Old Iron Woman* was a sour appraisal of the Falklands conflict and the stupidity and futility of war. Thatcher's quarrel was reduced to a disastrous and infantile fight over a trifle which left only 'the families of the dead [to tend] the graves'. Thatcher was presented as a grotesquely erotic swivel-eyed metallic giant, 'an old woman' who lived with 'lots of money and guns'. She was, as Briggs pointed, out 'not real', but a mere myth of her own making and of those around her. The book had been preceded by *When the Wind Blows*, the poignant and tragic tale of a middle-aged couple who die after a nuclear explosion they were convinced they might survive because of government propaganda. It is illuminating that some opposed to Thatcher's policies were reduced to the visceral immediacy of cartoon vitriol to express their distaste, as if it were no longer possible to put forward a rational argument.[2]

Thatcher embodied contradictions that were represented quite differently, both by herself and her publicists, as consistency. In 1960, having just been elected to Parliament, Thatcher promoted a freedom of information bill called the Public Bodies (Admission of the Press to Meetings) Bill. In this she was supported by E.P. Thompson and Barbara Castle. The Bill appeared libertarian, but it was not, being designed instead to break the secrecy of Labour council meetings, and proceedings in the actual Labour Party. It was sparked by a union strike at the time. Thatcher's stance had made her appear almost liberal in her views to those who would later rue the day that they had ever supported her.

Neither was Thatcher particularly homophobic. She was not so naive as to dismiss homosexuality, and, following the Wolfenden committee's report on the legalisation of homosexual acts, Thatcher supported the Sexual Offences Act of 1967, but only because it confined homosexuality to the private sphere and did not promote homosexual display in public. Thatcher's promotion of privacy over state interference was one of her constant themes and should be seen against Labour's growing state control and welfare communalism.

> The bureaucratic statism towards which Labour politicians increasingly drifted carried with it a rhetoric in which the State, in all its aspects, was seen as a public good, a defence of working people, or of the little man, against private vested interests. The dividing line between the Welfare State and the Police State became obscure, and bureaucracy, in every form, waxed fat in this obscurity.[3]

Ironically, the promotion of civil and private liberties required even greater state intervention, policing and interference. The secret state reached its peak in the early 1980s with every encouragement from the Prime Minister, who seemed to enjoyed secrecy and flirted with the intelligence services whom she flattered. Peter Wright's claim that the secret services 'bugged and burgled [their] way across London at the state's behest, while pompous bowler-hatted civil servants pretended to look the other way' was, according to one journalist specialising in spying, 'entirely credible'.[4]

Despite arguments to the contrary, Thatcher was no fascist either. Her continuing friendship with General Pinochet, even when he was under house arrest in Britain, was born of a mistaken belief that diplomatic and military expediency accorded with recognition of loyalty and services rendered. Thatcher used democracy and bent its rules, but the overtly authoritarian use of the military was always carefully guarded against despite the loose talk before she became Prime Minister. It was, of course, never needed. Troops were used in Ireland, where the police were themselves militarised, but were always kept out of sight on the mainland. It was no secret, however, that troops always stood by in times of emergency. They had done so for years. Thus during the 1979 Winter of Discontent, Home Secretary Merlyn Rees had been prepared to call out the troops.[5]

Troops were an option of last resort, and the Thatcher government never really interfered with the old emergency powers or how they might be enforced, taking a non-political approach to the issue. The army stood ready or actually became involved quite rarely, but did so during the three ambulance personnel strikes in 1979, 1981 and 1982. Military personnel were involved with Civil Service strikes and at two strikes at military installations in 1979 and 1981, to protect air and nuclear facilities. In November 1979, soldiers *were* used to break a picket line at Charing Cross Hospital and regular threats continued throughout 1980 and 1981 when ambulance crews went on strike against appalling pay and conditions, but were only used in Wales where soldiers answered emergency calls. Ambulance and other workers were not particularly incensed by the army working to break their strikes. What offended was the use of volunteers who were considered scab labour. Green Goddess fire engines were also wheeled out against firefighters when they went on strike in November 1980. In 1982, troops were deployed during a rail workers' strike, but their presence was minor and largely unnoticed. In 1983, the use of troops was threatened in the water workers' dispute, but volunteers were mobilised instead. Indeed, the strangest use of military personnel was the requisitioning of a Sealink ferry in 1983 which was 'hijacked' by the navy from Wallsend-on-Tyne after a pay dispute had caused running costs to rocket.

All this was small beer compared with the prison officers' dispute of 1980. Officers were on strike because of terrible conditions in overcrowded and run-down Victorian jails. One former director general of the prison service called conditions nothing less than 'abominable'.[6] The dispute left prisons unguarded, so the military was chosen to take up the job, because of its record in Northern Ireland.

To allow army personnel to run prisons, new legislation was quickly brought in. This was the Imprisonment (Temporary Provisions) Act 1980, called by the National Council for Civil Liberties 'one of the most dangerous laws to be put on the statute book'.[7] The original bill was put to Parliament after a defence council order authorised the use of troops under section 2 of the Emergency Powers Act 1964. The bill, once in law, was supposed to lapse after a year, but was renewed in 1981 as the strike dragged on. The bill was initially presented to Parliament by William Whitelaw and passed into law in a record thirteen hours and twenty minutes. The law was designed to allow:

> 'any place' as an 'approved place' for the detention of prisoners; removed the guar-
> antee that prisoners were entitled to certain statutory rights; gave the police the
> right to hold prisoners in police cells; and gave troops all the powers, authority,
> protection and privileges of a constable (while acting as warders), for the first time
> in British history.[8]

In all, approximately 1,000 specialised army personnel took part, guarding half-finished prison projects and army prisons such as HM Prison Frankland in County Durham with 600 prisoners, and army prison Rollestone near Salisbury Plain holding a further 352, a month before the strike ended.

Whatever she was, Thatcher was neither particularly racist nor personally discrimina-tory (in fact, very often the opposite), rather she was always an authoritarian populist who nevertheless flirted with the ideas of fascist regimes such as Chile and refused to condemn Rhodesian unilateralism or South African apartheid, the shadows of which determined attitudes to the economy and her attitude to the problems of the inner city which were dealt with as if they were a matter of colonial policing and where internal uprisings might be dealt with by police rather than the army which was trying to do the same thing on a daily and more deadly basis in Belfast and Londonderry.

The difference between left and right was clear: left-wing communities had to be destroyed as they created the culture of *moral degeneration* that was the real target of Thatcher's policies. Nowhere was this distaste more obvious than in clause 28 of the Local Government Act 1988, which banned the promotion of homosexuality in schools. The moral degeneracy that had been key to Westminster Council's secret deliberations was tolerated as long it followed a Thatcherite agenda, and as long as it could be hidden from the public, or, if exposed, the government could be exonerated of any wrongdoing. This led to terrible abuses of power undertaken in the name of liberalism, the most evident of which was the continuing toleration of Shirley Porter and the active promotion of Jimmy Savile, whose working-class mining credentials made him seem perfect proof that Thatcherism worked.

Savile was promoted (and promoted himself) as a personal friend of the PM and would frequently be entertained at Downing Street or Chequers. He was even employed, by Edwina Currie, as the director of Broadmoor Psychiatric Hospital in 1988 to break a strike and bring nurse/wardens into line, despite the fact that his now-notorious sex life was known about from at least 1972, the time coincidentally that Cyril Smith, who had allegedly abused boys for years, appeared on an MI5 list of possible 'homosexuals' and was therefore a potential communist mole. Smith's activities were ignored because David Steele the leader of the Liberal Party saw no harm in 'just spanking a few bottoms' and because those in charge of protecting public morals couldn't seem to imagine what paedophilia meant, whether it was at the Kincora Boys' Home in Northern Ireland or in Middlesbrough General Hospital years later.

Such sexual proclivities linked such people to organisations such as NCCL through the Paedophile Information Exchange and linked them also through the numerous networks of perversion that ran through Westminster. Everything needed to be hidden away, and the whistle-blowers put on trial lest others with secrets to hide were themselves exposed. Nothing was done in Smith's case, and Savile earned a knighthood. Some who abused children were treated as celebrities and courted. If it was true that those in the Labour and Liberal parties were under surveillance for deviant and possibly subversive behaviour, then it was also certainly true that the Conservative Party was not morally pure either.

In June 1986, the *People* exposed Harvey Proctor, MP for Billericay and one of the representatives of Thatcher's 'Essex Man'. He was accused of indulging in spanking sessions with underage male prostitutes and was forced to resign after a trial in 1987. Later, he set up a shirt-making shop in Richmond with investment money loaned by Conservative Party friends. Unsubstantiated rumours that a homosexual paedophile group operated or used Downing Street itself and that Thatcher turned a blind eye, continued to circulate into 2015.

More interesting perhaps, were the paedophile activities reportedly occurring at the Elm Guest House near Barnes Common and a 'holding' house in Mortlake. Elm House was used as a brothel involving children held in 'care' at the Grafton Close children's home in Richmond. Senior politicians were linked to the house and its uses throughout the 1970s and 1980s. In 1989, Labour MP Bernard Cohen named Leon Brittan as a visitor in a Commons question. He was told to be silent by the Speaker. Wild rumours suggested that Cyril Smith, Sir Anthony Blunt and Jimmy Savile and his brother were frequent visitors. Savile might have had connections to the security services through his activities at the guest house which would have made him a useful tool and allowed him to fantasise about his influence on VIPs and the royal family. Whether Smith was involved or not, sufficient intelligence had built up around his activities that when he was chosen to be knighted in 1988, the committee had 'some hesitation' due to information regarding allegations dating back to 1960 (there was plenty of other more recent evidence). Thatcher still offered Smith the knighthood perhaps to avoid awkward questions if he had not been knighted.

In 2012, the *Independent* reported that social worker Chris Fay had been shown pictures of naked boys and men by the owner of the property, Carol Casir, who apparently killed herself in 1990 with an overdose of insulin – which was itself suggestive of state agencies being involved, especially as she had incriminating photographs and possible videos of middle-aged politicians and young boys. Casir had previously been charged with running a 'disorderly house', but other charges were never pursued. The whole operation was supposedly run by the intelligence services as a useful way into blackmail, with Casir as merely a type of caretaker 'madam'. The disappearances of Martin Allen in 1979 and Vishal Mehrotra in 1981 were both linked in newspaper articles to activities at Elm House. On 16 August 1982, Attorney General Michael Havers intervened to put a stop to further reporting. Alternatively, Mehrota's disappearance may relate to another paedophile gang run by Sidney Cooke (Hissing Sid), whose activities included the murder of numerous other children and who may have once boasted of killing an 'Asian' boy. Cooke was arrested in 1989. The Mehrota case was reopened in June 2015 and shows the extreme caution needed in pursuing conspiracies of this sort.

According to the *Sunday People*, Thatcher was said to have had a secret meeting with one of her senior ministers in which she told him to 'clean up' his sexual activities with boys. More damaging accusations of a prime-ministerial cover-up have come from former Conservative worker Anthony Gilberthorpe, who claims that in 1989 he sent a forty-page dossier to Downing Street which accused Cabinet members of abusing children at parties. This has further been compounded by a separate source with links to Scotland Yard. The source told how an unnamed minister was accused of sexually abusing boys at the home of his agent some time in 1982. The minister was also apparently hauled before Thatcher, Whitelaw, a senior policeman and an MI5 officer and told to watch his behaviour. He was not disciplined or sacked. Was this the incident Edwina Currie was alluding to in her diary for 24 July 1990?

> One appointment in the recent reshuffle has attracted a lot of gossip and could be very dangerous: Peter Morrison has become the PM's PPS [Parliamentary Private Secretary]. Now he's what they call a 'noted pederast', with a liking for young boys; he admitted as much to [Conservative Party chairman] Norman Tebbit when he became deputy chairman of the party but added, 'However, I'm very discreet' – and he must be! She [Thatcher] either knows and is taking a chance, or doesn't; either way, it's a really dumb move.[9]

The case was reopened in 2012, when police again looked at the disappearance of Martin Allen. Despite reopening the investigation, the police only had a lead to a house in Liverpool where there was a supposed shrine to the boy in the home of a child abuser. Allen's death was, however, linked to Elm House. Nevertheless, the investigation again proved inconclusive and was wound down in 2013.

Earlier in 2012, the Metropolitan Police had begun a 'scoping exercise' into Elm House called Operation Fairbank, with the intention of deciding if an investigation was warranted. The result was a criminal investigation called Operation Fernbridge, begun in 2013. The investigation was part of a bigger operation intended to break international paedophile rings. Operation Fairbank had in fact been set up after the Labour

MP Tom Watson raised a question in the Commons on 24 October 2012 regarding a 'powerful paedophile network linked to Parliament and No 10'. Watson mentioned a Downing Street aide and a former Prime Minister, but named neither. It does appear that a very high-level paedophile ring, linking prominent politicians and celebrities, and protected by intelligence agencies, operated without hindrance from the 1970s into the 1980s because it was expedient to allow it to exist.

Then, in the summer of 2014, the allegations surfaced again. It was claimed that in 1983, Conservative MP Geoffrey Dickins showed Leon Brittan, then Home Secretary, a dossier containing 114 allegations of child abuse, naming eight prominent politicians. He was also meant to have shown the Director of Public Prosecutions, Sir Thomas Hetherington, the same document. Brittan first said that he did not recall reading the document and then 'remembered' that he had and had passed it to officials. That was the end, apparently, of his involvement despite the fact that the dossier had named very prominent people and the papers then went 'missing' or were deliberately shredded or 'lost'. In 2013, there had even been an interim report produced by the Home Office, but without reference to the original dossier or Brittan's response.

On the BBC's *Andrew Marr Show* on 6 July 2014, Norman Tebbit suggested that the dossier had been lost because 'it was more important to protect the system than make any effort to bring the perpetrators to justice'. His tone suggested that he too might have heard the rumours at the time. By coincidence, an accusation of rape (not, however, of paedophilia) was brought against Brittan, which itself coincided with the announcement of an inquiry by the Home Secretary Teresa May into the situation.

The government appointed Elizabeth Butler-Sloss to oversee an inquiry, but she immediately resigned amid 'chaos' because she was Michael Havers's sister. Her resignation was immediately followed by that of her successor Fiona Woolf because, it was claimed, she was too close to Leon Brittan. How much senior politicians and civil servants knew about the abuse and turned a blind eye to it might never be revealed, but the suggestion remains that very senior people indeed were aware of what they wilfully chose to ignore. The final choice was Justice Lowell Goddard from New Zealand.

More evidence emerged during the writing of this book. The man seen possibly talking to Martin Allen at Earl's Court Station may be linked to either David Smith, Jimmy Savile's chauffeur (who committed suicide before a scheduled court appearance in 2014), or Sidney Cooke, who both had connections with the car firm servicing the Australian embassy. Allen's father was also working for the same firm and numerous dignitaries, including Thatcher, knew the father and may have also known of his son. Allen disappeared on 5 Nov 1979. When the disappearance was reported Martin's brother Keith remembers a 'suave' policeman visiting and listening to accusations against prominent politicians and warning his parents not to pursue the case because, 'if you keep saying things like that you will be hurt'. The case remains unopened and unsolved.[10]

The case of Vishal Mehrota, abducted in 1981 around the Barnes area, also remains unsolved. His father Vishambar Mehrota is convinced he was killed in Dolphin Square or at the Elm Guest House.[11] The evidence was built upon allegations from another boy 'Nick', that one paedophile MP strangled and murdered a victim at Dolphin Square.[12] Cyril Smith and others were allegedly protected by police in on the opportunities offered by easy sex. In Smith's case it was Sergeant Don Mackintosh, another paedophile.[13]

As part of the current investigation the IPCC will look into whether there was any cover-up of a politician's involvement in a South London paedophile ring; the activities at Dolphin Square; the actions of senior police implicated in the activities at the Westminster flats; the altering and redacting of witness evidence; evidence suppressed by Special Branch; a conspiracy within the Metropolitan Police to end any investigation; the nature of communications between the police, politicians and others; lack of any prosecutions; surveillance of victim. Whether the alleged murders will be reopened for investigation or those involved will ever be named or allowed to die before naming is anyone's guess.

Leon Brittan who had two of his homes in Pimlico and Wensleydale raided as part of Operation Midland, the investigation into child sex abuse, died in 2015; his office is known to have mislaid four files relating to the case. At the same time police raided the home of the former head of the armed forces Lord Bramhall, whose carer opened the door. Lord Greville Janner was deemed too ill to stand trial in 2015 by Alison Saunders, the Director Of Public Prosecutions, whilst Sir Peter Hayman, who died in 1992, was an active member of the Paedophile Information Exchange (PIE) which also included at least fifteen other MPs and judges, all of whom are still to be named.[14]

By May 2015, 'Operation Hydrant' was investigating seventy-six suspects from politics amongst 1,433 others from various walks of life, but there were no figures as to investigations into the secret services or the police.[15] Harvey Proctor maintains that he has no connection with the current paedophile controversy.[16]

With all this in mind, the framing of Colin Wallace might not have been directly to do with his involvement in Clockwork Orange but more closely related to his investigation in the mid 1970s into the Kincora Boys' Home in which homosexual abuse of teenage boys had been combined with a terrorist organisation centred on William McGrath. On 1 August 2014, the subject again became a public issue when Brian Gemmel, an army intelligence officer at the time, broke silence about his own report into the home, which he said had been suppressed.

❧⁓❦⁓❧

Thatcherism was a moral crusade primarily and only an economic crusade secondarily, an attitude that, nevertheless, saw freedom as only possible within a strict code of ethical behaviour and economic individualism. This behaviour was firmly codified by

Mary Whitehouse and her group of vigilante moralists called the National Viewers'
and Listeners' Association. Thatcher had met their representatives and approved their
low-church evangelism. Their cause was to end the excesses of the media which they
considered corrupted by a diet of liberal attitudes. Their central mission was the curbing
of what they saw as rampant sexuality, which was undermining family values and which
had become an urgent issue since the invention of the home video recorder. In 1979,
home recorders were introduced in Britain allowing unrestricted and unsupervised
viewing and playback. The new technology was accompanied by an influx of films
made almost exclusively for home consumption, and this included a new generation
of more explicit horror movies, many of which showed scenes of extreme, but usually
rather slapstick, violence and sexuality.

One company sent its produce to the association, a stunt that sent Whitehouse off
on a crusade to ban what she termed 'video nasties'. Interestingly, the press lapped up
the possibility of talking about extreme violence and sexuality and its connections with
unsupervised children's viewing. The subsequent seizures and prosecutions for retail-
ing films 'liable to corrupt' became a type of witch-hunt against any form of deviance.
This led to ridiculous scenes of police officers being required to view pornographic
and horror films as part of their work. The introduction of a private member's bill by
Conservative MP Graham Bright in the House of Commons in 1983 finally meant
that Whitehouse's campaigning was made into law. Yet the video nasty campaign had
terrible repercussions far away from Westminster and years later.

In the early hours of 27 February 1991, a large force of police and social workers
raided four homes on South Ronaldsay in Orkney to 'rescue' nine abused children
and take them to 'places of safety' on the mainland. No explanations were given to
the families, all of whom were English, as to the official abduction of their children,
but books, play clothes, school masks, paperwork and twenty-eight videos were seized,
as was a broken crucifix and cloak from the local pastor, Reverend MacKenzie, who
was not one of the parents. The children were rounded up and herded away and the
parents kept in ignorance of the charges. Then the children were taken for questioning
and the families finally broken up as the children were sent to different foster homes.
The parents found themselves questioned about an old 'quarry', ritual dancing and
abusive activity, as did the children. The accusations of satanic rituals went back to a
previous case of actual child abuse on a neighbouring island and the psychotic fantasies
of one of the children involved. The initial case hung on this young girl's evidence
and little else. The police had even questioned the families over their religious beliefs.
One family was Quaker and their practices were considered highly suspicious as they
sat in silence in circles; another of the families were practising Jews who had the hor-
rifyingly déjà-vu experience of having their children taken away by uniformed police
without warning.

The charges emerged slowly and painfully, but they were only fully explained at
the internal inquiry. Paul Lee, the leader of Orkney's social work team, explained that

the children had been, 'interviewed separately, ... they had each told horrific stories of bizarre sexual abuse, ritual dancing and music after dark in an Orkney quarry ... including having sexual intercourse with a man dressed in a black cloak who was identified as Morris MacKenzie, the local minister from St Margaret's'.[17]

The explanation was gobbledegook concocted by the social workers to justify the seizures. The well-being of the children had been sacrificed to the importance of the case. Why?

It seemed that the video nasty scare of 1979 to 1983, which had supposedly encouraged all sorts of devil worship and even had an effect on dogs, had now spawned an industry of Satan-hunters determined to root out sin. It had begun in England with the discovery of paedophile activities in Cleveland and Nottingham. The first allegations of Satanic abuse were in October 1987 when a number of children were removed from their families in Broxtowe, Nottingham. In 1989 a family from the area was charged with child sexual abuse, neglect and Satanic abuse ritiuals. A 600-page report found no traces of Satanism. The case was the first in Britain to highlight growng suspicion that Satanism was part of recovered memory syndromw and multiple personality disorder, following the 1980 publication in the United States of *Michele Remembers* by Dr Lawrence Padzer. Its fountainhead was the new Evangelical Charismatic Movement which had identified the first Gulf War as a war against Satan. Anti-Satanic thinking penetrated social-work circles where Charismatics could operate quite legitimately. The movement had tentacles in Orkney too. At least one worker in the case was involved with the movement. One witness suggested:

It's known that there is one social worker in this very small department who does belong to a Charismatic Christian Fellowship. The history of this Fellowship in Orkney goes back to the early 1980s ... They've been living for the last ten years in an environment where they expect there to be a high level of occult activity in society. Coming from a background like that, I think those views would make a Charismatic social worker highly sympathetic to the views that he was receiving through the professional channels of the social service.[18]

The activities of this Charismatic group had surfaced during a summer camp in Orkney. Here, it was reported that 'Teenage girls returned from that camp with stories of speaking in tongues and exorcising evil spirits. Some of them had gone into trances, and questions were asked by many worried parents. Some of the children needed psychiatric treatment, and others received counselling by the orthodox Church of Scotland clergy.'[19]

The situation was exacerbated by the work of an American child counsellor called Pamala (or Pamela) Klein who was diagnosing satanic possession down the phone to senior police officers in Kent during 1988. Klein's approach was replicated in Britain by Maureen Davies who established the Reachout Trust in 1983 and advised social workers in Rochdale and Nottingham as well as speaking at a two-day seminar in Aberdeen which an Orkney social worker attended.

There can be little doubt that despite the refutations by social workers and those on the local council, the video nasty scare and the witch-hunts that followed were directly related to the new moral hysteria which had partially been whipped up by the media and promulgated by 'nutcases' who had official backing both in Parliament and in the government.

There was no proof whatsoever of satanic abuse nor of child cruelty or inappropriate sexual activity in Orkney. The children finally returned to their families. On 27 October 1992, Lord Clyde published his report on the Inquiry into the Removal of Children from Orkney in February 1991. It ran to 363 pages; a statement was read out by Ian Lang, Scottish Secretary, in the House of Commons. No one was prosecuted and no one resigned, despite the fact that there had been no evidence for the actions of the social workers and police, no code of practice for social work in Orkney, no procedures of any sort followed, no actual accusations made against the parents, no interest taken in the children's welfare. The methods employed also breached the European Code of Human Rights. The children had been taken away in secrecy and without warning to strange places including police stations, subject to isolation from the outside world, stripped naked and searched and even kept without food or professional witnesses until they agreed to answer leading questions put by social workers.[20]

By 1990, child abuse accusations had subtly changed course from discussion of who was doing the abusing to what the cause was of this 'type' of abuse, for now there was a wave of satanic ritual cases and the accusers were the social workers themselves. The NSPCC swallowed the line, but of 200 cases examined, only three seemed to fit even a vague profile.

Liz McClean was in charge of interviewing the children from Ronaldsay. She had also been at the centre of a supposed case of satanic ritual ubuse in Rochdale when twenty children were taken away. The case, like fourteen others in England and Wales, was dismissed as a fabrication:

> Liz McLean was later described by several of the children as a terrifying figure who was 'fixated on finding satanic abuse', and other children described how she urged them to draw circles and faces, presumably as evidence indicating abusive rites. One of the children later said of the interviews: 'In order to get out of a room, after an hour or so of saying, "No, this never happened," you'd break down.'
>
> Another child recalled as an adult that, 'I would never say that a child's testimony in the company of Liz McLean at the time [is reliable]. She was a very manipulative woman, and she would write what she wanted to write.'[21]

The children were deprived of the toys, letters and Easter eggs that poured in from well-wishers and were not allowed to write or communicate with their parents.

One of the child victims remembered the bullying tactics of both police and social workers who 'sniggered' at his continued defence of his parents' behaviour.[22] The return of the children on 4 April 1991, after the collapse of the court hearing, left some withdrawn and suspicious of strangers such as police and officials and others mentally scarred; the abuse came from ideologically motivated and unsupervised officials of whom no one was brought to account. Indeed, Lord Clyde suggested that Paul Lee's team were concerned with 'secrecy' rather than the well-being of the children, and Lee actually agreed.

Surprisingly, there was in the case little to distinguish it from the cases of interrogation in Northern Ireland. Although the children had been taken for their own good, the seizures had been motivated by ideological and evangelical missionary zeal. The children were seized without explanation and their parents vilified as abusers without any evidence. Their human rights were breached, but the action of social workers was kept a strict secret as unverifiable evidence was collected.

❧

Sexual abuse of children is as old as the hills, but, in the 1980s, it was a relatively new medical phenomena and entirely new in the press. By 1984, it was true that cases of rape had been treated much more sympathetically and the police were accepting training in matters of sexual violence. The abuse of children had a growing number of works of guidance, but was still mostly judged by the physical marks and sometimes by testimony. By 1987, there was a growing body of disturbing evidence and there were better investigative methods and better means of dealing with families at risk.

Yet this was all put at stake by the controversy surrounding the new techniques used by medical practitioners in Middlesbrough Hospital in Cleveland. Here, investigators had applied physical tests and observations on all children brought in for treatment. The methods they used were borrowed from forensic pathology in the morgue and were tests on the rectum and genital areas using 'anal dilation' as a proof of buggery. This method seemed to reveal that very young children were being abused by fathers, uncles and trusted members of the family. Such information was shocking and new. It was so radical as to be disbelieved by many outside the small group of professionals that made up the medical team. In 1985, even the Republic of Ireland had begun investigating rape cases more seriously. What emerged in the Republic as in England was that child abuse cases rapidly overtook other reported activity. In 1986, two Leeds paediatricians, Jane Wynne and Christopher Hobbs, had published a piece in the *Lancet* outlining buggery as a secret abuse of young children.

Following the article, Cleveland County Council decided to employ Sue Richardson as a consultant and Dr Marietta Higgs as consultant paediatrician at Middlesbrough General Hospital. Here Higgs carried out the observations first undertaken by Wynne and Hobbs. By June 1987, there had been 110 cases 'proved' and social services set up a children's resource centre at the hospital even though the evidence was now being hotly disputed by fathers (who formed a pressure group called Parents Against Injustice), the police, the local churches and councillors. The Labour MP for the area, Stuart Bell, allied himself with Reverend Peter Wright (not the author of *Spycatcher*) to fight the findings, which they accused of being an ideological witch-hunt by so-called experts. Bell, speaking in the House of Commons, accused Richardson and Higgs of a conspiracy against fathers and families. This was echoed in more ideological terms by Wright, who suggested there was:

> a strong element of evangelistic crusading coming across, in which the feeling was conveyed by people who are obviously women, many of them divorced or single parents, that families would be better off without fathers. That caused a great deal of anger. It may well have a lot to do with the fact that a lot of people involved are women. Certainly the line was being put across that families would be happier without fathers and this was laid at the door of feminism.[23]

Indeed, 'It was not lost on Dr Higgs that the press preferred to portray her as a solitary figure, a woman without relationships, without networks, without a neighbourhood. It became a familiar motif in the 1980s, the undomesticated working woman aloof from the world of the *real* woman, the family.'[24]

Meanwhile, Cleveland Police, the same police that were so determined to destroy the miners, were led by their chief constable in a revolt against Home Office guidelines on cases of violence against women (which was never circulated as directed by the minister) and refused to work with local social services or collect corroborating evidence.

In October 1987, an inquiry led by Elizabeth Butler-Sloss and held at Middlesbrough Town Hall was scathing about the inaction and indifference of the police force which had proved particularly truculent in regard to government directives considered too liberal to those who wished to protect good old-fashioned policing of the type approved by traditional moralists on both sides of the House. The force was suspected of wholesale corruption but was never investigated. Moreover, 'Secrecy was no stranger to the [Cleveland] police committee – it had had the habit of keeping two sets of minutes: when a sensitive matter was being discussed it often confined them to "confidentiality" and kept the records out of sight of elected members of the council.'[25]

The Cleveland child abuse scandal vilified professionals working with children as mad lesbians and 'witches' who hated men on principal and were the do-gooders that Thatcherism hoped to eliminate, exactly the same types that were helping the miners or camping outside airbases. They were identified not as trained and caring experts who had tried new methods to expose horrifying activities that many believed should remain hidden or that didn't even exist, and had for their troubles been universally demonised in the popular press.

One set of abuse cases was predicated on the importance of the religious mores of Christian evangelism, while the other was based upon professional diagnoses by medically qualified scientists. One set of cases was based on supernaturalism and the other on physiological investigation. The forensic methods of medical professionals proved a much easier target than satanism when it came to the media, police and local authorities to ridicule and members of Parliament to attack (the moral high ground was adopted both by Conservatives who disliked the new liberalism and the Labour right whose constituency was nevertheless the old Labour values of working-class respectability). The methods in Orkney proved the significance of state surveillance while the methods in Middlesbrough proved that the state was corrupted by 'enthusiasts' attacking the traditional values of family sanctity. The cases in Cleveland proved that some families were not stable and that, if the sort of individuals on which respectable liberal and stable society and community relied were acting indecently, then corruption had penetrated the heart of the Thatcher experiment. The last taboo was located not in communist takeover or the unions but in the tension between various forms of statism which could not be reconciled. These differences were located on the bodies of little children and signified where the last terrible secret was located: the 'respectable' families that were celebrated by Thatcher's ideologues.

All the children in the case in Orkney were left with psychological scars from what was, in effect, psychological torture by bureaucrats in the name of an unanswerable secret state, the same state that had attempted to destroy its own employees in Middlesbrough when they had attempted to 'enter' the sanctity of the family and deal with abuses in the heart of the one area that was taboo in Thatcher's Britain:

> Child torture came to haunt Thatcherism during the 1980s. The ghosts of dead children Jasmine Beckford, Tyra Kenry and Kimberley Carlile all destroyed by their fathers – smiled out from the newspapers, their photographs snipped from supposedly Happy Family albums while the texts alongside described bites, burns, broken bones and then death. These little martyrs to bad, mad men were handed over to a populist politics of punishment. It all seemed to vindicate Thatcherism's scorn for the busy-body welfare state. But not quite: these children died within the family, the institution sanctified by Thatcherism. The state had sinned by omission, not commission – families were kept intact, and children were killed.[26]

Amongst the most outlandish and paranoid claims around paedophilia scandals have been made by barrister Michael Shrimpton, a former air traffic controller. According to Shrimpton, in a long and eventful career he has been connected to British intelligence, the Labour Party and international diplomatic and military circles. He was General Pinochet's representative in 1999 and 2000. Shrimpton's claims are complex.

He suggests that there was, and still is, a highly secret German intelligence network operation to supply children and blackmail recipients throughout Europe. The organisation is called the Deutsches Verteidigungs Dienst, or German Defence Service (DVD), and it was set up by German spymaster Admiral Wilhelm Canaris before the Second World War in anticipation of Hitler's defeat. The DVD still exists under the name GO2 and is a deep-cover intelligence agency within Europe and the British secret services. According to Shrimpton there are 10,000 current employees.

Shrimpton has claimed that Edward Heath was not merely homosexual but also a paedophile who had boys murdered on his yacht after sexually abusing them. These victims were allegedly supplied by Jimmy Savile who had procured them from Haut de la Garenne in Jersey where, in 2008, police excavations were conducted for the graves of missing children. This traffic in young boys was then supposedly covered up by Cabinet Secretary John Hunt, allegedly also a paedophile. These 'facts' were known to Thatcher and yet she entertained Savile at Chequers. But blackmail hardly accounts for Thatcher's intimacy with Savile, when he could have simply been liquidated.

Despite training as a barrister and acting as an immigration appeals judge, Shrimpton appears to be paranoid and deluded. In 2014, for instance, he was prosecuted for falsely outlining a plot to steer an old German submarine up the Thames filled with a nuclear 'bomb' to be detonated at the Olympics opening ceremony.

In 2015 yet another satanic paedophile scandal threatened to emerge. The Bishop of Durham, Paul Butler, accused Enoch Powell of being both a paedophile and a satanist in a report into satanic abuse cases. He also named MP Leo Abse and both names were passed on to Operation Fernbridge for investigation. The names originated with overheard conversations by Dominic Walker, former Bishop of Monmouth when he was a parish priest. The accusations were strenuously denied by Powell's friends, such as Simon Heffer.[27] The story was exposed as a 'hoax' by David Aaronovitch in *The Times*.[28] He had a tip-off from blogger Richard Bartholomew regarding a confidence artist called Derry Mainwaring Knight who had been living in Brighton and spread a story to gullible vicars that he was a defecting Satanist willing to tell all about his colleagues from 'the Sons of Lucifer'. He made a large amount of money from his scam, but was finally caught and imprisoned for seven years.

27

VICARIOUS VICTIMHOOD

During the 1980s short-sightedness in government produced all sorts of contradictions in policy that were smoothed over or hushed up at the time. Dangerous, manipulative and abusive people were kept in power in order to protect the state from being brought into disrepute, and equally dangerous, manipulative and abusive people worked for the state and in the interests of the 'defence of the realm'. Thatcher's greatest enemies were those she saw as the terrorists who had murdered her friends and had tried to murder her in Brighton, but increasingly, those named as terrorists were nothing but legitimate opponents vilified because they opposed the nuclear industry or nuclear armaments. 'All governments,' suggests one commentator, 'need enemies. If there are not enough to go round they have to invent them … It is why they talk constantly of war.'[1]

Ultimately, there seemed to be no enemies left, so they were invented. Sir Antony Duff, director general of MI5 between 1985 and 1987, acknowledged that the internal threat to the state was over. There were no more enemies to fight.[2] Therefore, new enemies 'appeared'. Despite the fact that communism had collapsed in 1989, MI5 retained a counter-subversion operation going for another five years, and, by 1991, F Branch still had six officers, three managers and twenty support staff with nothing to do. Their targets, the Socialist Workers' Party, the Communist Party of Great Britain, Militant, the National Front, the BNP and Class War represented no threat whatsoever to the structures of the state. Not until 1994 when F2 was shut down did MI5 stop sending reports to ministers on subversive groups.

As MI5 floundered, the police grew in strength as guardians of morality. Who was left to keep watch on? In March 1985, as the miners' strike ground on, Thatcher saw a televised broadcast of Millwall and Luton fans fighting. It was yet another indication that English working-class men were out of control. On 11 May, Bradford City were about to play Lincoln City; an old stand caught fire and fifty-six people were killed. Three weeks later, thirty-nine people died when part of the Heysel Stadium in Brussels collapsed when Liverpool were about to play Juventus. Something was disastrously wrong with football and with those who followed the game.

Alcohol-fuelled hooliganism was blamed as a major factor in the Heysel tragedy and when the Public Order Bill was introduced in 1985 to create stronger measures against the growth of protest, there was a section devoted to the new criminalisation of drunkenness and missile throwing at football matches. The NCCL pointed out that the White Paper's approach was misplaced as the tragedy at Bradford was not related to drunkenness. The NCCL did recognise the problem of hooliganism, but considered the attempts to regulate the behaviour of fans was overly authoritarian and repressive, citing the 'temporary' provisions of the Terrorism Act which followed the Birmingham bombings in 1974 (and which had not been repealed) and had already had certain aspects of its provisions incorporated into normal police procedure. The current White Paper was the 'thin end of the wedge' in attacking personal freedom.[3] None of the arguments to the contrary made any difference. The debate over public order became a condemnation of football fans who were categorised more and more as a mob of hooligans. Football violence was seen as 'mass civil disorder'.[4]

The panic over hooliganism was a perfect opportunity for the police to find a new law and order role. The vilification of Merseyside since the time of Derek Hatton and Militant left it particularly vulnerable to accusations of hooliganism and drunkenness in the right-wing press and in right-wing ideology. On 15 April 1989, the FA Cup semi-final between Nottingham Forest and Liverpool, held at Sheffield Wednesday's Hillsborough ground at which there were 54,000 supporters, should have gone off without incident. But the ground was unmodernised and access was poor. There was a 'squeeze' point that could not be opened any wider on the Lepping Lane terrace 'pen'. The subsequent deaths of 96 Liverpool fans was the result of a crush that became a human avalanche.

The authorities had been expecting drunken crowds and rowdiness from the Liverpool supporters. They were the same South Yorkshire policemen that had been at Orgreave and ever since the miners' strike there had been a sense that all crowds, no matter what their intent, were inherently hostile. There had been much talk in the government and press regarding English fans abroad who had been at the centre of trouble and tragedies like that at Heysel. The tactics used at Orgreave and elsewhere therefore proved a dreadful blueprint for crowd control generally, and the methods used by the 1,122 officers that day were wholly unsuited to non-confrontational circumstances; but what was much worse was the indecision of senior officers who were unfamiliar with football crowds and unable to make critical choices.

The police might have acted more quickly, might indeed have apologised for not being prepared, might have put their own major incident plan into action. Instead they lied and obfuscated and blamed fan behaviour and the Liverpool fans particularly. The only real expert in the South Yorkshire force on football crowd control had been Chief Superintendent Brian Mole, and he had left after a recent scandal. He was replaced by Chief Superintendent David Duckenfield, who had no experience of commanding police at football matches and who was criticised in the subsequent inquiry for being unfit to command.

As the dead were gathered in a nearby gym, the coroner decided to take blood samples from all the bodies for alcohol traces. The implication was that the fans were drunk and pushed their way to their own deaths. Indeed, even as the first signs of trouble became apparent, the police were concocting a cover story. According to the story fed to John Motson, the BBC commentator, the problem was a crush outside which was followed by a 'break-in' by un-ticketed fans. It was a perfect excuse to let senior officers off the hook and the police immediately started a campaign to show that they had been blameless against Liverpool thuggery. The lie stuck and was peddled by every paper.

> The South Yorkshire Chief Constable ... blamed the initial crush outside the turnstiles on 'the late arrival of large numbers of people', which was reported as: 'between three and four thousand Liverpool fans turned up just five minutes before kick-off'.
> Effectively, the 'forced gate' theory was replaced by the 'conspiracy theory'. This implied that Liverpool fans, drunk and ticketless, planned to arrive immediately before kick-off, compelling the police to open exit gates. 'Hooligan hysteria', linked to the 'Heysel factor', turned Hillsborough into a public order issue.[5]

It was an easy line to follow given the demonisation of Liverpool. The *Evening Standard*, quite against any evidence, argued that the tragedy was the result of 'mindless passion' and the *Sun* was at one time even going to lead with the headline 'You scum'. The Police Federation stoked the lies with stories of theft and urination on bodies. Liverpool, rather than just its fans, had been successfully destroyed in the media through the drip of police black propaganda and the city now proved Thatcher's thesis that there was a deep social malaise. Indeed, Liverpool became the exemplar of northern working-class Neanderthal hooliganism. Bernhard Ingham, on a short visit to the Hillsborough ground, commented:

> I visited Hillsborough on the morning after the disaster. I know what I learned on the spot. There would have been no Hillsborough if a mob, who were clearly tanked up, had not tried to force their way into the ground. To blame the police is a cop-out ... They are the guilty ones. They caused the terrible disaster and I am astonished that anyone can believe otherwise.[6]

The subsequent inquiry headed by Lord Justice Taylor found no grounds for the police accusations or the newspaper headlines. His report was consigned to the bin as it did not fit the narrative. Lord Taylor found Duckenfield to be an incompetent and 'untruthful' officer who 'froze' at the moment of decision and whose subsequent actions only caused 'grave offence and distress' to the bereaved.[7] Insensitive handling of the dispute with the miners spilled into football. Taylor found 'not a single witness' to the police story concocted after the events.[8] At the new inquests, held during 2015 at Warrington, David Duckenfield finally admitted that his failure to keep the gates closed 'was the direct cause of the deaths of 96 people'. In giving evidence he further said that he 'froze' when he saw the result of opening the gate. He also admitted not submitting this in evidence to 'Operation Resolve', the police inquiry. Duckenfield admitted drinking in the run up to the Taylor Inquiry, and he was finally medically retired from the police with 'severe depression and post-traumatic stress disorder'; he'd already been suspended on a full pension.[9]

The evidence, however, did not defeat the received narrative. On 3 March 1993, the *Daily Telegraph* published Auberon Waugh's caustic assessment of Liverpool. In his article, Waugh commented, 'It is said that Liverpool's problems are all due to unemployment. I wonder what Liverpool's unemployment is due to. I fear it may be due to the stupidity as much as the unpleasant habits of the people who live there. All the clever people left it long ago.'[10] Brian Clough, former manager of Leeds and Nottingham Forest, mentioned in his 1994 autobiography, 'I will always remain convinced that those Liverpool fans who died were killed by Liverpool people. All those lives were lost needlessly.'[11] Later, even the Mayor of London, Boris Johnson, waded in, prompted by the death of Liverpudlian Ken Bigley in Iraq. Johnson considered that Liverpool 'wallowed in a sense of vicarious victimhood' which proved 'the mawkish sentimentality' of Liverpool culture.

The dominance of right-wing concerns *in advance of events* had not only ended up with at least one police force incorrectly trained and ideologically pre-programmed towards crowds of civilians, but had also created a ready-made narrative regarding drunken hooliganism that would be useful for covering up police incompetence and the cause of police corruption at the highest level.

☙◦❧

That there was an inability to distinguish duty from legal or even moral correctness at the very highest levels in many police forces including the South Yorkshire Police, the Metropolitan Police, the Greater Manchester Police and the RUC throughout the 1980s cannot really be doubted. One writer goes so far as to suggest, 'We had produced compelling evidence that the RUC had become, in part, a terrorist organisation employing the exact same methods as the terrorists in the Provisional IRA … members of a police force in the United Kingdom were running death squads.'[12]

The battles with youth in the inner cities and with the miners, and the harassment of gay people, Greenham Common women and the travelling community had a further deeply worrisome knock-on effect. This was the belief that the police were invulnerable from prosecution. Thus, when printers walked out at the News International site on 24 January 1986 over new working conditions, the tactics adopted by the police to control the strike were both grossly disproportionate, politically motivated and illegal, all based on their tactics in those previous disputes where they had appeared immune from the law: police tactics at Wapping on 3 May 1986 were, for instance, compared by many with those used at Orgreave.[13]

This was hardly surprising. Cleveland Police, whose chief constable Christopher Payne chaired the Association of Chief Police Officers' working party set up after the riots of 1981, helped draw up the secret manual of paramilitary tactics that was used to plan the 'ambush' of miners at Orgreave in the first place. The manual proved a blueprint for all other occasions, including action at Wapping, the police moving from uniformed citizens keeping the peace to activists in militarised operations.

To restrict the ability of the strikers to protest while still allowing News International lorries free access was effectively a political rather than a tactical decision which was accomplished by arbitrary use of roadblocks, refusal of right of way for vehicles, requirements that locals effectively carried identification or face refusal to allow them free passage home (in effect, 'stop and search') and the temporary sealing of the area as police felt fit. This angered both residents and protesters whose tactics became more desperate – stone throwing – which justified even harsher police tactics.

The police in 1986 still had no body whatsoever with which to be called to account. Operation Countryman, set up to trap 'bent 'coppers in 1978, was itself wound down in 1982 without one conviction and amid arguments that the officers undertaking the enquiries were themselves suspect. The had already taken over 2,000 statements and pursued over 200 lines of inquiry; the commissioner of the Metropolitan Police, Kenneth Newman admitted that at least 250 police might be corrupt.[14]

These were important steps, but even as Newman spoke of ridding the Metropolitan Police of subversion and corruption, a secret Masonic lodge known as the Manor of St James was undermining his words. Sir John Hermon took over as chief constable of the RUC. He should have taken over a strong, moral and incorruptible force. Instead he presided over a deeply corrupt organisation, which acted in an entirely partisan way and whose Special Branch was a type of assassination squad. Senior police officers were members of or had connections with Ulster's masons and worked within a network which operated on the basis of co-joined private vendettas. Hermon was also closely associated with Sir James Anderton, chief constable in Manchester, whose deputy was John Stalker.

Countryman and other failed attempts to curb police individual licence on one hand, and failure to discipline officers in crowd control on the other, had led to a culture of authoritarian entitlement which was itself a form of authorised corruption. Police could effectively act as free agents of the state.

The NCCL (now more commonly known as Liberty) concluded that there was no justification in police tactics which veered on the political. The problem was quite clear, the police were 'not accountable to anyone' as they could choose their own tactics in decisions which *legally excluded* the Home Secretary. 'The use of roadblocks,' stated the NCCL, was 'unnecessary and unacceptable' creating 'infringements of freedom of movement'; many actions were simply 'unlawful'.[15] During the 1980s, the police often acted beyond their remit and took on the role of a quasi-governmental agency, neither accountable to Parliament nor ministers and adopting tactics that were draconian, authoritarian, dubious and often illegal. Throughout the period discussed in this book, the government resisted any legislation that might curb the excesses of those in the security services, army or police, allowing criminal action by people who knew they were never going to be held to account.

Whatever the truth of such an assertion, it was certainly the case that those who delved too deeply into such affairs were likely to come off badly: Colin Wallace was framed, as was John Stalker; Fred Holroyd suffered a mental breakdown; investigative journalists such as Roger Bolton were smeared and accused of lying, or harassed like Duncan Campbell. Those who pried into nuclear affairs, such as Hilda Murrell and Willie McCrea, might find they were under constant surveillance, burgled or even to become the unwitting target of assassins. Those who were seen as too left-wing, such as Ken Livingstone, Derek Hatton and Arthur Scargill, were vilified as Marxists or Trotskyists, their voices drowned out by stories in the *Sun*, *Sunday Times* or *Telegraph* which periodically acted as mouthpieces for various ministries, intelligence services and even the Prime Minister's office. Black people were the subject of police racism and were disproportionally stopped on the streets.

One unforeseen repercussion of Thatcherite policies was the politicisation of a generation of women who had never encountered political activity before and who had previously been indifferent to the Cruise missile protests. It also seriously affected family relationships, often for the worse. Hence one miner Barry Fitzpatrick recalled the change in his wife Denise, whose political education led her to the barricades in East London:

> When police started pulling walls down and there were police throwing … big walling stones under cars, and ruddy soldiers there in uniform, soldier's uniform not police's, and they raced us all over bloody village as we were trying to get out of way. Well they got away with that without a thing being said, and I says to Denise, 'We've lost this strike, love'.
>
> I lost the strike and I lost me wife as well, 'cos she just started campaigning for this that and the other, when Wapping came up she were there organising T and G to go down. She knew we were going to lose this community, not just pits and jobs.[16]

❧

Today, even more people have their phones tapped and their personal behaviour put on file. This is especially true of those who are involved in legitimate protest and find themselves on databases of internal 'extremists'. Twenty-four years after the Hillsborough tragedy, there is still no justice, and the connection between public-order policing issues on the picket line and the disaster at the stadium is still denied. As late as 17 June 2014, the *Daily Mail* ran a column dismissing such a connection as 'an insult to … Liverpool fans', whereas it might be a realistic and truthful interpretation. It shows again the mendacious jockeying of the right-wing press to make sure, by twisting words, that the moral high ground remains theirs despite the evidence.

Thatcher's ultimate political dominance was born of her 144-seat majority following victory in the Falklands War, but it had been forged long before and, once tested, was to be turned on every hue of political and cultural foe as the enemies of that form of Thatcherism which had hatched in the 1970s. Each was identified and eliminated.

It is true, however, that the more overt violence and manipulation that had marked official behaviour in Northern Ireland by both the army and the RUC Special Branch was finally curbed in the late 1980s. There were other enemies, however, more terrifying than the IRA, and they lived among us. Oddly, the intelligence tactics in Northern Ireland impacted elsewhere in quite different circumstances and for quite other uses.

There can be no doubt that the era of Thatcherism was also the era of the strongest powers of the 'thought police' so denigrated in Thatcher's *1984* speech. In every walk of life, from the introduction of Clause 28, to the promotion of nuclear power, to attacking Travellers' convoys, to the application of the SUS laws and to the censorship of films seen in private, the law watched and waited. It was a peculiar irony that the 'golden age' of individual freedom was the period of greatest personal surveillance; non-conformity and lifestyle choices were now criminalised and *officially* punishable.

What remained were the cover-ups, official denials and the tarnishing of the reputations of those appointed to investigate what essentially had to remain out of sight. Throughout the 1980s, black propaganda was routinely used in the media to protect the guilty, and the press was subject to routine feeds of misinformation. Thatcher was no sadist. She expressly forbade torture to be used during the invasion of Iraq, but her ministers had no mechanism to scrutinise what was occurring or really to rein in abuses. Torture *was* used during the invasion of Iraq and was only exposed in the death of Baha Mousa in 2003. The incriminating document, Part II of *The Directive on Interrogation by the Armed Forces in Internal Security Operations*, which authorised forms of 'torture' and was produced in 1972, only came to light in 2008.[17]

Above all, Thatcher inherited people and systems that were ready and willing to use underhand means to further the market liberalism which she always encouraged. After the Brighton bombing, Thatcher delivered her speech to conference. 'This attack has failed,' she intoned, 'but … all attempts to destroy democracy by terrorism will fail.' Here, Thatcher might have been excused for forgetting her own authoritarian lessons and the unlawful and underhand methods employed to keep her brand of democracy in power.

These underhand methods had been legitimised in practice long before by Frank Kitson whose *Low Intensity Operations: Subversion, Insurgency and Peacekeeping* proved a type of blueprint for everything that followed. The fact that he became Commander-in-Chief of UK Land Forces in 1982 speaks volumes. His belief that there was a case for 'the disposal of unwanted members of the public' had sufficient nuances to allow every form of state intervention – interventions often publically disapproved of by Thatcher but winked at in private.

The case for Kitson being directly involved with commissioning assassinations, remained nevertheless unproven when Martin Dillon and Denis Lehane investigated the problem in 1973:

> Thus it would seem that at the time of the assassinations there did exist a structure within the Army that would fit the apparent description of assassination squads, and which did have at least some justification for such a policy in military terms behind them. But Kitson does not in his book refer to political assassination as a specific policy, and this is perfectly consistent. The primary concern of Kitson is with Military intelligence and the Army's preparedness to fight a psychological as well as a military campaign. It is clear that assassination for political purposes does come within the terms of reference given by Kitson to his Special Units, but the question one has to answer in Northern Ireland is whether this did indeed occur. On the basis of the evidence produced in this chapter the case against the Army must be declared unproven.[18]

Indeed, even the army might be mainly absolved:

> On the four clear cases [up to 1973] where the Army was involved in killing or attempted killing of Catholics by its plain-clothes troops, it is by no means certain that the soldiers' claim to have been fired upon first was not correct, even if the victims were not those responsible for the shootings.[19]

Forty years later, the case against Kitson and the army remains unproven.

Those who cannot escape blame in the war against the various wings of the IRA are those Protestant policemen, territorials and paramilitaries who continued to use illegal and secret terror against their fellow British citizens. That there was state-*inspired* murder now seems beyond doubt. The question remains, was it a deliberate policy or one of useful pragmatism made up as circumstances arose, which finally collapsed into the tacit approval of applied state terror, using armed (Irish) vigilante citizens who were being used to fight Britain's last colonial war against anarchy and Sovietism?[20]

28

MUMMSIE TIME!

The story ends on a minor note. Things have, for the most part, been forgiven or forgotten. Margaret Thatcher is dead and has been posthumously beatified, despite consistent rumblings from those who will never be reconciled with her legacy. The Franks Committee exonerated the government over the handling of the early stages of the Falklands War, as did the Scott Inquiry into the arms trade with Iraq and the Stevens Inquiries into corruption in Northern Irish policing. Thatcher's advisors too are dead, or keep mum, or rewrite their own part in history. Those who plotted the rise of Thatcherism long before it appeared as an ideology take pride in their achievement of changing the course of Britain and the defeat of the trade unions and, even, of world communism. Capitalism, so the argument went, was morally superior because it won the war, but it was a battle fought away from the ballot box, often in secret and always in deadly earnest, sometimes using the most corrupt methods. It demonstrated that naked power could be hidden by propaganda applied to every walk of life and that economic well-being and security acted as morphine to voters numbed into indifference as to the fate of those caught in the machinations of government policies.

The legacy of the ideologues of revival left Britain economically secure, but morally bankrupt. The corruption ran through five Prime Ministers starting in the 1970s and left an inheritance that was fully understood when Tony Blair came to power in 1997. In an off-the-record interview with New Labour's biographer Andrew Rawnsley, Blair 'recognised that much of the Labour Party suffered him only on the basis that he would deliver power', not that he would stick to socialist policies.[1] It left a historical vacuum and many unanswered questions. It proved, however, that economic liberalism was compatible with a largely secret and authoritarian state run as if it was offering greater democracy not less.

The architects of Thatcher's 'revolution' were sincere in their belief, but those charged with carrying out the experiment were not always as sincere nor as open in their aims. The aims of those early theorists leave no doubt that the new architecture of state would be built on market forces and military discipline, both enforced as necessary with doses of pragmatic authoritarian sticks and entrepreneurial individualistic carrots: society was to be atomised and the anarchy of the market encouraged by the fiats of governmental policy upheld by a silent and secret state willing to use pragmatic means learned from fighting Irish terrorists and union leaders.

No one has been brought to account for the deaths of Helen Smith, Jonathan Lewis, Jonathan Moyle, Willie McCrea or the workers who died in the secret electronics industry; no one has been brought to book for the multiple phone tappings, buggings, physical surveillance, intimidation, common assault, bullying and even gerrymandering which marked the period and that terrified so many victims for so long; only now in the first quarter of the twenty-first century (and after their deaths) have the crimes of those such as Jimmy Savile come to light, while Colin Wallace, Fred Holroyd and John Stalker remain tainted, their accusers allowed to live scot-free and even the recipients of honours and largesse.

Hilda Murrell's case remains 'unsolved' despite a conviction. It is probably the most famous mystery since the disappearance of Lord Lucan, with almost as much interest in the circumstances of her death as ever. Her nephew still pursues the case, although a correspondent with this author, who knew Commander Green during the initial investigation, considers that he was 'a bit freaky and going to séances to get Hilda to speak to him from the dead' which does little for his credibility, despite the evidence. The same correspondent nevertheless considers that 'the government must have been implicated in the whole affair'.[2]

The journalists who first investigated the stories detailed in this book have been largely ignored by the greater public. The nuclear fuel industry remains a closed secret and the action of the Greenham women in regard to nuclear weaponry merely a heroic memory. The police have only just been exposed for their use of undercover officers to destabilise legitimate organisations such as Greenpeace;[3] some are seemingly still corrupt enough to frame a politician for supposedly calling them 'plebs'. The Police Federation now also appears inherently 'corrupt', something the Home Secretary seems unable to curb.

The information leaked by Edward Snowden has shown how intelligence has created permanent surveillance on everyone. Snowden went public because '[the NSA was] building a system whose goal was the elimination of all privacy, globally', and in this GCHQ is its closest ally.[4] Perhaps, the United Kingdom's secret services and intelligence community are on better behaviour, but the complicit links with American plans regarding extraordinary rendition after the 9/11 attacks suggest that the situation is no better than before and that suspects held in Iraq after the invasion were handed over to the Americans without correct procedure by army intelligence. Files were provided to the Moroccans by MI5 in order to facilitate torture of a prisoner and MI6 had been involved in supplying information for interrogations in Pakistan.[5] Such situations are still subject to the same official denials as ever.

Commenting on Extraordinary Rendition on 13 December 2005, Jack Straw, then Foreign Secretary, could state straight-faced, 'Unless we all start to believe in conspiracy theories and that the officials are lying, that I am lying, that behind this there is some kind of secret state … there simply is no truth in the claims that the United Kingdom has been involved in rendition.'[6]

More recently, the scandal over GCHQ/NSA phone tapping suggests the intelligence services are simply trying harder to hide their misdeeds. Proposed legislation implies that the government wants much more, rather than less, cooperation with private industry; data protection laws are still regularly flouted by the police and intelligence agencies. The privatisation of data collection and surveillance still goes on apace.

The role of the SAS might also be perceived by some to need radical change. After the second Gulf War, it was becoming clearer that targets were no longer simply military or indeed military at all. Instead, technology creates new warfare scenarios where the combatants are 'as likely to be allies as enemies' and where 'everyone carries out industrial espionage against everyone else'.[7] For this type of warfare, the 'economic warriors of the future will be civilians', a 'ghost force' operating at the boundaries between peace and war, and targeting economic rather than military secrets.

> A token SAS could remain in existence as a Hereford tourist attraction, but in the tradition of the Regiment there would be a secret within the secret. Its true function would be to act as cover for a force that is deniable, invisible, unknowable and invincible, more deadly than the SAS … Ghost Force.[8]

Thus for former SAS soldiers there were always well-paid mercenary jobs. The world of derring-do hatched in the smoke-filled luxury of London's club land has not vanished since the days of David Stirling's Watchguard in the 1970s. It was alive and well as late as 2004, when ex-SAS officer Simon Mann was hired to lead a coup attempt against President Teodoro Mbasogo of Equatorial Guinea. He was to be replaced by a puppet leader called Severo Moto. The conspiracy was intended to allow exclusive access to Guinea's oil reserves, and the army of mercenaries, made up of former members of 32 Buffalo Battalion, South Africa's version of the SAS, was either supported or financed by a group that appeared to include Thatcher's former PR guru Tim Bell, the novelist and Conservative organiser, Jeffrey Archer, Ely Calil, a Lebanese oil billionaire, and Margaret Thatcher's own son, now *Sir* Mark Thatcher, whose code name was Scratcher. On 13 September 2005, Mark Thatcher was found guilty of helping to finance the coup by a South African court and given a four-year suspended sentence and fined US$560,000. The coup was known beforehand to both the British (Labour) and American governments, who simply denied any foreknowledge.

Long before his African adventure, Mark Thatcher was deeply involved with what was fast becoming the 'family' business. The Al-Yamamah arms deal signed in 1988, but whose three parts would not be completed until 1992, was laced with

commissions, bribes and sweeteners and netted the son of the Prime Minister
£12 million and profited his group by £240 million.[9] Thatcher must have realised
the profitable nature of working alongside his mother when he netted £50,000 in
1981 after the signing of a deal with Oman.

The accusation that Mark Thatcher was involved with problematic money deals
was first made in 1989 by Jeffrey Rooker MP, but did not surface until the allegations
reached the *Sunday Times* in 1994. Mark Thatcher was also involved with Carlos
Cardoen, whose office had large portraits of both General Pinochet and Saddam
Hussein, and he seems to have been deeply involved in the Malaysian arms deal,
which was disguised by the building of the Pergau Dam. Although Mark described
himself as 'a private businessman' without connections to his mother, it was clear
that he was often involved with deals either just in the background or fronting as
Thatcher's son. He was certainly deeply involved in some of the arms deals that
found their way to Iraq.

The complexity of his various business dealings meant that, in the end, he was
looked upon with suspicion by many in the industry and was moved to Lotus cars in
America where he would possibly do less harm. Here he worked for David Wickens,
a friend of Denis Thatcher and until 1986 a principle shareholder in the waste
disposal company Attwoods, of which Denis had been deputy chairman from 1983.
Attwoods was later investigated by the FBI for financial misdealing and connections
with the Mafia.[10]

Although he always represented himself as non-political, it is clear that Mark
Thatcher was used to further the Conservative Party's agenda. On one trade visit to
Hong Kong, he went out of his way to persuade those arms dealers who had dealt
with his mother's government to donate money to the Thatcher Foundation: 'It's
pay-up for mummsie time!'[11]

Thatcher junior was so significant to his mother because he was part of a second-
ary agenda not directly related to arms dealings. This was party fundraising for the
Conservatives, who would find their finances in dire straits throughout the 1980s.
Indeed, party fundraisers went on all the visits to different countries and on at least
sixteen missions to Hong Kong. So serious was the problem of raising money that the
Charter Movement and the Party Reform Steering Group approached Conservative
Party Treasurer Lord McAlpine (whose company had originally sponsored NAFF)
to demand information. McAlpine refused to give straight answers because, by this
point, a large proportion of Conservative Party donations were coming from foreign
arms dealers and speculators whose money might not have been too clean.

In 1992, there were £17.9 million worth of unaccounted donations, and, in the
years of arms dealing between 1985 and 1993, £71 million came in from various
payments which might have looked problematic if they had ever been investigated.
These included contributions such as that from Asil Nadir who ran the Polly Peck
Group but was also an arms dealer. He gave the Conservative Party £1.5 million.[12]

The largest donation by far came from Chinese billionaire Li Kash-ing of the Hong Kong and Shanghai Bank, which acquired Midland Bank at the centre of the arms-for-Iraq scandal.

Police cover-ups continue, protected by anonymous civil servants. So bad is the situation that, in 2014, Sir Bernard Hogan-Howe, Commissioner of the Metropolitan Police, employed a full-time image consultant to positively manage his personal media profile.[13]

Of all the deceptions that followed the Thatcher years, none has been more controversial than our relationship with Iraq, and, despite the Scott Report and the Hutton Inquiry, there is still no real sense of why Britain was entangled in the supply of arms, deceit and finally two wars, one of which was based on a document whose central information had been tampered with, nor why that led to the death (suicide or murder) of David Kelly; nor why an unelected press officer suddenly became the most important man in the government; nor, indeed, why Tony Blair acquiesced in his own political suicide.

In 2010, the summer riots replicated those of 1981 and 1985 and reminded us that things have not necessarily improved in our inner cities and that certain things had in fact become worse because of long-term neglect.

Since 2000, there has been a resurgence of non-parliamentary action groups, such as Wikileaks, Occupy and Anonymous, based on communal leadership, cooperation and street action. These groups no longer take their ideologies from Trotskyism or Leninism. They are mostly anarchist groups dedicated to social justice rather than parliamentary reform. It is partly because of the history of the years recalled in this book that 'real' politics has moved beyond Westminster where the government of the day is now seen as simply managing a corrupt economy and where party-political differences have been eroded and anyone who is not for the Big Society (Conservative) or for One Nation (Labour) is considered a type of cultural traitor.

Things are not entirely the same of course. The work of Peter Tatchell and others in exposing covert homosexuals who condemn other gay men and women has, on the whole, stopped corruption on those lines, and changes to the law have meant that there are no more (known) attempts at entrapping gay intelligence agents. Moreover, gay culture has thrived since 1997. Our enemies have changed. We are faced with terrorists who align themselves with no country. Their plots are murky and the Home Office is now more determined than ever to make the case for vigilance and help formulate new laws which have huge ramifications for the ordinary citizen and which are presented as our only safeguard from anarchy.

Political Islam has replaced the Soviet Union as the enemy without but for many the enemies within are now bankers and financiers rather than the government. The protest groups gathered to bring down capitalism are still monitored through the new social media, but are still mostly ineffectual. At the same time, there is a concerted attempt to withdraw from human rights legislation as the authoritarian state grows, even more CCTV appears on the streets and higher barriers are placed around Parliament and the entrance to Downing Street, restricting ordinary voters' direct access to the democracy they live in and providing twenty-four-hour surveillance of our everyday lives.

This book has been partly a para-history of ifs and maybes, hints and allegations. It has the substance of fact and sometimes the feeling of fiction. Nothing feels stable and coincidences and circumstantial evidence sometimes have to stand in for 'the truth'. The faceless spooks and unelected people who run the secret state and who work for the multiple agencies that service it, who are charged with designating the current 'enemies within', wouldn't themselves know where to look for clues to these lost years. All the trails have gone cold, all the political heat evaporated; many of the actual historical facts are lost or rewritten; and the past lies, as well as the current lies, misinformation and character blackening, are swallowed, as always, as fact or reproduced as paranoia and conspiracy. This situation is hardly new. In 1722, Daniel Defoe wrote, 'It seemed that the government had a true account of it ... but all was kept very private.'[14] What has changed is the intensity.

Thatcher was eventually slain by a sledgehammer of her own forging. The tragedy for Thatcher was that the 1987 election victory was so great it reinforced her hubristic side and armoured her in a carapace of apparent immunity. It was a sort of natural justice that her pursuit of left-wing institutions, coinciding as it did with the attempt to give greater responsibility to individuals, was that which, in the end, proved her downfall.

The community charge, colloquially known as the poll tax, was a personal Thatcher project to destroy the left once and for all in local government and at the same time reduce the bill to Whitehall for inefficient local services, education and local welfare. The left had never quite been extinguished in local councils. Indeed, it had often flourished as a counterweight to central policy. As the government hardened its attitudes, so Labour councils moved more to the left to protect services. Thatcher was determined to finish once and for all with left-wing localism, overspending and 'socialist' projects. At the party conference held at Bournemouth in October 1989, one speaker branded the London Borough of Brent a 'fascist left-wing junta'.[15] The manifesto itself spoke of 'the abuses of left-wing Labour councils ... The Labour Party leadership pretends that this is a problem in only a few London boroughs. The truth is that the far left control town halls in many of our cities.'[16]

There certainly was much to exercise the right, whose campaign to destroy the left in local councils had, it seemed, merely pushed them further into the one area the government was incapable of controlling. Horror stories in the media told of lunatic political correctness such as the alleged row in Lambeth over 'Baa, baa *white* sheep' (a fabrication), the appearance of local 'nuclear-free zones' and money going to lesbian and gay support groups; Scargill-Livingstone-Hatton was the triple-headed monster that kept Tories awake at night, and Thatcher was determined that it should be slain once and for all. Others, such as Ted Knight at Lambeth, offered themselves to slaughter when they were eventually surcharged for not paying the new tax. Ironically, Conservative Westminster Council, whose activities had been actually illegal, was left unpunished.

The poll tax as it finally emerged was meant to be the 'flagship of the Thatcher fleet' for the coming term of office; Thatcher had claimed it as such at the party conference. This was the final brick in her edifice of social engineering which was designed to make (socialist) social engineering impossible in the future. The actual community charge had taken years and much debate and gestation to arrive in its present form. The process had begun at Chequers in 1981 and taken almost eight years to create. The charge itself was renamed and renamed again, the ministers responsible themselves changing like the seasons.

On the surface, it all seemed very reasonable; a tax to assuage the many 'widows' who were being bled dry by rates; but Thatcher was also acutely aware of problems with her own constituent old ladies if the cost of the new tax was too high.[17] Thatcher thought that rates were 'manifestly unfair and unConservative [sic]', a tax on home improvements and on property per se.[18] The tax proposed was designed for those who paid for local council services rather than those who merely used them. This made some sense but it proved a tax on those people who voted, were abstemious and self-motivated – ideal Conservative voters, in fact.

> Many people benefit from local services yet make little or no contribution towards them: this throws too heavy a burden on too few shoulders. There is much wrong with the present system of domestic rates. They seem unfair and arbitrary … We will tackle the roots of the problem. We will reform local government finance to strengthen local democracy and accountability. Local electors must be able to decide the level of service they want and how much they are prepared to pay for it. We will legislate in the first session of Parliament to abolish the unfair domestic rating system and replace rates with a fairer Community Charge.[19]

The rebellion began in Scotland. After a punishing re-evaluation of the rates and a disaster at the election, Scotland was a lost cause ripe for some experimentation even if Scottish Conservatives were deeply opposed to the new tax. It was a gift to the Scottish National Party when the tax was finally imposed. The SNP campaigned unashamedly for non-payment of a tax that actually considerably raised the payment threshold. Labour was under pressure for its inactivity as Jim Sillars 'defected' to the SNP in the Glasgow Govan by-election and overturned his previous majority as a Labour MP by 19,500 votes. The majority of people registered for the tax as instructed, but a very significant number simply vanished from the electoral roles to avoid payment. In Glasgow, 26,000 people ceased to officially exist. The cost of the poll tax was soon rising, and a petition with 300,000 signatures was sent to Parliament while protests and marches were organised.

By September 1989, the Anti-Poll Tax Federation led by Militant had persuaded almost a million people not to register from a population of 3.8 million; the refusal ranged between 15 and 20 per cent in some areas. The courts were overwhelmed trying to deal with defaulters, and the hated bailiffs were harassed at every opportunity. The cost of getting back what was owed far outweighed the original charge.

The whole sorry poll tax affair had been pioneered and organised by Nicholas Ridley, a chain-smoking maverick who was very much 'one of us'. Ridley had already been at the heart of 'revolutionary' Thatcherite policy. He had devised a plan years before to defeat strikes in the power industries. The Ridley Plan or Ridley Report was drawn up after the miners' strike of 1974. The plan was prepared in secret during 1977 specifically to consider how to deal with the unions in nationalised industries. Nicholas Ridley was one of the Selsdon group of extreme free marketeers. In his paper he suggested contingency planning to defeat a challenge from trade unions such as might occur in the aftermath of free market reforms. He recognised that the mobilisation of the middle classes, as occurred during the General Strike of 1926, may no longer be a possibility, hence, he reasoned, the government should be prepared for a conflict with the unions and should be alert to the threat from the miners in particular. Thus coal stocks should be built up at power stations; coal should be imported from non-union foreign ports and non-union lorry drivers should be employed to carry it; and dual coal- and oil-firing generators should be installed. Moreover, the government should seek to 'cut off the money supply to the strikers [Ridley called them 'the mob'] and make the union finance them'. He also suggested that there was a need to train and equip a mobile police force large enough to deal with riots and violent picketing. The plans proved a blueprint for later action. They were, however, leaked to *The Economist* and published on 27 May 1978.

Ridley's current poll tax plans were *opposed*, nevertheless, by Nigel Lawson, one of the original converts to the Thatcher ideal. If two dyed-in-the-wool Thatcherite monetarists argued over the tax, what would happen when it was rolled out in England and Wales? By October 1989, opinion polls in England showed that 63 per cent of the electorate opposed the community charge. Of these, it was Essex Man, those in the economic bracket C1 and C2 who had enjoyed the fruits of Thatcherism, who felt that they might suffer most. 'The front-line troops of the Thatcher revolution were about to be attacked by their own side.'[20]

The poll tax rebellion achieved its ends not through the many town-hall protests, clashes with bailiffs or actual rioting in Trafalgar Square on 31 March 1990 (which ended with 341 people arrested followed by another 150 later); it was not the involvement of Class War or Militant in the civil disobedience which marked the hard left's final revenge on Thatcher and Thatcherism, but the simple fact that Thatcher's flagship had been sunk by those deep and traditional Tories who could not stomach extra taxation when they had been promised less. Like the *Belgrano*, the ship had sunk with its captain.[21] The charge was repealed in 1991 and replaced by a new council tax in 1993.

A Prime Minister may lie, deceive and curtail civil liberties for years and happily survive, but a Prime Minister who has lost the power to raise taxes will inevitably fall. After the resignation of Geoffrey Howe over her stance on Europe, Thatcher was reduced to what she saw herself as – a beleaguered martyr who had succumbed to those in her own party who were the secret enemies within.

Some historians have tended to think of the Thatcher years as an aberration or type of 'episode' to which British politics is only semi-attached and which faded to some extent with the leaving of the main character from the stage. Others have seen Thatcher as leaving a legacy that forced later Prime Ministers into a straightjacket of imitation. Both views hold water, but, in this book, I have tried to show something a little different. For me, the Thatcher years represent the end of a long tradition in British political life of attitudes to state intervention.

The last third of the nineteenth century had seen a conflict between individualist-libertarians and collectivists. The individualists had argued for a free contract between equals which required greater democracy and greater freedom to enter the marketplace, but, by the later nineteenth century, this goal had been largely lost sight of through the aggregation of industry into larger and larger units and the growth of cities which could no longer be left to voluntary or charitable intervention. The collectivisation of industrial and merchant life led inevitably to the creation of collectivism among the workers who banded together in unions to protect their standard of living. Thus working-class collectivism was precisely the mechanism for protecting working people's individual needs.

Almost none of these changes had any real relationship to socialism which, for the most part, remained a minority interest. Society and parliamentary reform followed these lines into and after the First World War. Nevertheless, the Bolshevik revolution gave huge impetus to socialism and, by the 1920s, socialism and communism became the revolutionary forces behind extra-parliamentary change. The Labour Party, the strongest and largest working-class political organisation in the country, was on the whole free from Bolshevik tendencies, but its collective welfarism gave it the veneer of collaboration with communist subversion.

In the nineteenth century, a secret service would have been unthinkable and a threat against an Englishman's very liberty of movement or thought. No Prime Minister would countenance spying on fellow Britons. The creation of the Irish Special Branch was itself the product of very specific circumstances. By the Edwardian period, tales of British spies, German and French invasions and Russians with snow on their boots marching through the capital were just amusing fictions. The First World War changed all this and military spying became a necessity, but what kept the intelligence networks going from the 1920s was the 'red menace', something which only finally died with the fall of the Berlin Wall in 1989. The creation of an 'independent' nuclear deterrent and the coincidental bonds with American paranoia over Russian intentions after the Second World War embedded secrecy as a way of life in British politics.

Those who first devised Thatcherism in the 1970s were the inheritors of 100 years of debate and frustration over what philosophy should be the guiding light of government policy. The whole weight of economic, military and diplomatic effort was put to this question. The Falklands War and the war in Ireland were the last vestiges of Britain's colonial inheritance; the battle with the miners put an end to the industrial revolution; the nuclear bomb defended Britain against the communist menace; the secret state made sure that there were no dissenting voices.

Every aspect of Thatcherism took on a parasitical life of its own until Thatcher herself became the embodiment of the enemy of the very philosophy which was named after her. The state's role and the government's refusal, or incapacity, throughout the 1980s to curb its excesses were part and parcel of a trend that was internal to the Conservatives themselves, where the defence of traditional freedoms could only be won by the application of repressive state machineries and bureaucracies.

⌾⌾⌾

Tam Dalyell was a good snoop, even though he sometimes made mistakes. Perhaps he should have dogged the Prime Minister more exhaustively! Thatcher was always able to appear to stand for morality and freedom. She was a 'conviction' politician, that is, not a politician at all, in fact, but a higher moralist who just happened to be in the supreme position of power. She was, of course, political through and through. In this respect she was the embodiment of the moral contradiction that was Thatcherism.

As a politician, she appeared to have known something about some very dirty practices, before and during her premiership, which she chose to ignore for the sake of the 'system', the protection of HMG, the support of the arms industry and 'UK Ltd' or in order to protect a regime in Northern Ireland which she could not challenge because it was fighting terrorism.

If she was amost caught out over the sinking of the *Belgrano*, she was peculiarly lucky to have resigned before further questions might have destroyed what she stood for. Thatcher was able to avoid accusations of knowing full well about the export of the constituents of both armaments and poison gas to Iraq (which fell into John Major's lap during the Matrix-Churchill trial and Scott Inquiry), or of being reasonably aware of the underhand methods being used by the RUC Special Branch which had been only partially exonerated by the Stevens Inquiries, or of the various cover-ups to hide government complicity in the murder of British citizens by other British citizens (in Northern Ireland), or the apparent position she was in to stop child abuse by her colleagues. As a moralist, Thatcher was never able to rise above the dirty politics she was embroiled in, but which she *convinced herself* were moral actions rather than political decisions. The contradiction was corrosive.

The tradition that Thatcher fought for was always contradicted by the means for attaining it. By the time Thatcher had come to power, secrecy had become normal and beyond comment in every form of government transaction and in the free hand offered to the state as long as it followed government desires. By the end, the organs of the state had started to act independent of government will. The Thatcher government was certainly not the only one that found comfort and security in lying both to Parliament and to the voter. Hers was a regime born from the peculiar circumstances of the 1970s Cold War and the Irish troubles, where conspiracy was seen as somehow central to everything and where economic policy led directly to the sale of weapons of mass destruction to Saddam Hussein as a central plank of Britain's export drive in the 1980s. It may be inferred that it was this knowledge (rather than any 'dodgy dossier' or 'sexed up' intelligence report) that allowed Tony Blair and his advisors to talk with such assurance of the threat of WMDs – simply because they knew the potential of what had been sold ten years before.

By 2006, there arose a new version of accountability. Driven by the secret state and the ideas of those advising Gordon Brown, but in almost all aspects based on Thatcher's distrust of dissent as somehow traitorous, the reform of public services was based upon the responsibility of the citizen to the government rather than the government to the citizen. This new form of 'transformational government' based upon the 'totality of the relationship with the citizen' was intended to create 'identity management' and 'a single source of truth' with each of us.[22] A government report highlighted the use of IT to keep records, but suggested no safeguards as to privacy.

❧

Thatcher's Secret War has been concerned with the charged political atmosphere of suspicion that surrounded the many unexplained and irregular deaths that happened in the era and that occurred in the computer warfare sector, the world of English rose growers and Scottish nationalists, in the coalfields of England and the holding cells of police stations. But it also includes the strange deaths of airmen and intelligence experts on a remote hillside, the peculiar circumstances surrounding a dead tycoon and a dead banker, the many deaths during the Irish troubles and the hushed-up deaths of football supporters; here too are famous politicians and little-known ex-pats who died in mysterious circumstances in Saudi Arabia. Each death reveals something of the state of politics in the period from 1979 through to the end of the Cold War, and each is a model of obfuscation and deceit, of smoke and mirrors and of paranoid projections and conjecture that left those in opposition to the state and Thatcher governments bewildered and frustrated.

This book has focused on an important thread of paranoia hitherto disregarded or sidelined by other histories. It is not an alternative history of Thatcher's premiership, but a history which accounts for an atmosphere which worsened throughout the

1980s, and covers both the reality of secrecy and the perception of conspiracy by
those affected. It has also looked at the paranoia and suspicion that marked the right
at the end of the 1970s and that was central to the siege mentality that was the mark
of both Thatcher and her premierships, and that was confirmed by the leadership
crisis that engulfed her in the winter of 1990 when her own party rejected both the
lady and, to an extent, her political philosophy. Yet the siege mentality that was the
quintessence of Thatcher also marked the ideology named after her. Thatcherism
was never quite Thatcher, and Thatcher was always coy (if flattered) about conflating
the two, but it did mean that Thatcherite ideologists could act in ways they thought
were compatible with the Prime Minister's wishes.

Covert surveillance has now been accepted as necessary to protect against unspeci-
fied threats which are now and again 'thwarted' by clever boffins working for our best
interests. In 2000, the government passed the Regulation of Investigatory Powers
Act, but it only institutionalised the intrusion into privacy, something that the coali-
tion government under David Cameron made no effort to roll back. In 2006 and
2007 there were over 800 separate bodies which could intrude into the privacy of
the home, including 474 local authorities, while in 2014, it was revealed that there
had been 2,760 warrants to tap private communications and 514,608 warrants to
examine communications metadata.[23] In attempting to protect the privacy of the
home and the individual, Thatcherism began the process of unravelling all the pro-
tections against abuse. By Thatcher's passing, Edward Coke's comment of 1628, that
'everyone's home is to him his castle', was only true in as much as the castle now had
people looking in at every window.

NOTES

Chapter 1

1 *Daily Mail*, 27 June 2009. Interestingly, Teresa Gorman thought that Thatcher was always surrounded by aristocratic civil servants. See Teresa Gorman, *The Bastards* (London: Pan Macmillan, 1993), 5

2 Coleman, Terry, *Great Interviews of the Twentieth Century* (London: Guardian, 1971, 2007), 7

3 Dalyell, Tam, Hansard 29 October 1986, Col. 389

4 Foot, Paul, *Who Framed Colin Wallace?* (London: Pan, 1989), 366

5 Aaronovitch, David, *Voodoo Histories: The Role of the Conspiracy Theory in Shaping Modern History* (London: Jonathan Cape, 2009)

6 Ranelagh, John, *Thatcher's People: An Insider's Account of the Politics, the Power and the Personalities* (London: Fontana, 1992), 35

7 Foot, 346

8 Ibid., 46

9 Ibid., 398

Chapter 2

1 Dalyell, Tam, *Misrule: How Mrs Thatcher Has Misled Parliament from the Sinking of the 'Belgrano' to the Wright Affair* (London: Hamish Hamilton, 1987), 22–4

2 Smith, Michael, *New Cloak, Old Dagger: How Britain's Spies Came in from the Cold* (London: Victor Golancz, 1996), 16

3 Ibid., 17

4 Ibid., 9

5 Smith, Graham, *Death of a Rose-Grower: Who Killed Hilda Murrell?* (London: Cecil Woolf, 1985), 83–4

6 Ibid., 93

7 Ibid., 84

8 Ibid., 86

9 Ibid., 86

10 chrisryansas.blogspot.co.uk/2012/07/ive-been-asked-if-increment-is-real-and.html

11 Bruce, Paul, *The Nemesis File* (London: Blake Publishing, 1995)

12 Report of the Independent Commission of Inquiry into the Dublin and Monaghan Bombings, December 2003, 179

13 Ibid., Mr Justice Henry Barron's statement to the Oireachtas Joint Committee, 203

14 Fiennes, Ranulph, *The Feather Men* (Harmondsworth: Penguin, 1998)

15 Murray, Gary, *Enemies of the State* (London: Simon & Schuster, 1993), 113

16 Ibid., 113

17 Rushton, William, *Spy Thatcher: The Collected Ravings of a Senior MI5 Officer* (London: Pavilion, 1987), 31

18 Andrew, Christopher, *Secret Service: The Making of the British Intelligence Community* (London: Sceptre, 1992), 696

19 Andrew, Christopher, *Defend the Realm: The Authorised History of MI5* (New York: Alfred A Knopf, 2009), XIX

20 Lawson, Nigel, *The View From No. 11: Memoirs of a Tory Radical* (London: Corgi, 1992), 314

21 Penrose, Barrie and Courtiour, Roger, *The Pencourt File* (London: Secker & Warburg, 1978), 8

22 Ibid., 9

23 Ibid, 13

24 Ibid., 65

25 Freeman, Simon and Penrose, Barrie, *Rinkagate: The Rise and Fall of Jeremy Thorpe* (London: Bloomsbury, 1996), 206

26 Ibid., 162

27 Penrose and Courtiour, 178

28 Freeman and Penrose, 176

29 Ibid., 72–3

30 Ibid., 122

31 Ibid., 359

32 Ibid., 359

33 Ibid., 291

34 Ibid., 295

Chapter 3

1 Foot, Paul, *Who Framed Colin Wallace?* (London: Pan, 1989), 77

2 Ibid., 394

3 Andrew, Christopher, *Defend the Realm: The Authorised History of MI5* (New York, Alfred A Knopf, 2009), 641

4 Ibid., 642

5 Ibid., 642

6 Porter, Bernard, *Plots and Paranoia: A History of Political Espionage in Britain 1790–1988* (London: Unwin Hyman, 1989), 211

7 Andrew, 666

8 Ibid., 701

9 Thatcher, Margaret, *The Path to Power* (London: Harper Collins, 1995), 412–13

10 Dorril, Stephen, *MI6: Fifty Years of Special Operations* (London: Fourth Estate, 2000), 743

11 Ibid., 742

12 Foot, 764

13 Murray, Gary, *Enemies of the State* (London: Simon & Schuster, 1993), 112, and Foot 397

14 Ibid., 103

15 Ibid., 165

16 Ibid., 165

17 Ibid., 394

18 Ibid., 165

19 Foot, 394

Chapter 4

1 These were the original council members of what was then called the National Association for Freedom. They included figures as varied as Field Marshal Sir Gerald Templer, the constitutional expert Lord Blake and the cricketer Alec Bedser. Norris McWhirter, 'A Brief History of the Freedom Association', 2003, accessed from freedomassociation.typepad.com/the_freedom_association/files/hiso1; Andy Beckett, *When the Lights Went Out: Britain in the Seventies* (London: Faber & Faber, 2009) p.377

2 1975 Nov 28 HC PQ [Private Notice Question: Mr Ross McWhirter (Shooting)], www.margaretthatcher.org

3 Cosgrave, Patrick, *Thatcher: The First Term* (London: Bodley Head, 1985), 9

4 Routledge, Paul, *Public Servant Secret Agent: The Elusive Life and Violent Death of Airey Neave* (London: Fourth Estate, 2002), 256

5 Cosgrave, i–ix, 4

6 Routledge., 262

7 Ibid., 263

8 Ibid., 270

9 Ibid., 272

10 McCamley, Nick, *Cold War Secret Nuclear Bunkers* (Barnsley: Pen & Sword Books, 2013), 149

11 Hoe, Alan, *David Stirling: The Authorised Biography of the Creator of the SAS* (London: Little, Brown & Company, 1992), 97

12 *Britain's State Within the State* (London: New Park Publications) 1979–1980, 6

13 Ibid., 9

14 Kitson, Frank, *Low Intensity Operations: Subversion, Insurgency and Peacekeeping* (London: Faber & Faber, 1971), 3 and 199

15 Ibid., 69

16 Ibid., 25

17 Ibid.,189

18 wikipedia.org/wiki/Robert Nairac. See also John Parker, *Death of a Hero: Captain Robert Nairac, GC and the undercover war in Northern Ireland* (London: Metro, 1999)

19 Ibid.

20 Cadwallader, Anne, *Lethal Allies: British Collusion in Ireland* (Cork: Mercier Press, 2013), 330

21 For the full details of the death of Pat Finucane in 1989 and the collusion of the intelligence agencies with Loyalist assassins see Justin O'Brien, *Killing Finucane: Murder in Defence of the Realm* (Dublin, Gill and Macmillan,2005)

22 Parker, John, *Death of a Hero: Captain Robert Nairac, GC and the undercover war in Northern Ireland* (London: Metro, 1999), 192

23 Hart-Davis, Duff, *The War That Never Was: The True Story of the Men Who Fought Britain's*

Most Secret Battle (London: Arrow, 2012), 16

24 Hoe, Alan, *David Stirling: The Authorised Biography of the Creator of the S.A.S.* (London: Little, Brown & Company, 1992), 424–6

25 James, Gerald, *In the Public Interest* (London: Little, Brown & Company, 1995), 51

26 Ibid., 49

27 Hoe, 435

28 Ibid., 439

29 *Britain's State Within the State*, 29

30 Ibid., 39

31 Ibid., 41

32 Ibid., 43

33 Hackett, General Sir John, *The Third World War: August 1985: A Future History* (London: Sidgwick & Jackson, 1978), 253

34 Shipway, George, *The Chilian Club* (London: Mayflower, 1972)

35 Ibid., 30

36 Ibid., 28

37 Dalyell, Tam, *Misrule: How Mrs Thatcher Has Misled Parliament from the Sinking of the 'Belgrano' to the Wright Affair* (London: Hamish Hamilton, 1987), 131

38 Routledge, 279

39 Ibid., 290

40 Ibid., 295

41 Ibid., 297

42 Cadwallader, 126

43 Ibid., 127

44 Cadwallader, 163

45 Routledge, 300

46 Ibid., 300

47 Ibid., 300

48 Bolton, Roger, *Death on the Rock and Other Stories* (London: W.H. Allen, 1990), 307–9

49 Conservative Party Archive: CCOPR 432/79 March 1979

50 *The Herald*, 13 April 2013

Chapter 5

1 McWhirter Norris, *In Defence of Freedom: The Ross McWhirter Memorial Essays* (London: Systems Publications, 1978), 8

2 Ibid., 13

3 Ibid., 11

4 McWhirter, Norris, *Ross: The Story of a Shared Life* (London: Churchill Press, 1976), 183

5 McWhirter, *In Defence of Freedom*, 2

6 Ibid., 4 and 5

7 Ibid., 2

8 Ibid., 5

9 McWhirter, Norris, *Ross: The Story of a Shared Life*, 218

10 Margaret Thatcher, Speech to Finchley Constituency, 31 January 1976

11 Walker, Sir Walter, *The Next Domino?* (London: Corgi, 1982), 291

12 Ibid., 287

13 Ibid., 285

14 Bloom, Clive, *Violent London: 2000 Years of Riots, Rebels and Revolts* (Basingstoke: Palgrave Macmillan, 2003), 387–8

15 Gouriet, John, *Hear Hear! Collected Articles and Letters, 1999–2009* (Milton Keynes: Authorhouse, 2010), forward by Norman Tebbit [npn]

16 Crozier, Brian, *Free Agent: The Unseen War 1941–1991* (New York: Harper Collins, 1993), 121

17 Ibid., 188

18 Hougan, Jim, *Spooks: The Private Use of Secret Agents* (London: W.H. Allen, 1979), 65

19 Hutber, Patrick, *The Decline and Fall of the Middle Class and How It Can Fight Back* (Harmondsworth: Penguin, 1976), 108

20 Ibid., 110

21 Ibid., 1

22 See Gretton, John and Jackson, Mark, *William Tyndale: Collapse of a School – or a System* (London: George Allen Unwin, 1976). See also Ellis, Terry, et al, *William Tyndale: The Teachers' Story* (Tiptree: Anchor Press, 1976).

23 Hutber, 19

24 Ibid., 24

25 Ibid., 22

26 Ibid., 29–30

27 Ibid., 30

28 Ibid., 162

Chapter 6

1 Beckett, Andy, *Pinochet in Piccadilly: Britain and Chile's Hidden History* (London: Faber & Faber, 2002), 113

2 Ibid., 185–6

3 Moss, Robert, *The Collapse of Democracy* (London: Abacus, 1977), 110

4 Ibid., 116

5 Crozier, Brian, *Free Agent: The Unseen War 1941–1991* (New York: Harper Collins, 1993), 196

6 Lawson, Nigel, *The View From No. 11: Memoirs of a Tory Radical* (London: Corgi, 1992), 14

7 Ibid., 14

8 Campbell, John, *Margaret Thatcher, Volume Two: The Iron Lady* (London: Jonathan Cape, 2007), 22

9 Jenkins, Simon, *Thatcher & Sons: A Revolution in Three Acts* (London: Allen Lane, 2006), 55

10 Ibid., 155

11 Ibid., 55

12 Beckett, 184 and 195

13 Pincher, Chapman, *The Secret Offensive* (London: Sidgwick & Jackson, 1985), 184

14 Ibid., 185

15 Ibid., 187

Chapter 7

1 The *Daily Express* was a Conservative newspaper which nevertheless appealed to working-class Labour voters.

2 Pincher, Chapman *The Secret Offensive* (London: Sidgwick & Jackson, 1985), 189

3 Ibid., 189

4 Campbell, John, *Margaret Thatcher, Volume One: The Grocer's Daughter* (London: Jonathan Cape, 2000), 97

5 Ibid., 97–8

6 Thatcher, Margaret, Address to the Backbench 1922 Committee, July 1984

7 *Britain's State Within the State* (London: New Park Publications, 1979–1980), 4

8 Ibid., 5

9 Jenkins, Simon, *Thatcher & Sons: A Revolution in Three Acts* (London: Allen Lane, 2006), 126

10 Ibid., 154

11 Ibid., 122

12 Ibid., 102

13 Moore, Charles, *Margaret Thatcher: The Authorized Biography Volume One* (London: Allen Lane, 2013), 329

14 margaretthatcher.org: Margaret Thatcher archive, CCOPR 1748

15 Ibid.

16 Ibid.

17 Ibid.

18 Ibid.

19 Ibid.

20 Ibid.

21 Ibid.

22 Ibid.

23 Moore, 359

24 Ibid., 359

Chapter 8

1 Ponting, Clive, *Whitehall: Tragedy & Farce* (London: Sphere Books, 1986), 110

2 Ibid.

3 Kinnock, Neil, *Making Our Way: Investing in Britain's Future* (Oxford: Basil Blackwell, 1986), 182

4 Ponting, 121

5 Kinnock, 188

6 Ponting, 33

7 Ibid., 33

8 Renwick, Robin, *A Journey With Margaret Thatcher: Foreign Policy Under the Iron Lady* (London: Biteback, 2013), 124

9 Moorcock, Michael, *The Retreat From Liberty: The Erosion of Democracy in Today's Britain* (London: Zomba Books, 1983), 28

10 Ibid., 59

11 Ibid., 8

12 Ibid., 10

13 Ibid., 24

14 Bolton, Roger, *Death on the Rock and Other Stories* (London: W.H. Allen, 1990), 143

15 Ibid., 9

16 Oborne, Peter, *The Rise of Political Lying* (London: The Free Press, 2005), 16

17 Ibid., 15

18 Bilton, Michael and Kosminsky, Peter, *Speaking Out: Untold Stories from the Falklands War* (London: Andre Deutsch, 1987), 9

19 Ibid., 14

20 Ibid., 31

21 Ibid., 33

22 Dalyell, Tam, Misrule: *How Mrs Thatcher Has Misled Parliament from the Sinking of the 'Belgrano' to the Wright Affair* (London: Hamish Hamilton, 1987), 18

23 Prebble, Stuart, *Secrets of the Conqueror: The Untold Story of Britain's Most Famous Submarine* (London: Faber & Faber, 2012), 256

24 Ibid., 102

Chapter 9

1 Moore, Charles, *Margaret Thatcher: The Authorized Biography*, Volume One (London: Allen Lane, 2013), 532

2 Ibid., 533

3 Ibid., 533

4 Ibid., 347

5 Ibid., 346

6 Ibid., 348

7 Ibid., 348

8 Ibid., 349

9 Ibid., 349

10 margaretthatcher.org/document/105502

11 Ibid.

12 Coleman, Terry, *Great Interviews of the Twentieth Century* (London: Guardian, 1971, 2007), 14

13 Ibid., 9

14 Oborne, Peter, *The Rise of Political Lying* (London: The Free Press, 2005), 15

15 Ponting, Clive, *Whitehall: Tragedy & Farce* (London: Sphere Books, 1986), 5

16 Manningham-Buller, Eliza, *Securing Freedom* (London: Profile Books, 2012), 39

17 Ibid., 41 and 86

18 Collins, Tony, *Open Verdict: An Account of 25 Mysterious Deaths in The Defence Industry* (London: Sphere Books, 1990), 244

19 Manningham-Buller, 44 and 92

Chapter 10

1 Stewart, Graham, *Bang! A History of Britain in the 1980s* (London: Atlantic Books, 2013), 227

2 Ibid., 227

3 Golding, John, *Hammer of the Left: Defeating Tony Benn, Eric Heffer and Militant in the Battle for the Labour Party* (London: Politico's, 2003), 185

4 Ingham, Bernard, *Shoot the Messenger* (London: Harper Collins, 1991), 17

5 Ibid., 18

6 Moore, Charles, *Margaret Thatcher: The Authorized Biography Volume One* (London: Allen Lane, 2013), 349

7 Ponting, Clive, *Whitehall: Tragedy & Farce:* (London: Sphere Books, 1986), 178

8 Benn, Tony, *The End of an Era: Diaries 1980–90* (London: Arrow Books, 1992), 407

9 Ibid., 407

10 Heffer, Eric, *Labour's Future: Socialist or SDP Mark 2?* (London: Verso, 1986), 28

11 Ibid., 408

12 Heffer, XIII

13 Ibid., XII

14 Ibid., 11

15 Shipley, Peter, *Revolutionaries in Modern Britain* (London: Bodley Head, 1976), 20

16 Golding, 226

17 Ibid., 280

18 Ibid., 275

19 Ibid,. 334

20 Ibid., 337

21 Ibid., 327

22 Ibid., 340

23 Ibid., 344

24 Shipley, 97

25 Andrew, Christopher, *Defend the Realm: The Authorised History of MI5* (New York: Alfred A Knopf, 2009), 660

26 Butler, David; Adonis, Andrew and Travers, Tony, *Failure in British Government: The Politics of the Poll Tax* (Oxford: Oxford University Press, 1994), 130

Chapter 11

1 Kettle, Martin and Hodges, Lucy, *Uprising! The Police, the People and the Riots in Britain's Cities* (London: Pan, 1982), 97

2 James, Nicki, and Allison, Eric, *Strangeways 1990: A Serious Disturbance* (London: Larkin Publications, 1995), 96

3 Thatcher, Margaret, *The Downing Street Years* (London: Harper Collins, 1993), 143–4

4 Ibid., 144

5 Ibid., 145

6 Ibid., 147

7 Ibid., 146

8 Benn, Melissa and Worpole, Ken, *Death in the City: An Examination of Police Related Deaths in London* (London: Canary Press, 1986)

9 Frost, Diane and North, Peter, *Militant Liverpool* (Liverpool: Liverpool University Press, 2013), 47

10 See PRO T466/22 Measures to Assist Merseyside and Regional Policy including 'Managed Decline' in Liverpool.

11 Crick, Michael, *Militant* (London: Faber & Faber, 1984) 154

12 Frost and North, 97

13 Carvel, John, *Citizen Ken* (London: Hogarth Press, 1984), 10

14 Ibid., 69

15 Ibid., 74

16 Ibid., 21

17 Livingstone, Ken, *You Can't Say That: Memoirs* (London: Faber & Faber, 2011), 192

18 Ibid., 258

19 Hosken, Andrew, *Nothing Like a Dame: The Scandals of Shirley Porter* (London: Granta, 2006), 154

20 Ibid., 73

21 Ibid., 81

22 Ibid., 135

23 Ibid., 325

24 Ibid., 325

25 Ibid., 323

26 Livingstone, 258

Chapter 12

1 Routledge, Paul, *Public Servant Secret Agent: The Elusive Life and Violent Death of Airey Neave* (London: Fourth Estate, 2002), 72

2 Ibid., 47

3 Crick, Michael, Militant (London: Faber & Faber, 1984), 1

4 MacGregor, Ian, *The Enemies Within: The Story of the Miners' Strike 1984–5* (London: Collins, 1986), 11

5 Routledge, 129

6 Ibid., 129

7 Milne, Seumas, *The Enemy Within: The Secret War Against the Miners* (London: Verso, 2004), 342

8 Adeney, Martin and Lloyd, John, *The Miners' Strike 1984–5: Loss Without Limit* (London: Routledge & Kegan Paul, 1988), 208

9 Milne, 344–5

10 MacGregor, 13, and Haggar, Nicholas, *Scargill the Stalinist?* (London: Oaktree, 1984), 8

11 Hollingsworth, Mark and Fielding Nick, *Defending the Realm: MI5 and the Shayler Affair* (London: Andre Deutsch, 1999), 77

12 Milne, 325

13 Ibid., 331

14 Graef, Roger, *Talking Blues: The Police in Their Own Words* (London: Fontana/Collins Harvill, 1990), 69

15 Lloyd, Cathie, 'A National Riot Police: Britain's "Third Force"'? in Bob Fine and Robert Millar, eds, *Policing the Miners' Strike* (London: Lawrence & Wishart, 1985), 67

16 Graef, 73

17 Lloyd, 66

18 Graef, 75

19 Ibid., 74–5

20 For the last time this law was formulated as part of an enquiry see, Scarman, Lord Justice, *Report of Inquiry under the Rt Hon Lord Justice Scarman OBE into a dispute between Grunwick Processing Laboratories Limited and Members of the Association of Professional, Executive, Clerical and Computer Staff* (London: HMSO Cmnd 6922, 1977)

21 farleys.com/blog/rioting-and-the-law-the-legal-definition-and-associated-penalties#sthash.BxIfyDp5.dpuf

22 Christian, Louise, 'Restriction Without Conviction: The Role of the Courts in Legitimizing Police Control in Nottinghamshire' in Fine and Millar, 135

23 Graef, 81

24 Ibid., 81

25 Bassett, Philip, *Strike Free: New Industrial Relations in Britain* (London: Papermac, 1987), 2
26 Milne, 343

Chapter 13

1 Margaret Thatcher 'Winston Churchill Memorial Lecture' (Luxemburg) 18 October, 1979
2 Ibid.
3 Ibid.
4 Smith, Dan and Smith, Ron, 'British Military Expenditure in the 1980s' in E.P. Thompson and Dan Smith, eds, *Protest and Survive* (Harmondsworth: Penguin, 1980), 195–6
5 Ibid., 197
6 McCamley, N.J., *Secret Underground Cities* (Barnsley: Leo Cooper, 1998), 1
7 Ibid., 5
8 McCamley, Nick, *Cold War Secret Nuclear Bunkers* (Barnsley: Pen & Sword Books, 2013), 1
9 Ibid., 58
10 Ibid., 4
11 Renwick, Robin, *A Journey with Margaret Thatcher: Foreign Policy Under the Iron Lady* (London: Biteback, 2013), 125
12 Ibid., 131
13 Ibid., 151
14 Ibid., 151
15 Ibid., 147–8
16 McCamley, Nick, 166
17 Seagrave, Sterling, *Yellow Rain: Chemical warfare – the deadliest arms race* (London: Abacus, 1982), 177
18 Ibid., 206
19 Ibid., 201
20 Ibid., 202
21 Ibid., 202
22 Ibid., 55
23 Murphy, Sean; Hay Alastair and Rose, Steven, *No Fire, No Thunder* (London: Pluto Press, 1984), 92

Chapter 14

1 HMSO, Civil Defence: Manual of Basic Training, Volume II: Atomic Warfare Pamphlet No. 6 (London: HMSO, 1950), 11, 25–6
2 Grant, Matthew, *After the Bomb: Civil Defence and Nuclear War in Britain, 1945–1968* (Basingstoke: Palgrave Macmillan, 2010), IX
3 Thompson, E.P., *Protest and Survive* (London: Campaign for Nuclear Disarmament, 1980), 2
4 Ibid., 33
5 Ibid., 7
6 Ibid., 22
7 Ibid., 24 and 22
8 Ibid,. 25
9 Ibid., 25

10 Ibid, 10
11 Ibid., 23–4
12 Ibid., 32
13 Liddington, Jill, *The Road to Greenham Common: Feminism and Anti-Militarism in Britain since 1820* (New York: Syracuse University Press, 1991, 214
14 Duff, Peggy, *Left, Left, Left: A Personal account of six protest campaigns 1945–65* (London: Allison & Busby, 1971), 154
15 Pettitt, Ann, *Walking to Greenham: How the Peace-camp began and the Cold War ended* (Aberystwyth: Honno, 2006), 25
16 Ibid., 41
17 Ibid., 67
18 Ibid., 281
19 Ibid., 286
20 Barber, Ed, *Peace Moves: Nuclear Protest in the 1980s* (London: Hogarth Press, 1984), author's note
21 Zoe Fairbairns in Barber [npn]
22 Ibid.
23 Ibid.

Chapter 15

1 Holden, Triona, *Queen Coal: Women of the Miners' Strike* (Stroud: Sutton Publishing, 2005), XI
2 Salt, Chrys and Layzell, Jim, *Here We Go! Women's memories of the 1984/85 Miners Strike* (London: Co-operative Retails Services Ltd [nd]), 4
3 Holden, 91
4 Sutcliffe, Lealy and Hill, Brian, *Let Them Eat Coal: the Political Use of Social Security During the Miners' Strike* (London: Canary Press, 1985)
5 Walker, Martin, *A Turn of the Screw: The Aftermath of the 1984–85 Miners' Strike* (London: Canary Press, 1985), 102
6 Worthington, Andy, ed., *The Battle of the Beanfield* (Devon: Enabler Publications, 2005), 9
7 Ibid., 17
8 Ibid., 17
9 Ruesch, Hans, *Slaughter of the Innocent* (London: Futura, 1978), 366
10 Worthington, 24
11 Ibid., 27
12 Ibid., 60
13 Ibid,. 60–1
14 Deacon, Richard, *The French Secret Service* (London: Grafton, 1990), 307
14 Dalyell, Tam, Misrule: *How Mrs Thatcher Has Misled Parliament from the Sinking of the 'Belgrano' to the Wright Affair (*London: Hamish Hamilton, 1987), 76
15 Ibid, 76
16 Ibid., 77
17 McCamley, Nick, *Cold War Secret Nuclear Bunkers* (Barnsley: Pen & Sword Books, 2013), 277

Chapter 16

1 Collins, Tony, *Open Verdict: An Account of 25 Mysterious Deaths in the Defence Industry* (London: Sphere Books, 1990), 139

2 Ibid., 173

3 Ibid., 139

4 Ibid., 46

5 Ibid., 105

6 Ibid., 161

7 Nick Davies, *The Guardian*, 5 October 1999

8 Collins, 221

9 Ibid., 229

10 McRae, Ron, *Mind Wars: The True Story of Secret Government Research Into the Military Potential of Psychic Weapons* (New York, St Martin's Press, 1984), XVIII

11 Ibid., 62

12 Ibid., 62

13 Ibid., 136

14 Hougan, Jim, *Spooks: The Private Use of Secret Agents* (London: W.H. Allen, 1979), 18

15 Collins, 243

16 McRae, 124

17 Ibid., 125

18 slavery.org.uk/Beulahbaruch/killed.htm

19 beulahbaruch.org.uk

20 urbandictionary.com/define.php?term=gang%20stalking

21 taknbsorbemwon5.wordpress.com/tag/darrim-daoud

22 wikipedia.org/wiki/Usenet_celebrity

Chapter 17

1 West, Nigel, *The Secret War for the Falklands* (London: TimeWarner, 2002), 80

2 Carter, Miranda, *Anthony Blunt: His Lives* (London: Macmillan, 2001), 471–6

3 Cole, D.J., *Geoffrey Prime: The Imperfect Spy* (London: Robert Hale, 1998), 25

4 Ibid., 59

5 Foot, Paul, *Who Framed Colin Wallace?* (London: Pan, 1989), 396–7

6 *Irish Echo*, January/February 1993

7 Aldrich, Richard J., *GCHQ: The Uncensored Story of Britain's Most Secret Intelligence Agency* (London: Harper Press, 2011), 421

8 Ibid., 422

9 Ibid., 422

10 Ibid., 423

11 Ibid., 428

12 Ibid., 431

13 Ibid., 432

14 Ibid., 432

15 Ibid., 435

16 Ibid., 435

17 Ibid., 436

18 Dalyell, Tam, *Misrule: How Mrs Thatcher Has Misled Parliament from the Sinking of the 'Belgrano' to the Wright Affair* (London: Hamish Hamilton, 1987), 96

19 Ibid., 109

20 Ibid., 106

Chapter 18

1 Foot, Paul, *The Helen Smith Story* (London: Fontana, 1983), 90

2 Ibid., 102

3 Ibid., 109

4 Miller, Davina, *Export or Die: Britain's Defence Trade with Iran and Iraq* (London: Cassell, 1996), 2

5 Brooke, Heather, *The Silent State* (London: William Heinemann, 2010), 99 and 102

6 *The Guardian*, 25 February 2003

7 kuna.net.kw/ArticleDetails.aspx?id=1171386&language=en

8 Ibid.

9 wikipedia.org/wiki/Abu_Nida

10 onlinepublishingcompany.info/content/sitenewsreadmore/infobox/news/template/default/active_id/746

11 Ibid.

12 Ibid.

13 Deacon, Richard, *The French Secret Service* (London: Grafton, 1990), 307

14 Wright, Peter, *Spycatcher: The Candid Autobiography of a Senior Intelligence Officer* (New York: Viking, 1987), 187

15 West, Nigel, *The Secret War for the Falklands* (London: Time Warner, 2002)

16 Thomas, Gordon and Dillon, Martin, *The Assassination of Robert Maxwell: Israel's Superspy*, (London: Robson Books, 2002), 42

17 Davies, Russell, *Foreign Body: The Secret Life of Robert Maxwell* (London: Bloomsbury, 1995), 39

18 Thomas and Dillon, 352

19 Davies, 212

20 Thomas and Dillon, 278

21 Davies, 25

22 Andrew, Christopher, *Defend the Realm: The Authorised History of MI5* (New York: Alfred A Knopf, 2009), 690

23 Cobain, Ian, *Cruel Britannia: A Secret History of Torture* (London: Portobello Books, 2012), 282

24 Davies, 219

25 Ibid., 218

Chapter 19

1 Milne, Seumas, *The Enemy Within: The Secret War Against the Miners* (London: Verso, 2004), 86

2 Ibid., 91–2

3 James, Gerald, *In the Public Interest* (London: Little, Brown & Company, 1995), 102

4 Sweeney, John, *Trading with the Enemy: Britain's Arming of Iraq* (London: Pan, 1993), 95–6

5 Leigh, David, *Betrayed: The Real Story of the Matrix Churchill Trial* (London: Bloomsbury, 1993), 14

6 Ibid., 15

7 Ibid., 15

8 Scott, the Right Honourable Sir Richard, Report of the Inquiry into the Export of Defence Equipment and Dual-Use Goods to Iraq and Related Prosecutions (HMSO, Ord 341002, 1996)

9 James, 152

10 For the story of the Westland Affair see Magnus Linklater and David Leigh, *Not With Honour: the Inside Story of the Westland Scandal* (London: Sphere Books, 1986)

Chapter 20

1 Hall, Tony, *Nuclear Politics: The History of Nuclear Power in Britain* (Harmondsworth: Penguin, 1986), 47–8

2 Ibid., 49

3 Murray, Gary, *Enemies of the State* (London: Simon & Schuster, 1993), 156

4 Ibid., 124

5 Smith, Graham, *Death of a Rose-Grower: Who Killed Hilda Murrell?* (London: Cecil Woolf, 1985), 44

6 Ibid., 45

7 Murray, 128–9

8 Ibid., 141

9 Ibid., 134–5

10 Hall, 63

11 Ibid., 166

12 Ince, Martin, *Sizewell Report: What Happened at the Inquiry?* (London: Pluto Press, 1984), 180

13 Ibid., 22

14 Ibid., 138–9

15 Hall, 186

16 Ince, 65

17 Ibid., 3

18 Hall, 145

19 Ibid., 145

Chapter 21

1 Ponting, C., *Secrecy in Britain* (London: Basil Blackwell, 1990), 54

2 Stewart, Graham, *Bang! A History of Britain in the 1980s* (London: Atlantic Books, 2013), 210–11

3 Aaronovitch, David, *Voodoo Histories: The Role of the Conspiracy Theory in Shaping Modern History* (London: Jonathan Cape, 2009), 186

4 Ibid., 164

5 Green, Robert, *A Thorn in Their Side* (London: John Blake, 2013), 23–4

6 Ibid., 45

7 Ibid., 137

8 Ibid., XV

9 Murray, Gary, *Enemies of the State* (London: Simon & Schuster, 1993), 220

10 Ibid., 219

Chapter 22

1 Turner, Arthur, *Scottish Home Rule* (Oxford: Basil Blackwell, 1952), 1
2 Ibid., 2
3 Ponting, C., *Secrecy in Britain* (London: Basil Blackwell, 1990), 54–5
4 Thatcher, Margaret, *The Path to Power* (London: Harper Collins, 1995), 321
5 Ibid., 321
6 Ibid., 322
7 Ibid., 322
8 Ibid., 323
9 Ibid., 323
10 Ibid., 324
11 Ibid., 325
12 Cosgrave, Patrick, *Thatcher: The First Term* (London: Bodley Head, 1985), 29
13 Thatcher, *The Path to Power*, 430
14 Cosgrave, 59
15 Ibid., 61
16 Thatcher, *Path to Power*, 624
17 Bloom, Clive, *Restless Revolutionaries: A History of Britain's Fight for a Republic* (Stroud: The History Press, 2010), 253, 257
18 Murray Scott, Andrew and Macleay, Iain, *Britain's Secret War* (Edinburgh, Mainstream, 1990), 114

Chapter 23

1 Thatcher, Margaret, *The Downing Street Years* (London: Harper Collins, 1993), 618
2 Ibid., 618
3 Ibid., 619
4 Ibid., 619
5 Ibid., 624
6 Chalmers, Malcolm and Walker, William, *Uncharted Waters: The UK, Nuclear Weapons and the Scottish Question* (East Linton, East Lothian: Tuckwell Press, 2001), 15
7 Ibid., 23 and 28
8 Ibid., 38–9
9 SNP Statement of Defence Policy, December 1976, in Chalmers and Walker, 38
10 Murray, Gary, *Enemies of the State* (London: Simon & Schuster, 1993), 211

Chapter 24

1 O'Connor, Ulick, ed., *Skylark Sing Your Lonely Song: An anthology of the writings of Bobby Sands*, (Dublin and Cork: Mercier Press, 1982), 149
2 Ibid., 16
3 Ibid., 12
4 Wright, Peter, *Spycatcher: The Candid Autobiography of a Senior Intelligence Officer* (New York: Viking, 1987), 304
5 Cobain, Ian, *Cruel Britannia: A Secret History of Torture* (London: Portobello Books, 2012), 141–2

6 Ibid., 154
7 Ibid., 155
8 Cadwallader, Anne, *Lethal Allies: British Collusion in Ireland* (Cork: Mercier Press, 2013), 27
9 Taylor, Peter, *Stalker: The Search for the Truth* (London: Faber & Faber, 1987), 66
10 Stalker, John, *Stalker* (Harmondsworth: Penguin, 1988), 33
11 Ibid., 38
12 Ibid., 131
13 Ibid., 74
14 Cadwallader, 160

Chapter 25

1 Adams, James, Morgan, Robin and Bambridge, Anthony, *Ambush: The War Between the SAS and the IRA* (London: Pan, 1988), 90
2 Bolton, Roger, *Death on the Rock and Other Stories* (London: W.H Allen, 1990), 37
3 Ibid., 49
4 Ibid., 132
5 Ibid,. 265–6
6 Adams, Morgan and Bambridge, 179
7 Bolton, 247
8 Ibid., 296
9 wikispooks.com/wiki/Mull_of_Kintyre_RAF_Chinook_crash
10 The *Guardian,* 14 June 2000
11 Slessor, Tim, *Lying in State: How Whitehall Denies, Dissembles and Deceives* (London: Aurum, 2005), 136
12 Ibid., 136
13 Ibid., 143
14 Ibid., 167
15 Ibid, 178
16 BBC News, 3 November 2006
17 Slessor, 187–8

Chapter 26

1 Hannan, Patrick, *When Arthur Met Maggie* (Bridgend: Poetry Wales Press, 2006), 11
2 Briggs, Raymond, *The Tin-Pot General and the Old Iron Woman* (London: Hamish Hamilton, 1984) and *When the Wind Blows* (London: Penguin, 1983)
3 Vincent, David, *The Culture of Secrecy: Britain 1832–1998* (Oxford: Oxford University Press, 1998), 244
4 Smith, Michael, *New Cloak, Old Dagger: How Britain's Spies Came in from the Cold* (London: Victor Golancz, 1996), 17
5 Peak, Steve, *Troops in Strikes: Military Intervention in Industrial Disputes* (London: Cobden Trust, 1984), 140
6 Ibid., 149
7 Ibid., 149
8 Ibid., 151

9 Currie, Edwina, *Diaries 1987–1992* (London: Little, Brown & Company, 2002), 195

10 *Evening Standard*, 14 May 2015

11 *Metro*, 17 March, 2015

12 *Sunday People*, 16 November 2014

13 *Daily Mail*, 20 March 2015

14 *Times*, 17 March 2015

15 *Mirror*, 21 May 2015

16 *London Evening Standard*, 5 March 2015

17 Black, Robert, *Orkney: A Place of Safety?* (Edinburgh: Canongate Press, 1992), 150

18 Ibid., 71–2

19 Ibid., 72

20 Ibid., 129

21 The *Guardian*, 22 August 2006; wikipedia.org/wiki/South_Ronaldsay_child_abuse_scandal/
    BBC News, 22 August 2006; Addley, Esther (21 October 2006) 'Interview: Esther Addley meets'

22 Black, 132

23 Campbell, Beatrix, *Unofficial Secrets: Child Sexual Abuse: The Cleveland Case* (London:
    Virago, 1988), 50

24 Ibid., 54

25 Ibid., 93

26 Ibid., 118

27 *Daily Mail*, 30 March 2015

28 *The Times*, 2 April 2015

Chapter 27

1 Hannan, Patrick, *When Arthur Met Maggie* (Bridgend: Poetry Wales Press, 2006), 9

2 Hollingsworth, Mark and Fielding Nick, *Defending the Realm: MI5 and the Shayler Affair*
   (London: Andre Deutsch, 1999), 89

3 Thornton, Peter, *We Protest: The Public Order Debate* (London: National Council for Civil
   Liberties, 1985), 70

4 Scraton, Phil, *Hillsborough: The Truth* (Edinburgh and London: Mainstream Publishing,
   2009), 33

5 Ibid., 116

6 Ibid., 119–120

7 Ibid., 124

8 Ibid., 125

9 *The Times* 18 March 2015

10 Scraton, 250

11 Ibid., 157

12 McPhilemy, Sean, *The Committee: Political Assassination in Northern Ireland* (Niwot,
    Colorado: Roberts Rinehart, 1998), 83

13 Policing Monitoring and Research Group, *Policing Wapping: An Account of the Dispute
    1986/7, Briefing Paper 3* (London: London Strategic Policy Unit [nd]), 11

14 McLagan, Graeme, *Bent Coppers: The Inside Story of Scotland Yard's Battle Against Police
    Corruption* (London: Orion, 2003), 16

15 Thornton, 14

16 Holden, Triona, *Queen Coal: Women of the Miners' Strike* (Stroud: Sutton Publishing, 2005), 43

17 Cobain, Ian, *Cruel Britannia: A Secret History of Torture* (London: Portobello Books, 2012) 163

18 Dillon, Martin and Lehane, Denis, *Political Murder in Northern Ireland* (Harmondsworth: Penguin, 1973), 318

19 Ibid., 318

20 Punch, Maurice, *State Violence, Collusion and the Troubles: Counter Insurgency, Government Deviance and Northern Ireland* (London: Pluto Press, 2012), 85

Chapter 28

1 Rawnsley, Andrew, *Servants of the People: the Inside Story of New Labour* (Harmondsworth: Penguin, 2001) 4

2 Gerry Gable email, 10 May 2013

3 Evans, Rob and Lewis Paul, *Undercover: the True Story Behind Britain's Secret Police* (London: Faber & Faber, 2013) [np]

4 Evening Standard, 15 May 2014

5 Tyrie, Andrew, Gough, Roger and McCracken, Stuart, *Account Rendered: Extraordinary Rendition and Britain's Role* (London: Biteback, 2011), 83–5

6 Cobain, Ian, *Cruel Britannia: A Secret History of Torture* (London: Portobello Books, 2012), 204

7 Connor, Ken, *Ghost Force: The Secret History of the SAS* (London: Weidenfeld and Nicolson, 1998), 344

8 Ibid., 348

9 James, Gerald, *In the Public Interest* (London: Little, Brown & Company, 1995), 62

10 Ibid., 104

11 Ibid., 144

12 Ibid., 113

13 *Metro*, 1 July 2014

14 Daniel Defoe, *Journal of the Plague Year* (1772), Chapter 1

15 Butler, David; Adonis, Andrew and Travers, Tony, *Failure in British Government: The Politics of the Poll Tax* (Oxford: Oxford University Press, 1994), 101

16 Ibid., 105

17 Thatcher, Margaret, *The Downing Street Years* (London: Harper Collins, 1993), 644–7

18 Ibid., 644

19 Butler, 105

20 Ibid., 141

21 Burns, Danny, *Poll Tax Rebellion* (London: AK Press, 1992), 105

22 Raab, Dominic, *The Assault on Liberty: What Went Wrong With Rights* (London: Fourth Estate, 2009), 91

23 Ibid., 93

BIBLIOGRAPHY

Primary sources

Books and articles

Aaronovitch, David, *Voodoo Histories: The Role of the Conspiracy Theory in Shaping Modern History* (London: Jonathan Cape, 2009)

Adams, James, *The Financing of Terror* (London: Hodder and Stoughton, 1986)

Adams, James; Morgan, Robin and Bambridge, Anthony, *Ambush: The War Between the SAS and the IRA* (London: Pan, 1988)

Adeney, Martin and Lloyd, John, *The Miners' Strike 1984–5: Loss Without Limit* (London: Routledge & Kegan Paul, 1988)

Aldrich, Richard J., *GCHQ: The Uncensored Story of Britain's Most Secret Intelligence Agency* (London: Harper Press, 2011)

Andrew, Christopher, *Secret Service: The Making of the British Intelligence Community* (London: Sceptre, 1992)

— *Defend the Realm: The Authorised History of MI5* (New York: Alfred A Knopf, 2009)

Barber, Ed, *Peace Moves: Nuclear Protest in the 1980s* (London: Hogarth Press, 1984)

Bassett, Philip, *Strike Free: New Industrial Relations in Britain* (London: Papermac, 1987)

Beckett, Andy, *Pinochet in Piccadilly: Britain and Chile's Hidden History* (London: Faber & Faber, 2002)

Benn, Melissa and Worpole, Ken, *Death in the City: An Examination of Police Related Deaths in London* (London: Canary Press, 1986)

Benn, Tony, *The End of an Era: Diaries 1980–90* (London: Arrow Books, 1992)

Bilton, Michael and Kosminsky, Peter, *Speaking Out: Untold Stories from the Falklands War* (London: Andre Deutsch, 1987)

Black, Robert, *Orkney: A Place of Safety?* (Edinburgh: Canongate Press, 1992)

Bloom, Clive, *Violent London: 2000 Years of Riots, Rebels and Revolts* (Basingstoke: Palgrave Macmillan, 2003)

— *Restless Revolutionaries: A History of Britain's Fight for a Republic* (Stroud: The History Press, 2010)

Bolton, Roger, *Death on the Rock and Other Stories* (London: W.H. Allen, 1990)

Britain's State Within the State [Anon], (London: New Park Publications, 1979–80)

Briggs, Raymond, *When the Wind Blows* (London: Penguin, 1983)

— *The Tin-Pot Foreign General and the Old Iron Woman* (London: Hamish Hamilton, 1984)

Brooke, Heather, *The Silent State* (London: William Heinemann, 2010)

Bruce, Paul, *The Nemesis File* (London: Blake Publishing, 1995)

Burns, Danny, *Poll Tax Rebellion* (London: AK Press, 1992)

Butler, David; Adonis, Andrew and Travers, Tony, *Failure in British Government: The Politics of the Poll Tax* (Oxford: Oxford University Press, 1994)

Butler, David and Kavanagh, Dennis *The British General Election of 1987* (Basingstoke: Macmillan Press, 1988)

Cadwallader, Anne, *Lethal Allies: British Collusion in Ireland* (Cork: Mercier Press, 2013)

Campbell, Beatrix, *Unofficial Secrets: Child Sexual Abuse: The Cleveland Case* (London: Virago, 1988)

Campbell, John, *Margaret Thatcher, Volume One: The Grocer's Daughter* (London: Jonathan Cape, 2000)

— *Margaret Thatcher, Volume Two: The Iron Lady* (London: Jonathan Cape, 2007)

Carter, Miranda, *Anthony Blunt: His Lives* (London: Macmillan, 2001)

Carvel, John, *Citizen Ken* (London: Hogarth Press, 1984)

Chalmers, Malcolm and Walker, William, *Uncharted Waters: The UK, Nuclear Weapons and the Scottish Question* (East Linton, East Lothian: Tuckwell Press, 2001)

Cobain, Ian, *Cruel Britannia: A Secret History of Torture* (London: Portobello Books, 2012)

Cole, D.J., *Geoffrey Prime: The Imperfect Spy* (London: Robert Hale, 1998)

Coleman, Terry, *Great Interviews of the Twentieth Century* (London: Guardian, 1971, 2007)

Collins, Tony, *Open Verdict: An Account of 25 Mysterious Deaths in the Defence Industry* (London: Sphere Books, 1990)

Connor, Ken, *Ghost Force: The Secret History of the SAS* (London: Weidenfeld & Nicolson, 1998)

Cook, Judith, *Who Killed Hilda Murrell?* (London: New English Library, 1985)

Cornwell, Robert, *God's Banker: The Life and Death of Roberto Calvi* (London: Counterpoint, 1984)

Cosgrave, Patrick, *Thatcher: The First Term* (London: Bodley Head, 1985)

Crick, Michael, *Militant* (London: Faber & Faber, 1984)

Crozier, Brian, *Free Agent: The Unseen War 1941–1991* (New York: Harper Collins, 1993)

Currie, Edwina, *Diaries 1987–1992* (London: Little, Brown & Company, 2002)

Dalyell, Tam, *Misrule: How Mrs Thatcher Has Misled Parliament from the Sinking of the 'Belgrano' to the Wright Affair* (London: Hamish Hamilton, 1987)

Davies, Russell, *Foreign Body: The Secret Life of Robert Maxwell* (London: Bloomsbury, 1995)

Deacon, Richard, *The French Secret Service* (London: Grafton, 1990)

Dillon, Martin and Lehane, Denis, *Political Murder in Northern Ireland* (Harmondsworth: Penguin, 1973)

Dorril, Stephen, *MI6: Fifty Years of Special Operations* (London: Fourth Estate, 2000)

Duff, Peggy, *Left, Left, Left: A Personal Account of Six Protest Campaigns 1945–65* (London: Allison & Busby, 1971)

Eckert, Nicholas, *Fatal Encounter: The Story of the Gibraltar Killings* (Dublin: Poolbeg Press Ltd, 1999)

Ellis, Terry et al, *William Tyndale: The Teachers' Story* (Tiptree: Anchor Press, 1976)

Evans, Rob and Lewis, Paul, *Undercover: The True Story Behind Britain's Secret Police* (London: Faber & Faber, 2013)

Fiennes, Ranulph, *The Feather Men* (Harmondsworth: Penguin, 1998)

Fine, Bob and Millar, Robert, eds, *Policing the Miners' Strike* (London: Lawrence & Wishart, 1985)

Foot, Paul, *The Helen Smith Story* (London: Fontana, 1983)

— *Who Framed Colin Wallace?* (London: Pan, 1989)

Freeman, Simon and Penrose, Barrie, *Rinkagate: The Rise and Fall of Jeremy Thorpe* (London: Bloomsbury, 1996)

Frost, Diane and North, Peter, *Militant Liverpool* (Liverpool: Liverpool University Press, 2013)

Golding, John, *Hammer of the Left: Defeating Tony Benn, Eric Heffer and Militant in the Battle for the Labour Party* (London: Politico's, 2003)

Gorman, Teresa, *The Bastards* (London: Pan Macmillan, 1993)

Gouriet, John, *Hear Hear! Collected Articles and Letters 1999–2009* (Milton Keynes: Authorhouse, 2010)

Graef, Roger, *Talking Blues: The Police in Their Own Words* (London: Fontana/Collins Harvill, 1990)

Grant, Matthew, *After the Bomb: Civil Defence and Nuclear War in Britain 1945–1968* (Basingstoke: Palgrave Macmillan, 2010)

Green, Robert, *A Thorn in Their Side* (London: John Blake, 2013)

Gretton, John and Jackson, Mark, *William Tyndale: Collapse of a School – or a System* (London: George Allen Unwin, 1976)

Grist, Caroline and Ferguson, Katy, *No Way in Wapping* (London: National Council for Civil Liberty, 1986)

Hackett, General Sir John, *The Third World War: August 1985: A Future History* (London: Sidgwick & Jackson, 1978)

Haggar, Nicholas, *Scargill the Stalinist?* (London: Oaktree, 1984)

Hall, Tony, *Nuclear Politics: The History of Nuclear Power in Britain* (Harmondsworth: Penguin, 1986)

Hannan, Patrick, *When Arthur Met Maggie* (Bridgend: Poetry Wales Press, 2006)

Hart-Davis, Duff, *The War That Never Was: The True Story of the Men Who Fought Britain's Most Secret Battle* (London: Arrow, 2012)

Heffer, Eric, *Labour's Future: Socialist or SDP Mark 2?* (London: Verso, 1986)

Hennessy, Peter, *The Secret State: Preparing for the Worst, 1945–2010* (Harmondsworth: Penguin, 2010)

Hinton, James, *Protests & Visions: Peace Politics in 20th Century Britain* (London: Hutchinson Radius, 1989)

HMSO, *Civil Defence: Manual of Basic Training, Volume II: Atomic Warfare Pamphlet No. 6* (London: HMSO, 1950)

Hoe, Alan, *David Stirling: The Authorised Biography of the Creator of the SAS* (London: Little, Brown & Company, 1992)

Holden, Triona, *Queen Coal: Women of the Miners' Strike* (Stroud: Sutton Publishing, 2005)

Hollingsworth, Mark, *The Ultimate Spin Doctor: The Life & Fast Times of Tim Bell* (London: Hodder & Stoughton, 1997)

Hollingsworth, Mark and Fielding, Nick, *Defending the Realm: MI5 and the Shayler Affair* (London: Andre Deutsch, 1999)

Hosken, Andrew, *Nothing Like a Dame: The Scandals of Shirley Porter* (London: Granta, 2006)

Hougan, Jim, *Spooks: The Private Use of Secret Agents* (London: W.H. Allen, 1979)

Hutber, Patrick, *The Decline and Fall of the Middle Class and How It Can Fight Back* (Harmondsworth: Penguin, 1976)

Ince, Martin, *Sizewell Report: What Happened at the Inquiry?* (London: Pluto Press, 1984)

Ingham, Bernard, *Shoot the Messenger* (London: Harper Collins, 1991)

James, Gerald, *In the Public Interest* (London: Little, Brown & Company, 1995)

James, Nicki, and Allison, Eric, *Strangeways 1990: A Serious Disturbance* (London: Larkin Publications, 1995)

Jenkins, Simon, *Thatcher & Sons: A Revolution in Three Acts* (London: Allen Lane, 2006)

Kettle, Martin and Hodges, Lucy, *Uprising! The Police, the People and the Riots in Britain's Cities* (London: Pan, 1982)

Kinnock, Neil, *Making Our Way: Investing in Britain's Future* (Oxford: Basil Blackwell, 1986)

Kitson, Frank, *Low Intensity Operations: Subversion, Insurgency and Peacekeeping* (Faber & Faber, London, 1971)

Lawson, Nigel, *The View From No. 11: Memoirs of a Tory Radical* (London: Corgi, 1992)

Leigh, David, *Betrayed: The Real Story of the Matrix Churchill Trial* (London: Bloomsbury, 1993)

Liddington, Jill, *The Road to Greenham Common: Feminism and Anti-Militarism in Britain since 1820* (New York: Syracuse University Press, 1991

Linklater, Magnus and Leigh, David, *Not With Honour: the Inside Story of the Westland Scandal* (London: Sphere Books, 1986)

Livingstone, Ken, *You Can't Say That: Memoirs* (London: Faber & Faber, 2011)

MacGregor, Ian, *The Enemies Within: The Story of the Miners' Strike 1984–5* (London: Collins, 1986)

McCamley, Nick, *Cold War Secret Nuclear Bunkers* (Barnsley: Pen & Sword Books, 2013)

McCamley, N.J., *Secret Underground Cities* (Barnsley: Leo Cooper, 1998)

McCutcheon, Campbell, *Protect and Survive: Civil Defence Manual of Basic Training* (Stroud: Tempus, 1949, 2007)

McLagan, Graeme, *Bent Coppers: The Inside Story of Scotland Yard's Battle Against Police Corruption* (London: Orion, 2003)

McPhilemy, Sean, *The Committee: Political Assassination in Northern Ireland* (Niwot, Colorado: Roberts Rinehart, 1998)

McRae, Ron, *Mind Wars: The True Story of Secret Government Research Into the Military Potential of Psychic Weapons* (New York: St Martin's Press, 1984)

McWhirter, Norris, *In Defence of Freedom: The Ross McWhirter Memorial Essays* (London: Systems Publications, 1978)

— *Ross: The Story of a Shared Life* (London: Churchill Press, 1976)

Manningham-Buller, Eliza, *Securing Freedom* (London: Profile Books, 2012)

Miller, Davina, *Export or Die: Britain's Defence Trade with Iran and Iraq* (London: Cassell, 1996)

Milne, Seumas, *The Enemy Within: The Secret War Against the Miners* (London: Verso, 2004)

Minnion, John and Bolsover, Philip, eds, *The CND Story: The first 25 years of CND in the words of people involved* (London: Allison & Busby, 1983)

Moorcock, Michael, *The Retreat From Liberty: The Erosion of Democracy in Today's Britain* (London: Zomba, 1983)

Moore, Charles, *Margaret Thatcher: The Authorized Biography Volume One: Not for Turning* (London: Allen Lane, 2013)

Moss, Robert, *The Collapse of Democracy* (London: Abacus, 1977)

Murphy, Sean; Hay, Alastair and Rose, Steven, *No Fire, No Thunder* (London: Pluto Press, 1984)

Murray, Gary, *Enemies of the State* (London: Simon & Schuster, 1993)

Murray Scott, Andrew and Macleay, Iain, *Britain's Secret War* (Edinburgh, Mainstream, 1990)

Oborne, Peter, *The Rise of Political Lying* (London: The Free Press, 2005)

O'Brien, Justin, *Killing Finucane: Murder in Defence of the Realm* (Dublin: Gill and Macmillan Ltd, 2005)

O'Connor, Ulick, ed, *Skylark Sing Your Lonely Song: An anthology of the writings of Bobby Sands* (Dublin and Cork: Mercier Press, 1982)

Parker, John, *Death of a Hero: Captain Robert Nairac, GC and the undercover war in Northern Ireland* (London: Metro, 1999)

Peak, Steve, *Troops in Strikes: Military Intervention in Industrial Disputes* (London: Cobden Trust, 1984)

Penrose, Barrie and Courtiour, Roger, *The Pencourt File* (London: Secker & Warburg, 1978)

Pettitt, Ann, *Walking to Greenham: How the Peace-camp began and the Cold War ended* (Aberystwyth, Honno, 2006)

Pincher, Chapman, *The Secret Offensive* (London: Sidgwick & Jackson, 1985)

Policing Monitoring and Research Group, *Policing Wapping: An Account of the Dispute 1986/7, Briefing Paper 3* (London: London Strategic Policy Unit)

Ponting, Clive, *The Right to Know: The Inside Story of the Belgrano Affair* (London: Sphere Books, 1985)

— *Whitehall: Tragedy & Farce* (London: Sphere Books, 1986)

Ponting, C., *Secrecy in Britain* (London: Basil Blackwell, 1990)

Porter, Bernard, *Plots and Paranoia: A History of Political Espionage in Britain 1790–1988* (London: Unwin Hyman, 1989)

Prebble, Stuart, *Secrets of the Conqueror: The Untold Story of Britain's Most Famous Submarine* (London: Faber & Faber, 2012)

Punch, Maurice, *State Violence, Collusion and the Troubles: Counter Insurgency, Government Deviance and Northern Ireland* (London: Pluto Press, 2012)

Raab, Dominic, *The Assault on Liberty: What Went Wrong With Rights* (London: Fourth Estate, 2009)

Ranelagh, John, *Thatcher's People: An Insider's Account of the Politics, the Power and the Personalities* (London: Fontana, 1992)

Rawnsley, Andrew, *Servants of the People: The Inside Story of New Labour* (Harmondsworth: Penguin, 2001)

Renwick, Robin, *A Journey With Margaret Thatcher: Foreign Policy Under the Iron Lady* (London: Biteback, 2013)

Routledge, Paul, *Public Servant Secret Agent: The Elusive Life and Violent Death of Airey Neave* (London: Fourth Estate, 2002)

Ruesch, Hans, *Slaughter of the Innocent* (London: Futura, 1978)

Rushton, William, *Spy Thatcher: The Collected Ravings of a Senior MI5 Officer* (London: Pavilion, 1987)

Salt, Chrys and Layzell, Jim, *Here We Go! Women's memories of the 1984/85 Miners Strike* (London: Co-operative Retails Services [nd])

Scott, the Right Honourable Sir Richard, *Report of the Inquiry into the Export of Defence Equipment and Dual-Use Goods to Iraq and Related Prosecutions* (London: HMSO, Ord 341002, 1996)

Scraton, Phil, *Hillsborough: The Truth* (Edinburgh and London: Mainstream Publishing, 2009)

Seagrave, Sterling, *Yellow Rain: Chemical warfare – the deadliest arms race* (London: Abacus, 1982)

Shipley, Peter, *Revolutionaries in Modern Britain* (London: Bodley Head, 1976)

Shipway, George, *The Chilian Club* (London: Mayflower, 1972)

Sinclair, Andrew, *Secret Service: The Making of the British Intelligence Community* (London: Sceptre, 1985)

Sinker, Charles, ed., *Hilda Murrell's Nature Diaries 1961–1983* (London: Collins, 1987)

Slessor, Tim, *Lying in State: How Whitehall Denies, Dissembles and Deceives* (London: Aurum, 2005)

Smith, Dan and Smith, Ron, 'British Military Expenditure in the 1980s', in E.P. Thompson and Dan Smith, eds, *Protest and Survive* (Harmondsworth: Penguin, 1980)

Smith, Graham, *Death of a Rose-Grower: Who Killed Hilda Murrell?* (London: Cecil Woolf, 1985)

Smith, Michael, *New Cloak, Old Dagger: How Britain's Spies Came in from the Cold* (London: Victor Golancz, 1996)

Stalker, John, *Stalker* (Harmondsworth: Penguin, 1988)

Stewart, Graham, *Bang! A History of Britain in the 1980s* (London: Atlantic Books, 2013)

Sutcliffe, Lealy and Hill, Brian, *Let Them Eat Coal: The Political Use of Social Security During the Miners' Strike* (London: Canary Press, 1985)

Sweeney, John, *Trading with the Enemy: Britain's Arming of Iraq* (London: Pan, 1993)

Taylor, Peter, *Stalker: The Search for the Truth* (London: Faber & Faber, 1987)

Thatcher, Margaret, *The Downing Street Years* (London: Harper Collins, 1993)

— *The Path to Power* (London: Harper Collins, 1995)

Thomas, Gordon and Dillon, Martin, *The Assassination of Robert Maxwell: Israel's Superspy* (London: Robson Books, 2002)

Thompson, E.P., *Protest and Survive* (London: Campaign for Nuclear Disarmament, 1980)

Thornton, Peter, *We Protest: The Public Order Debate* (London: National Council for Civil Liberties, 1985)

Turner, Arthur, *Scottish Home Rule* (Oxford: Basil Blackwell, 1952)

Tyrie, Andrew; Gough, Roger and McCracken, Stuart, *Account Rendered: Extraordinary Rendition and Britain's Role* (London: Biteback, 2011)

Vincent, David, *The Culture of Secrecy: Britain 1832–1998* (Oxford: Oxford University Press, 1998)

Walker, Martin, *A Turn of the Screw: The Aftermath of the 1984–85 Miners' Strike* (London: Canary Press, 1985)

Walker, Sir Walter, *The Next Domino?* (London: Corgi, 1982)

West, Nigel, *The Secret War for the Falklands* (London: Time Warner, 2002)

Worthington, Andy, ed, *The Battle of the Beanfield* (Devon: Enabler Publications, 2005)

Wright, Peter, *Spycatcher: The Candid Autobiography of a Senior Intelligence Officer* (New York: Viking, 1987)

Websites

arrse.co.uk/wiki/Paul_Bruce; arrse.co.uk/community/threads/the-nemesis-file-ffs-not-again.155511

beulahbaruch.org.uk

dailymail.co.uk/news/article-1128630/Death-SAS-fantasist-Was-Tom-Carew-murdered--did-fake-death.html

fantompowa.net/Flame/william_mcrae.htm

farleys.com/blog/rioting-and-the-law-the-legal-definition-and-associated-penalties#sthash.BxIfyDp5.dpuf

huffingtonpost.co.uk

johnblakepublishing.co.uk/e-store/search.php?mode=search&page=1

kuna.net.kw/ArticleDetails.aspx?id=1171386&language=en

margaretthatcher.org

onlinepublishingcompany.info/content/sitenewsreadmore/infobox/news/template/default/active_id

slavery.org.uk/Beulahbaruch/killed.htm

taknbsorbemwon5.wordpress.com/tag/darrim-daoud

urbandictionary.com/define.php?term=gang%20stalking

wikipedia.org/wiki: South Ronaldsay child abuse scandal; Fred Holroyd; Robert Nairac; Michael John Smith; Michael Bettaney; Cathy Massiter; Usenet celebrity; Abu Nida

wikispooks.com/wiki/Mull_of_Kintyre_RAF_Chinook_crash

Secondary sources

Books and articles

Ambler, Ken, *A Coalfield in Chaos* (East Yorkshire: Ken Ambler [nd])

Arthurs, Alan, 'GCHQ and the changing face of staff relations in the Civil Service', *Industrial Relations Journal* vol. 16, no. 2, summer 1985, pp. 26–33

Baker, Norman MP, *The Strange Death of David Kelly* (London: Methuen, 2007)

Barnett, Anthony, *Iron Britannia: Why Parliament Waged its Falklands War* (London: Allison & Busby, 1982)

Beckett, Andy, *When the Lights Went Out: What Really Happened to Britain in the Seventies* (London: Faber & Faber, 2009)

Beckett, Francis and Hencke, David, *Marching to the Fault Line: The Miners' Strike and the Battle for Industrial Britain* (London: Constable, 2009)

Bellamy, Alison, *How About That Then? The Authorized Biography of Jimmy Savile* (Great Northern Books, 2012)

Bicheno, Hugh, *Razor's Edge: the Unofficial History of the Falklands War* (London: Weidenfeld & Nicolson, 2006)

Bloom, Clive, *Violent London: 2000 Years of Riots, Rebels and Revolts* (London: Palgrave Macmillan, 2003, 2010)

— *Riot City: Protest and Rebellion in the City* (London: Palgrave Macmillan, 2012)

Bowden, Tom, *Beyond the Limits of the Law: A Comparative Study of the Police in Crisis Politics* (Harmondsworth: Penguin, 1978)

Brock, George et al, *Siege: Six Days at the Iranian Embassy* (London: Macmillan, 1980)

Bunyan, Tony, *The History and Practice of The Political Police in Britain* (London: Quartet Books, 1977)

Chippindale, Peter and Leigh, David, *The Thorpe Committal: The Full Story of the Minehead Proceedings* (London: Arrow, 1979)

Chomsky Noam, *Hegemony or Survival: America's Quest for Global Dominance* (London: Penguin Books, 2004)

Cliff, Tony, *The Crisis: Social Contract or Socialism* (London: Pluto Press, 1975)

Corby, Susan, 'The GCHQ Union Ban 1984–1997: The union's strategy and the outcome', *Labour History Review*, 65, winter 2000, pp. 317–32

Coulter, Jim; Walker, Susan and Walker, Martin, *State of Siege; Miners' Strike 1984* (London: Canary Press, 1984)

Cowell, David; Jones, Trevor and Young, Jock, *Policing the Riots* (London: Junction Books, 1982)

Danczuk, Simon and Baker, Matthew, *Smile for the Camera: The Double Life of Cyril Smith* (London: Biteback, 2014)

Darlington, Ralph and Lyddon, Dave, *Glorious Summer: Class Struggle in Britain 1972* (London: Bookmarks, 1972)

Davies, Barry, *SAS Rescue* (London: Sidgwick & Jackson, 1996)

Davies, Dan, *In Plain Sight; The Life and Lies of Jimmy Savile* (London: Quercus Publishing, 2014)

Davies, Nicholas, *Dead Men Talking: Collusion, Cover-Up and Murder in Northern Ireland's Dirty War* (Edinburgh and London: Mainstream Publishing, 2006)

Dorrill, Stephen and Ramsan, Robin, *Smear! Wilson and the Secret State* (London: Fourth Estate, 1991)

Dunn, Douglas, *Poll Tax: The Fiscal Fake* (London: Chatto & Windus, 1990)

Elliott, Brian, *The Miners' Striker, Day by Day* (Barnsley: Wharncliffe Books, 2006)

Ferris, Paul, *The New Militants: Crisis in the Trade Unions* (Harmondsworth: Penguin, 1972)

Firmin, Rusty and Pearson, Will, *Go! Go! Go! The SAS. The Iranian Embassy Siege. The True Story* (London: Phoenix, 2011)

Frost, Diane and Phillips, Richard, *Liverpool '81: Remembering the Riots* (Liverpool: Liverpool University Press, 2011)

Gibbon, Peter and Steyne, David, *Thurcroft: A Village and the Miners' Strike* (Nottingham: Atlantic Highlands, 1986)

Gilmour, Ian, *Inside Right: Conservatism, Policies and the People* (London: Quartet Books, 1978)

Grant, Ted, *History of British Trotskyism* (London: Wellred Publications, 2002)

Hain, Peter, *Political Trials in Britain: From the Past to the Present Day* (Harmondsworth: Penguin, 1984)

Hall, Stuart and Jacques, Martin, eds, *The Politics of Thatcherism* (London: Lawrence & Wishart, 1983)

Hayek, F.A., *The Road to Serfdom* (London and Henley: Routledge & Kegan Paul, London, 1944)

Humphries, John, *Freedom Fighters: Wales's Forgotten 'War', 1963–1993* (Cardiff: University of Wales Press, 2008)

Kahn, Peggy et al, *Industrial Disputes, Tactics and the Law* (London: Routledge & Kegan Paul, 1983)

Kavanagh, Dennis and Seldon, Anthony, eds, *The Major Effect* (London: Macmillan, 1994)

Keith Michael, *Race, Riots and Policing: Lore and Disorder in a Multi-racist Society* (London: University College London Press, 1993)

'Kelvedon Hatch Secret Nuclear Bunker, The: RGHQ 5.1' (Kelvedon Hatch Nuclear Bunker, nd)

Khabaz, D.V., *Manufactured Schema: Thatcher, the Miners and the Culture Industry* (Leicester: Troubador Publishing, 2006)

King Roger and Nugent, Neill (eds), *Respectable Rebels: Middle Class Campaigns in Britain in the 1970s* (London: Hodder and Stoughton, 1979)

Lang, John and Dodkins, Graham, *Bad News: The Wapping Dispute* (Nottingham: Spokesman, 2011)

Layton-Henry, Zig, *The Politics of Race in Britain* (London: Allen & Unwin, 1984)

Leigh, David, *The Wilson Plot: The Intelligence Services and the Discrediting of a Prime Minister 1945–1976* (London: Heinemann, 1988)

Lightman, Gavin, Q.C., *The Lightman Report on the N.U.M.* (London: Penguin, 1990)

McSmith, Andy, *No Such Thing as Society: A History of Britain in the 1980s* (London: Constable & Robinson, 2011)

Melman, Yossi, *The Master Terrorist: The True Story Behind Abu Nidal* (London: Sidgwick & Jackson, 1992)

Mullin, Chris, *A Very British Coup* (London: Hodder & Stoughton, 1982)

Northam, Gerry, *Shooting in the Dark: Riot Police in Britain* (London: Faber & Faber, 1988)

Norton-Taylor, Richard; Lloyd, Mark and Cook, Stephen, *Knee Deep in Dishonour: The Scott Report and its Aftermath* (London: Weidenfeld & Nicolson, 1996)

Pimlott, Ben, *Harold Wilson* (London: Harper Collins, 1993)

'Protect and Survive' (Home Office, London, 1976 (reprinted 1980)

Rice, Desmond and Gavshon, Arthur, *The Sinking of the Belgrano* (London: Secker & Warburg, 1984)

Riddell, Peter, *The Thatcher Decade* (Oxford: Basil Blackwell, 1989)

Rossiter, Mike, *Sink the Belgrano* (London: Corgi Books, 2007)

Sandbrook, Dominic, *State of Emergency: The Way We Were: Britain 1970–1974* (London: Penguin, 2010)

— *Seasons in the Sun: The Battle for Britain, 1974–1979* (London: Penguin, 2012)

Savile, Jimmy, *Love is an Uphill Thing* (London: Coronet, 1976)

Scott Murray, Andrew and Macleay, Iain, *Britain's Secret War: Tartan Terrorism and the Anglo-American State* (Edinburgh: Mainstream Publishing, 1990)

Skidelsky, Robert, ed., *Thatcherism* (Oxford: Basil Blackwell, 1988)

South, Nigel, *Policing for Profit: The Private Security Sector* (London: Sage, 1988)

Stephenson, Hugh, *Mrs Thatcher's First Year* (London: Jill Norman, 1980)

Taaffe, Peter and Mulhearn, Tony, *Liverpool: A City that Dared to Fight* (London: Fortress Books, 1988)

Taylor, Roger; Ward, Andrew and Newburn, Tim, *The Day of the Hillsborough Disaster, a Narrative Account* (Liverpool: Liverpool University Press, 1995)

Thornett, Alan, *Inside Cowley: Trade union struggle in the 1970s: who really opened the door to the Tory onslaught?* (London: Porcupine Press, 1998)

Tomlinson, John, *Left, Right: The March of Political Extremism in Britain* (London: John Calder, 1981)

Torrance, David, *We in Scotland: Thatcherism in a Cold Climate* (Edinburgh: Birlinn, 2009)

Tumber, Howard, *Television and the Riots* (London: British Film Institute, 1982)

Turner, Alwyn W., *Crisis? What Crisis? Britain in the 1970s* (London: Aurum Press, 2009)

Urban, Mark, *Big Boys' Rules: The Secret War Against the IRA* (London: BCA, 1992)

Vinen, Richard, *Thatcher's Britain: The Politics and Social Upheaval of the 1980s* (London: Pocket Books, 2009)

Williams, David L., *Siege* (Shepperton: Ian Allan, 1993)

Reports

Gifford, Lord, Q.C., *Broadwater Farm Revisited: Second Report of the Independent Inquiry into the disturbances of October 1985 at the Broadwater Farm Estate, Tottenham* (London: Karia Press, 1989)

Scarman, Lord Justice, *Report of Inquiry under the Rt Hon Lord Justice Scarman OBE into a dispute between Grunwick Processing Laboratories Limited and Members of the Association of Professional, Executive, Clerical and Computer Staff* (London: HMSO Cmnd 6922, 1977)

Trades Union Council documents

GCHQ – Special Meeting of the General Council, 29 February 1984

TUC Press Release, Circular 167, 1 March 1984

TTUC Press Release, 5 March 1984

TUC Press Release, 6 August 1984

TUC Press Release, 19 October 1984

TUC Press Release, Circular 9, 20 October 1988

Speakers' Notes, GCHQ Day, 20 October 1988

Letter to Margaret Thatcher from Norman Willis, 16 October 1984

Letter to Francis Blanchard, Director General of the International Labour Organisation, from Norman Willis, 18 October 1984

Letter to Council of Civil Service Unions from Sir Robert Armstrong, Secretary of the Cabinet and Head of the Home Civil Service, 19 July 1984

Nigel Jones, Speech notes, 23 January 1993

Norman Willis, Speech, 23 January 1993

Pamphlets

Anarchy 29: The Spies for Peace Story (Vol. 3. No. 7) (London: 1963)

Emergency Powers: A Fresh Start, an informal group Fabian tract 416 (London: Fabian Society, 1972)

GCHQ – the Story of the Ban (Council of Civil Service Unions [nd])

Poll Tax Riot: 10 Hours that Shook Trafalgar Square (London: Acab Press, 1990)

The Poll Tax Rebellion in Haringey (London: Haringey Solidarity Group, 1999)

Report of the Working Party on Community/Police Relations in Lambeth (London: Brixton, Public Relations Division, 1981)

Bambery, Chris, *Scotland's National Question* (London: Socialist Workers Party, 1990)

Brown, Michael Barratt, *The Background to the Miners' Strike: What really happened to the Coal Industry* (Nottingham: Institute for Workers' Control, 1972)

Coates, Ken and Morgan, W. John, *The Nottinghamshire Coalfield and the British Miners Strike 1984–85* (Nottingham: University of Nottingham Press, 1990)

Cook, Robin, *No Nukes!* (London: Fabian Tract 475, Fabian Society, 1981)

Cook, Robin and Smith, Dan, *What future in NATO?* (London: Fabian Research Series 337, Fabian Society, 1978)

Cook, Robin et al, *Defence Review: An Anti-White Paper* (London: Fabian Research Series 323, Fabian Society, 1975)

Douglass, D., *Tell Us Lies About the Miners* (private publication, 1985)

Emerson, Tony, *Mass Communication – or Mass Deception* (London: Key Issue Publications, 1975)

Farrow, Stephen and Chown, Alex, eds, *The Human Cost of Nuclear War* (Cardiff: Medical Campaign Against Nuclear Weapons, 1983)

Flood, Michael and Grove-White, Robin, *Nuclear Prospects: A Comment on the Individual, the State and Nuclear Power* (London: Friends of the Earth, 1976)

Jones, Mark, *The Story of David Gareth Jones* (London: New Park Publications, 1985)

Mitchison, Naomi, *Oil for the Highlands?* (London: Fabian Research Series 315, Fabian Society, 1974)

Reid, Betty, *Ultra Leftism in Britain* (London: Communist Party [nd])

Reid, Lorna, *Poll Tax: Paying to be Poor* (London: Larkin Publications, 1990)

Sweet, Colin, *Anti Nuclear Campaign: The Costs of Nuclear Power* (Sheffield: Anti Nuclear Campaign, 1982)

Thompson, E.P., *The Defence of Britain* (London: European Nuclear Disarmament [nd])

Ephemera

GCHQ Trade Unions Bulletin, August 1984 (Trade Union Archive JN457)

Paper Boys: One Man's Account of Picketing at Wapping [npub, nd]

Warning Signal, November 1997, no. 150 (Trade Union Archive JN451)

Websites

belfasttelegraph.co.uk/news/local-national/legal-action-could-lift-the-lid-on-northern-irelands-freemasons-28496618.html

theguardian.com/theguardian/2006/sep/04/features5

theguardian.com/uk/2012/nov/16/miners-strike-police-battle-orgreave

thejusticegap.com/2012/10/from-orgreave-to-hillsborough-south-yorkshire-police-out-of-control/

mirror.co.uk/news/uk-news/battle-of-orgreave-south-yorkshire-police-1393586

telegraph.co.uk/news/obituaries/3401849/Sir-John-Hermon.html

INDEX